UNDERSTANDING SOCIAL LIFE: AN INTRODUCTION TO SOCIOLOGY

Frances A. Boudreau
Connecticut College

William M. Newman
University of Connecticut

West Publishing Company
Minneapolis/St. Paul ■ New York ■ Los Angeles ■ San Francisco

Copyediting: Caroline Ries
Text Design: John Edeen
Composition: Parkwood Composition Services, Inc.
Art: David Farr, ImageSmythe
Cover Design: Lori Zurn
Cover Image: Umberto Boccioni, *La strada entra nella casa,* 1911. Sprengel Museum Hannover.
Production, Prepress, Printing, and Binding by West Publishing Company.

WEST'S COMMITMENT TO THE ENVIRONMENT

In 1906, West Publishing Company began recycling materials left over from the production of books. This began a tradition of efficient and responsible use of resources. Today, up to 95 percent of our legal books and 70 percent of our college and school texts are printed on recycled, acid-free stock. West also recycles nearly 22 million pounds of scrap paper annually—the equivalent of 181,717 trees. Since the 1960s, West has devised ways to capture and recycle waste inks, solvents, oils, and vapors created in the printing process. We also recycle plastics of all kinds, wood, glass, corrugated cardboard, and batteries, and have eliminated the use of styrofoam book packaging. We at West are proud of the longevity and the scope of our commitment to our environment.

PHOTO CREDITS: **7** AP/Wide World Photos; **10** Reuters/ Bettmann; **14** © Sidney Harris; **37** AP/Wide World Photos; **40** © Joel Gordon 1992; **42** © John Feingersh/Stock Boston; **54** Reuters Bettmann; Reuters/Bettmann, UPI/Bettmann, AP/Wide World Photos, Reuters/Bettmann; **61** Reuters/Bettmann; **69** AP/Wide World Photos; **82** AP/Wide World Photos; **92** © Mary Kate Denny/Photo Edit; © Bob Daemmrich/Stock Boston; **97** UPI/ Bettmann; **100** Reuters/Bettmann; **116** AP/Wide World Photos; **123** The Bettmann Archive; **125** Bettmann; **144** © Dave Schaeffer/Photo Edit; **150** © Elizabeth Crews/ Stock Boston; **160** Library of Congress; **188** AP/Wide World Photos; **195** UPI/Bettmann; **217** AP/Wide World Photos; **243** © Jim Harrison/Stock Boston; **246** AP/Wide World Photos; **249** © David Young-Wolff/Photo Edit; **265** © Jeff Albertson/Stock Boston; **283** © Lionel Delevingne/ Stock Boston; **287** Reuters/Bettmann; **300** © Alexander Tsiaras/ Photo Researchers; **311** © Tony Freeman/Photo Edit; **318** AP/Wide World Photos; **323** Reuters/Bettmann

610 Opperman Drive
P.O. Box 64526
St. Paul, MN 55164–0526

Printed in the United States of America

00 99 98 97 96 95 94 93   8 7 6 5 4 3 2 1 0

Library of Congress Cataloging-in-Publication Data

Boudreau, Frances A.
Understanding social life: an introduction to sociology:
Frances A. Boudreau, William M. Newman
p. cm.
Includes bibliographical references and index.
ISBN 0-314-01187-0 (pbk. : alk. paper)
1. Sociology. I. Newman, William M. II. Title
HM51.B765 1993
301—dc20

92–30979
CIP

ABOUT THE AUTHORS

Frances A. Boudreau holds a B.A. (1971) and M.A. (1973) from the University of Rhode Island, and a Ph.D. (1980) from the University of Connecticut. She is an Associate Professor and Chair of the sociology department at Connecticut College in New London, Connecticut. Dr. Boudreau is co-editor of *Sex Roles and Social Patterns* (Prager, 1986), as well as a contributor of book chapters and journal essays focusing on issues in social psychology, family, and gender studies. She resides in Norwich, Connecticut, with her husband, Dr. William M. Newman.

William M. Newman holds a B.A. (1965) and M.A. (1967) from Syracuse University, and a Ph.D. (1970) from the Graduate Faculty of the New School for Social Research. He is a member of the sociology faculty at the University of Connecticut. Dr. Newman is the author of *American Pluralism* (Harper 1973), editor of *The Social Meanings of Religion* (Rand McNally 1974), and is co-author with geographer Peter L. Halvorson of a series of books on American religious trends. The most recent of these is *Atlas of Religious Change in America, 1952–1990* (Glenmary 1993). Dr. Newman is a past Series Editor of the Monograph Series of the Society for the Scientific Study of Religion, and is a frequent contributor of book chapters and journal essays focusing on intergroup relations and religious trends. He resides in Norwich, Connecticut, with his wife, Dr. Frances A. Boudreau.

CONTENTS

CHAPTER 3

CULTURE: WHAT MAKES HUMANS UNIQUE? 58

CHAPTER 4

SOCIAL STRUCTURE AND SOCIAL INTERACTION 85

CHAPTER 5

Social Institutions: Patterns in Transition 110

CHAPTER 6

Selves, Others, and Social Interaction 137

CHAPTER 7

The Processes of Social Deviance 167

CHAPTER 10

SOCIAL CHANGE: MACROSOCIOLOGY 274

CHAPTER 11

MODERNITY: BUREAUCRATIZATION, SECULARIZATION, AND METROPOLITANIZATION 308

PREFACE

Our many years of teaching both large and small classes of introductory sociology have bred more than a little dissatisfaction with textbook offerings. Large reference-type texts contain more material than can be covered in a one-semester course. Moreover, few students are pleased about purchasing an expensive text, much of which won't even be assigned. In contrast, our experience with mini-texts is that often they are so brief they fail to show students how basic sociological ideas can be applied and how sociological analysis is undertaken. Simplistic styles of presentation lull students into believing that they've grasped complex ideas, when they have not.

This eleven-chapter treatment has a number of unique features, the result, in part, of a topical reshuffling of the sociological deck. First, like most of the larger texts, theory and research are given early placement in a separate chapter (Chapter 2). Second, unlike many basic sociology texts, this book does not confine the treatment of social institutions to a few chapters at the end of the book. Rather, institutional analysis (of family, religion, education, and others) provides illustrations throughout the book. Our closest attempt at an "institutions" chapter (Chapter 5) contains an in-depth analysis of the most important of all institutions, the family. Third, a number of topics that normally receive chapter-length treatment in larger books are examined here in two chapters on social change (Chapters 10 and 11). Among these topics are social movements, demography, technology, urbanization, and bureaucracy.

Surely any basic text attempts to combine traditional concepts with illustrations from contemporary research and current events. Our focus on traditional concepts should be readily apparent, with culture, social structure, social psychology, deviance, social stratification, and status relations (minorities) all receiving chapter-length examinations. We've attempted to create a text that provides illustrations and examples drawn from the life experience of today's students. Applications and case study sections at the end of each chapter are designed to provide a special edge in showing students how basic sociological concepts are "alive" in everyday events and social issues. In the midst of it all, one reviewer noted: "It may not show from the table of contents, but these people really have tried to do something different here." We hope that difference will help open the door to sociological thinking for the students who read the book.

If occasionally it is important for students to know who said what, it is equally important for them to know *when* certain things were said. Accordingly, reference materials are cited by their original dates of publication with current editions and translations noted in the individual bibliographic entries at the end of each chapter. In matters of English usage and style, we've opted for the Chicago Manual of Style rather than the *Time* magazine version of the language. We hope this book will demonstrate to students that standard English grammar and usage still are powerful tools for clear and concise communication.

We've incurred many debts in the process of inventing this book. Classroom reactions of students, both at Connecticut College and the University of Connecticut, have been invaluable in helping us understand what does and does not "work." We wish to thank Connecticut College in New London, Connecticut, for the luxury of a year's sabbatic leave for Boudreau, during which the key elements of the book were conceptualized. The people at West Educational Publishing have shaped this book in more ways than we can count. We are pleased to thank editor Clark Baxter, developmental editor Joe Terry, Caroline Ries who copyedited the text, Sarah Bennett in promotions, and production editor Kara ZumBahlen, whose skills with manuscripts and people transformed a lot of ink on paper into this book.

We also have had sound counsel from peers who reviewed successive drafts of the manuscript. We are pleased for the opportunity to thank Ansaruddin Ahmed (Monroe Community College), Ben Austin (Middle Tennessee State University), Susan Blackwell (Delgado Community College), Jacqueline Boles (Georgia State University), Diana A. Bustamante (New Mexico State University), Jerry Clavner (Cuyahoga Community College), Lois Easterday (Onondaga Community College), David Edwards (San Antonio College), Irwin W. Epstein (University of Missouri—Rolla), Christopher C. Ezell (Vincennes University), Rudolph C. Harris (Des Moines Area Community College), Gary Hodge (Collin County Community College), Fred O. Jones (Simpson College), Michael Keen (Indiana University at South Bend), Michael Kleiman (University of South Florida), Jerry Lewis (Kent State University), Anthony V. Margavio (University of New Orleans), Gloria J. Milton (Glendale Community College), Carole A. Mosher (Jefferson Community College), Gustave G. Nelson (Berkshire Community College), Brother Tri Van Nguyen (LaSalle University), S. Fernando Rodriguez (University of Texas–El Paso), Rita Phyllis Sakitt (Suffolk County Community College), William Spinrad (Adelphi University), George F. Stine (Millersville University), Ralph W. Wedeking (Iowa Central Community College), and Ronald T. Wohlstein (Eastern Illinois University).

Finally, we wish to thank a large black Newfoundland named Dury who waited patiently through much of the writing, and from time-to-time beckoned us to "come and play" when she either got bored or sensed that comic relief was in order. Woof!

FAB & WMN
July 4, 1992
Norwich, Connecticut

CHAPTER 1

THE ART AND SCIENCE OF SOCIOLOGICAL ANALYSIS

CHAPTER OUTLINE

LEARNING OBJECTIVES

WHAT IS SOCIOLOGY?

Turning to the first chapter in any introductory textbook is very much like being parachuted into an unknown foreign land. The language is different. You don't know how to get from one place to the next. It is not altogether clear what kinds of things can be taken for granted, or what sorts of things you are expected to know. Each of the chapters in this text begins with a discussion of learning objectives and concludes with a chapter summary. These might be viewed as a road map for your excursion into the field of sociology. More specifically, the discussion of learning objectives focuses upon the questions that are addressed in each chapter and thus identifies the kinds of issues with which you should be conversant after studying the chapter. The chapter summary provides the central themes that answer these questions as well as the concepts from which the answers are constructed.

Chapter one examines the question, what is sociology? What sorts of things do sociologists study, and for what purpose? Why is sociology both a basic and an applied science? This chapter will introduce you to the art and science of sociological analysis. It examines some of the historical developments that led to the blossoming of the science of sociology in this, the latter half of the twentieth century. Finally, this chapter examines some differences between the sociological view of social reality and everyday understandings of social life.

After reading and studying this chapter you should be able to discuss answers to the following questions:

1. What is sociology, and why should anyone bother studying it?
2. What kinds of things do sociologists study?
3. What are the most important features of the subject matter of sociology, social reality?
4. How may sociology be understood as both an art and a science?
5. What are the social and historical conditions that have given rise to the sociological perspective?
6. How can sociology be both a basic and an applied science?
7. Why do some people find sociological insights difficult to understand, and how can these barriers to thinking sociologically be overcome?

THE SOCIOLOGICAL ENTERPRISE

Frequently, in both the popular press and the electronic media, the term "sociology" is heard in connection with such issues as family violence, poverty, and crime. The impression emerges that the only phenomena in which sociologists are interested are social arrangements that somehow don't work properly. While it is true that these sorts of social problems are of interest to sociologists, they are only one part of what sociologists study. This popular view of sociology as simply the study of social problems does not begin to capture the complexity of the sociological enterprise. Accordingly, the first questions addressed in this book are what is sociology? why do we bother studying it? and what types of things do sociologists study? The first section of this chapter provides some preliminary answers to these questions, answers that are explored in greater depth in the remaining sections of the chapter.

SOCIOLOGY DEFINED

Sociology

Sociology is the scientific study and interpretation of social life. It is a science because, like all basic sciences, it is guided by specific rules of investigation and has the goal of explaining what is found. It is interpretative because the "facts" of scientific work rarely speak for themselves. All sciences involve interpreting what is found. For instance, most persons have had an X-ray taken at one time or another. But, an X-ray picture of the body means little until an expert interprets the picture and declares its meaning and significance. Ultimately, the X-ray technician and the physician determine whether the picture taken indicates disease or health, cause for deep concern, or nothing about which to worry. Similarly, social phenomena involve meanings and require interpretation.

For instance, the birth rate in country "B" may be many times greater than that in country "A." But, what are the consequences of that high birth rate? What will it mean in the future for the people living in country "B?" It may not immediately be apparent to the people in country "B" that a high birth rate may mean a scarcity of food and health services, that in the context of economic scarcity, they may experience starvation, high infant death rates, and other social miseries. Interpretation always is an important part of the scientific act.

Sociology investigates and seeks to explain *social* reality. The sociologist wishes to know how and why social arrangements and social patterns are as they are. This emphasis upon the word "social" means that sociology is not a study of individual persons, but rather the study of individuals as participants in collective patterns of social life. Thus, the subject matter of sociology includes all the things that people do, think, and feel that involve or result from life with other people. Said differently, sociology focuses upon the ways in which social conditions and social settings influence human thought, feelings, and behavior. Our thoughts, actions, and feelings are intelligible and "make sense" because of meanings we attach to them, meanings that are shared with other persons in society.

MICRO- AND MACROSOCIOLOGY

In their approach to the study of social reality, sociologists focus upon different levels of social phenomena, resulting in what is called micro- and macrosociology. Micro- and macro- refer to the size and scope of the phenomena to be investigated. For example, some sociologists focus upon the characteristics of total societies, and even world systems of events. *The study of large-scale social*

Macrosociology

phenomena is called macrosociology. There are many important questions at this level of analysis. How do societies develop? How are they organized, and how do they change? How do the patterns of social structure in one society compare to those of another? Are there processes of social development that affect all societies similarly? How do certain predominant themes in cultural values or political ideology shape societies differently? Why do some societies produce more dramatic and severe patterns of social inequality, poverty, and wealth than others? Different as these questions may be, they all involve studying and analyzing rather large-scale social phenomena, and thus, all are instances of macrosociology.

On the other hand, some sociologists prefer to study small-scale social units, such as the development of the social self, family relationships, friendship groups, or classroom patterns. *This study of small-scale social units is called microsociology.* There are many important and interesting sociological questions at this level of analysis as well. How are people shaped and influenced by cultural patterns and social structural settings? Do different societies produce qualitatively different types of persons? How does the social self develop? What are the processes through which individuals adopt the traditions and values of society? What leads to conformity in some persons and deviance in others? What kinds of interactions occur in different microsocial settings? For example, how does the number of persons in a small group affect the sorts of relationships between persons? Small-group sociologists have found that as groups increase in size from dyads, to triads, to quadrads, and larger groups, people's communication patterns change and their degree of satisfaction arising from group participation decreases.

Microsociology

Additionally, microsociology examines the emergence, change, and consequences of meaning systems. For instance, why do various religious cults and sects behave differently, with some retreating from society into self-contained communes, while others send out missionaries to seek converts and spread the "good news?" These are but a few illustrations of the smaller-level phenomena studied by microsociologists.

Between these two levels of analysis, of course, lies a broad range of social phenomena not easily classified as either micro- or macro-. For example, studies of community life, professional associations, and business corporations fall somewhere between these two levels of analysis. At least one prominent sociologist (Merton 1949) has suggested using the term "middle range" to describe the substantial quantity of sociological work that is not clearly either micro or macro.

THE SUBJECT MATTER OF SOCIOLOGY

In at least one important regard, today's beginning college or university student is set adrift in a bewildering intellectual supermarket. Courses seem to be offered on every academic (and sometimes not so academic) subject imaginable. Unfortunately, relatively little is said about how these many different courses and subjects relate. In a holistic sense, what is the larger message about the human condition that is to be learned from all this? Surely, a first text in sociology is not the place to address in depth such a complex question; but, it is important to locate sociology within the scheme of the human sciences. What is the place of sociology's subject matter in the modern social science curriculum?

Obviously, sociology's focus upon social behavior is shared with other social sciences, yet each of the other social sciences examines human behavior in specialized contexts. For example, economics is concerned with economic aspects of social life and with humans as economic actors. Political science studies political systems and humans as political actors. However, sociology focuses upon the patterns and processes of social relations in all spheres of social life, as well as the various interconnections among them. In other words, sociology claims to be the most general of the social science perspectives.

The precise aspects of the social landscape studied depend upon the sociologist's specific interests and areas of specialization. Because the expansion and proliferation of knowledge in today's technological society make it difficult to study systematically the entirety of complex phenomena, there are many subdisciplines and specializations within sociology: among them are political sociology, family sociology, and urban sociology. Sociologists also specialize in the study of educational and religious institutions, deviance, and stratification, to name but a few. Many areas of interest and investigation necessarily overlap those of the other social sciences. However, in spite of this overlap, there are important differences among the various social sciences in their approaches to the subject matter. Each of the social sciences views social life with concepts central to its own discipline. Each looks at the world through a particular lens, focusing upon the subject matter in a distinctive way. The special features of sociology's particular lens is the concern of the rest of this chapter.

In summary, sociology is the scientific study and interpretation of social life. Sociologists focus upon individuals only to the extent that they participate in, and are shaped by, collective social patterns. Sociologists search in these collective patterns for explanations of human behavior. Macrosociology examines rather large, societal or even global questions. Microsociology focuses upon smaller units of social life, such as family relations and religious practices. Within this context, the things that sociologists study are exceedingly diverse. While sharing its focus on human behavior with the other social sciences, sociology brings a unique perspective to the study of social life, what might be called the art of doing sociology. The remaining sections of this chapter explore these themes in greater detail.

The Art of Sociological Analysis

What is involved in the art of sociological analysis? Typically, when people think about scientific activity, regardless of whether that science is physics or sociology, biology or psychology, a number of images are brought to mind. Science is said to be a method of study involving the collection of information or data, a rational process in which hypotheses are tested. The "facts" logically emerge from this rational process of comparing hypotheses and data. Surely, to some extent, each of these notions—that science is a method, that it is rational, and that it involves data collection and analysis—is a reasonable view of what science is and what scientists do.

However, these images of science tell only part of the story. Science is more than a rational application of certain methods and techniques. As Robert

Nisbet (1962) has suggested, the most important advances in science are produced, not through the use of sophisticated methodological tools, but rather through thought processes that characterize both art and science—creativity and discovery. They involve an ability to think about the subject matter in new and imaginative ways, a drive to understand and interpret, and a desire to communicate that understanding to others.

The art of sociological analysis involves a distinctive approach to the subject matter, what various writers have called the "sociological imagination." It begins with a willingness to look beyond the obvious and take a fresh look at "taken-for-granted" familiar things. It revolves around a quest to discover and illuminate social reality. Peter Berger (1963) has described this as a "passion to understand." While this chapter will explore the more rational features of sociology as a science, we begin here with the more creative elements of the sociological perspective.

Let's examine the ideas of three sociologists, each of whom has attempted to capture the uniqueness of the sociological view of social reality. Each has explained, a bit differently, what is involved in the art of sociology. The 19th century French sociologist Emile Durkheim focused upon the process of discovering social facts and understanding the role of social forces in our lives. The late C. Wright Mills, an American sociologist of the 1950s and early 1960s, describes what he calls the "sociological imagination." Mills demonstrates the importance of locating everyday events within a social-historical framework. Finally, a more contemporary sociologist, Peter L. Berger, suggests that sociology "unmasks" apparent social realities by looking beyond the obvious. Each of these three images provides a unique insight into the art of sociological analysis. Each offers clues about how one enters into the process of acquiring a uniquely sociological perspective.

DISCOVERING SOCIAL FACTS: EMILE DURKHEIM

Individual facts

Social facts

The idea that sociology involves the discovery of "social facts" is a major contribution of Emile Durkheim (1858–1917). In his book *The Rules of Sociological Method* (1895), Durkheim distinguishes between *individual facts* and *social facts. Individual facts are specific psychological and biological traits internal to individuals, while social facts are collective social forces that are external to individuals and exert control over them.* Social facts result from social participation. As people participate in social life, specific social forces emerge that become part of the larger culture and social structure which, in turn, influence individual behavior. Social facts are not simply the sum total of individual facts. Rather, social life constitutes a distinctive level of reality that is not interpretable in terms of the characteristics of individuals.

Let's examine a concrete example of this. In a typical fast food restaurant a remarkably ordered set of activities unfolds. There is the appearance of a high level of coordination and commitment. As one person takes orders at the drive-up window, several other persons are cooking and packaging food to go. Other members of the work team are taking cash and making change, cleaning the work areas, and performing related tasks. Yet, this well-orchestrated collective activity does not result from the combined psychic activities of the individuals participating in it. In fact, Josh and Laurie, while busily cooking burgers and fries, actually are bored and are more interested in each other than the work at hand. Paul, who is taking orders at the take-out window, is counting the minutes until he can leave to join his friends at a party. Gayle, the assistant manager, dislikes the entire operation and has been thinking of getting another job. The point, then, is that each of the individual workers in the restaurant is participating in a collective social happening that is something more than, and something different from, the sum total of their individual motives and states of mind. Social facts cannot be equated with or reduced to psychic facts. Durkheim argued that sociology's purpose is to discover and understand the underlying social forces that make social life possible.

Durkheim did not deny the reality of psychological facts, nor did he underestimate the usefulness of psychology in understanding the human condition. Rather, he argued that, while individual facts explain individual behavior, social facts may be explained only by reference to other social facts—characteristics of the social structure and culture. He illustrated this basic sociological principle in his study *Suicide* (1897) by showing that even an apparently individualistic act (suicide) can be understood in terms of the social context in which it takes place. Durkheim observed that there were consistent differences in suicide rates among different categories of persons in several Western European nations. For example, suicide was more common among single and divorced than married persons. He asked, if suicide is the consequence of individual psychic flaws, why do these patterns of difference exist among such categories of persons? Rather than seeing the act of suicide as an individually unique experience, Durkheim's strategy of sociological discovery involved looking for characteristics these categories have in common. He found that one social fact, differential rates of suicide, could be explained in terms of another social fact: the degree of social integration. Durkheim discovered, for example, that married persons benefit from the supporting social network of the family group (a mechanism of social integration) in ways that divorced and single persons do not. Accordingly, the latter became more probable candidates for suicide.

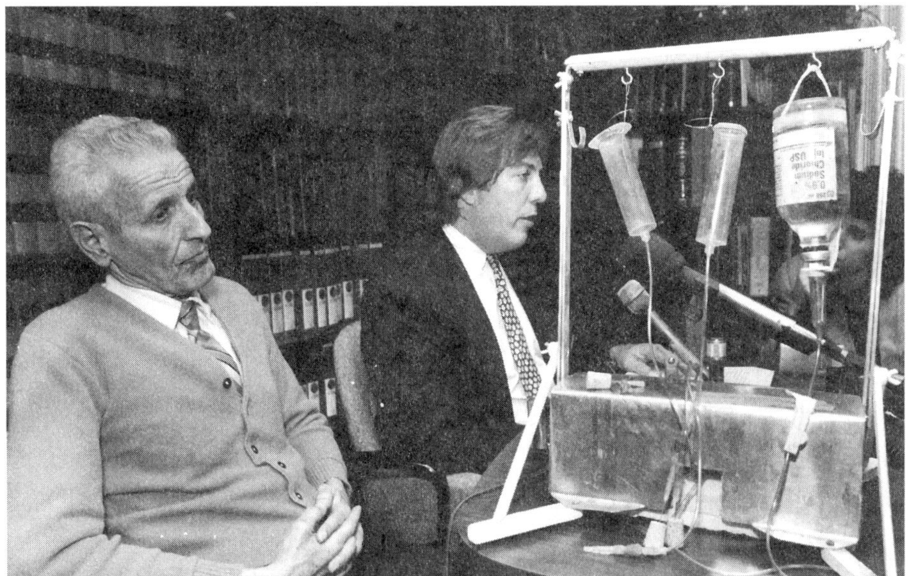

FIGURE 1.1
Dr. Jack Kevorkian and his "suicide machine." Hero or villain?

In observing that the degree of social integration influences rates of suicide, Durkheim did not argue that psychological factors have no place in understanding why a particular individual commits suicide. Rather, he argued that psychology and sociology provide different types of insight. Psychology explains the individual act. Sociology explains how the individual act is shaped by social forces.

Yet another example of social forces influencing individual experience is found in the work of sociologist Mark Zborowski (1952). In interviewing hospital personnel, Zborowski learned that members of different ethnic communities respond to pain quite differently. Italian and Jewish-Americans openly express the discomfort of pain, while so-called "old-Americans" or Nordics respond to pain rather stoically, with little open complaint. Recognizing that pain thresholds are quite similar in all humans, Zborowski concluded that how one responds to pain involves group norms that are learned in ethnic subcultures. Thus, while for each of us pain is a highly personal and individual experience, our ways of responding to pain involve social facts. Zborowski, like Durkheim, discovered underlying collective elements in individual behavior and experience.

THE SOCIOLOGICAL IMAGINATION: C. WRIGHT MILLS

A different view of the art of sociology analysis is found in the work of the late C. Wright Mills. In his essay *The Sociological Imagination* (1959), Mills suggests that understanding social forces requires a special kind of creative "imagination" that captures the complexity of the relationship between individual lives and the sociohistorical context in which those lives are lived. In developing a sociological imagination the observer must "stand back" from the immediate events or happenings of any social situation or social problem. Specific events must be understood as part of a larger social landscape. The sociological imagination enables us to see how the difficulties and dilemmas experienced by individuals are part of broad sociohistorical processes in which patterns of cause and consequence unfold. For Mills, *the sociological imagination involves seeing this larger picture; developing a holistic framework; and asking what produces these social happenings, what has preceded them, and what kinds of consequences flow from them?* This entails a search for sociohistorical linkages that may not be immediately apparent.

Sociological imagination

Mills distinguishes between "personal troubles" and "public issues," and describes the interconnections between the two. Personal troubles are problems experienced by individuals; public issues entail collective social facts and transcend individual experience. Troubles raise private concerns, while issues raise public concerns. According to Mills, a sociological imagination allows us to see the extent to which personal troubles are a manifestation of public issues.

Let's consider a specific case. Mary Smith is a divorced mother of two children, aged 4 and 6. Prior to her divorce, Mary was a full time homemaker, living in a nice home in a middle class suburban neighborhood. Today, she is having difficulties "making ends meet." She lives in a small apartment and works in a rather low-paying job. While she receives support payments for the children from their father, these funds do not cover the costs of raising two children. After childcare and living expenses, there is little money left for nonessentials. Mary's ex-husband is a successful businessman. When Mary reflects upon her economic situation, she tends to view it in personal terms, perhaps as a result of her experience with a selfish or irresponsible ex-husband who does not provide sufficient support for her and the children, or perhaps even as a consequence of her own failings. She may ask herself, "Where did I go wrong?" or blame herself for not finishing college. When Mary thinks of solutions, they also tend to be individualistic.

Yet, Mary's personal troubles are part of a widespread social trend. Mary is one of a growing number of divorced women trapped in what has been called the "feminization of poverty" (i.e. the tendency for those in poverty in the United States to be female). In a 10-year study of the effects of California's pioneering no-fault divorce law, sociologist Leonore Weitzman (1985) encountered some unanticipated social consequences of the new no-fault practices. She found that divorce has dramatic effects upon people's standard of living, most especially upon their disposable incomes. However, husbands and wives are not affected equally. After divorce, women and their minor children experience a 73 percent decline in their standard of living. Conversely, on average, divorced men experience a 42 percent improvement. In the context of Weitzman's research, what Mary experiences as a personal trouble is also a collective social problem.

No-fault divorce was designed to reduce the bickering that is so common in the traditionally adversarial legal system, and to provide a reasonable 50/50 division of community property. However, lawmakers did not consider that gender discrimination in the job market or differential labor force participation would make it extremely difficult for women to recover financially from divorce. Men not only hold better paying jobs, but usually do not have the financial and practical concerns of raising the children from their failed marriages. Thus, while no-fault divorce was a well-intentioned idea, it produced some major societywide problems that were not anticipated.

Weitzman's study illustrates Mills' sociological imagination at work. She places the institution of no-fault divorce laws within a social and historical perspective, demonstrating how the broader social context of these changes in the legal system shapes the consequences. What is gained by doing this? From a sociological perspective, it provides greater understanding of the complex relationship between individual experience and the larger social structure. As Mills suggests, patterns of social cause and consequence are brought into focus, giving new social meaning to things that initially seemed to be only individual troubles.

UNMASKING APPARENT REALITIES: PETER L. BERGER

A third way of understanding the art of sociological analysis is suggested by sociologist Peter L. Berger. In his essay *Invitation to Sociology* (1963), Berger observes that people tend to take for granted the world in which they live and accept rather unquestioningly the view of reality that has been socially constructed for them. Yet, as Berger notes, there is more to social life than meets the eye. Conventional or official interpretations about the world are not always correct, and even when correct, don't always present the "whole story" of events. In other words, what everybody "knows" and accepts as true does not always represent all of what actually exists. Social reality involves levels of meaning, not all of which are immediately apparent. The art of sociological analysis involves looking beyond commonly accepted or officially defined interpretations in order to more fully understand the complexities of the social world. *The art of what Berger calls "unmasking" social reality requires looking at the familiar in a new light, taking a critical look at commonly accepted phenomena in order to more fully understand the complex nature of social reality.* The sociological perspective involves searching for what else is there.

Unmasking social reality

Let's consider an example of how this is done. Kristen Luker's study *Abortion and the Politics of Motherhood* (1984) demonstrates how sociologists look beyond apparent reality to discover what else is really there. It frequently is claimed that differences in people's attitudes toward abortion stem from differences in religious beliefs. However, religious values are only part of the story. Luker's study of women in the prochoice and prolife movements demonstrates how a variety of life experiences, such as education, income, occupation, and family background shape the values and actions of abortion activists. While there are religious differences between the two groups of women, Luker discovers that differences in attitudes toward abortion are grounded in diametrically opposed definitions of motherhood and the social role of women.

Those who oppose abortion tend to believe that women are inextricably linked to biological roles, while those who support abortion believe that biology should not be the primary determinant of women's lives. For prolife activists, motherhood is seen as the most important function women perform. Prochoice activists, on the other hand, view motherhood as only one of the many roles available to women. Most importantly, Luker finds that these different value systems are related to different life situations. The passion with which each side defends its position is, to a great extent, a defense of their own personal life choices and lifestyles. Women who oppose abortion typically are full-time homemakers, while prochoice activists tend to choose another life-

FIGURE 1.2
Understanding people's behavior requires one to consider the social context.

style. Clearly, women's attitudes toward abortion are outcomes of, and in part, justifications for, the different life choices they've already made. Religious values, while important, are also situated in this larger web of life choices. Thus, Luker's study illustrates the process Berger calls "unmasking." It shows how the sociologist can look beyond the "taken-for-granted" to see what else is propelling events.

In summary, the art of sociological analysis has been examined here through the ideas of three prominent sociologists. Writing at the turn of the century, Emile Durkheim showed that sociological analysis involves a process of discovery. Social facts, which are different from psychic facts, are the hidden forces in which individual experience always is embedded. For Durkheim, sociology is the art of searching for and discovering social facts.

In the middle of the 20th century, C. Wright Mills argued for the use of our sociological imagination. He maintained that personal troubles can be understood only by viewing their connections to social issues. The individual experience is part of a broader social-structural and social-historical pattern.

Finally, the contemporary sociologist Peter L. Berger maintains that the art of sociological analysis involves unmasking apparent realities. The sociologst must look beyond the obvious for what else is happening. The poet Samuel Taylor Coleridge has suggested that literature is "the willing suspension of disbelief." Similarly, the art of sociological analysis begins with a "willing suspension of belief." It is a conscious decision to ask what lies behind "taken-for-granted" realities, what are the consequences of observed social arrangements, and what are the meanings of social patterns?

The Science of Sociological Analysis

In many different ways science and the products of scientific work have become part of the everyday experience of modern life. We hear and read about one sort of scientific discovery or another in the daily news reports. Television commercials constantly invoke scientific evidence and testimony in support of the products we are asked to buy. Like much of our daily experience, the very idea of science is taken for granted. Without really pausing to examine this idea, it is assumed that we know what science is. After all, why should such a question concern us? Most of the time people's actions stem from a "pragmatic motive" (Berger 1963). Our quest for knowledge or information springs from practical concerns involved in our day-to-day activities. For instance, most people need to know how to operate an automobile but have little interest in knowing how or why the car runs when the ignition key is turned. Typically, our interest in science is limited to what the results of a particular scientific activity may do for us in a specific situation. Will a certain new drug help cure my cold? Will a nutritional discovery such as Nutrasweet let me eat sweets and candy without getting fat? Will a new fuel additive make my old car run faster?

For the moment we shall depart from this "pragmatic motive" and examine the concept of science. Unless we understand what science is, we cannot fully comprehend the idea of sociology as a basic science. *Science is distinguished by its focus upon a very unique set of goals or purposes. Specifically, science* **Science** *attempts to seek explanations for empirically available phenomena. It does this through a variety of procedures and methods based on the principle of replication. Most importantly, all scientific work adheres to the norm of objectivity.* These goals and purposes make scientific thought and activity somewhat different from the kinds of things that most people do most of the time. Let's examine each of these four essential aspects of science.

EXPLANATION

Explanation

All basic science has the goal of e*xplanation, which is to tell why or how something happens.* Sociologists are primarily concerned with learning about the causes (why) and processes (how) through which patterns of social life are established or altered. Patterns of social consequences are a related concern. This search for explanations involves a very different approach to the social world than that which most people adopt on a daily basis. Specifically, it involves questioning the things that most people simply take for granted. Just as the chemist asks how the compound H_2O is formed, or the biologist questions how cell reproduction occurs, so the sociologist wishes to examine the causes and typical processes that result in both order and change in the social world.

EMPIRICAL AVAILABILITY

Empirical availability

Not all things are suited to scientific study. In the sciences, the concept of *empirical availability means that the things being studied must be available for observation and/or measurement.* The idea of empirical availability is a bit more complex than it may appear at first glance. It does not mean that the subject matter under study must be available to the naked eye. Rather, in some way, we must be able to observe and measure the phenomena being studied. For example, in biology the processes of cell division cannot be examined with the naked eye. A microscope makes these invisible processes visible. It makes things that are too small to be observed by the human eye empirically available. In both psychology and sociology, attitudes and opinions are not immediately observable. Yet, through careful questioning techniques it is possible to study the ideas, opinions, and attitudes hidden in people's minds. Thus, like cell division, political attitudes and racial prejudice may not be directly observable. However, they are empirically available.

Not all phenomena are empirically available. All the microscopes and questioning techniques in the world will not help deliver a scientific answer to the question "How many angels fit on the head of a pin?" Like all human activities, science has its limits. Some questions we would like to answer cannot be answered scientifically because the features of the subject must be "taken on faith," not on empirical evidence. Obviously, this is why there are so many different brands of religion and so many different political philosophies. Each of these begins with matters that are not empirically available, but that must be taken on faith.

REPLICATION

How is something actually known in science? One of the most frequently heard misconceptions is the claim that "facts" are established in science through the use of statistics. But statistics are only a tool of research and study. In all sciences statistics are used because they summarize information. Statistics are a kind of shorthand. For example, rather than analyzing the long list of salaries for members of the Carpenters' Union in the United States, one might examine one number, the mean, or average salary figure. The statistical mean summarizes a great part of the information that might be obtained by inspecting the entire list of salary information. However, just because a person uses numbers does not mean that the claims being made are accurate.

What, then, is the essential mechanism by which scientific facts are established? In the final analysis, the establishment of scientific facts is based upon replication. *Replication is the ability to repeat or to do something again. In the sciences, replication is the ability of different scholars or researchers to arrive at the same research conclusions, independently of one another.* It is here that scholarly journals and periodical research publications enter the picture. Through such volumes as the *New England Journal of Medicine,* the *Annals of the American Association of Geographers,* or the *American Journal of Sociology,* scholars can make independent inspections of the research findings of other scientists. In this way, the publication of research findings serves as a form of replication in modern sciences. Whether it be through the publication of studies or through actual replication research, it is the act of agreement among experts that creates scientific facts. In this regard, it may be useful to think about science, not as a body of facts or storehouse of information, but as a continuing process of discovery and replication.

Replication

OBJECTIVITY

As described thus far, sociology may be understood as a search to explain patterns of stability and change in society. In that search, sociologists, like all scientists confine their work to phenomena that are empirically available and rely upon accepted standards of replication in determining the accuracy of their research. One all-important goal characterizes these activities: all scientific work should proceed under the norm of objectivity. *The term objectivity means that something is free from bias, prejudgement, or extraneous values.* To operate under a norm of objectivity means that once a topic has been chosen for study, personal bias, individual values, likes and dislikes, should not influence the work being done.

Objectivity

This does not mean that scientists do not have strong personal interests in, and concerns about, the phenomena they study. Can you imagine a Jonas Salk spending years of his life searching for a vaccine for polio if he were not personally committed to that search? Would Madame Curie have discovered radium with something less than the enduring interest and concern that sustained her over many years of research effort? The Swedish scholar Gunnar Myrdal certainly had a passionate concern about racism, a concern that resulted in his landmark study *An American Dilemma* (1944). Yet, once a piece of scientific work has begun, once the act of research has been undertaken, unbending standards of objectivity should prevail. Scientists must make a conscious effort to prevent bias and personal values from intruding into their work.

In summary, sociology, like physics, chemistry, and botany is a science. Like all sciences, it has a distinct subject matter. For sociologists, it is the social rather than the physical world that demands explanation. The act of doing soci-

FIGURE 1.3
THEN A MIRACLE HAPPENS

"I THINK YOU SHOULD BE MORE EXPLICIT HERE IN STEP TWO."

SOURCE: © 1977 Sidney Harris, *American Scientist Magazine.* Used with permission.

ology, of learning how and why social reality appears as it does, is governed by the same norms and characteristics as all other sciences. Scientists attempt to confine their work to issues and questions for which data or information is empirically available. Scientific learning and discovery are gradual processes through which experts inspect and scrutinize each other's work, and, through replication, arrive at explanations of things upon which the experts agree. Finally, all science operates under the norm of objectivity, the idea that individual values and prejudices should not enter into the activity of research and interpretation.

THE ORIGINS AND GROWTH OF SOCIOLOGY

Modern sociology is a direct outgrowth of the 17th century movement known as the Enlightenment. Two specific Enlightenment developments contributed to the rise of sociological thought. First was the very idea of science. The older idea, that human history is little more than a reflection of the will of the gods, was replaced by the belief that the physical and social world exhibit a natural order subject to reasoned understanding. That is, humans can understand and explain events in their environment through the use of rational empirical methods. The second theme of Enlightenment thought influencing the development of sociology was philosophical humanism. Humanism emphasized the perfectibility of humankind. It anticipated social progress and a betterment of the human condition. In the 18th and 19th centuries these two Enlightenment themes were merged into *scientific humanism, the idea that rational science is a tool for social improvement.* These two concerns, rational explanation and social reform, would become alternate and sometimes competing goals in contemporary sociology.

Scientific humanism

Although humanism and scientific thought were both well established by the late 18th century, most historians of science agree that sociology as a distinct discipline did not emerge until the latter half of the 19th century. Only when the social problems accompanying the political and industrial revolutions in Europe became increasingly apparent did the new sociological movement blossom. The stability of whole societies was being disrupted. In the face of these upheavals, social analysts began to focus more closely on the nature of social order and social disorganization. The attempt to analyze and understand societies signaled the beginning of a sociological consciousness. Let's take a closer look at these developments.

EUROPEAN BEGINNINGS

What were the social conditions under which sociological thought first emerged? As sociologist Robert Nisbet has observed, by the middle of the 19th century the old social order was collapsing "under the twin blows of industrialism and revolutionary democracy" (Nisbet 1966, 21). On the political front, by the turn of the 19th century, democratic revolutions in France and America, as well as political reform in England, had brought new forms of self-government into existence. With these new governments came new social and cultural practices, and a new social order. Societies were being changed dramatically. Today, we take for granted political democracy, freedom of association, and the various cultural traditions that surround these principles. In the day of sociology's founders, however, these arrangements were considered revolutionary and were dramatic breaks with political and social traditions. The new science of sociology focused upon the causes and consequences of these new patterns of social life.

The industrial revolution with its accompanying urbanization was sweeping through many Western societies. People were leaving the land and migrating to cities to work in factories. For the first time, large-scale separation of home and work occurred. What would later be called "the great transformation" was disrupting traditional ways of doing things. People's relationships to the land, to their kinship system, and to the church were undermined. Social cohesiveness was replaced by a growing emphasis on individualism. Because people migrated to the cities at rates faster than could be absorbed, a host of new social problems afflicted the growing urban-industrial landscape. New patterns of urban poverty, industrial pollution, crime, and inadequate housing were rampant.

Within this framework, it is understandable that sociology developed when it did, and why it took the direction it did. Sociology's founders were both rationalists (the scientific view) and social reformers (humanists) who examined society from a unique historical vantage point. The incredible rate of social and political change allowed them to see the fragile underpinnings of social order. In their quest to understand the social and political changes around them, in their desire to make society better, they focused upon the nature of society itself. In other words, they invented the science called sociology out of a desire to understand and improve their social world (Becker 1968).

While the French scholar August Comte (1798–1857) frequently is referred to as the "father of sociology" because he gave the discipline its name, it is a bit misleading to think of him in this way. Sociological thinking is not the product of a single intellectual parent. Rather, the sociological perspective was the creation of an entire generation of European scholars. Today, those pioneering sociological thinkers are referred to as "the classic tradition" in sociological thought. The most noteworthy of these classical period authors were the two German writers Karl Marx (1818–1883) and Max Weber (1864–1920), and the French sociologist Emile Durkheim (1858–1917). In responding to the rapidly changing social order, each of them made lasting contributions to modern sociological thought.

Durkheim was deeply concerned with the disorder in society stemming from rapid industrialization and urbanization. These humanistic concerns led him to examine the special contributions of religious, educational, and family institutions in creating moral solidarity in modern societies (Wallwork 1972). Consequently, the sociological question of how social order is created and maintained in societies is a central theme running throughout his works. In the face of apparent social disorder and political chaos, Durkheim asked how social integration and social consensus are possible.

Durkheim's understanding of the functional interdependence among the highly specialized institutions in modern societies (1893) became a central theme of *structural-functional theory* in modern sociology. According to

Durkheim, in simple nontechnological societies, the central institution of the family fulfills most societal needs. However, as societies become more industrialized and urbanized, other social institutions, among them, education and government, acquire greater functional importance. Durkheim viewed modern society much like a biological organism, composed of interdependent, coordinated, and complementary parts. Each part contributes a specialized function for the survival of the whole. In modern sociology, *structural-functional theory emphasizes the functional contribution each social institution makes to the general condition of social order and stability.*

Structural functional theory

In Germany, two related sociological traditions were spawned following the works of Karl Marx and Max Weber respectively. These traditions form the basis for *social conflict theory. Modern social conflict theorists focus upon processes of change and group opposition in societies.* Marx was a social economist who is best known for his critique of industrial capitalism. Like Durkheim, Marx was disturbed by the changes taking place in society. He was especially concerned with changes in working conditions and their consequences for the emerging social order. He argued that the new system of capitalism that accompanied industrialization enslaved and alienated the working classes (1867). In his critical analysis, Marx placed much emphasis upon the force of the economic system in shaping the social structure. He believed that the way a society allocates ownership of the means of production is the primary determinant of how wealth and power are distributed. Thus, Marx began a tradition of analyzing social inequality and stratification in societies (see Chapter 8). He developed a theory of social change based on class conflict and predicted that the *proletariat,* the industrial workers, would eventually revolt against the *bourgeoisie,* the capitalists, leading to a classless society. As a humanist, Marx's social philosophy of communism was his response to the question "How can a better society be created?" Although some of Marx's political predictions (i.e. a classless society) have not proven correct, he made an enormous contribution to the sociological understanding of economic and power conflicts in societies.

Social conflict theory

Not all of German sociology followed the Marxian path. Without question, the most important attempt to extend the analysis of social change and conflict beyond Marx's ideas was the work of the social historian Max Weber. While Weber shared Marx's interest in social conflict, he believed that social conflicts occur over much more than just economic interests. He examined how groups and individuals often fight over such things as political ideologies, religious doctrines, and even issues of lifestyle. He is best known for his essay *The Protestant Ethic and the Spirit of Capitalism* (1904–1905), in which he demonstrated that religious ideas and values played an important role in the emergence of industrial-capitalist society. Like both Durkheim and Marx, Weber was deeply troubled by the kinds of social changes that marked the transition into modernity. He was concerned with the loss of traditional values and believed that the overriding characteristic of Western society was its rationality (see Chapter 11). Changes in society had brought with them a social consciousness in which great emphasis was placed on the rational calculation of the most efficient means of achieving desired goals. Weber believed that the processes set in motion would lead to the depersonalization and dehumanization of social life. He studied these trends in bureaucracies, religious institutions, legal systems, and stratification processes. Throughout, his sociology emphasizes the decline of traditional values and the conflict of values in modern societies. While

Weber, like Marx, was critical of the new social order, he was much more restrained than Marx in stating his social and philosophical views. Unlike Marx, his humanistic concerns did not influence any political movements. However, his sociological legacy is very great.

AMERICAN DEVELOPMENTS

The origins of American sociology greatly resemble the European trends just described. In the late 19th century, scientific humanism was a prevalent view among social reformers and "do-gooders" who envisioned the new sociology as an instrument of social reconstruction. Like their European counterparts, America's first generation of sociologists was deeply disturbed by the new social problems of urban-industrial society. To many, the scientific study of society held the promise of resolving the dilemmas created by industrialization and urbanization. However, by the turn of the century, American sociology was no longer just the tool of the social reformers. Instead, it was becoming an established scientific discipline taught in colleges and universities throughout the nation (Turner & Turner 1990, Vidich & Lyman 1985).

The rapid growth of sociology in America during the first half of the twentieth century involved a great many developments in both theory and research. From the present vantage point, four developments are noteworthy. The first of these is the emergence of the "Chicago school" sociologists. In the first quarter of the 20th century, sociologists at the University of Chicago approached the surrounding city of Chicago as a laboratory for studying in detail many of the problems of urban-industrial society. The Chicago sociologists, among them Robert Park (1864–1944), William Ogburn (1886–1959), Ernest Burgess (1886–1966), and Louis Wirth (1897–1952), produced a wide range of pioneering empirical studies. From these writers would come the first sociological understanding of demography and population change, racial patterns and ethnic relationships, and the social ecology of urban life. It might well be argued that the Chicago sociologists brought an arsenal of empirical research techniques to the same issues the Europeans had examined primarily with theories. Thus, many subfields in modern sociology owe a debt to the ground-breaking studies of these Chicago sociologists.

Social psychology

A second, very different development at Chicago also made a lasting contribution to the fast-growing science of sociology. This was the emergence of the field of *social psychology*. Perhaps because psychology already was an established discipline, the classical period European sociologists wrote relatively little about the connection between the individual and the social structure. However, in the United States, the philosopher George Herbert Mead (1863–1931) addressed the issue of the connections between thought, action, and social structure. He was particularly interested in the development of the social self and the meanings that individuals attach to social events. Because of his influence, today, sociology shares with psychology the interdisciplinary field of social psychology.

Symbolic interactionism

Although social psychologists trained in both sociology and psychology have some common interests in the relationships between the individual and the social structure, they study these things from different perspectives. Mead's students at Chicago would build the social psychological tradition in sociology known as symbolic interactionism. *Symbolic interactionism is a microsocial perspec-*

tive in sociology that views social life as a shared, symbolic meaning system. Emphasis is placed upon the ways in which words, gestures, and labels influence both individual behavior and social processes. Symbolic interactionism has taken its place alongside structural-functionalism and social conflict theory as a theoretical approach that asks an important set of questions about social life.

A third American development occurred at several Eastern Universities. At Yale University, a distinguished group of sociologists under the leadership of Lloyd Warner (1898–1970) began a series of community studies, aimed, among other things, at the question of the class structure. Warner, in his several studies of a place he called "Yankee City" (Warner & Lunt 1941, Warner 1949), and August Hollingshead, in his study of "Elmtown" (1949), provided empirical tests of Marx and Weber's ideas on social stratification. At Columbia University in New York City, Robert and Helen Lynd pursued similar issues in their study of "Middletown" (1929). These writers also developed some important directions in qualitative and case-study research methods. These studies of American community life would become a baseline to which all subsequent studies of community organization and the class system would be compared.

Finally, no picture of American sociology through mid-century would be complete without considering the work of Talcott Parsons (1902–1979). More than any other scholar, he was responsible for introducing the ideas of the European theorists, especially Weber and Durkheim, into American sociology. Parsons would use these ideas, particularly those of Durkheim, in his formulation of structural-functional theory. This approach provided an empirical research agenda in the 1940s and more so in the 1950s for examining the functional aspects of many institutions in American society, religion, family, medicine, education, law and many others.

Today, most sociological work is grounded in one of three theoretical perspectives: structural-functionalism, social conflict theory, and symbolic interactionism. As shown in Table 1.1, each theory focuses upon different aspects of social reality, and accordingly, each depicts different social processes as important.

TABLE 1.1

THREE SOCIOLOGICAL THEORIES

Name of Theory	Founding Writers	Focus Upon	Social Life Is Viewed As
Structural-Functional Theory	E. Durkheim T. Parsons	Macro-level	Interdependent structures yielding social order and continuity
Social Conflict Theory	K. Marx M. Weber	Macro-level	Conflicting material interests and values resulting in conflicts and change
Symbolic Interactionism	G. H. Mead	Micro-level	Shared meanings and symbols shaping patterned social interaction processes

SOCIOLOGY SINCE MIDCENTURY

Certain developments in academic sociology during the latter half of the 20th century deserve mention here. First, during the 1960s a general abandonment of structural-functional analysis occurred. This does not mean that this line of sociological study ceased. Rather, it took a back seat to a rebirth of interest in social conflict, patterns of social inequality, and social change processes. The reasons for this shift are easily discerned. In the United States, the 1960s were a period of both social turmoil and social awareness. The Kennedy administration's Peace Corps and VISTA (Volunteers in Service to America) programs and the Johnson administration's "War on Poverty" focused attention on both domestic and world social problems. Developments within sociology reflected these trends. Specifically, sociologists became interested in such social problems as poverty, urban decay, and social inequality. Worldwide dilemmas of war, population explosion, and the plight of underdeveloped nations were the newer social concerns of the times, and of some sociologists as well. Thanks to the writing of C. Wright Mills (1956, 1959) and others, some of the basic ideas of Marxian sociology gained new popularity.

A second development during this period was the codification and extension of the ideas of George Herbert Mead. Role theory and reference group theory arose as variations of symbolic interactionism and characterized the growth of social psychology as a major segment of the field of sociology. Finally, in the 1970s and 1980s, a new movement called *clinical sociology* became a component in some graduate training programs and a visible element in the meetings and publications of the American Sociological Association. This trend reflects the fact that many sociologists work in nonacademic settings, as city planners, organizational consultants, and evaluation researchers. They do such things as measure the success or failure of government social programs and help corporations design employee development programs. Some have established family counseling practices. *Clinical sociologists are applied scientists who use sociological knowledge to improve social arrangements in a diversity of social institutions and settings in both the public and private economic sectors.* Thus, in the 1970s and 1980s, one branch of sociology became more of a professional practice, not just a basic science. Today, this diversity is reflected in both the professional organization of sociology as well as in its literature and research publications.

Clinical sociology

TWO SOCIOLOGIES, BASIC AND APPLIED

If one dates sociology by August Comte's coinage of the word in the 1840s, sociology is now 150 years old. In retrospect, sociologists seem to have vacillated between two different, though related, conceptions of sociology: as a basic science and as an applied science. What is meant by this distinction? As noted earlier, *basic sciences have the purpose or goal of explanation.* In sociology this means the quest to understand how and why social reality becomes the way it is and is changed. Thus, *a sociological problem or question is a question about how and why social structures and social processes occur, how they are sustained and how they are changed.* In contrast, *applied sciences attempt to remedy or cure things.* Said differently, applied sciences attempt to solve real life problems. Unlike sociological problems, which involve explaining social trends, their causes, and con-

Basic science

Sociological problem

Applied science

Social problem

sequences, *social problems are problems that have social causes and require collective social solutions. Social problems refer to situations in which people are experiencing pain, suffering, or dislocation. Social problems are the focus of applied sociology.* Let's consider how these two kinds of scientific concerns apply to a specific social trend.

Racism is a social phenomena entailing both basic scientific questions and applied scientific concerns. The basic science questions about racism focus on explaining how and why racism occurs and understanding the consequences of racism for the oppressors, the oppressed, and society as a whole. Because racism occurs in most societies, our sociological imagination suggests that it must involve some rather fundamental aspects of social structure and culture. Obviously, the applied science questions about racism are quite different. Here, viewing racism as a negative force in the social structure, we wish to know how to reduce and even prevent racism. Applied sociology is concerned with intervention in the processes that sustain racist thought and practices. In this particular example there is a rather close connection between basic and applied sociological concerns. After all, by understanding the fundamental causes of racism, we might stand a better chance of preventing or eliminating it. Here a knowledge of causes and an ability to intervene may be closely related.

Of course, this close connection between sociological and social problems does not always exist. While some situations allow asking both basic and applied science questions, the distinction between sociological questions and social problems should not be blurred. The concerns of basic and applied science are different, and thus, the kinds of questions they ask, even about the same social phenomena, will be different. Obviously, both approaches have a place in modern sociological practice. However, this text, like most introductory college courses in sociology, stresses the basic science aspects of sociology.

In summary, this section of the chapter has identified some central themes in the development of sociological thought. Sociology emerged in the 19th century as a reflection of both scientific rationalism and humanism. The functional theory of Durkheim and the conflict theories of both Marx and Weber all were responses to the rise of urban-industrial society. Similarly, in America, sociology first emerged from the dual motive to both explain and repair society. The first half of the 20th century saw four major developments. The Chicago sociologists contributed a rich tradition of empirical studies on urban life. Also at Chicago, George Herbert Mead would begin an approach to the field of social psychology that later would be known as symbolic interactionism. At Yale University, Lloyd Warner and others began a tradition of community studies and an examination of stratification and other social structural issues. Finally, the Harvard-based sociologist Talcott Parsons refined and developed the sociological theory called structural-functionalism.

While sociology has undergone many changes since mid-century, three have been examined here. First, largely due to the rediscovery of significant social problems, there has been a gradual eclipse of structural-functional theory by conflict theories. Second, both role theory and reference group theory have provided major developments within symbolic interactionism. Finally, the emergence of clinical sociology has stressed the role of sociology as an applied, not just as a basic, science.

BARRIERS TO SOCIOLOGICAL THINKING

Although a sociological perspective may provide a distinctive way of viewing the social world, there are a number of frequently encountered barriers that stand in the way of developing such a perspective. Several features of Western, and especially American, cultural traditions run counter to a sociological view of things. Certain "habits of thought" stress interpretations of social life that make it difficult, at first, to view society from a sociological perspective. The following discussion identifies and makes explicit some of these features of everyday thought. By developing an awareness of them, we can begin to neutralize their tendency to block our developing a sociological view of society.

INDIVIDUALS AS CAUSES

A first such barrier is the tendency to view social life in individualistic terms. Ours is a highly psychologized culture. This means that social events in general, and especially the patterns of success or failure that persons experience, are explained in terms of individual traits and characteristics. Let's consider an example.

Harry Lewis of Detroit, Michigan is one of the thousands of individuals in the United States who is homeless. Harry frequents the local soup kitchen for his main meal. In the evening, he lines up with dozens of others trying to get shelter at the local Salvation Army facilities. If he's lucky, he gets a bed. If not, he retreats to the most sheltered spot he can find. How might Harry's situation be understood? The cultural tendency is to see Harry as a loser, someone who either is lazy, unmotivated, or who wants to live on the streets. After all, if only Harry would get a job, he could earn enough money to live in a home just like everyone else. Everyone knows it's easy to find work if a person really wants to work. That's one way of viewing it.

Actually, Harry is a bright, hardworking, skilled craftsman. He was an automotive worker at a major plant until three years ago when he was laid off. His unemployment benefits were exhausted after the first year. For the next year, he was able to live on the savings he had put aside. However, these, too, have been exhausted. The truth of the matter is that, today, Harry *is* working. He has a job as a dishwasher in a local restaurant that pays minimum wage. Harry didn't work for the first year, waiting to be called back to the auto plant. When he wasn't recalled, he began looking for work. However, automobile factories were not hiring. Because of foreign car competition, and the automation of manufacturing techniques, the American automobile industry needs fewer workers. When Harry looked elsewhere for work, his skills did not transfer easily into another high paying job. Harry took a job at a fast food outlet. However, the money he earned was not enough to cover the rent on his apartment and the payment on his car. Harry continued to search for a better paying job but was caught in a downward financial spiral. Harry sold his car, then gave up his apartment, and finally sold his household possessions. Harry would have moved to an inexpensive apartment. However, the landlord required a security deposit, plus first and last months' rent before Harry could move in. This amounted to about $1,000.00, something Harry, with his limited resources, could not afford. Harry began living on the streets, attempting to save some of the necessary money. However, it's not easy staying clean and neat on the streets. Harry lost his job at the fast food outlet because of his "unkempt" appearance. Since it's difficult looking for work under street conditions, Harry took the only work available, his dishwashing job which pays less than his previous job. Harry is a hard worker trapped in a situation over which he has little control. We need to understand Harry's situation, and the situation of others like Harry, not only as an individual problem but as the consequences of some broad social trends. Imported cars, a slowdown in American automobile production, the high cost of housing, and the minimum wage are not things Harry controls, nor does he have a lot of options immediately available to him.

This example demonstrates that an individualistic view prompts a different understanding of events than a sociological one. The individualistic view, in a sense, blames individuals for the things that befall them. Individuals' traits and characteristics are seen as causes of the things that happen to them. For example, in the United States, most children are taught in both their family and in schools that the individual can accomplish anything that her or his potential will allow. Such a perspective blinds us to the impact of collective, social forces in our lives. It is true that individual actions always have consequences, and that some of the messes we create in life are very much of our own making. However, it is essential to separate individual from social causes. The ability to make this distinction is a goal of sociological consciousness.

EVERYONE'S AN EXPERT

A second barrier to sociological thinking stems from the fact that the people, places, and events of everyday life are the subject matter of sociological study. Social reality is constantly right in front of our eyes to be seen and studied. Sociologists are not working with corpuscles and capillaries, atoms and electrons, salts and compounds, the structures of which are invisible to the naked eye. Rather, sociologists examine the world of the familiar.

However, herein lies the problem. Because all of us live in society, and all of us constantly participate in social life, we assume that we are experts about social life. After all, everyone is intimately familiar with the "things" sociologists study—people, groups, families, religious practices, and political events. Everyone's an expert on this sort of stuff, so it would seem. However, this really is not so. All people may be experts at living in society, but few are experts in answering scientific questions about society. As we've already seen, science focuses upon the task of explanation, and sociology seeks to explain the collective aspects of human behavior. These are not the kinds of tasks about which most people have expertise.

Developing a sociological perspective requires a realization that not everything about familiar social happenings is immediately apparent. Sociology involves discerning the unfamiliar causes and conditions that are embedded in familiar events. It might be argued that just like those corpuscles and capillaries, social structures and processes are invisible until social life is placed under the microscope of the sociological perspective.

I ALREADY KNEW THAT

A third barrier to sociological thinking is closely related to the previous idea that because things are familiar to us we have expertise about them. However, here the very language used by sociologists requires consideration. Because sociology uses everyday language to describe everyday events, it may sound as though nothing new is being said. This is quite different from the situation in physical science.

Because the physical, chemical, and biological realities studied in these sciences are not the stuff of everyday experience, the opportunity arises for inventing new terms to describe these phenomena. For instance, chemists work in laboratories with polymers and hydrocarbons. While polymers and hydrocarbons actually are parts of everyday life, they are not included in everyday discourse or language. Blood corpuscles are part of everyone's life experience. Yet, since people don't see them, they don't think or speak about them as such. The situation with social life and the language for describing it is quite another matter. Because social sciences use the same language to describe social reality that is used in everyday life, it sometimes sounds like nothing new is being said. However, sociological insights are much more than "common sense" observations about social life. Unless one reads and thinks carefully, there is the tendency to think "I already knew that." Indeed, just as chemicals in the laboratory are often labeled "handle with care," so we might say that social science textbooks should be labeled "read with care." The words are familiar, but the meanings are not everyday meanings.

HUMAN BEHAVIOR CAN'T BE PREDICTED

A fourth barrier to developing a sociological perspective is the belief that human behavior cannot be predicted. Yet, social life is not random and chaotic. Rather, social reality has an underlying order and predictability. While the assumption of order and predictability in the universe is true of all science, many people cannot accept this when it is applied to human beings. Surely, there is a certain self-interest involved in all of this. After all, if human behavior is patterned and predictable, and I am a human being, then my own actions must be predictable. That is not a very comforting thought. At the very least, it conflicts with my image of myself as a unique individual. Moreover, from our individual life experiences, each of us usually can find an exception to what the sociologist claims is the rule. We can find at least one instance where the prediction does not hold true. So, can human behavior be predicted or not? Let's consider some actual cases.

Suppose we compare the income of a particular female with that of a particular male, or of an individual black person with that of an individual white person? We may find that this one particular female earns more money than the male, or this individual black person earns more money than the individual white person. However, there also is a general pattern in which females and blacks as aggregates earn less money than do males or whites. Even though it does not pertain in 100 percent of the cases, there is an underlying general pattern requiring explanation. How can these individual cases and the general pattern which is different from these individual cases both make sense?

Probability

The existing general pattern is a probabilistic fact. *Probabilities are things that most of the time, all things being equal, tend to happen with regularity.* Upon inspection, probable patterns exhibit understandable causes. Exceptions to these probabilities exhibit unique circumstances. In other words, the individual cases vary from the general pattern because of special conditions. Let's return to our case examples. In America today, most black persons earn less than most white persons. Similarly, most females earn less than do most males. Both the general pattern and the individual cases are true because the general pattern is one of probability. Such patterns of probability are equally present in the physical sciences. There is a direct causal relationship between smoking and lung cancer. However, 100 percent of smokers do not develop lung cancer. This does not negate the general finding that smokers are more likely to develop lung cancer than nonsmokers. It would be foolhardy to believe that the exceptions disprove this rule. Exceptional cases reflect unique circumstances.

Therefore, saying that human behavior is predictable does not rob us of our individualism. Social life, like physical phenomena, exhibits general tendencies. All of us are caught in such trends or tendencies, but only to the extent that in any situation our particular case may fit or vary from the probable typical case. From moment to moment, we are all free, to some extent, to alter in one way or another the circumstances of our lives and the paths that we traverse. However, the consequences of those choices are routinely predictable. They follow probable patterns.

In summary, we have examined four important reasons why it may be difficult for the beginning student to grasp sociological thinking. First, since it is assumed that individuals are "masters of their own destinies," we tend not to look for the collective social bases of human thoughts, actions, and feelings. Second, since we all live in society, we commit the error of thinking we are experts about society. Third, because sociology examines social phenomena with which we are familiar, we mistakenly believe that the information sociology supplies is not new. Finally, in maintaining that human behavior can't be predicted, beginning students often ignore the reality of social patterns.

APPLICATIONS

WHY STUDY SOCIOLOGY?

What can be gained from studying sociology? After all, most students taking an introductory sociology course are not going to become professional sociologists. However, a Ph.D. in sociology is not required to use the tools of sociology in everyday life situations. An awareness of how social forces affect your life, and the lives of others, is a valuable asset. The sociological perspective supplies insights into everyday interactions and increases our understanding of the events and persons that populate our lives. It enables us to see commonplace events in a new light and to notice things not noticed before.

By way of illustration, each chapter of this text concludes with an "applications" discussion in which some of the basic concepts of the chapter are applied to contemporary events. For this first "applications" discussion, we've selected a rather remarkable event in the world of publishing, a publishing event that quickly became a social controversy, and that reveals some dramatic social facts in present-day American society.

CASE

DYING IN AMERICA

In March of 1991, author Derek Humphrey published a handbook on how to commit suicide entitled *Final Exit.* The book produced immediate public debate in the press and electronic media. Should this book be banned? Is it ethical to publish such a book? Will people harm themselves with the information in it? How could a person in good conscience publish this kind of material?

To the sociological eye the interesting event was not so much the book's publication, but its robust sales. By August of 1991, the publisher reported that the book was "sold out" and "back ordered" by 150,000 copies (Ames, *et al.* 1991). It even topped the *New York Times Book Review* "Paperback Best Sellers" list in the "Advice, How-To and Miscellaneous" category. What do the sales of this book reveal about American society? Why is a suicide handbook such a hot item?

Clearly, committing suicide is a highly personal act. However, understanding why substantial numbers of people want knowledge of the techniques for committing suicide requires using what C. Wright Mills calls a "sociological imagination." To what extent is the present-day interest in the "how-to's" of suicide a manifestation of what Mills terms a "public issue?"

Through technological intervention, people can be kept alive by artificial means far beyond the time their bodies could survive independently. The growing use of "life support" systems has raised a question. When should a person be allowed to die? Some state governments have intervened in the attempts of families to remove loved ones from life support systems. What was once a private issue for families and their physicians has become a wide-spread public issue.

TABLE 1.2

SELECTED POPULATION CHARACTERISTICS FOR THE UNITED STATES, 1920–2000*

Year	Percent of Population Age 65 & Older	Population Size in Millions	Life Expectancy At Birth (years)	
			Men	Women
1920	4.7%	105,711	53.6	54.6
1940	8.1%	131,669	60.8	65.2
1960	9.2%	179,323	66.6	73.1
1980	11.3%	226,504	70.0	77.4
1990	12.7%	249,975	72.1	79.0
2000	13.0%	268,266	73.5	80.4

SOURCE: *Statistical Abstract of the United States,* Washington, D.C., Government Printing Office (annual editions).

*Statistics for the year 2000 are estimated projections, middle series.

As seen in Table 1.2, between 1920 and 1990, the proportion of the American population aged 65 and older has nearly tripled (from 4.7 percent to 12.7 percent). Moreover, because the size of the United States population grew so much between 1920 and 1990 (from approximately 105 million to 250 million) the actual number of older Americans has increased by a factor of eight, from just under 4 million to nearly 32 million persons. Life expectancy for men (72 years) and women (78 years) are both at record highs. But, these trends raise "quality-of-life" versus "quantity-of-life" issues. Is longevity desirable if it is accompanied by pain and suffering? It is not surprising that many people are concerned about the timing of their death and having control over death (suicide). Additionally, today, people are aware of the financial costs of health care and may prefer to die rather than to have their families exhaust their funds postponing an inevitable event.

These issues are apt to remain controversial for a substantial time because modern societies have not yet formulated clear moral and ethical guidelines about these matters. Until such societal norms are established, suicide is apt to remain a relevant choice.

Suicide is a very personal act, but a sociological perspective reveals that it also has become a major social issue in modern societies. The publication and sales of *Final Exit* show that American society may be undergoing a period of change regarding both social practices and cultural values about life and death matters.

Chapter Summary

1. Sociology is the scientific study and interpretation of social life. Accordingly, sociologists study a wide range of phenomena including all the things that people do with other persons. Collective patterns are the focus of sociological study. Individuals are of interest through their participation in groups, culture, and social structure.

2. Sociological subject matter is divided into macro- and microsocial categories. Macrosocial topics are large, such as how entire social systems work, what kinds of social stratification occur, or how patterns of modernization and development are produced. Microsocial topics are small and focus either upon specific institutions, such as religious or family units, or upon connections between the individual and the group.

3. There is an art to sociological analysis. This art derives from the unique approach to the subject matter involved in the sociological perspective. Durkheim saw this as the process of discovering social facts and social forces. C. Wright Mills described that art as a sociological imagination in which sociohistorical patterns of cause and consequence are examined. Peter L. Berger speaks of this art as the process of unmasking reality and looking beyond the obvious.

4. Sociology is a science because it shares certain key characteristics with all scientific investigation: the goal of explanation, the focus on empirically available phenomena, the use of techniques of replication, and the norm of objectivity.

5. Sociology, which began in the middle of the 19th century, was, in part, conditioned by questions and concerns stimulated by rapid social changes. In both Europe and America, sociology has moved between two different kinds of scientific models: basic and applied science. While the former seeks explanations, the latter attempts to remedy. Clinical sociology is the most recent applied science development in modern sociology.
6. Common ways of viewing society can be barriers for beginning students first developing a sociological perspective. One must search for general, not individual, causes of events. While we all live in society, this does not make us social science experts. While sociological terms seem familiar, the scientific findings they convey are much more than "common sense" claims. Social reality and human behavior, like physical phenomena, reveal probable causes and patterns and are thus predictable.
7. While few people pursue sociology as a career, the sociological perspective is a useful component in anyone's education. By understanding social structures and social processes, we become better equipped to navigate through social life.

Key Concepts

applied science
basic science
clinical sociology
empirical availability
explanation
individual facts
macrosociology
microsociology
objectivity
probability
replication
science
scientific humanism
social facts
social conflict theory
social problem
social psychology
sociology
sociological imagination
sociological problem
structural-functional theory
symbolic interactionism
unmasking social reality

Bibliography

Ames, Katrine *et al.*
1991. "Last Rights," in *Newsweek*, (August 26): pp. 40–41.

Becker, Ernest
1968. *The structure of evil: An essay on the unification of the science of man.* New York: George Braziller.

Berger, Peter, L.
1963. *Invitation to sociology.* Garden City: Doubleday.

Durkheim, Emile
1893. *The division of labor in society.* Translated by George Simpson, 1933. New York: Macmillan.

1895. *The rules of sociological method.* Translated by Sarah Solovay & John H. Mueller, Edited by George E. G. Catlin, 1938. New York: Free Press.

1897. *Suicide: A study in sociology.* Translated by George Simpson, 1951. New York: Free Press.

Hollingshead, August B.
1949. *Elmtown's Youth.* New Haven, Connecticut: Yale Unviersity Press.

Humphrey, Derek
1991. *Final exit.* New York: The Hemlock Society.

Luker, Kristen
1984. *Abortion and the politics of motherhood.* Berkeley and Los Angeles, California: University of California Press.

Lynd, Robert, S. & Helen Merrill Lynd
1929. *Middletown.* New York: Harcourt, Brace, Jovanovich.

Marx, Karl
1867. *Capital.* Translated by Samuel Moore and Edward Aveling, 3 volumes, 1967. New York: International Publishers.

Merton, Robert
1949. On sociological theories of the middle range. In *Social theory and social structure.* (Enlarged edition, 1968). New York: Free Press.

Mills, C. Wright
1956. *The power elite.* New York: Oxford University Press.

1959. *The sociological imagination.* New York: Oxford University Press.

Myrdal, Gunnar
1944. *An American Dilemma.* New York: Harper & Row.

Nisbet, Robert A.
1962. "Sociology as an art form." *Pacific Sociological Review,* Vol. 5, No. 2 (Fall), pp. 67–74.

1966. *The sociological tradition.* New York: Basic Books.

Turner, Stephen Park & Jonathan H. Turner
1990. *The impossible science: An institutional analysis of american sociology.* Newbury Park, California: Sage Publications.

Vidich, Arthur J. & Stanford M. Lyman
1985. *American sociology: Worldly rejections of religion and their directions.* New Haven, Connecticut: Yale University Press.

Wallwork, Ernest
1972. *Durkheim: Morality and milieu.* Cambridge, Mass.: Harvard University Press.

Warner, Lloyd
1949. *Social class in america.* Chicago: The Social Science Research Association.

Warner, Lloyd & Paul S. Lunt
1941. *The social life of a modern community.* New Haven: Yale University Press.

Weber, Max
1904–1905. *The Protestant ethic and the spirit of capitalism.* Translated by Talcott Parsons, 1958. New York: Scribner.

Weitzman, Leonore J.
1985. *The divorce revolution.* New York: The Free Press.

Zborowski, Mark
1952. "Cultural components in responses to pain," *Journal of Social Issues,* Vol. 8, No. 4, pp. 16–30.

CHAPTER 2

DOING SOCIOLOGY: THEORY AND RESEARCH

CHAPTER OUTLINE

LEARNING OBJECTIVES

All scientists theorize and build general bodies of knowledge about their subject matter, which requires empirical research and carefully assembling the data with which theories may be tested. How are these things done in sociology? This chapter examines the role of theory in guiding research and the role of research in building sociological theories. It also examines the various ways in which sociologists conduct social research and collect data for scientific analysis. Unlike the physical sciences, which rely heavily upon a single research strategy (the laboratory experiment), the social sciences use a broad range of methodologies. In most physical sciences, the uniformity of the subject matter justifies a uniformity of method. In contrast, the social sciences must contend with a high degree of complexity and diversity of subject matter. For these reasons, sociologists have developed a variety of research methods for studying social life.

The purposes of this chapter are to provide an understanding of the relationship between theory and research, an overview of the ways in which sociological research is conducted, and an inventory of the various research methods available. If sociologists must choose from a variety of methods, how do they decide which ones are to be used, and why? What factors enter into these decisions? What are some of the practical and ethical issues that must be faced by social researchers in all research situations?

The beginning student in sociology has little need to become an expert in research methods. However, an understanding of the role of theory in research, and how the various research techniques "fit" different kinds of research questions about social life are important ingredients in a sociological perspective. This chapter provides some elementary lessons in sociological research methods, including some examples of the things sociologists study and how they study them. You will become a more informed and sophisticated consumer of sociological information and research findings.

From reading and studying this chapter, you should be able to answer the following questions:

1. How do social research and sociological theory promote and fulfill basic scientific goals?
2. What is the relationship between theory and research in the process of doing sociology?
3. What are the specific links in the chain of events that connect theory and research findings?
4. As sociologists enter the field to collect research data, what sorts of questions must be answered to insure quality control? How can we know that the research is well-designed, and how do sociologists decide whom they will study?
5. Why do sociologists use so many different research methods? How are these methods related to the subject matter of sociology?
6. What are the specific research methods or techniques used in sociological research, and what criteria determine their selection and use?

Building Sociological Theories

What does it mean to do sociology? What sorts of activities are involved, and what kinds of concerns guide and shape those activities? Sociology, like all other basic sciences, focuses upon the goal of explanation and does so through the analysis of empirically available phenomena. The first section of this chapter explores in greater depth the scientific activity of explaining events through the analysis of empirically available information. We turn first to the nature of, and relationships between, sociological theory and social research. These two activities are linked by a chain of ideas. Concepts, theory propositions, nominal definitions, research hypotheses, variables, and operational definitions are the links in this chain. We also shall consider some criteria for assessing the quality of these links. The matters of validity, reliability, and the use of population samples will be explored.

THEORY AND RESEARCH

Theory

What is a sociological theory? *A theory is a set of logically related general statements that describe, explain, and predict occurrences in an entire class of events.* Typically, theoretical statements reflect the collection and analysis of relevant empirical information. Moreover, theories are general in nature because they attempt to explain not simply specific happenings, but entire classes of events. The importance of studying and understanding classes of events rather than just particular events is illustrated by recent medical research on the disease of AIDS. Once it was understood that AIDS fit a category of events, i.e., viral disease, aspects of the syndrome that were puzzling became intelligible. In a sense, once a category of events is identified, researchers know what kinds of information to seek. The typical life-cycle of events fits a pattern and may be compared to, and explained with, other similar cases in its class. Sociological theories generalize about the ways entire classes of social phenomena occur. For example, while sociologists may begin by studying a friendship group, a small work group, or even the members of an athletic team, the object is to make generalizations about small groups as a category of events.

What are the respective roles of theory and research? Theory describes the apparent logical relationships that exist in the events being studied, while research provides the means for testing whether or not those relationships actually exist. Theory provides direction and focus to research activities. It identifies things of importance, sharpens the questions to be asked, and specifies the types of information required for answering those questions. Research, of course, is the actual collecting of information. There is, then, a reciprocity between theory and research. Let's examine that reciprocity more closely.

Deductive method

Inductive method

Theory and research interact in a never-ending cycle, and philosophers of science have debated the issue of where that cycle ought to begin. Those debates have focused upon the deductive and inductive approaches to research. *In the deductive method, scientific activity begins with a theory and research tests that theory. In the inductive method, the collection of information or data is the initial act, and theories result from the analysis of research data.* In actuality, both sorts of activities occur in the research process. As seen in Figure 2.1, beginning

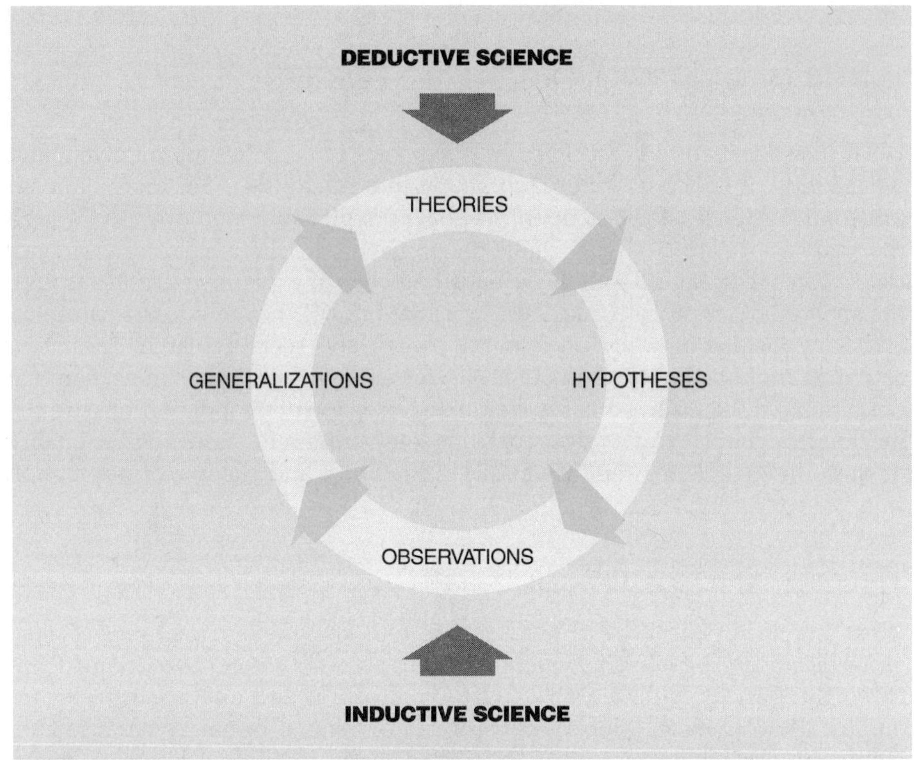

FIGURE 2.1
THE WHEEL OF SCIENCE

SOURCE: Adapted and reprinted with permission from Walter L. Wallace, *The Logic of Science in Sociology*, New York, Aldine de Gruyer, copyright 1971 by Walter L. Wallace.

with the deductive side of the process, theories generate hypotheses. Hypotheses suggest data-gathering techniques, which lead to observations, from which generalizations are formed. The result is modification or support for the initial theory. However, starting from the inductive side, the researcher begins with specific observations. This suggests generalizations that tentatively spawn a theory, which then is tested through the formulation of hypotheses. The difference between induction and deduction is the point at which one breaks into the cycle. In practice, researchers may break into this cycle at various points, depending upon the amount and type of information or data available.

In this context it may be noted that sociology, like other sciences, offers a number of different theoretical perspectives. Each perspective, namely, structural-functionalism, social conflict theory, and symbolic interactionism, provides a different model for examining social life. Each contains different assumptions, directs the researcher toward different aspects of social phenomena, and asks different research questions. In this sense, different theories are like different windows in a room. To see what's in the room, one must look through the windows. However, each window provides a different point of view, revealing distinct aspects of the room while obscuring others. Taking full account of the room requires a consideration of all the images provided by the different windows. The act of sociological analysis is quite similar. Specific investigations of social reality typically proceed from a single theoretical perspective. Different theories and the research activities they produce supply information on different aspects of the whole.

Finally, it should be recognized that although research may demonstrate that a theory is *false*, it never can prove that a theory is *true*. Even if the research yields information conforming to the predicted relationships of the theory, it can only be said that the research *supports* the theory. This is because a theory is an abstraction about an entire range of phenomena, and it is impossible to test a theory against all possible events within that range. On the other hand, it is possible to disprove a theory. If research does not discover the expected relationships, the theory is rejected, not supported. At best, the theory may be modified to conform with the findings. In this sense, research scientists are very much like persons sitting on a jury. Jurors must decide, within a reasonable doubt, if an accused person is guilty. The jurors cannot directly say that the available evidence proves innocence. They can only say within reason that the evidence supports a theory of guilt. Of course, as noted in Chapter 1 (pp. 12–13), theory testing rarely depends upon a single piece of research. Rather, support or rejection of a theory is produced through replication.

PROPOSITIONS, CONCEPTS, AND NOMINAL DEFINITIONS

We've seen thus far that there are two kinds of activities involved in doing sociology, research and theory-building. What are the actual tools by which these two activities are accomplished? While these things may be grouped in a variety of ways, we shall focus here upon six tools involved in doing sociology. Three of these stem from the theoretical side of the ledger. They are concepts, propositions, and nominal definitions. The other three pertain more directly to the research act. They are operational definitions, variables, and hypotheses.

Propositions

While theories are sets of logically related statements about categories of events, *individual theoretical statements are called propositions. They describe relationships among relevant concepts.* For example, we may suspect that religious activity and age are related. A specific proposition may be that the frequency of religious behavior increases with aging. In this instance, the proposition has described the anticipated relationship between two concepts, religious behavior and age. *Concepts are linguistic symbols representing entire categories of phenomena. Concepts allow categorizing the things to be studied.* Concepts do not refer to specific phenomena or events. Rather, precisely because of their general nature, concepts may include a number of different criteria or characteristics common to a general category of phenomena. Concepts reveal how the things in a given class are alike. As such, concepts serve an important "sensitizing" function (Blumer 1954). Concepts not only sensitize us to things that share certain properties, but also help us exclude those things that ought to be subsumed under a different conceptual category. Thus, in the example given here, the concept of "religious behavior" focuses our attention upon activities growing from a belief in a supernatural being. At the same time, economic, political, educational, and other patterns of activity are excluded from examination.

Concepts

However, because of their level of abstraction, concepts are not immediately useful for research purposes. Rather, every researcher must move from the level of abstract concepts to a specification of exactly what will be studied. This is called a nominal definition. *A nominal definition identifies a specific range, type, or category of real life events or activities that fall within the general concept.* Concepts always must be nominally defined before beginning actual research. Doing so establishes the boundaries for collecting data. In the simplest terms, nominal definitions name the kinds of phenomena and events to be studied.

Nominal definition

Thus, in the example given earlier, religious behavior might be defined nominally as all behavior related to the belief in a supernatural that occurs within religious institutions, such as churches, temples, synagogues, and mosques. For the purposes of the present research, it is understood the religious behavior consists of the things people do in churches, temples, synagogues, and mosques. Obviously, much has been excluded from this nominal definition of religious behavior. Moreover, it is not being claimed that other kinds of religious activities are not significant. Rather, the nominal definition operates under two provisos. First, it is impossible to study everything about religion (or for that matter anything else) all at once. Second, the definition proposed is consistent with, and appropriate for, the theoretical proposition formulated.

HYPOTHESES, VARIABLES, AND OPERATIONAL DEFINITIONS

Variables, hypotheses, and operational definitions perform essential tasks on the research side of the sociological chain of activities. These three elements of the research act answer the questions: Exactly what will be studied? How will it be measured? and What specific patterns do we anticipate finding (Babbie 1986, 37)?

Variable

A variable is any phenomenon, the characteristics, properties, or attributes of which change (or vary) from case to case in terms of amount, degree, or type. Said differently, when a theoretical concept is brought into the field of research it is called a variable. Variables may change in value both quantitatively and qualitatively. For example, the question, "How often do you attend church?" elicits a quantitative measure of religious behavior, such as once per week, twice per month, or once per month. In contrast, the question "What is your religious preference?" produces qualitative categories of response, such as Protestant, Catholic, Jewish, Moslem, or none of these. These are qualitative variations because they are different in kind. On the other hand, quantitative variations are differences of degree or extent, not type or kind. Both sorts of variables are studied in sociological research.

Operational definition

While a variable tells what will be measured, *an operational definition specifies exactly how a variable is to be measured in a particular study.* This "operationalization" of the original theoretical concept is one of the last steps in the research process before entering the field to collect data. In the illustration we've been using here, religious behavior may be operationalized as the number of times each month that a person attends prayer services. Of course, once the variables and operational definitions have been provided, it is also possible to specify the precise research hypotheses to be tested. *A research hypothesis states the expected pattern and relationships among the variables.* For instance, we may hypothesize that young persons, meaning those under 35 years of age, attend prayer services fewer times each month than middle aged persons, meaning those 36–55 years of age. The research hypothesis contains the exact dispositions of variables and measures through which the original general theoretical proposition will be tested. Thus, through hypotheses, variables, and operational definitions, the links in the chain connecting theory to research are joined to each other.

Research hypothesis

Why is it important to be cognizant of these several links in the chain? Obviously, any general theoretical proposition may be tested through quite a number of research hypotheses. Any concept may be nominally and operationally defined in various ways. Differences in the extent to which a research effort supports a theory can be created at various steps in this process. Therefore, as an informed consumer of sociological information, you should not simply ask "What was found?" Rather, you should begin asking "How was this found?" It is not enough to be satisfied that a chain of connective links has been established leading from a theory to en empirical test of it. Rather, the quality of those links in the sociological chain ought to be examined. That examination, what might be thought of as scientific quality control, proceeds according to well-established criteria. Those criteria are the focus of the next section of this chapter.

In summary, we have seen that the tasks of research and theory-building are intimately related. Propositions, concepts, and nominal definitions are critical links on the theory-building side of the chain of sociological work. Hypotheses, variables, and operational definitions form the research links in that chain. Regardless of whether the process begins inductively with data collection, or deductively with the formulation of propositions, all of these activities are included in the process of doing sociology.

Some Complexities of Measurement

There is an old adage that "a chain is only as good as its weakest link." How may we evaluate and test the strength of the links that connect theoretical issues and research findings in sociology? The answer lies in determining the validity and reliability of the measures used, and in the careful selection of appropriate sampling techniques.

VALIDITY AND RELIABILITY

Validity

Validity means that a measure accurately reflects the meaning of the concept it is intended to measure. In assessing validity, the question becomes: Has the researcher measured what he or she intended to measure, or has something else been measured? Any concept may be operationalized by a number of valid measures. While a valid measure of that concept need not be the only valid measure of that concept, it is essential that all measures used in empirical research be valid. An invalid measure could lead to an inaccurate claim of support for a theory.

Let's return to the concept of religious behavior, nominally defined as actions and events that stem from a belief in a supernatural being and that take place in religious institutions. Could this concept be measured by the amount of money persons give to religious institutions? Is this a valid measure of religion, as defined here? Clearly, it is not. What would be measured is financial behavior, and financial behavior as it may be religiously motivated. Giving money to religious institutions is neither a sufficient nor necessary indication of belief in the supernatural. Some persons may give substantial sums to religious institutions because they feel those organizations do good work, or because they feel that giving is an obligation of membership. But, these motives are not included in the concept of "religious behavior" provided here. This does not prohibit using such a measure should the concept be defined differently. In contrast, people's attendance at worship services bears a logical relationship to the definition of religious behavior used here. In fact, the activity of prayer makes little sense in the absence of religious belief. When there are common sense connections from the concept to the nominal definition to the actual measure, the measure is valid.

Reliability

In addition to being valid, measures also must be reliable. The same measure, when used in similar studies of similar events, should yield similar results. *Reliability refers to the consistency of a measure.* The constancy or reliability of a measure is of critical importance. Without reliable measures, replication would not be possible, and without replication in some form, it would be impossible to gain a consensus about research findings. Stated differently, if the measures used are not reliable, then the different studies using such measures cannot be compared.

Measures can be reliable and invalid, but not the reverse. They cannot be unreliable and valid. In other words, the question "How much money do you give to religious institutions?" is probably quite reliable and would yield similar response patterns within different religious communities. However, it measures financial not religious behavior. The question "Do you pray to Jesus Christ?" is neither a valid nor a reliable measure of the concept "religious behavior." If this question were asked of Christians, Jews, and Moslems, they'd all respond differently. One can say "no" to this question and still be engaging in religious activity. This is because the question measures *Christian* belief, not the *general* belief in a supernatural being. The question "Do you pray to a supreme being?" would operationalize the concept "religious behavior" and would produce similar response patterns among Catholics, Protestants, Jews, and Moslems. Therefore, it is both a reliable and valid measure of this concept.

Consider another illustration; the incidence of rape within a community. The number of rapes as measured by police statistics on convicted rapists is a reliable measure. It surely will produce comparable statistics from researcher to researcher. However, it is an invalid measure. This is because it measures convictions, not rapes!

Validity and reliability are criteria that should be applied in assessing the strength of the links in the chain of theory and research. Assessing validity and reliability involves looking for common sense uniformities in the transition from concepts to measures. While these uniformities help answer the question of how sociologists collect data, a related question is "From whom do they collect it?"

SAMPLES: RANDOM, STRATIFIED, AND PURPOSIVE

How do sociologists decide who to include in a given study? What determines the selection of persons who will be included in the research or data collection activities? The concepts with which a study begins provide a first clue. Those concepts, you will recall, describe classes or categories of events or persons. The goal of social research is to construct general theoretical understandings of those classes or categories of persons, events, or activities. Operational definitions identify real instances through which the general concept is measured, and also

Population universe

specify the population to be studied. *A population, universe, or population universe describes all those person or events in the general category about which one wishes to theorize.* For example, the concept "religious behavior" discussed here was to be measured in the population universe of members of religious institutions.

Sample

What are samples, and what is the relationship between populations and samples? Why do scientists use samples? *A sample is a systematic selection of cases from the total universe or population being studied.* The use of samples results from a very practical dilemma faced by all scientists. It rarely is possible to include in a study all the persons or events in the population of interest. For instance, it simply is not possible to ask all members of religious institutions in the United States about their activities. Even if this were possible, it hardly would be practical. Samples are a practical solution for this dilemma. Samples are "stand-ins" or substitutes for the population universes from which they are drawn. Accordingly, a sample is said to be representative if it accurately reflects the characteristics of the population from which it is drawn, or at least those characteristics relevant to the particular study at hand. The ability to generalize about a population based upon studying a sample from it hinges on the care with which a sample is selected. Sample selection procedures, not the size of the sample, determines its usefulness.

FIGURE 2.2
Sociologists are not the only people who use the idea of random selection.

Because scientists in all fields of study rely so heavily upon samples, sampling techniques have become the focus of a highly specialized subfield in research methodology. However, all researchers must understand the major sampling techniques and the kinds of research situations for which they are suited. While there are many sampling techniques, three basic ones are discussed here, random, stratified, and purposive samples.

Random sample

Perhaps the best known sampling procedure is random sampling. *A random sample is a selection of persons, cases, or events from a universe in such a manner that each one has an equal chance of being chosen.* Random sampling techniques are used when the goal is to produce the same profile or body of information that would be obtained if the entire population or universe were to be included in the study. Selecting a random sample assumes that the researcher could include the entire population if time, funds, and other practical considerations allowed. There are many ways of randomizing the selection process. For a small population, this could entail something as simple as placing everyone's name in a hat and blindly selecting a sample of persons. For large populations, a computer-generated table of random numbers could be used. Each week, in many states, public lotteries use randomizing techniques for selecting winning combinations of numbers. In all these instances, the basic principle is that all cases have an equal chance of being selected.

Stratified sample

A second type of technique produces a stratified sample. *A stratified sample is a selection of homogeneous subpopulations of persons, events, or cases from a population in a manner that insures certain desired proportions of subpopulations in the sample.* Stratified sampling is done when it is known that an important variable is not evenly distributed in the population being studied. Its purpose is to insure adequate representation of subpopulations. For example, in the United States, whites greatly outnumber blacks, Hispanics, Asians, and other subpopulations. A random sample might produce too few members of these subpopulations to allow adequate representation. To correct this, a stratified sample is drawn. Moreover, it is possible to combine both random and stratified sampling techniques.

Purposive samples

A third technique is called purposive sampling. *Purposive samples are composed of persons, cases, or events exhibiting known characteristics of special relevance for the research question being studied.* In other words, the research is not aimed at large general populations. Its goal is to understand things about persons or events that share rather unique or particular characteristics. For example, to learn about the things that happen to victims of crime does not require random sampling from the general population. Rather, a purposive sample of crime victims is the best source of this information. Purposive samples are representative precisely because persons or events are selected, not randomly, but on the basis of special characteristics that are the subject of the research. Some other examples of purposive samples are criminal offenders, members of religious cults or sects, leaders of particular organizations, and teenage mothers. In some instances, it is useful to compare data collected from such special populations with that from general populations or control groups. In this manner, it is possible to simulate an experimental research design.

METHODOLOGICAL CHOICES

Doing sociology requires making a series of decisions. We've seen that sociologists make decisions about broad theoretical concerns (propositions and concepts) and also about operational techniques (measuring variables and drawing samples). The latter of these decisions concerns the precise strategies of data collection. How will the research be conducted? Will it involve talking to people, observing them, mailing them questionnaires, or some other strategy? These choices in research method stem from the nature of the sociologist's subject matter. Let's reexamine that subject matter for a moment.

Human life exhibits three distinct aspects: action, cognition, and emotion. People act, have beliefs and ideas, and experience feelings. The scientific study and interpretation of social life requires access to all three realms of human experience. All science, of course, is predicated upon the empirical availability of the subject matter. To be studied, phenomena must be either directly observable or measurable in some way. In the physical sciences, this usually means observations done in laboratory settings. Much of the physical world is directly observable, and we do not disrupt physical reality by bringing some of it into the laboratory for observation. These things are not true of social life.

Of the three realms of human life—action, cognition, and emotion—only human action is directly observable. Accordingly, techniques of direct observation are a first basic category of research techniques. Cognition, taken to include thoughts, attitudes, opinions, beliefs, commitments, knowledge, and ideologies, constitutes the second major realm of human life. These things seem to be hidden from scientific observation. They are packed away in people's heads. Similarly, emotional categories of experience are equally elusive to observational research methods. While, on occasion, people are unable to hide their emotions, for instance, when persons blush, cry, or smile, most emotional states, like some cognitive phenomena, are not suited to examination through observational research techniques. One way to gain information about something that cannot be observed is to ask about it.

Finally, there are many things that sociologists wish to know about social life that cannot be ascertained through either direct observation or direct question research. For example, if the research question involves history, one can neither ask questions nor observe directly. Rather, techniques of indirect observation must be introduced. Indirect observation entails analyzing existing records or data files rather than collecting new data. These techniques frequently are practical alternatives for studying present-day social life as well.

In summary, we've seen that validity and reliability are two tests of the strength of the research act. A valid measure accurately reflects the meaning of the concept it is intended to measure. A reliable measure does its job consistently from one research situation to the next. Because it rarely is practical to study all members of a population or population universe, sociologists frequently study samples. A random sample, in which all members of a population have an equal chance of being selected, is used when one wishes to generalize about the characteristics of a large population. A stratified sample consists of specified subpopulations and compensates for elements of bias likely to result in a simple random sample. Purposive samples consists of persons exhibiting known social characteristics of relevance to the research.

Direct question, direct observation, and indirect observation are the three categories of research strategies with which sociologists gather social data. The remaining sections of this chapter examine in detail the specific research techniques in each of these three categories.

DIRECT QUESTION METHODS

Direct question

Direct question methods pertain, in the first instance, to the study of things that are not readily available for observation. Both the cognitive and emotional realms of human experience are the subject matter of sociological inquiry. However, there are other kinds of actions requiring direct question methods. Some activities, such as sexual conduct or other intimate aspects of family life, typically are not observed by outsiders. In order to gain such information, people must be questioned. Additionally, some activities while not occurring in private settings, develop over long periods of time. Researchers may ask people to reconstruct these events to describe what happened and why it happened. There are two general strategies of direct question research, the survey and the in-depth interview. Additionally, surveys may be administered in three different ways: through self-administration, through telephone interviews, and through face-to-face interviews. Each direct question strategy and method of administration has advantages and disadvantages as well as specific requirements for successful use.

SURVEYS, THREE TECHNIQUES

Survey

A survey is a direct-question research strategy that uses a standardized questionnaire to which a relatively large sample of persons respond. Surveys provide an efficient way of fulfilling certain kinds of research goals. First, when coupled with appropriate sampling techniques, survey methods facilitate the collection of information from which generalizations about large populations may be made. This is why opinion polls and attitude surveys are so often used by national television networks. The rapid administration of standardized questions to a population sample allows broadcasters to characterize public opinion or public sentiment on issues of current interest. Second, while surveys occasionally are used to examine issues in depth, survey research is most appropriate for descriptive studies. Political preferences, consumers' likes and dislikes, levels of prejudice, and a host of other attitudinal variables may be described with survey techniques. Third, compared to in-depth interviews, survey techniques are inexpensive and fast. Survey research is the most frequently used direct question strategy.

The format of survey questionnaires is uniform. That is, the same set of questions is presented in the same order, and in the same words, to all respondents. Specific questions (items) often are pretested for reliability and validity and usually are precoded and formatted for ease of computer processing. This minimizes the time between data collection and data analysis. The designing of survey items is a skilled craft and an art. Questions must be unambiguous, be free of hidden biases, and avoid the implicit suggestion of right or wrong answers to the respondents. There are three methods of survey administration. They are self-administration, telephone, and face-to-face questioning. Let's briefly examine the strengths and weaknesses of each.

Self-administration, in which people are asked to complete the survey themselves, is the most commonly used technique of collecting survey data. Questionnaires may be either mailed or delivered, return-mailed or retrieved by the researcher. Even with the ever-increasing costs of paper, printing, and postage, the self-administered mailed questionnaire remains an inexpensive and rapid data collection technique. Self-administered surveys also have the advantage of allowing respondents to be anonymous. For this reason, they are a logical choice when the sensitivity of the information sought may negatively affect people's willingness to participate in a study.

FIGURE 2.3
Surveys often focus on people's opinions.

Self-administered questionnaires may range in length and complexity from the short set of questions you may have been asked to answer on the guarantee card for the "boom-box" you purchased last year to the several pages of questions some persons are asked to complete for the United States Census. However, all self-administered research situations assume that the people being studied are literate. This is a major weakness of the self-administration technique. Even in nations where the literacy rate is high, literacy may vary greatly by geographic region and social class. This may lead to a biased sample, since only those who can read and write with fluency will complete the self-administered questionnaire. A related problem of the self-administered questionnaire is the potential for low response rates. Response rates (the percent of the sample that participates) affects the ability to generalize from the findings of a study. Mailed studies sometimes receive response rates as low as 10 percent, and a 50 percent response rate is considered minimally adequate (Babbie 1986). The self-administered survey remains the most common direct-question research strategy. Its low cost, speed of administration, and anonymity account for its popularity. Its limitations are the potential for low response rates, and the requirement of a literate population or sample.

An alternative method of collecting survey data is the interview technique, in which trained interviewers read questions to respondents and record their answers. This may be done either by telephone or face-to-face. Obviously, both of these approaches introduce labor expenses beyond those involved in self-administration. Let's first look at the *face-to-face interview.*

Face-to-Face interview

Generally, the advantages and disadvantages of the face-to-face survey are the reverse of the self-administered questionnaire. Face-to-face surveys allow one to study more complex topics and obtain greater detail in responses. In other words, the face-to-face survey produces a richer body of information than self-administered surveys. Nonverbal aspects of communication and demeanor can be "read" by the interviewer. Moreover, the need for a literate population is eliminated. Face-to-face surveys also obtain higher response rates than self-administered surveys. This is because people are less likely to refuse an in-person request for an interview than they are to simply discard a mailed questionnaire.

On the other hand, this method of collecting survey data is time consuming and costly. While some large research organizations regularly use the face-to-face interview, for many individual researchers, this is prohibited by the high labor costs of such a procedure. Interviewing is a special skill, and skilled interviewers command substantial pay.

Telephone interview

In many ways, the *telephone interview* represents a compromise between face-to-face interviewing and the self-administration. Like the latter, the telephone interview is relatively inexpensive and can be administered quickly. As telephone companies never tire of saying, it's easier and cheaper to "let your fingers do the walking." Information may be gathered quickly. And, like the self-administered questionnaire, it offers a certain degree of anonymity lost in the face-to-face interview. Like the face-to-face interview, it allows some degree of probing people's responses and exploration of their understanding of questions. However, it cannot be equated with the face-to-face interview, since one cannot "observe" over the telephone. Telephone interviews simply convey less depth of communication than do face-to-face interviews. It is a less intimate form of communication.

FIGURE 2.4
Applying modern technology to direct question research techniques.

One of the major disadvantages of the telephone survey is, of course, that not everyone has a telephone, and not everyone with a telephone is listed in the telephone book. Consequently, sampling techniques based on telephone listings are flawed. Also, as a general rule, telephone surveys must be shorter than either self-administered or face-to-face interview surveys. This, in turn, substantially reduces the amount of data that can be collected. The telephone interview is an unanticipated interruption in the daily household routine, and under such circumstances, the duration of the interview and the depth of its questions must be limited.

In recent years, the telephone interview has become the method of choice for both market researchers and political pollsters. For instance, most of the opinion surveys conducted for national television networks by such commercial polling agencies as the George Gallup Poll, the Louis Harris Poll, and the Yankelovich Poll are of this type. During the 1988 national elections in the United States, so many polls were done so quickly and frequently that politicians complained that these research activities had become part of the political process rather than being simply a technique for studying it (see discussion pp. 53–55). Whether the telephone technique gradually will displace self-administered questionnaires and the face-to-face interview remains to be seen. Surely, this would be entirely consistent with the general spread of electronic technologies in American culture.

UNSTRUCTURED INTERVIEWS

Most surveys, even when well-designed and sophisticated, do not provide complex reasoning and first-hand testimony about why people do particular things. Survey techniques simply are not well-suited for probing into people's reasoning processes or the depths of their emotional experiences. It is difficult for persons to explain why they support or oppose such things as abortion or the death penalty by checking a few boxes on a questionnaire. Even when surveys contain some unstructured items that attempt to measure the reasons why people have responded as they did, one is unlikely to get the "whole story." For this type of information another direct question method is more appropriate, the unstructured interview.

Unstructured or in-depth interview

Unlike survey research, which relies upon the standardized questionnaire, the *unstructured or in-depth interview* does not require that questions be asked in the same words or the same order. Rather, the unstructured interview is an extended interaction between the interviewer and the respondent in which, ideally, the respondent does most of the talking. The interviewer may have a general plan of inquiry that establishes a general direction for the conversation, but also will pursue topics raised by the respondent. One of the special strengths of the unstructured interview is its flexibility. With this type of interview, there is an ability to "shift gears" so to speak. Answers evoked by the interviewer's initial questions suggest areas to be pursued further. It allows people to talk about their own thoughts, beliefs, feelings, and past actions in their own words. It is an essential technique for probing into what lies behind surface attitudes and opinions, what kinds of justifications people have for some of the actions they undertake, or what meanings and emotions govern certain situations for people.

For example, sociologist Alan M. Klein wished to understand the motives, experiences, and life-styles of women who entered the once male-dominated world of bodybuilding. His essay "Pumping iron" (1985) is based upon four years of "hanging out" at Gold's Gym in Venice, California, and upon dozens of unstructured interviews with female bodybuilders. The meanings of this somewhat unique career for these women could not have been grasped very easily through a survey.

However, this technique is not without its disadvantages. First, it may be costly to staff the research unless the principal researcher is conducting all the interviews. Second, for several reasons, this is a slow, time-consuming research process. Minimally, an in-depth interview consumes several hours, not counting the time required to arrange for the interview. Even with the help of modern tape recording equipment (in the "old days" interviewers took notes at a furious pace), the information collected must be coded, that is placed in useful analytical categories. Typically, transcribing and categorizing data from in-depth interviews consumes far more time than does conducting the interviews. All of these activities require effort, time, and money.

To summarize, surveys in their various forms, and the unstructured interview are two different strategies for conducting direct-question research. Surveys, whether self-administered, mailed, face-to-face, or conducted by telephone, are relatively inexpensive and fast procedures. Surveys are the most frequently used sociological research strategy and are best suited for the collection of descriptive information. In contrast, in-depth interviews are much more costly but allow the collection of complex information.

Direct Observation

Direct observation

Whenever the patterns of conduct to be studied are available for observation, the simplest research strategy is to look. Thus, the various forms of observational research are focused on patterns of activity, conduct, or behavior. Observational techniques may be divided into two categories, experiments and field studies. Additionally, there are three types of social research experiments: laboratory experiments, field experiments, and natural experiments. Finally, field studies may involve either participant observation, where researchers become part of the actions they study, or uninvolved observation, in which researchers observe without participating in the events observed. There are advantages and disadvantages to each observational technique.

EXPERIMENTS

Most persons are familiar with the experimental design from its use in the physical sciences. Typically, a test variable, or independent variable, is introduced into a situation so that its effects upon a dependent variable may be observed. The logic of the experimental research design in the physical and social sciences requires that observations be made both with and without the presence of the independent variable thought to be producing the results of interest. The most conventional way to do this is through the use of control groups. That is, the independent variable is introduced into one group (the experimental group) but not the other (the control group). An important criterion for assessing the impact of the independent variable is, of course, that the experimental and control groups be similar in terms of factors except the variable being introduced. In the social sciences, this similarity is accomplished either through matching, that is, selecting people with similar social characteristics, or through random assignment of persons into either the experimental or control groups. This allows assessing the impact of the experimental or independent variable as compared to other variables that might be influencing the outcome. If the experimental group changes in some way, while the control group does not, the change can be attributed to the introduction of the independent variable.

These techniques are used frequently in medical research where the experimental group is administered a new drug or treatment while the control group is given no treatment or a "placebo." If the experimental group improves while the control group does not, one can say with reasonable certainty that the new drug treatment caused the observed change. Without a control group, the researcher is left to wonder whether the improvement in the experimental group is due to the treatment, or due to some other extraneous factor. There are three types of experimental research conducted in sociology. They are: the laboratory experiment, the field experiment, and the natural experiment. Let's briefly examine each of the them.

Laboratory experiments

As in the physical sciences, *laboratory experiments are instances in which the subject matter to be studied is brought into the special setting of the laboratory.* This setting allows researchers to manipulate conditions in order to observe the specific influence of one variable upon another and to control the influences of extraneous variables. While the laboratory technique enjoys nearly universal popularity in the physical sciences, it is the least frequently encountered method within sociology. In fact, the field of psychology, which in many ways attempts to emulate the physical sciences, is the only social science that relies heavily upon laboratory experiments. Why is the practice of observing people in well-controlled laboratory settings not very common in sociology?

First, sociologists tend to view social life as multicausal. In other words, it is believed that people act as they do because of the rather complex interplay of many social variables. While laboratory settings may be useful in demonstrating some very basic properties of social life, these artificial situations simply do not re-create accurately the complexity of real life situations, nor the interplay of the many different variables that can influence people's actions. Accordingly, most, though not all, sociologists contend that it is precarious to form generalizations about real social situations based on laboratory research (Locke 1986).

Second, the laboratory setting is best suited to those situations where the focus of inquiry is upon one person at a time or upon small groups of individuals. Most sociologists are concerned with collective, not individual, phenomena. Their research simply is not suited to laboratory conditions. Finally, placing people in laboratory settings and exposing them to various stimuli raises some difficult ethical questions. Most sociologists argue that, given the wealth of direct question and observational techniques available, there is little justification for treating human beings like guinea pigs. In fairness, however, it must be acknowledged that various techniques have been developed to minimize the negative effects of experiments on participants, and most colleges and universities have adopted strict guidelines that protect human subjects involved in experimental research.

Finally, several factors can make the laboratory experiment a financially costly procedure. First, special facilities may be required. Second, even when student populations are used, it is usually necessary to pay people for their participation. Third, much laboratory research requires a great deal of administrative coordination, making it more of a team research approach as opposed to something done by an individual researcher.

Having stated these cautions, under what circumstances do sociologists use laboratory experiments? Obviously, the special setting of the laboratory is used when there is a high degree of concern about controlling variables, that is, when it is imperative that extraneous variables be excluded from the research situation, or when more naturalistic social settings do not provide reasonably good observational opportunities. In actual practice, the laboratory experiment has been used most by social psychologists in sociology because of their special interest in the impact of specific social forces and situational variables upon individuals. Since the laboratory setting allows close scrutiny of individuals as units of observation, there is a good "fit" between this methodological technique and the kinds of research questions asked by social psychologists. As the unit of observation shifts from individuals to groups, strata, and populations, the likelihood of the laboratory experiment being used by sociologists greatly decreases.

Perhaps one of the most widely publicized laboratory studies is that of social psychologist Philip Zimbardo (1972), whose controversial work has been presented on network television. Zimbardo was interested in how people's actions are shaped by the social environments in which they are situated. Some twenty-one college males were recruited and paid to play the roles of prisoners and guards in a mock prison setting. The men were randomly assigned to be either prisoners or guards. During the six days of the experiment, some "prisoners" became withdrawn and others rebellious, while the guards became alarmingly hostile and aggressive. The researchers stopped the experiment in the sixth day because they feared psychic and even physical injury to the participants. The experiment was a dramatic demonstration of the influence of environment upon people's actions. It also placed some of the participants at serious risk. Did the scientific goal justify that risk? Critics argue that Zimbardo's experiment demonstrated something already well recognized by social scientists—that social environments shape people's actions in very direct ways. From this perspective, there was little special need to subject people to the dangers of this experimental situation.

In another controversial experiment, social psychologist Stanley Milgram (1963, 1965) studied the apparent willingness of people to inflict pain on others, especially when such actions are legitimized by persons in positions of authority. The wartime situations of Nazi concentration camps and the My Lai tragedy in Vietnam both are examples of behavior in which people rationalized "I was only following orders." Milgram wished to know if such actions were exceptional. He created a laboratory situation in which people believed they were administering painful shocks to other humans, even to the extent of believing that they had seriously injured those being shocked. When it appeared that the participants could not, or would not, continue, Milgram told them that the experiment required their continuance, and that he would take responsibility for the outcome. He found that the majority of persons were willing to follow such orders, even to the point of presumably killing someone! Actually, no one was harmed. Yet, the situation seemed so "real" that some participants pleaded with the experimenter to let them stop giving the shocks and to be let out of the experiment. Many appeared to experience as much pain as those they thought were being "shocked." Although they were told after the experiment that they had not really hurt anyone, the knowledge that they were capable of doing so was extremely painful to them. While follow-up research demonstrated that none of the participants experienced lasting psychological damage from their participation, Milgram's research raised serious ethical considerations, and provoked considerable controversy over his methodology. To many, the finding of the research, which only replicated some tragic real life situations, did not justify the potential damage to the participants. While interesting and engrossing, the kinds of laboratory experiments conducted by Zimbardo and Milgram illustrate the ethical dilemmas of this genre of research.

A second experimental technique in sociology is the field experiment. The field experiment attempts to overcome the problems of artificiality in the laboratory experiment by studying people in their normal social settings. *The field experiment involves introducing some experimental condition into a normal social setting and assessing its effects.* Although applying experimental conditions in the field can be difficult, it is frequently done. Field experiments follow the same general strategy as laboratory experiments. For example, in so-called bystander intervention studies, researchers create a situation where someone needs help and then observe the conditions under which help is given and by whom. Although this type of experiment has the advantage of more closely approximating real life than the laboratory experiment, it doesn't allow for the same degree of control of other variables that might be influencing the outcome. Depending upon the complexity of the study, field experiments may involve all of the same logistical and coordination problems of laboratory experiments. In some cases it means gaining access to research settings not readily available. This can be both time-consuming and costly.

Field experiment

A third type of experiment is the natural experiment. *Natural experiments are real-life situations that provide experimental design conditions without human intervention.* In other words, the situation is not contrived by the researcher. Natural field settings that offer differences in key variables are located and observed without any intervention by the research team. For instance, Kasl *et. al.* (1981) studied the impact of the Three Mile Island (TMI) nuclear accident upon nuclear plant workers. They compared the attitudes toward working in nuclear power plants of those who had been working at TMI at the time of the accident and those who worked in other nuclear power plants were accidents had not occurred. The experimental variable was the nuclear accident. Those who worked at TMI were the experimental group, and those who worked at other nuclear plants not experiencing an accident were the control group. Since in this type of research one cannot assign people to either the experimental or control groups, extreme care must be taken to ensure that both the experimental and control groups are comparable on characteristics other than the experimental variable.

Natural experiments

Experiments, be they in the field or in the laboratory, provide excellent opportunities for studying causal processes. However, they are but one set of direct observational techniques. Field studies represent a very different set of research options.

FIELD STUDIES

The second major observational research approach in sociology is the field study. *In the field study, the researcher goes directly to the social phenomenon under study and observes it as closely and completely as possible.* The field study is the least structured and most flexible of all observational research methods. Doing field studies requires the researcher's being sensitive to all the subtle nuances of human behavior. The basic tool of the field researcher is the "field journal" in which field researchers record, either at the time of observation or immediately thereafter, everything that has been observed. The field study may be as uncomplicated as observing people in publicly available activities and settings such as bars, shopping malls, and playgrounds, or as complex as gaining access to private settings among such groups as the Ku Klux Klan, religious cults, or the boards of directors of large corporations.

Field study

Field studies involve a variety of decisions about the role assumed by the researcher. Will you identify yourself to the people being studied? Will you choose to participate in the events being observed? Identifying yourself to those you are studying may affect their behavior. On the other hand, is it ethical to deceive the people you are studying by not revealing your real purpose in the situation? Sociologists distinguish between the participant observer and the complete observer. These two research roles represent two very different approaches to field observation. Let's examine each of them.

For *the complete observer,* the key element is *the ability of the researcher to observe a social process without becoming involved in it in any way.* Opportunities for this type of research are numerous. Shopping centers, public office buildings, public recreation areas such as parks and beaches, private recreation areas like baseball and football stadiums, night clubs, cafes, and amusement parks all provide examples of settings for this type of research.

Complete observer

For example, sociologist Barry Schwartz became interested in how even the least organized aspects of social life exhibit societywide rules, values, and status distinctions. In order to examine such things, he studied what happens when people must wait in line. His book *Cueuing and Waiting* (1975) describes his field notes taken over many evenings of sitting in his parked car in front of a movie theater. He learned, for example, that men can break social rules and cut into the line far more easily than can women. Clearly, this is a reflection of the societywide dominance of men over women. Also, he found that groups of persons can break into the line more easily than can individuals. These patterns illustrate the effect of numbers upon norm-breaking in all social situations. Thus, through the unobtrusive technique of the complete observer, watching people in line and taking careful field notes, Schwartz learned much about the surrounding culture and social structure.

This type of field study offers many advantages. First, it does not require the coordination of the activities of different persons, and therefore, is ideal for one-person research projects. Additionally, since there is no large research staff, no subjects to be hired and paid, and no need for special equipment, this is a relatively inexpensive research technique. Unless one chooses to observe in costly locations, such as expensive restaurants or cruise ships, the basic expense is the researcher's time.

However, what if the activities requiring examination occur in a relatively private setting? What if it is a situation into which "members only" may enter? What if having a stranger (the researcher) standing around taking notes, or even asking questions, would interfere with the very activities to be studied? The technique known as participant observation allows studying these kinds of situations. The participant observer may be a genuine participant in the events being studied, or may pretend to be a participant for purposes of the research.

Participant observation

Participant observation is a type of field study in which the researcher joins the group or community for the purpose of studying it. Participant observation has become a method of choice under several distinct circumstances. Among these are occasions when the activities to be studied occur in restricted or private settings to which only group members have access. Participant observation also is used in circumstances when it is believed that group members don't have useful subjective knowledge of the things the researcher wants to know, or when it is clear that questioning people will produce reconstructed or distorted responses. Let's consider an example of the latter situation.

During the middle 1950s, the leader of a small and unique religious group in a midwestern university community announced the exact day and time several weeks hence when the earth would come to an end. Moreover, it was claimed that a ship from outer space would arrive just before the predicted apocalypse and take all the "true believers" to the biblical Promised Land. Social psychologist Leon Festinger and his associates reasoned that these events would not happen, and they wondered what effect this failed prophecy would have upon the faith of these believers. Festinger believed that the cognitive processes to be studied here required first-hand observation. Festinger and the other research team members joined this group in order to study it. In the book *When Prophecy Fails* (1956), they report on their observations made as participant observers.

Clearly, participant observation is a strategy of data collection requiring substantial commitment by the researcher. Depending upon the setting, it also can be a costly form of social research. For instance, in Becker and Geer's study *Boys in White* (1961), several researchers became full-time medical school students for the purpose of studying the professional socialization processes that occur in the school setting. These researchers remained committed through several years of participant research activity. Because the participant observer is, in essence, a spy, and is masquerading as something he or she is not, there are special ethical questions surrounding this observational research technique. One is the question of informed consent. Do people have a right to know that they are being studied? Is it ethical to allow people to confide in you in a way they might not if they knew you were a researcher? Do the scientific goals of the particular research project mitigate such ethical considerations? Ultimately, such questions must be resolved by each individual researcher. Although the American Sociological Association has addressed these questions, the norms established by this professional association are rather ambiguous when applied to specific situations. These issues not withstanding, it is clear that participant observation yields extremely rich field information.

In summary, experiments and field studies are two general categories of direct observational research methods. Experiments may be created in the laboratory, may occur naturally in field situations, or may be created in the field by introducing a controlled variable. For numerous reasons, the laboratory experiment is the research technique least frequently used by sociologists.

Field studies provide occasions for in-depth observation of "real life" events. The technique of uninvolved field observation can be both unobtrusive and inexpensive, and is most appropriately used in public settings. In contrast, participant observation is a technique for studying actions in private or restricted settings. It can be a relatively costly research technique in terms of time and money and can raise ethical dilemmas for the researcher as well.

INDIRECT OBSERVATION

Indirect observation

Indirect observation is the use of documents, previously assembled records, and various types of cultural artifacts to study social patterns both past and present. Indirect observation has the advantage of being entirely unobtrusive. Most other research techniques require some intrusion on the part of the researcher into the lives or environments of the persons being studied. Indirect observational techniques, of course, are well-suited to historical topics, and in the past several decades, there has been significant convergence between the work of sociologists and historians. Both fields have been innovative in finding new ways of using various kinds of archives and historical records to depict social practices in earlier historical periods. However, the use of indirect observation is not limited to historical questions. There are two categories of indirect observational techniques frequently used to examine research questions about both historical and contemporary events. They are content analysis and secondary analysis. Content analysis will be examined here first.

CONTENT ANALYSIS

Content analysis

Content analysis is the examination of a class of social artifacts, including both written or pictorial documents, for the categories of social and cultural experience within them.

Private and public communications of all sorts may be assembled and analyzed. Moreover, sampling techniques may be applied to universes of documents in the same ways they are with human populations. Let's turn first to the use of private documents.

During the early 1900s, large numbers of Europeans emigrated to these shores. Typically, the male head of the family arrived first and sent for his loved ones only after becoming established. This process could easily take several years. Two sociologists at the University of Chicago, William Thomas (1863–1947) and Florian Zanecki (1882–1958), became interested in the plight of these European fathers, sons, and husbands and especially wondered what this difficult experience of separation from their families was like for them. Of course, in the days before inexpensive telephone rates, the inventions of television, and other electronic media, people sent, received, treasured, and saved handwritten letters. When the families of these men joined them in the United States, treasured collections of handwritten letters arrived with them. Thomas and Zanecki traveled through the ethnic neighborhoods in Chicago collecting many of these letters. Their content analysis of them forms the book *The Polish Peasant in Europe and America* (1918–1920) which tells the emotionally rich story of the immigrant experience.

Of course, content analysis is not limited to these types of private documents. One may examine public documents, such as political speeches, official records, books, magazines, newspapers, popular song lyrics, and legal codes. For example, in researching the study *Megatrends* (1982), author John Naisbitt and his associates routinely content-analyzed on a monthly basis some 6,000 local newspapers. Similarly, the content of television programs and advertisements provide a wealth of data about our popular culture and social structure (National Institute of Mental Health 1982). Several public interest research groups have done content analyses of the extent of violence in television programs. Sociologist Leonore Weitzman and her associates (1972) have content-analyzed children's picture books to determine how male and female social roles are portrayed in them. Content analysis also is useful for comparative historical work investigating sociocultural change patterns.

A key advantage of content analysis is economy of time and money. It can be done easily by a single researcher and requires neither staff nor special equipment. In fact, the major requirement of most content analysis is access to the documents or artifacts. Through content analysis, sociologists can study the macrostructures of societies without ever visiting them. In a sense, it allows the researcher to "revisit" events that happened in the distant past and "interview" persons who are no longer living. However, such "interviews" are limited to the most literate members of past societies. In other words, content analysis tends to supply information about elite rather than common populations. A major flaw of research based upon content analysis is that, like all indirect observations, the research is confined to the limitations of "pre-existing" information.

SECONDARY ANALYSIS

Secondary analysis

Secondary analysis is any use of existing data to address a research question not intended by those collecting the data. Content analysis is one way this is sometimes done. However, secondary analysis more frequently entails reshaping the data, bringing together new combinations of question items to form new variables, or using new techniques that were not available when the data were originally collected. Durkheim's study *Suicide* (1897) is an early example of secondary analysis. Using data collected for administrative purposes, Durkheim supplied his own conceptual framework and explored the causal role of variables that were of little concern to the government bureaucrats who collected the data.

Public documents contain a storehouse of information about social life. Government reports are the richest public source of such materials, and the most prized government source is the work of the United States Census Bureau. In addition to conducting the Census study every ten years, the Census Bureau, which is part of the United States Department of Commerce, administers a wide range of Current Population Studies. The 1967 Freedom of Information Act provided that all United States government statistics and reports, except those "classified" for security reasons, are in the public domain. Census data may be reanalyzed or may be correlated with the data from sample surveys. Demographers, social scientists who specialize in population analysis, have a particular interest in these Census materials.

There are, of course, many other government sources of useful social science data. Criminologists make substantial use of the Uniform Crime Reports released periodically by the Justice Department. Medical sociologists focus on the wide variety of public health statistics that emanate from the Centers for Disease Control and the United States Department of Health and Human Services. State and local governments also possess useful records and data files.

Today, most major universities participate in one of the several national social science data banks that archive information collected in all sorts of studies. Rather than undertaking new research, a sociologist may conduct a search of existing data files to determine if the information needed has already been collected. For instance, the public opinion surveys frequently conducted by such firms as the George Gallup Poll, the Louis Harris Poll, and the Yankelovich Poll, are available to researchers for secondary analysis.

Examples of secondary analysis abound in sociological literature. For example, Newman and Halvorson (1980) used membership statistics collected by national religious denominations to study changing patterns of religious pluralism in the United States. The question of religious pluralism was not of concern to those who originally collected the membership statistics. Many studies of the deterrent effect of the death penalty have relied upon the government's Uniform Crime Reports.

The advantages and disadvantages of secondary analysis are readily apparent. This is a relatively inexpensive research strategy and also is less-time consuming than nearly all primary research activities. Through secondary analysis, researchers gain access to large data files that might otherwise be unavailable. On the other hand, there is no control over the selection and gathering of materials. Flaws in the data, such as the reliability and validity of measures and the sample selection techniques, cannot be repaired. When such problems emerge difficult research decisions must be made.

In summary, indirect observational research encompasses the use of a rich and diverse assortment of materials. Regardless of whether the research question is historical or contemporary, whether the data to be analyzed are taken from public or private sources, indirect observational approaches provide wide latitude for sociologists to be inventive, imaginative, and creative in shaping the "datum of human experience" into sociological data. Private and public documents from any media and data collected for various purposes may be used to study a variety of sociological questions. The artifacts and records from nearly everything people do may be conceptualized as data and be collected and analyzed in a scientific manner. The three major categories of social research methods and the specific techniques within each of them are summarized in Table 2.1. Clearly, there are important relationships between the kind of research questions asked, and the research techniques employed.

APPLICATIONS
THE ETHICS OF SOCIAL RESEARCH

Science has a special aura. The fact that scientists attempt to be objective and the notion that somehow scientific work advances the human condition (progress?) may lead us to forget that science, like everything else people do, is a human and social activity.

Because science is something people do, it is permeated with ethical implications, and frequently with explicit ethical judgments and decisions. Sociologists long have recognized this intrusion of values and judgments into the act of doing sociology. Each of the research techniques discussed in this chapter in some way has an ethical dimension.

Let's consider some examples. In most direct question research, participants are not told the precise reasons why they are being studied. It is claimed that to do so would influence people's consciousness about what is being studied, with the result that accurate measurement would become impossible. At best, less than the entire truth is told to the participant by the survey researcher

TABLE 2.1

METHODOLOGICAL CHOICES

The Research Questions Are	The Primary Approach Is	Choices Available
Behavioral Patterns	Direct Observation	(1) Experiment a. Laboratory b. Field c. Natural (2) Field Study
Cognitive or Emotional Patterns	Direct Question	(1) Survey a. Self-administered b. Telephone c. Face-to-Face (2) In-Depth Interview
Past Events	Indirect Question	(1) Content Analysis (2) Secondary Analysis

or interviewer. We've already noted (pp. 44–46) that laboratory experiments raise some ethical concerns about manipulating human behavior. The controversial studies of both Milgram (1963, 1965) and Zimbardo (1972) highlight these concerns. Finally, it should be obvious that the participant observer sometimes is a spy. The participant observer frequently conceals from most, if not all, of the persons being studied the real purpose of his or her presence in the situation. Accordingly, the participant observer may become privy to information that is potentially damaging to those being studied (Humphries 1970).

The ethical dimensions of social research rarely become apparent to the lay person. However, in recent American history there is at least one important exception: the role of pollsters taking exit polls *during* the election process. Let's examine this very public dilemma of the use of social research.

CASE
Elections and Exit Polls

During the 1960s and 1970s, two powerful electronic technologies grew in tandem: communications technology, especially television, and computer or data processing technology. The Kennedy-Nixon debates of 1960 became America's first televised Presidential campaign. By the mid 1970s, computerized research in the form of exit polls had caught up with televised campaigns. With high-speed data processing it became possible to conduct surveys with voters leaving the polls, and to broadcast predictions about the election's result on the network news even before the election was over. Indeed, as the six o'clock news is broadcasting on the American East Coast, millions of people on the West Coast have not yet voted, and have another three hours to decide if they will vote.

The use of exit polls by news networks began in 1960 when the Harris Poll was hired by CBS. However, as network correspondent Roger Mudd observes (1987), exit polls were not used to predict the results of a national election until CBS did so in 1968, followed by NBC in 1974 and ABC in 1976. On the night of the 1980 Presidential election, the NBC News organization did something that would elevate concern over exit polls from a mildly interesting issue to a first rate ethical controversy. At 8:15 P.M. Eastern Standard Time, NBC, based on its exit polls, declared Ronald Reagan the winner of the Reagan-Carter Presidential contest. However, on the West Coast, where it was only 5:15 P.M., the polls were still open with millions of people yet to cast their votes.

This raised the question: To what extent had survey research in the form of exit polls become a part of the event it was designed to study? For example, if a given candidate was losing by a large margin by mid afternoon West Coast time, and this was broadcast, potential voters who might have reversed that trend would become discouraged and decide not to vote. Conversely, in a close election, knowledge of the afternoon voting trend might encourage people who rarely vote to converge on the voting booths to change the predicted result. In either case, a serious ethical issue was facing the survey researcher and the broadcasting industry: Is it ethical to broadcast the findings of exit polls prior to the close of an election?

Perhaps for justifiable reasons, both state and federal governments were not content to wait for the research and broadcast professions to resolve this difficult ethical issue. In 1983, the State of Washington passed a law forbidding journalists and researchers from approaching voters within 300 feet of a polling place. Prior to this legislation, it was illegal in that state to solicit voters within 100 feet of a polling place for any purpose, political or not. The new Washington law effectively made voters inaccessible to interviewers. In the space of 300 feet the people to be interviewed have dispersed and vanished!

ABC, CBS, NBC, the *New York Times,* and the *Daily Herald* filed suit claiming that the Washington law violated the First Amendment freedoms of speech and press. While the district court initially upheld the new law, in 1988 the U. S. Court of Appeals ruled it to be an unconstitutional restriction of free speech and public debate (United States Court of Appeals 1988). The United States House of Representatives seems to have anticipated this finding. In 1983, the House held hearings on the issue of exit polls, and subsequently passed a nonbinding resolution against the practice of releasing exit poll results during an election. In research as elsewhere, what is legal is not always what is morally right.

In 1985 the three major television networks signed a voluntary pact to refrain from broadcasting projections of election results based on exit polls until the voting booths have closed throughout the nation. Thus, the research continues, but the use of the data is subject to a voluntary ethical norm. Ironically, in 1988 an editorial in the *New Republic* criticized the practical results of this voluntary pact. On "Super Tuesday," when a large number of state-level Presidential primary elections were conducted, the networks wasted a great deal of time pretending that they were unable to "call" the result of primary elections that actually had rather obvious outcomes. What the *New Republic* (1988) called "fake tension-builders" and "hours of bogus suspense" created, at best, boring television.

In retrospect, it might be asked, does it really matter? Do exit polls have any effect upon the electorate? What little research has been done suggests that, in fact, it does matter. For example, a study of the 1980 Presidential election (Carpini 1984) found that the release of exit poll data had the effect of depressing the turnout of Democratic voters for both Presidential and Congressional candidates. Thus, there is support for the idea that exit polls might have an effect on close contests. If some people didn't bother to vote because they knew their Presidential candidate already had lost the election, those uncast

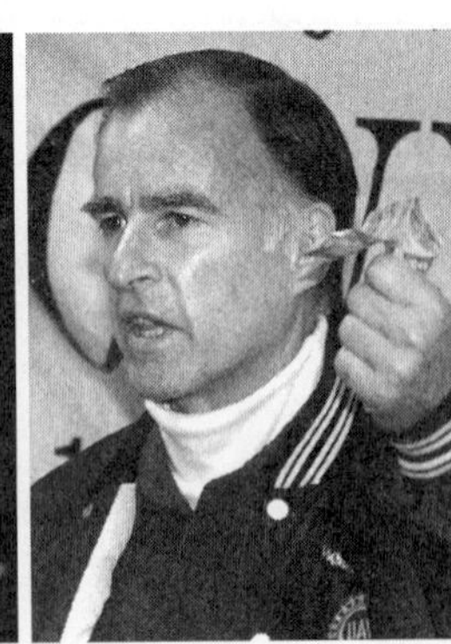

FIGURE 2.5
Did the media influence the outcome?

votes in a close contest may have cost that party's Congressional candidate the election.

All research situations involve ethical issues. Few of them involve issues of Constitutional scope. Whether the broadcasting industry and the survey research companies that work for them behaved "appropriately" in the exit-poll controversy remains an interesting question. As in all ethical questions, which of course, involve values, there are legitimate differences of opinion.

Chapter Summary

1. Doing sociology consists of two related activities, building sociological theories and conducting social research. Theories are general-level descriptive, explanatory, and predictive statements. Research is the act of collecting information or data with which theoretical claims may be tested.
2. It is useful to envision a chain of links connecting research and theory-building activities. Three links emanate from the theory side of the chain: propositions about relationships between phenomena, concepts that define categories of events, and nominal definitions that identify ranges of events within the general concept. Links in the research side of the chain include variables (telling what will be measured), hypotheses (describing anticipated relationships between variables), and operational definitions (telling how the variables will be measured).
3. Like any human work activity, research involves certain quality control techniques. It is important that measures of social things have validity, that we actually measure what we intend to measure. Similarly, research measures must be reliable, measure the same thing consistently from one situation to the next. Much social research uses samples, selections of persons from large populations. Random, stratified, and purposive sampling are three widely used techniques of selecting persons for participation in sociological studies.
4. Unlike the physical sciences that rely primarily upon one standard research technique (the experiment), sociology has a variety of research techniques. Direct questioning, direct observation, and indirect observation are the general strategies for doing social research. Questioning techniques are prevalent when studying cognitive or emotional phenomena. Observational techniques are a probable choice for studying people's actions.
5. The two major direct-question techniques are surveys and unstructured interviews. Surveys, which are the most commonly used social research techniques, may be self-administered, conducted by telephone, or conducted face-to-face. Unstructured or in-depth interviews allow collection of much richer information than do surveys.
6. The two major categories of direct observational research are experiments and field studies. Experiments may be conducted in laboratory settings, in field locations, or may even occur naturally in the course of events. For both practical and ethical reasons, sociologists do not often conduct laboratory

experiments. Field studies may be either participant observer- or complete observer-based. In participant observation, researchers join groups and communities for the purpose of studying them. This technique is appropriate for studying private social settings. The complete observer is an unobtrusive, nonparticipating observer. The latter can be done in a wide variety of public settings.

7. Indirect observation entails the use of existing documents or records for research purposes. Content analysis entails the systematic scrutiny of documents and records for the categories of social experience in them. Content analysis is one example of secondary analysis, the technique of using existing information to answer new questions.

Key Concepts

complete observer
concepts
content analysis
deductive method
direct observation
direct question
face-to-face interview
field experiment
field study
indirect observation
inductive method
laboratory experiments
natural experiments
nominal definition
operational definition
participant observation
population universe
propositions
purposive samples
random sample
reliability
research hypothesis
sample
secondary analysis
stratified sample
survey
telephone interview
theory
unstructured or in-depth interview
validity
variable

Bibliography

Babbie, Earl
1986. *The practice of social research.* Belmont, California: Wadsworth.

Becker, Howard, and Blanche Geer
1961. *Boys in white.* Chicago: University of Chicago Press.

Blumer, Herbert
1954. What's wrong with social theory? *American Sociological Review.* Vol. 19, No. 1: 3–10.

Carpini, Michael X. Delli
1984. Scooping the voters? The consequences of the networks' early call of the 1980 Presidential race. *Journal of Politics.* Vol. 46, No. 3: 866–85.

Durkheim, Emile
1897. *Suicide.* Translated by J. A. Spaulding and G. Simpson, 1951. Glencoe, Illinois: Free Press.

Festinger, Leon, Henry Riecken, and Stanley Schachter
1956. *When prophecy fails.* New York: Harper & Row.

Humphries, Laud
1970. *Tearoom trade: impersonal sex in public places.* enl. ed. 1975. Chicago: Aldine.

Kasl, Stanislav, Rupert Chisolm, and Brenda Eskenazi
1981. The impact of the accident at Three Mile Island on the behavior and well-being of nuclear workers. *American Journal of Public Health.* Vol. 7, No. 5 (May): 484–95.

Klein, Alan M.
1985. Pumping iron. *Society.* Vol. 22, No. 6 (September–October): 68–75.

Locke, Edwin A., ed.
1986. *Generalizing from laboratory to field studies.* Lexington, Massachusetts: Lexington Books.

Milgram, Stanley
1963. Behavioral study of obedience. *Journal of Abnormal and Social Psychology.* Vol. 67: 371–78.

1965. Some conditions of obedience and disobedience to authority. *Human Relations.* Vol. 18, No. 1: 57–76.

Mudd, Roger
1987. Television network news in campaigns. In *Political persuasion in presidential campaigns.* Edited by Patrick Devlin, pp. 85–92. New Brunswick, New Jersey: Transaction Books.

Naisbitt, John
1982. *Megatrends.* New York: Warner Books.

National Institute of Mental Health
1982. *Television and behavior: 10 years of scientific progress and implications for the eighties.* Vol. 1. Washington, D.C.: U. S. Government Printing Office.

Newman, William M., and Peter L. Halvorson
1980. *Patterns in pluralism: A portrait of American religion, 1952–1971.* Washington, D. C.: Glenmary Research Center.

New Republic
1988. Potemkin election night. *New Republic.* Vol. 198 (March 28): 4 & 42.

Schwartz, Barry
1975. *Cueuing and waiting.* Chicago: Univ. of Chicago Press.

Thomas, William I., and Florian Zanecki
1918–1920. *The Polish peasant in Europe and America.* 5 vols. Boston: Richard G. Badger.

United States Court of Appeals
1988. *The Daily Herald Company v. Munro,* The United States Court of Appeals, 9th Circuit, 838 f.2d: 380.

Weitzman, L. J., D. Eifler, E. Hokada, and C. Ross
1972. Sex Role Socialization in Picture Books for Pre-school Children. *American Journal of Sociology.* Vol. 77, No. 6: 1118–41.

Zimbardo, Phillip
1972. Pathology of imprisonment. *Society.* Vol. 9 (April): 4–8.

CHAPTER 3

CULTURE: WHAT MAKES HUMANS UNIQUE

CHAPTER OUTLINE

LEARNING OBJECTIVES

We've already seen (Chapter 1) that one of the most difficult first lessons in sociology is the realization that things are not always quite what they seem (Berger 1963). Some of the basic notions that prevail in popular culture and in everyday life, upon closer inspection, are found to be not true. As the basic concepts of culture and social structure are examined in this chapter and the next, this clash between the "things everyone knows" and the findings of social science will become readily apparent. The idea that innate biological forces shape and control human life continues to be a very popular one in contemporary society despite evidence to the contrary. For instance, it is often claimed that outstanding athletes possess an "instinct" for the game. Similarly, people allege that certain behaviors associated with females and males are instinctual in nature, and therefore, are not easily changed. Much thinking about so-called race is characterized by this same sort of biological determinism. The basic claim behind all such ideas is that people do the things they do because of biological programming rather than learning. It is thought that different categories of people—men and women, blacks and whites, athletic stars and normal folks—differ from one another because of innate biological factors.

Yet, one of the central themes of modern sociology is that this commonly heard basic assumption about human life is not quite so. While surely the human animal is an animal, and thus its life is shaped in certain basic ways by its biological make-up, human life also is influenced uniquely by nonbiological forces. Humans, unlike dogs and cats, birds and monkeys, are cultural animals. That is, unlike other animal populations, human beings invent the solutions to life's daily problems and pass this social heritage to new generations.

This chapter and the one after it explore these themes by focusing upon the most fundamental sociological concepts: culture, social structure, and social interaction, which are the building blocks of social reality.

After reading and studying this chapter, you should be able to discuss answers to the following questions.

1. What are the relative influences of biological and nonbiological forces in shaping human life?
2. In what ways is human life similar to and different from that of other animal populations? Is the human animal unique, and if so, in what ways?
3. What is culture and what are its distinguishing characteristics?
4. What is social interaction? and what are the connections between social interaction processes and culture?

5. What are some of the more important consequences of the fact that humans are cultural animals?
6. What are some of the complexities of cultural systems and the resulting complexities involved in studying and understanding cultures?

THE BIOLOGICAL MATRIX

Since the emergence of the social sciences in the middle of the 19th century, scholars have debated the so-called nature-nurture question. Simply stated, the issue is, how much of human social life is determined by biological forces, and how much may be attributed to human invention and learning? To what extent are people's patterns of living preordained by a biological code, and to what degree do humans produce their own social arrangements and ways of living? For modern sociology, the answer to these questions is unambiguous. While it is recognized that human beings are animals, and that certain aspects of the organism are biologically determined, collective patterns of social and cultural life are humanly produced. Humans are unique in the degree to which their patterns of living are self-manufactured, socially created, and constructed.

Most of this chapter is focused upon human culture, the "stuff" of human social life. However, before even attempting a definition of culture, it is first necessary to consider the role of biological forces in shaping human behavior. Both physical and social scientists agree that in its basic aspects most animal life is influenced by three distinct phenomena, reflexes, drives, and instincts. However, humans differ from the rest of the animal kingdom. While human populations unquestionably exhibit both drives and reflexes, they do not exhibit instincts. Rather, among humans, culture plays the role that instinct plays for other animals. Each of these phenomena, reflexes, drives, instincts, and culture, requires careful examination.

REFLEXES

Reflexes

A reflex is a simple, involuntary action of an organism. Human beings execute a number of reflexive actions. Some of these, like breathing and blinking, are involuntary actions and appear to be critically important to the well-being of the organism. Others, like lifting a foot when stepping on a sharp object, seem to be involuntary responses to external stimuli. For instance, when a truck backfires producing a loud bang, the several small birds feeding on a nearby lawn take flight instantaneously. This action, simple and direct, seems to be reflexive. The birds are in flight in a fraction of a second. Indeed, the young man standing on the sidewalk also jumps a bit as the truck backfires. This, too, happens in a flash. No thought or reasoning is involved.

Reflexes are automatic. They happen with no conscious effort because the animal's nervous system is in a sense "wired" in a particular way. Reflexes are distinguished by the fact that people cannot will them away. For instance, a person cannot simply stop breathing as a matter of will or desire. Hold your breath long enough and you will pass out before you stop breathing. Suppressing a reflex requires some complex technological intervention, which is why the act of suicide typically involves some rather gory details! Reflexes are involuntary and beyond our control. Breathing, flinching, and blinking are but a few examples of reflexes. Moreover, most biologically programmed, simple reflexive activities contribute to the well-being of the organism.

DRIVES AND INSTINCTS

Drives

Drives represent a somewhat more complex area of animal life. *A drive is a felt need of an organism.* Unlike a reflex, a drive is not an action. Rather, it is something to which the organism must respond. In this sense, a drive, unlike a reflex, is not directly observable. Typically, scientists infer from the response that a drive is present. It is useful to think of a drive as a problem requiring a solution. Biologists and psychologists agree that most complex animal populations experience four such drives: namely, hunger, thirst, rest, and sex. Each of these drives creates a problem for the organism, a problem that is solved when the drive is satisfied.

Among *most* animal populations, these needs or problems are solved through the genetic code. In other words, a genetic program called an instinct provides solutions to the problems created by the drive systems. Let's look more closely at the concept of instinct.

Instincts

An instinct is an unlearned, complex pattern of behavior that is common to all members of a species. Unlike simple reflexive actions, instinctual patterns of activity are complex and are intimately connected to the system of drives or experienced needs. That is, it requires a series of coordinated activities aimed at the attainment of a particular goal. Moreover, to be instinctive, the particular

FIGURE 3.1
Some claim it is genes and instinct. She knows it's training and determination.

solution to a drive in any species or animal population must be common to all normal members of that species. For instance, in the Spring, the great steelhead salmon begin the arduous migration from the sea, up the streams and rivers to the place of their own birth. This action is complex. It takes a long time and requires conquering barriers on the river, such as waterfalls and dams. Genetic programming has provided these fish with an instinctual response to a drive. Once in the stream of their birth, and only in that place, these fish respond to their sexual drive and mate, thus producing more salmon who, in time, will respond to these same drives with these *exact* instinctual patterns.

For these same reasons, some species of birds build nests, and among nest-building birds, different kinds of birds build different kinds of nests. Each species is programmed by its instincts to use its own particular style of architecture. Nest-building among birds, like the seasonal migrations of some species of both fish and birds, is a complex activity, more than a simple reflex. Among nonhuman animal species then, drives and the instinctual activities that respond to the drives are intimately connected. Most importantly, these instincts produce patterns of behavior that are universal within each species and are species specific. All steelhead salmon make exactly the same trek upstream to the place of their birth in order to mate, just as all birds of the same species build the same architecturally distinctive nests before laying eggs and incubating them.

But what of humans? Do humans, like other animal populations, exhibit biologically programmed, complex patterns of activity common to all humans? Here, the answer must be an unqualified no. While certainly, there are some universal reflexes shared by all humans, truly complex patterns of activity among human populations are characterized, not by commonality, but by diversity. While it may be argued that most human societies contain similar types of institutions such as families, political organizations, and religious practices (see Chapter 5), the important point is that the specific shape and content of these institutions differ greatly from one society to the next, and even from group to group within the same society. This diversity, this lack of universal patterns of conduct, is a first clue that human social life is structured not by instinct, but by human invention. Let's consider the diversity of human responses to some of the basic drives mentioned earlier.

Unlike salmon, who satisfy their sexual urges in the same instinctively precise manner, human societies express wide variability in terms of what is sexually arousing, what types of sexual activities take place, and even which sexual orientations are considered proper. For instance, in many societies, homosexual behavior is socially acceptable under some circumstances, while in others it is disapproved. Monogamy is the norm in most Western societies, yet even within these societies some religious traditions have allowed a man to have many wives and experience sexual intercourse with all of them. Physical appearance seems to be an important aspect of sexual attractiveness in all societies. Yet, what constitutes physical attractiveness differs substantially from one society to the next. Clearly, in matters of sexuality, there is no single, universal pattern of response to the drive. Instincts, unlearned complex patterns of behavior common to all members of the species, do not prevail here. Rather, there is a fascinating diversity of sexual practices and preferences influenced by cultural customs and meanings.

The matter is no different with the hunger drive. What kinds of things are considered edible, how often one should eat, and how much one should eat differ among societies. To be sure, all humans experience the hunger drive.

Most babies, depending upon what they are fed, demand food every few hours. This, of course, is not so convenient for adults. Accordingly, children gradually are taught to take food at the same times as adults. In the United States, this is three times per day, a convenient arrangement that just happens to conform to the needs of an eight hour work day! In Mexico, the heaviest meal is at midday, and is followed by a wonderful rest period called a *siesta* (nap). In traditional Italian culture, a series of seven or eight small meals per day are eaten, with the largest consumed in the evening. Nomadic tribal societies eat when they can find food and eat better during some seasons than others. At certain times in the ancient world, it was common to regurgitate the food eaten during the meal so one could keep eating. This cultural practice of "throwing up" is not considered to be good social form, even on feast days (such as weddings and family reunions) in modern cultures!

The point then, is that while all humans experience the hunger drive, how often people respond to that drive, and with what kinds of foods differs from one cultural setting to the next. We even learn to be hungry at culturally approved times. Many things are called "instinctive" because they seem to occur so naturally. However, they appear natural because of social learning.

There are many popular misconceptions about so-called human instincts. For instance, some persons claim that humans have an instinct for survival. Yet, few infant animals are as helpless and as unsuited to unassisted survival as the human infant. Changing tables have straps for tying the infant, and playpens have been designed to restrain the child precisely because of the self-destructive potentials of the young human child. Only after a rather long period of social learning (see the discussion of socialization in Chapter 6) by human children do adult humans begin to have some confidence that their offspring will avoid self-injury and destruction. Even in adult life, there is much activity that contradicts the notion that people are genetically programmed for survival. The number of persons in the United States who die each year from smoking cigarettes (over 300,000 persons), driving automobiles (approximately 50,000), or committing suicide (approximately 30,000) suggests a serious malfunction in the alleged survival instinct.

Thus, while the term "instinct" is frequently heard in everyday conversation, there is no pattern of conduct among humans that fits the scientific definition of that term. Among humans, drives are satisfied by many different complex patterns of learned conduct that vary widely from one human community to the next. These complex patterns of conduct are all part of human culture.

CULTURE

Here then is a first payload, a first lesson gleaned from nearly one hundred and fifty years of thinking and studying in the social sciences. What is it that makes people different from other animals? The difference is culture. Humans are the only animal population that invent their own culture and teach it to each succeeding generation. Humans are the only animals that have escaped the determinism of the biological code so completely.

The key feature of human life is its plasticity (Cooley 1909, Becker 1962). The marvelous thing about plastic is that it may be shaped and molded to nearly any form, and to suit any environment. So it is with human life. Human patterns of living have been shaped in thousands of different ways that reflect, not simply the biological shape of the organism, but, more importantly, human inventiveness. A host of diverse ways of living have sprung from the different continents and seasons in which human life has flourished on the planet. Culture does for humans what instincts do for other animal populations. Culture provides solutions to the problems of daily living. Culture provides meaning and pattern to everyday life. Yet, unlike instinctual patterns among some animals which exhibit unbending uniformity within each animal species, culture is marked by its wide variation. This is the most salient clue to the fact that social reality is humanly constructed. Indeed, if the biological code of inherited instincts is signaled by its sameness within each species, then the diversity of human culture is the hallmark of human invention.

This chapter began with a rather complex question. How much of human life is shaped by biological factors, and how much is shaped by things other than biology? A first answer to this question is now at hand. As in all animal life, biological forces are the foundation of human existence. Human beings are, after all, part of the animal kingdom. They respond to the environment in simple reflexive ways and experience basic drives that require complex responses. Clearly, the biological and physiological constitution of the human animal shapes the context in which the daily problems of living must be solved. At the same time, every individual represents a slightly different arrangement of genetic material setting it apart from the next. Each person appears a bit different from the next and no doubt experiences life in subtlely different ways precisely because each person (excepting identical twins) is a unique assortment of genes and inherited characteristics.

Perhaps a cautionary word is in order here. Culture does not *determine* human nature. Rather, culture *shapes* human nature. Genetic inheritance sets boundaries on the types of human behavior that are possible. For example, humans cannot fly like birds. They are limited by the type of animal they are. In order to fly, humans had to invent a technology that made flight possible. From this perspective, it may be said that the influence of biology is twofold. First, it provides a common framework for living for the entire species, *homo sapiens*. Second, it constructs that framework in subtle ways a bit differently for each genetically unique individual member of the species. Clearly, the human being's complex adaptations to the environment, and the diversity of satisfactions of the drive systems, are not genetically given. These ways of living, these "patterns of culture" (Benedict 1934) are socially manufactured.

In summary, humans, like all animals, exhibit reflexes and experience basic drives. Reflexes are simple involuntary actions. Drives are felt or experienced needs. Unlike other animals, humans do not respond to those drives with instinctual behaviors. Instincts are unlearned patterns of complex behavior common to all members of a species, and humans do not have any. To understand the complexity of patterns of human life requires seeing that beyond setting the basic dilemmas, biology is not the prevailing influence. Rather, culture is.

CULTURE

So far, this chapter has taken a first look at the role of culture in the general biological matrix of the animal kingdom. A next task is to narrow the focus.

Specifically, what is culture? What is included in this unique, humanly invented stuff of social life, and from whence does it come? This last question may be answered by considering the role of social interaction in producing cultural phenomena. As we begin exploring the social world and asking fundamental questions about how social reality happens, how social life is produced, the answer rests with social interaction. The following discussion addresses three basic issues. First, what is culture? Second, how does its linkage with social interaction produce social reality? Third, what kinds of forces shape and influence cultural formation?

DEFINING CULTURE

Culture

Culture consists of all of the appropriate and/or required modes of thought, action, and feeling in societies, as well as the material productions that result from people's life together. Human life exhibits three basic properties: cognition (thinking, believing, and imagining), emotion (feelings), and action (behavior or conduct). People's patterns of action, emotion, and cognition all are shaped by their culture. Additionally, the technologies that are developed in different cultures result in different inventories of material objects that also are part of the culture. From this definition, one can see that culture is indeed an inclusive phenomenon. It encompasses the things that people think, their patterns of activity, their emotional states, and the material objects they create.

Given this rather enormous scope of cultural activities and objects, it also is apparent that a people's culture is something that typically is not studied all at once. Rather, sociologists are more likely to study specific parts of a culture at any given time. Family practices, religious traditions, youth gangs, school systems, political activities, occupational groups, and sexual practices are but a few specific examples of parts of the culture that may be studied.

CULTURE AND SOCIAL INTERACTION

As stated previously, cultural arrangements are human creations, existentially produced rather than genetically mandated. Thus far, however, we have avoided a difficult question. Where does culture "come from?" How does this process of social invention happen? What does it mean to say that people construct their own social world? The answer to this question requires an examination of the processes of social interactions.

Social interaction

Social interaction is the on-going process of social relationships between people. Regardless of the task at hand, processes of social interaction are the conduits of social life. If it is asked what is the origin of culture, the answer is social interaction. However, that answer is deceptively simple and requires closer scrutiny.

Let's imagine that we were present when that hypothetical first society was being invented. If the evolutionary theorists are correct, we are examining the hunting and gathering activities of early humans. As these early humans "eke out" an existence, they must develop ways of adapting to their environment and solving their daily problems. Once successful ways of doing this are found, they become habitual. That is, faced with similar situations, they rely on activities that in the past have worked for them. Moreover, these activities are named (through signs and language), are easily recognized, and no longer require negotiation or clarification. Once these patterns of activity are repeated as a matter of routine, and new generations are taught these routine ways of doing things, institutionalization has occurred. A pattern of activity is said to be *institutionalized* when, *in a given circumstance, it happens with regularity and is accepted widely throughout the population.* Institutionalized activities are imbued with meaning, and these meanings form the "pieces" of culture that provide the basis for social reality.

Institutionalized

Later in this chapter we shall explore the question of exactly how language enters the picture. But for the moment, it is not difficult to imagine how humans began naming familiar objects and patterns of living and imbuing them with meaning, given the complexity of the vocal cords, the size of the human brain, and a little spirit of invention. Thus, a pattern of social life has begun to be established in our little hunting and gathering clan. In a certain sense these residual products of interaction patterns have taken on a life of their own. They've become what Durkheim called "social facts."

Moreover, the processes of social interaction have a twofold significance in relation to human culture. First, cultural practices, habits of living, traditions, and the values inherent in them all spring from interaction processes. If we could have studied that hypothetical first human community, that little hunting and gathering society, we might have observed the emergence of cultural practices from routine patterns of social interaction. In this sense, it may be said that human culture is "embedded" in social interaction processes.

Second, cultural life not only has its origin in social interaction, but constantly is reproduced or re-enacted through interaction processes. Social psychologists have placed great emphasis on the fact that social reality is negotiated. It is not simply "given." Cultural meanings and the institutionalized patterns of living that accompany them always are open to negotiation. New patterns of interaction may result in new cultural patterns. Thus, regardless of whether the consequences of those new patterns are minor and subtle (men once were not fully dressed unless they wore a hat) or substantial ("let's dump all that tea in Boston Harbor"), social interaction processes always hold the potential for cultural change.

There is a continuous and intimate connection between culture and social interaction processes. Social interaction is the ebb and flow, the life blood of a group, community, or society. Social interaction is the on-going social relationships between people, the comings, goings, and doings in a human community. Culture consists of the institutionalized practices and patterns of living and the meanings attached to them that spring from our social interactions with one another. Yet, these same interactional processes always hold the potential for the institutionalization of new cultural patterns.

SHAPING INFLUENCES

It has been seen thus far that unlike other animal populations, human beings invent their own way of life. Culture apparently does for humans what instincts do for other animal populations. Culture springs from processes of social interaction. Yet, it also is clear that human cultures are not invented in a vacuum. Rather, the great diversity of and variation among human cultures demonstrates not only that people create them, but that environmental factors of many different types influence patterns of cultural development. Geography, climate, human physiology, and a host of other factors push and pull cultural practices in one way or another. As humans invent their life together and attempt to solve the practical problems of daily living, the environmental setting and the time and place in history provide some of the raw materials out of which a culture, a system of values, a way of life will be shaped. Let's consider some of these influences.

The geographic setting is one of the most powerful influences upon cultural development. For instance, nomadic societies are a frequent result of extreme climate in which it is difficult to maintain a constant food supply. As a result, continual movement becomes the way of life. While the geographic setting may influence the culture in very general ways, it also may set the pattern for very specific aspects of the culture. Among some North American Eskimo populations in the Arctic the language contains many different terms describing snow. Since the animals on which the Eskimos feed are highly sensitive to snow conditions, the ability to distinguish subtle changes in the environment becomes a requirement for survival. In a variety of ways, cultural practices and values become fitted to the pressure of the environmental setting. This process is called *cultural adaptation.*

Cultural adaptation

The natural resources of the physical settings are yet another powerful factor that can shape cultural traditions, tastes, and practices. For example, anyone who travels throughout the United States may observe that the physical resources in different parts of the country have produced variations in types of housing preferences. Wood frame structures are characteristic in the Northeast and Northwest where lumber was plentiful. However, homes of brick and masonry products predominate in the South and Southwest because of the availability of the component raw materials. In the Northeast, some industrial buildings are constructed of cinderblock, which is not viewed as an attractive building material. Yet, in Arizona, where cinderblock insulates well against the desert heat, and where the raw materials for making them are plentiful, many new luxury homes are constructed from these same cinderblocks. Clearly, the availability and practicality of building materials have shaped cultural tastes in the Northeast and the Southwest differently.

The same sorts of observations apply to culturally defined tastes in food. The American diet is exceedingly diverse, due, in large part, to the rather unique capability of the soil and climate to produce diverse and plentiful agricultural products. This wealth of natural resources has earned the United States the name of "the world's bread basket." Americans traveling in other parts of the world soon tire of the copious amounts of fish eaten in Scandinavia, and the quantities of rice typically consumed in Asian nations. Tastes in food are greatly shaped by what can be produced cheaply in quantity in a given environmental setting. Clearly, natural resources influence cultural formation.

Such factors as population density and both age and gender distributions in a population can exert influences upon cultural trends. For example, the dramatic growth in the number of older persons in American society has had readily apparent cultural effects. Mature Americans have become an important economic market. Television advertisements that once featured "teeny-boppers" in bikini bathing suits during the baby-boomer's teenage years now focus upon more mature audiences. The youth culture so predominant in the late 1960s and 1970s is less noticeable. Being older is no longer unfashionable. Accordingly, television commercials feature Americans over "thirty-something"extolling the virtues of everything from new cars to

FIGURE 3.2
CULTURAL FORMATION

CULTURE
COLLECTIVELY SHARED PATTERNS OF THOUGHT, ACTION, AND FEELING.

SOCIAL INTERACTION
1. SOLVING PROBLEMS IN DAILY LIVING
2. REPEATED PATTERNS THAT "WORK" ARE INSTITUTIONALIZED

THE BIOLOGICAL MATRIX
PHYSICAL LIMITS AND POTENTIALS OF THE SPECIES

PHYSICAL ENVIRONMENT
1. GEOGRAPHY
2. CLIMATE
3. NATURAL RESOURCES

"improved" breakfast cereals. Thus, age distribution is but one of a variety of characteristics of human populations that exert substantial influence upon the formation and change of cultural values and practices.

In summary, culture consists of all the appropriate and/or required modes of thought, action, and feeling in societies, as well as the material productions that result from people's life together. Social interaction is the on-going process of social relationships between people. Culture may be viewed as the meanings that are assigned to interaction patterns as those patterns become institutionalized. Finally, geography, natural resources, and population characteristics are but three of a wide range of factors that influence the specific patterns of culture. Culture, while a human invention, *always is* shaped by specific physical, environmental, social, and historical circumstances.

Figure 3.2 provides an overview of the information about cultural formation discussed in the preceding two sections of this chapter. The biological matrix, the physical environment, and social interaction processes each make unique contributions to cultural patterns. Both the biological features of the human animal and the setting of the physical environment provide a general context in which the all-important processes of human social interaction occur. The next section of this chapter examines the essential features of culture, among them language, symbols, and shared meanings.

THE CHARACTERISTICS OF CULTURE

Thus far, this chapter has placed the concept of culture within the general scheme of phenomena studied by social scientists. A closer look at culture and its characteristics is next in order. All human culture exhibits certain important features or characteristics. Through an examination of these characteristics of culture we may glean an even more satisfactory answer to the basic question of this chapter—how is life among people different from life among other animals?

LANGUAGE

Language is the root of all cultural systems, and without language, culture is not possible. Why is this fact so important? After all, we've been trying in this chapter to understand some basic ways in which human life differs from that of other animals. On the one hand, we've seen that humans, unlike monkeys, dogs, cats, and whales, do not seem to have any instincts. Also, humans, unlike other animal populations, possess culture. Language, a critical aspect of culture, is the essential mechanism through which humans manufacture culture. Language is common to all parts of the human species, while being absent among all other species. People are the only animal population with language.

But, wait—what about all those studies with apes and monkeys? Haven't these studies disproved the claim that *homo sapiens* are unique? Surely, the flood of studies by primatologists in the fields of psychology, anthropology, and zoology that began in the 1950s and continue today have revealed much. There now are dramatic chronicles of social life and social organization among the chimpanzees at Gombe Stream in Tanzania (Goodall 1971), among the baboons of Kenya (Strum 1987), and among the Great Apes, the gorilla families of the Virunga Mountains on the borders of Zaire, Rwanda, and Uganda (Fossey 1983). These valuable field studies reveal complex patterns of social structure among these different primate communities. Most importantly, there is convincing evidence that some of these social patterns are invented, learned, and taught in these populations, not simply provided by the genetic code. Apes and monkeys are both inventive and technological. Technology refers to ways in which animals extend the reach of their bodies to control their environment. Obviously, humans are an extremely technological animal. Though not to the extent of humans, apes do attempt technological control of their environment, and, to some degree, succeed. Thus, the once-popular view that humans are unique in their manufacture of social life must be rejected. It is clear that other primates also invent some of their life patterns, and thus reach beyond what is genetically given.

FIGURE 3.3
Are they more like us or different from us?

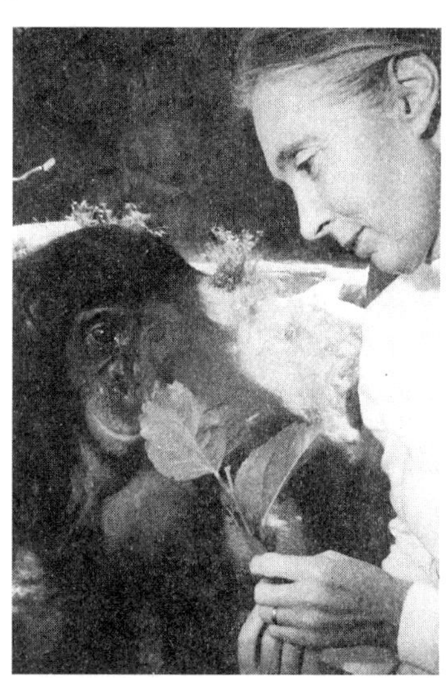

But does this mean that these "lower" primates also have language and culture? The answer to this critical question is not found in the naturalistic setting beside Gombe Stream, nor in the Mountains of Uganda, but in the various laboratory studies with chimps and other primates here in the United States. Beginning with a chimp named Washoe (Gardner and Gardner 1971) and extending through the work with such "celebrities" as Sarah (Premack 1971), Lana (Rumbaugh 1977), and Koko (Patterson 1981), it has been shown that other primates are able to converse with humans by using American Sign Language, or various sign and symbol codes on a board or computer terminal. These studies are so interesting, and at times surprising, that we may forget to stay focused upon what the folks in the business schools call "the bottom line." What is the most important thing learned from these kinds of studies?

Two critical things have *not* happened in these primate studies. First, neither Washoe, Koko, nor any other gorillas, apes, or monkeys have invented any new language of their own. Yes, they do connect and combine some of the previously learned signs and symbols, thus showing a sophisticated ability to manipulate meanings already acquired. But no new ones are invented. Obviously, both the size of the human brain and the possession of complex vocal cords give humans a tremendous advantage in the language-inventing game. One only need watch some of the "stupid dog tricks" on David Letterman's "Late Night" television show. While some owners surely think their dogs talk and sing, the clear lack of dog language and dog music is overwhelming. Second, none of these studies show other primates routinely teaching language to members of their own species. Again, some of these studies do show chimps sharing with one another some of the information they learn in these experiments. However, this is a far cry from human language invention, language acquisition, and socialization practices. Monkeys don't manufacture language. Nor do they routinely teach it to one another. That's the "bottom line."

Only human animals manufacture language and teach it to one another. While the reasons for this lie partly in matters of physiology (the brain and vocal cords), there is another element involved. Language is part of the symbolic aspect of culture.

SYMBOLS

Symbols

All language is symbolic, and all symbolic culture is linguistic. *A symbol is an arbitrary invention with which meaning is bestowed and which therefore stands for something outside itself.* Symbolic culture includes linguistic items (i.e., words), material objects, or even patterns of human action. Moreover, language conveys the conventional and arbitrary meanings that imbue both physical objects and human actions with their symbolic content. For instance, the word "chair" is a symbol. It is arbitrary because there is no natural connection between the word "chair" and the actual four-legged object upon which people sit. Chairs might just as easily have been called "desks," "tables," "sinks," or anything else. What something is called is far less important than the act of agreement in naming it. In this sense, all culture is said to be conventional (literally by agreement) rather than natural (biologically or physically determined in some way).

Language

Language is the working substance of all cultural systems, and accordingly, language may be understood as a rather enormous collection of conventional, symbolic terms or meanings. The abstract symbol "chair" points to something outside of itself, the physical object that is described. This is not so with a mere sign.

Let's return for a moment to the research on other primates. For Washoe, Koko, Sarah, and the others (Sebeok and Umiker-Sebeok 1980, Savage-Rumbaugh 1986), each item on the electronic keyboard, each plastic token, is essentially a sign, not a symbol. Signs, unlike symbols, are not quite so arbitrary. There is a natural connection between a sign, even a linguistic sign, and the object or action it describes.

Signs

Signs exhibit very specific and particular connections to the objects and acts they describe. For instance, for the very young human, the visual sign of the mother's breast or the baby bottle is a sign that the food is on the way, and thus, the youngster stops crying once the sign is presented. Obviously, there is a very direct connection between the breast/bottle and the feeding activity. But genuine symbolic meaning is both arbitrary and abstract. When this same youngster becomes a bit older and acquires not just signs, but symbols, the parent can abate the crying with a symbolic communication. "We are going for burgers and fries in five minutes." This rather complex assortment of abstract symbolic units (words) does for the symbol-comprehending animal what the less complex sign did for the pre-symbolic infant. It conveys meaning. Most researchers agree that apes and monkeys never quite arrive at this level of symbolic comprehension. This abstract (i.e., non-naturalistic) quality of words is what makes language so fully portable, at least within any specific cultural system.

Finally, even if future research does manage to demonstrate symbolic and culture-forming abilities among other primate populations, both the degree of human reliance on culture and the corresponding absence of instinctively guided action will continue making humans rather unique in the animal kingdom.

SHARED AND LEARNED

Culture is an attribute of individuals only as members of collectivities, that is, groups and communities. Culture is a "social fact," something in which individuals participate but which, in the final analysis, resides outside the individual. Let's consider an example.

In the typical college classroom, the events that transpire, collective cultural events, are not simply the summation of the individual psychic facts of the persons present. Adam really is waiting for class to end so he can meet Kathy for a date. Kim does not like sociology, but knows the class is required for graduation in her business major. John dislikes college and finds all classes dull. However, he'd rather be in class than working for a living. Josh and Vicki really like sociology, and both look forward to this class. Pat doesn't understand much of the sociology lecture, but she does nod and smile at the professor occasionally, thus giving the impression that she is involved in the events of the class. If we add together all the psychic states of mind of these individuals, the result is not the well-ordered, culturally patterned classroom experience. This is precisely because individual psychic facts and cultural facts are different (see the discussion in Chapter 1, pp. 5–8). The cultural event is collective, and is composed of shared traditions, values, and expectations. While individuals participate in these cultural realities, cultural events and practices should not be equated with individuals. It is for this reason that psychology, the study of individual personality systems, is a different science from sociology and anthropology, both of which focus upon the shared collective systems of meaning and activity in which individuals participate.

All culture is learned. From the fact that humans don't have instinctually patterned solutions to life's challenges and problems, it follows that human-made ways of life must be learned. This fact sounds too obvious to require discussion. But, the implications of this fact are momentous. First, it is through learning culture that humans become "human." Culture consists of the appropriate or required modes of thought, action, and feeling in a society. Thus, becoming a person, acquiring what people erroneously call *"human nature,"* is a cultural process. Humans learn how to be human from other humans. Genes do not provide that information. To use an analogy from the world of computers, in *homo sapiens,* genes only provide the equipment, the hardware. The programs are manufactured culturally. Every new member of the species must become socialized to the expected and required ways of living and being in his or her group, tribe, clan, community, or nation.

Human nature

This points to a second implication of the fact that culture is learned. The process of learning one's culture is intricate, complex, and subtle. That eventually this task of cultural learning is mastered by most humans, disguises the extent of this complexity. As will be seen in Chapter 6, the process of socialization, learning culture, *literally* becoming social, requires scientific scrutiny to be fully understood. Social psychologists focus on this fragile connection between the individual and the collective. The way in which the social self or human personality system is produced, the nature of social interactions and social relationships between persons, and the differences between early childhood or primary socialization, as compared to adult or secondary socialization, all are important topics that stem from the observation that culture is learned. The social psychologist wishes to know exactly how, in what ways, and under what circumstances the processes of cultural learning occur. Not only the social psychologist, but applied social scientists—social workers, psychiatrists, family therapists, and guidance counselors—need to understand the consequences when these socialization processes misfire or are incomplete.

STATIC AND DYNAMIC

All culture exhibits a dual profile. Cultures are full of static elements that seem to resist change from one generation to the next. At the same time, cultures also are in the continual process of change and alteration. Some aspects of culture change rapidly, while other aspects are prone to stability and longevity. In general, it may be argued that the more inclusive the system of cultural values or set of behavioral mandates, the more stability it will exhibit. In other words, the more persons who are affected by a value or behavioral requirement, the more stable it will be.

In most societies, religions stipulate highly inclusive values that apply equally to all members of the cultural unit, and thus religious values are very resistant to change. Even in religiously diverse or pluralistic societies like the United States, where there are many different religious subgroups (Catholic, Jewish, and many different Protestant communities) certain very general religious values in which all groups participate have prevailed in the culture for a long time. This is so because these overarching value systems provide meaning in a culture. They provide interpretations of the meaning of life on the planet, or of the place of the nation in history. While people sometimes joke about the American creed of "God, apple pie, motherhood, and country," most people recognize that there are serious risks in publicly attacking God, motherhood, and country. This is because broadly encompassing values are involved in such challenges.

Similarly, political values and traditions are highly resistant to change because political systems, like the ultimate religious conceptions in a culture, are broadly applicable to the members of the culture. While religious systems provide interpretive meanings, political values stipulate rules for the control and allocation of scarce rewards and resources in society. How people obtain wealth, respect, and power are embodied in political culture. As will be explained in greater detail in Chapters 8 and 9, such things are not easily altered.

Less inclusive parts of the culture are much more open to change: hair and clothing styles, fads in music, tastes in food, and a wide range of other things which do not involve tampering with the ultimate meanings or the patterns of access and control. It may be argued that the causes and consequences of stability and change are the heartland of sociological analysis. Much of sociology, and thus, much of this text is focused upon the development of concepts that promote the understanding of stability and change in both culture and social structure.

OMNIPRESENT

In the life of the human animal, culture is omnipresent. One can no more envision humans out of culture, than fish out of water. The analogy is frightfully graphic. Few things are as graceful as the motion of a school of fish in the water. Fish appear to move through the water effortlessly, large numbers of them shifting direction and changing speed together almost like a single being. Drag them up on shore or into a boat in a net and everything changes. They are no longer graceful. They gasp for the oxygen which their gills can extract only from water. The graceful movement created by the motion of their fins in water is transformed on dry land into rather clumsy flips and flops. This is because the fish obtains its most characteristic behavioral qualities through interaction with its environment. Alter that environment, and you've altered the apparent "nature" of the animal.

The essential functions of the cultural environment of humans works in exactly the same way. While culture is humanly manufactured, it also "acts back upon" and manufactures our "humanity." Culture is the medium through which people relate to one another. It conditions our thoughts, actions, and feelings. These actions and expressions are sensible to one another precisely because they are in and of the culture. Sadly, persons with severe brain damage provide a glimpse of humans slightly out of the culture. Either because of impaired motor skills or reduced mental ability, some persons with severe brain damage don't fulfill our cultural expectations. Their movements appear twisted and at times grotesque, and often we can't understand their strained attempts at speech. The same may be said of persons with severe mental illness. Again, nonimpaired members of the culture have great difficulty deciphering the actions and intentions of those who suffer from severe mental illness. As Szasz (1961) and others have observed, it is precisely the inability to fulfill cultural expectations that provides the recognizable symptoms of what is called "mental illness." The mentally ill don't seem to share everyone else's cultural expectations.

The point here is not that the mentally ill or the retarded are somehow not human beings. They are human. But, the often shameful ways in which these populations have been treated demonstrates the point that if humans are stripped of culture, even minimally, some people will cease viewing them as human. The fish out of water is still a fish, though in need of help. The human slightly out of culture is still a human, though in need of compassion and assistance. For physically and mentally normal members of the species *homo sapiens*, culture is omnipresent. Our ways of thinking, acting, and feeling, whether in public or in private, in groups or alone, are shaped, coded, and made meaningful by the culture. Culture is omnipresent.

In summary, language and symbols are the hallmarks of human cultural life distinguishing humans from the apes and monkeys. While our primate cousins, the chimps and gorillas, are able to learn signs, perhaps acquire a limited number of symbols, and even share some of them with one another under laboratory conditions, they don't manufacture language, nor do they routinely teach symbolic communication to one another. Only humans, through language, invent an arbitrary, abstract, and conventional world.

Culture exhibits a number of important characteristics. Culture is both learned and shared. It does not result from the biological code. It is invented by collective effort rather than individual endeavor. Additionally, culture is static and dynamic. Its more inclusive elements exhibit remarkable stability and resistance to change. Less inclusive parts of human cultures exhibit much fluidity and change. In many ways, the sociology of culture involves a focus on the causes, conditions, and consequences of these two basic cultural processes.

Finally, culture is omnipresent. It is a constantly present medium through which people recognize each other's humanity. Whether in groups and communities or alone, an individual's thoughts, actions, and feelings still follow cultural patterns.

Some Consequences of Being a Cultural Animal

It has been shown thus far that humans are unique in the animal kingdom because of their use of culture, and, of course, because of their freedom from instincts. Additionally, it has been seen that culture has some very distinctive features. Most important among these is its symbolic character. To all of this one might say, so what? Does it really matter if, after all, culture merely does for humans what instincts do for other animal species? But the matter is really not quite that simple. Indeed, human life is very different in many ways from the animal life among dogs, cats, and fish. It stands to reason that if humans are unique in their manufacture of this very special stuff called culture, there must be some consequences to all this. What sorts of things result from the human's cultural constitution?

Philosophers have long recognized that much of human life is characterized by a dilemma formed by the opposite polarities of freedom and order. Every social institution, every cultural practice, to provide order in our lives, must sacrifice freedom; and conversely, every freedom enjoyed is gained at the sacrifice of order. This dialectic provides a useful set of categories for examining the consequences of the cultural character of the human animal. Some features of cultural life may be understood as liberating and enabling. These aspects of culture expand the possibilities for thought, action, and feeling. Other aspects of cultural life may be viewed as restrictive and limiting. These features tend to reduce options and possibilities. Let's consider each of these two kinds of consequences of culture.

CULTURE AS LIBERATING

All culture is at once symbolic, conventional, and portable. These important features mean that so long as a person remains within any given cultural system, an inventory of standard meanings remains in place, ready to provide ease of communication and understanding between individuals and groups. This unique arrangement, what might be called reality by social agreement, has some very important taken-for-granted consequences. Two of these consequences are examined here. They are the ways in which culture provides a predictable and reliable social environment, and the way in which a shared culture facilitates the expression of individualism.

First, the very arbitrary and conventional feature of culture means that people within a cultural system can rely upon a predictable universe of meanings. Since people take for granted this feature of cultural reality, initially it seems not particularly significant or noteworthy. However, what would life be like if people were required to negotiate meanings and understandings anew in every situation encountered? The question is not quite so hypothetical. For persons traveling in a foreign culture, the experience of "culture shock" is quite real. The meanings of one culture are so different from those of another, that one must adjust to the newly acquired customs of the new cultural environment. The more different a foreign culture is from one's own, the more effort is required to negotiate meanings and communicate with other persons. The traveler in a foreign land finds the practical difficulties of negotiating reality quite exhausting until the new culture, like one's own host culture, begins to become a sort of "second nature." The problems of culture shock only begin to dissipate as one acculturates to the taken-for-granted cultural realities of the new culture.

The providing of a predictable universe of meanings is a truly significant consequence of cultural life. It even might be argued that a human being's "comfort" in the cultural environment contributes to a sense of psychic well-being. The discomfort that people sometimes experience in an uncommon subcultural setting, such as a different ethnic or religious community, illustrates this point. Through culture, then, people are provided with a reliable and predictable universe of meanings and events, all of which contribute to a sense of comfort and well-being.

A second, and perhaps ironic, feature of cultural life is that the more individuals share culture, the more they can express their own and perceive other people's individual and unique characteristics. Each individual person is unique, both as a genetic event and as a system of personality traits. It is the remarkable accomplishment of cultural life, through the process called socialization, that biologically unique individuals are conditioned to think, act, and feel in culturally common ways. Yet, at the very moment a shared culture makes people similar to one another, it also equips them to express their innate, individual differences from one another. Culture may be understood as a repertoire. It is a standard set of meanings, actions, and situations, all of which, through the process of socialization, become part of the stock of knowledge that each member of a particular culture possesses. Precisely because different individuals in a culture share this same body of information about appropriate or required modes of thought, action, and feeling, it is possible for each to recognize the more subtle, individual ways in which culturally expected norms are expressed. Conversely, when different individuals do not share much of the same culture, quite a lot of what each of them does seems unique to the other. Under such conditions it is, indeed, difficult to separate the individually unique from the culturally foreign aspects of what the other person says or does.

CULTURE AS RESTRICTING

In contrast to the liberating consequences of culture, all cultural systems impose constraints and limits upon their members. Two such limiting features are examined here. They are the tendency of persons to conform to the prevailing culture, and the ways in which cultures reduce options for alternate patterns of action, thought, and feeling.

First, while few persons like to admit it, one of the most evident consequences of cultural conditioning is the tendency to conform. To be sure, society offers people many inducements for conforming, among them a modicum of material well-being, and on some occasions wealth. The approval of other people is a reward for our doing what they expect us to do. Culture is, after all, an entire system of connected expectations about who should do what kinds of things and under what circumstances. It consists of appropriate or required modes of action, belief, and feeling. By fulfilling the appropriate, the required, and the expected, people get the approval of others. That approval ranges from the pat on the head a child gets for obeying his or her parents' command, to the raise in salary that an employee gets for "doing a good job."

There is a significant element of reciprocity in all this social conformity. Most persons, most of the time, prefer a predictable universe of events. Few of us would be pleased with a social experience of constant surprise. People like to be able to "count on" things being the way they expect them to be. So our own social conformity begets the conformity of others around us, and vice versa. This, in a sense, explains why most people, most of the time, conform to each other's expectations. Moreover, this extent of social conformity has some hidden social functions. Culture, it must be remembered, is a system of shared meanings, definitions of situations, and understandings of shared social realities. If one oversteps the boundary of those shared meanings, one runs the risk of being misunderstood. Thus, to a degree, the extent to which people conform to cultural expectations determines their ability to be understood unambiguously.

Second, culture always has the effect of reducing people's options for patterns of thought, action, and feeling. From a sociological point of view, among human populations, to paraphrase the French existentialist philosopher Jean-Paul Sartre (1943), "all things are possible." Said differently, there are few ways of responding to life's basic drives that have not been tried somewhere, sometime, by some human community. Yet, in contrast to this nearly unlimited range of human options for patterns of thought, action, and feeling, each single cultural system is finite and limited.

It might be said not simply that human nature is cultural, but that each culture stipulates a different model, a different idea of what the human animal is, and a different set of standards for what kinds of actions, thoughts, and feelings are appropriate. In this sense, each culture places stringent constraints and limits upon its members. What is "normal" in one culture may be viewed as deviant or even inhumane by another. Foods considered delicious in one culture sometimes are seen as repulsive in another. Practices that are sinful in one culture are viewed as sacred in another. In such ways each culture limits the human animal. Each individual must be him or herself only in culturally mandated ways. Would you be the same person you are today if you had been raised in a very different cultural environment? Who would Michael Jackson or Bruce Springsteen be today if they had been born in cultures that don't value rock music?

In summary, the cultural constitution of the human animal has important consequences, some liberating and some restricting. Culture is liberating because it provides members of any cultural community with a predictable and reliable social environment. Additionally, the more individuals share culture, the more their uniqueness can be expressed and perceived. In contrast, culture is restrictive because it induces conformity. Also, it limits the ways in which we can be ourselves because each culture is but one selection from a diverse universe of possibilities. Culture reflects the age-old dilemma of freedom and order. These counterbalancing tendencies are knit together differently in every culture.

STUDYING CULTURE: LESSONS FROM ANTHROPOLOGY

Most people assume that studying social life will be a rather simple and easy task. After all, people live in society all of their lives, and therefore, must develop some expertise in understanding social patterns and culture. Yet, the very fact that people are cultural animals, and that their ways of acting, habits of thought, and feelings are shaped by the cultural environment creates some special problems for studying the cultural environment. How is it possible to study, from an objective scientific standpoint, the very cultural traditions that have shaped our own ways of thinking, feeling, and acting? How can social scientists become liberated from their own cultural conditioning long enough to undertake objective analyses of other cultures? The following discussion examines some of these special problems involved in studying culture and human social life.

ETHNOCENTRISM

By the middle of the 19th century, British anthropologists had already launched a rather ambitious program of studying different cultures. Colonialism, economic imperialism, military conquest, and economic exploitation all led to British dominance over a wide assortment of peoples in Africa, Asia, the Middle East, and elsewhere. Wherever the British army went, British anthropological scholars followed. Sometimes they collected physical artifacts, such as native works of art, implements of warfare, eating utensils, and even human remains (consider the mummies of ancient Egypt). Museums in England were filled with the cultural products of these tribal societies, some of which would soon perish from the "progress" of "civilization." The popular Harrison Ford adventure film *Raiders of the Lost Ark* was remotely based upon such anthropological exploits.

Physical anthropology was not the only beneficiary of these military and economic forays of the British Empire during the 19th century. Cultural anthropologists focused upon the seemingly unique nonmaterial cultural life of these many foreign places. The political organization of the tribe, family, kinship relationships, and puberty rituals were all topics of great interest and fascination. These pioneering anthropologists were seeing for the first time social practices of enormous range and variation. Yet, as anthropologist Marvin Harris observes in his book *The Rise of Anthropological Theory* (1968), the early students of these newly-discovered cultures produced very little useful knowledge. They saw these "primitive" cultures as "grotesque" and "irrational." Native religious practices were interpreted as mere superstition and not truly religious. The problem, of course, was that the early British anthropologists were blinded by their own ethnocentrism.

Ethnocentrism

What is ethnocentrism? *Ethnocentrism is the tendency to view one's own cultural standards and cultural practices as best. From a scientific standpoint it is to commit the error of judging others' cultural traditions by the standards of one's own.* It is the habit of assuming that one's own culture is the way things ought to be in all cultures.

Just as a certain genetic fault may make some people "color-blind" (physically unable to see some colors), similarly it might be argued that ethnocentrism creates a sort of culture-blindness, an inability to understand and appreciate the meanings of another culture. Clearly, this was the situation of the early British anthropologists. Patterns of culture and social organization that differed greatly from those in their homeland were seen as irrational and unintelligible. Religious ethnocentrism, the belief that Christianity was the only "true" religion, prevented these observers from understanding that religious thoughts and practices, like all other social institutions, are of various kinds, and that the religious practices of other cultures are no less "religious" than those found in Christendom. Gradually, anthropologists recognized this ethnocentric flaw of the early 19th century scholars. Emile Durkheim's *Elementary Forms of the Religious Life* (1912), a study of the religion of Arunta society in Australia, is recognized as valuable by both sociologists and anthropologists for this very reason. Unlike the early British anthropologists who dismissed non-Christian religious practices in other cultures as insignificant, Durkheim attempted to use the example of Arunta religion to demonstrate the important social functions of all religions for the societies in which they are found.

Ethnocentrism is ever-present. It is a tendency about which every student in the social sciences must be cognizant. We cannot understand the practices of other societies, or even different social groups within the same society, in terms of our own values. To do so is very likely to misunderstand the phenomena studied. Rather, social scientific analysis, the study of culture, requires a special perspective to counteract ethnocentrism. That perspective is called cultural relativism.

CULTURAL RELATIVISM

One of the truly great anthropological scholars of the 20th century, the late Margaret Mead (1901–1978) is given much of the credit for clarifying the idea of cultural relativism. Mead, who did extensive field work in other cultures, argued that the specific cultural practices of any society must be understood and interpreted in the context of that society's culture alone. As another major figure in anthropology, Ruth Benedict (1887–1948) discovered, one could not understand the cultural life of the Kwakiutl Indians in British Columbia by evaluating their traditions according to Western Christian moral standards and values (Benedict 1934).

Cultural relativism

Cultural relativism is the practice of suspending the moral standards and judgements of one's own culture for the purpose of gaining a scientific understanding of other cultures. It allows the researcher to interpret specific cultural practices in the context of the culture in which they are found. It entails a recognition of the fact that values and moral judgements differ from culture to culture and are not universal. Since each person subscribes, to some degree, to the moral standards of his or her own culture, it is inevitable that some traditions in other cultures will seem morally repugnant. For instance, among some Native American tribes it was common practice to leave disabled elderly members of the tribe alone to die of starvation. In the context of present-day Western values this seems a cruel and morally offensive practice. Yet, for the people in these tribes this was a meaningful and dignified way to die. The dying person was spared the psychic distress of being a burden to loved ones. Indeed, to these people, no doubt, hospitalization and the death rituals of modern cultures might seem meaningless and cruel.

Every culture designs a way of life consistent with its own system of morals, values, and life contingencies. Understanding different cultural ways of life requires temporarily suspending one's own cultural values and adopting a stance of cultural relativism.

CULTURAL MYTHS

Ironically, the shedding of our own ethnocentrism, and the adoption of a cultural relativist standpoint is an important step in studying one's own culture as well. Precisely because culture is conventional and symbolic, it provides a collective ability to create ideas about reality that have varying degrees of "fit" with the way things actually are. Said differently, culture allows the human animal to imagine, to wish, and even to fantasize. Humans are able to invent conceptions not only about what is, but about what we'd like to be, and what we'd like to think we have been. It is here that cultural myths become apparent. *A myth is a collective view, a tale, a story, or a legend that provides an interpretation of what a people have been, are, or will become. Cultural myths typically contain cultural heroes or archetypes.* While cultural myths may not be true in the literal sense, they provide important clues to the political and social identities of nations and human communities of all types.

Myths

Anthropologists contend that myths have important functions for all societies. Cultural myths and heroes provide value and goal systems for societies. They also provide more cosmic meanings in the face of life's day-to-day routine. Cultural myths must be understood and in some sense demythologized. *To demythologize a myth is to search for the cultural significance, meanings, or functions of its less literal elements.* Let's consider a modern American cultural myth.

It is claimed that America is a "land of opportunity" in which all persons are "created equal" and in which anyone willing to work can achieve the "American dream" of "the good life." Yet, as many sociological studies show (see Chapter 8) these are ideals not realities. From the Civil War era to the last quarter of the 20th century, one percent of the American population has continued to own over a quarter of all the wealth in the nation (Zeitlin 1978). In spite of the women's movement, in 1988 less than one percent of the chief executive officers of American corporations were women. In spite of alleged Civil Rights gains, the black unemployment rate in 1988 was twice that of whites. For the entire decade of the 1980s, the gap between average white and average black incomes in the United States widened (U.S. Bureau of the Census 1991). A middle-range estimate of homelessness in the United States on any given night is between 250,000 and 350,000 persons (Peroff 1987).

Is all this stuff about "a land of opportunity" simply a pack of lies? Not quite. The American myth of equality is an important meaning system, a set of goals. It sustains some persons who don't become millionaires or who don't even quite enter the middle class. It helps motivate and propel other persons into the middle and upper classes. While all people are not treated equally in the United States, relatively few of the world's many national cultures embrace this myth or goal. If one wants to understand much of what happens in America, one must recognize this powerful myth. Recognizing this American myth of equality and the related myth of the attainability of "the good life," helps us understand why some parents make great economic sacrifices for their children, why people from other lands continue to immigrate here, and why some people work several jobs even though they don't seem to get rich doing so. Indeed, some of the things people do in search of the "American dream" don't seem especially rational. Yet, an insight into the myths that guide people's actions is essential in order to understand how these actions are meaningful and why they happen.

CULTURAL COMPLEXES, INTEGRATION, AND SUBCULTURES

Cultural unit

Cultural complex

From all that has been said about culture in this chapter, it should be apparent that cultures are not random assortments of ideas, ideals, practices, and material objects. Rather, the individual "units" of a culture are sewn together into a well-knit fabric called a cultural complex. *A cultural unit is any singular practice, idea, or material object in a culture. A cultural complex is a meaningfully related set of cultural practices, ideas, and objects.* For example, the activity of hitting a baseball is a cultural unit, and the baseball glove is a physical cultural unit. When the activities (pitching, batting, fielding) are viewed with the related objects (gloves, bats, bases) and the values involved in this game, we see a meaningful, comprehensible cultural complex. Why is the concept of cultural complexes useful?

Cultural integration

A common concern of students of both culture and social structure is the degree of diversity or consistency in cultural and structural systems. Generally, higher degrees of consistency and cultural integration are found in societies that have fewer cultural complexes. *Cultural integration refers to the degree to which different cultural complexes and value systems reinforce and support one another.* In the extreme case, such as a tribal society, one central cultural complex is encountered, and thus, the degree of cultural integration across different institutions (politics, family, religion, and occupation) is very high. It is not surprising that societies with a small number of well-integrated cultural complexes also exhibit little differentiation in their social structure. There are important correspondences between cultural diversity and structural diversity in societies. While social change may begin in either the cultural or structural realm, change in one will eventually lead to change in the other. Changes in the number of cultural complexes or in the cultural integration of a society should be connected to levels of differentiation in the social structure.

Subculture

In the case of less well-integrated cultural systems, those in which cultural complexes have proliferated, it is likely that actual subcultures will emerge. *A subculture is a cultural complex that exists within the context of a host cul-*

ture, but which has its own unique norms, values, and even life style. Obviously, subcultures are not commonly encountered in highly integrated cultural systems. In highly integrated cultural systems the cultural complexes tend to reinforce one another, or reflect similar values and traditions. Subcultures are just the reverse of this. Subcultures provide different lifestyles and traditions that are followed by different subgroups. They are found in societies that exhibit high levels of structural diversity or social differentiation. In practice, those who study modern societies use the term subculture to characterize these divergent values, lifestyles, and traditions that appear in different class groupings—in ethnic and religious communities, and, in some cases, in different occupational groupings. Thus, the term subculture is frequently encountered in the sociology of modern societies.

In summary, we have examined some of the complexities of human cultural systems and encountered some of the pitfalls involved in studying culture. In the historical development of the social sciences, ethnocentrism, the tendency to value one's own culture more than others, prevented objective analyses of different cultures. A cultural relativist orientation overcomes this difficulty. Analyzing culture requires a recognition of the important role of cultural myths. These are collective visions about what a people are, have been, or wish to become. Finally, levels of integration in cultural systems are important indicators of what is happening in a society. While traditional societies exhibit few major cultural complexes, modern societies contain many different cultural complexes. The most independent or "value distinct" of them are called subcultures.

APPLICATIONS

The Life and Death of Myths and Heroes

One of the most important themes of this chapter has been that language and culture are instruments with which humans invent their world. These creative cultural activities of the human animal are most dramatically highlighted by cultural inventions that depart from the strictly empirical. Cultural myths and heroes are prime examples of cultural productions beyond the strictly empirical.

As was noted earlier, a myth is a collective view, a tale, a story, or a legend, that provides an interpretation of what a people have been, are, or hope to become. Additionally, cultural myths are populated by cultural heroes. A nation's heroes, real or imagined, say much about a nation's identity.

Just as culture is both static and dynamic, so the myths of a nation are subject to change and alteration. However, myths and heroes do not die easily. Indeed, if myths and heroes involve our hopes and dreams, then the killing of myths and heroes entails the killing of our dreams. Mythic change in a society is a painful and tragic social process. Mythic rebirth, at best, is a healing one.

CASE

The Vietnam Vets and the Persian Gulf War

Between 1964 and 1975 the United States became ensnared in an agonizing killing activity. It is difficult to judge whether America did more harm to Viet-

FIGURE 3.4
Participating in mythic rituals can be vitally important even in modern societies.

nam than America itself. What were the consequences of the Vietnam conflict for America?

The immediate consequences of the Vietnam War are easily recounted for much has been written about them. The war killed over 50,000 young Americans, bankrupted the American economy, and destroyed a presidency. But, the war also destroyed a myth and killed a hero. The myth of American superiority and invincibility died in Vietnam. The idea of the American soldier as hero and the innocence of American youth died with it. Our heroes were killed shockingly before our eyes in a vividly televised war. As never before, our heroes were seen to be flesh and blood, and at times much more human than heroic.

The death of this myth and the slaughter of its heroes were painfully slow. For America, the funeral included the dedication of the Vietnam Memorial in Washington, D.C., and the formation of a network of Vietnam Veteran Centers throughout the land. Here America's wounded heroes, victims of Vietnam Syndrome, at least could convene with each other. Vietnam was the only war in American history in which the returning veterans were no longer heroes.

In January of 1991 the United States launched a spectacular military assault on the Iraqi forces of Saddam Hussein. In a matter of days, one of the world's largest armies had been decimated. This time, in a much less freely televised war, a hero was reborn and a myth was resurrected. Remarkably, on the Fourth of July, 1991, when thousands of American communities celebrated "Honor America Day," scores of Vietnam veterans wearing their tattered 20-year-old uniforms marched alongside the high-tech heroes of the Gulf War.

It is important to understand that, unlike real humans who live and die, cultural heroes can be reborn, but only upon the return of the cultural myth in which they participate. In the summer of 1991, many persons were disconcerted by the crude militarism and the chauvinism of the Gulf War celebrations. To be sure all of it may be viewed as political theater at its worst. Indeed, the Iraqi army was outgunned from the start, and in the end, we did not even remove the man President Bush called "a Hitler."

Yet, Honor America Day was a healing day precisely because of what it did for the Vietnam vets, and for rekindling a myth in which they could participate. The Gulf War provided the Vietnam veterans, and America as a nation, with the heroic "day in the sun" that the Vietnam War could not. Whatever else the Gulf War was, it has become a mythic event. It provides an epoch tale—a healing of wounded living heroes and a rebirth of mythic heroes.

CHAPTER SUMMARY

1. While all animals exhibit reflexes and experience drives, humans differ from other primates because there are no human instincts. Culture does for humans what instincts do for other animals. Since humans invent their own cultures, biological factors are not the prevailing influence in shaping the social life of humans.

2. Culture consists of all the appropriate and/or required modes of thought, action, and feeling in a society. Culture and social interaction are intimately

related. Social interaction, the on-going life of a community, is the origin of patterns of culture. When interaction patterns have regularity and enjoy acceptance among a population, institutionalization has occurred. Many different factors influence the specific contents of culture. Geography, natural resources, and population characteristics are a few of the major culture-shaping influences.

3. All culture is symbolic, linguistic, learned, shared, dynamic, static, and omnipresent. Each of these characteristics of culture, separately and together demonstrate that "human nature" is not a set of biological traits but is culturally determined.

4. Every culture represents a compromise between the extreme possibilities of complete freedom and complete order. On the one hand, culture liberates people by providing a predictable and reliable world and by facilitating the expression of individualism. In contrast, culture induces people to conform and confines patterns of thought, action, and feeling to the specific cultural choices within any one cultural system.

5. Studying culture requires a cultural relativist standpoint in which one avoids cultural bias and ethnocentrism. The analysis of culture requires an understanding of the key place of myth, patterns of cultural integration, cultural complexes and subcultures.

Key Concepts

culture
cultural adaptation
cultural relativism
cultural complex
cultural integration
cultural unit
drives
ethnocentrism
human nature
instincts
institutionalized
language
myths
reflexes
signs
social interaction
subculture
symbols

Bibliography

Becker, Ernest
1962. *The birth and death of meaning*. New York: Free Press.

Benedict, Ruth
1934. *Patterns of culture*. 1959 ed. New York: New American Library.

Berger, Peter L.
1963. *Invitation to sociology*. New York: Doubleday.

Cooley, Charles Horton
1909. *Human nature and the social order*. 1956 ed. New York: Free Press.

Durkheim, Emile
1912. *The elementary forms of the religious life*. 1965 ed. New York: Free Press.

Fossey, Diane
1983. *Gorillas in the mist.* Boston: Houghton Mifflin.

Gardner, Beatrice, T., and R. Allen Gardner
1971. Two-way communication with an infant chimpanzee. In *Behavior of nonhuman primates.* Edited by Allan M. Shrier and Fred Stollnitz, 117–83. New York: Academic Press.

Goodall, Jane
1971. *In the shadow of man.* Boston: Houghton Mifflin.

Harris, Marvin
1968. *The rise of anthropological theory.* New York: Thomas Y. Crowell.

Patterson, Francine, G.
1981. *Conversations with a gorilla.* New York: Holt, Rinehart & Winston.

Peroff, Kathleen
1987. Who are the homeless and how many are there? In *The homeless in contemporary society.* Edited by Richard Bingham *et al.*, 7–13. Beverly Hills, CA: Sage Publications.

Premack, David
1971. On the assessment of language competence in the chimpanzee. In *Behavior in nonhuman primates.* Edited by Allan M. Shrier and Fred Stollnitz, 186–228. New York: Academic Press.

Rumbaugh, Duane, M., ed.
1977. *Language learning by a chimpanzee: The LANA project.* New York: Academic Press.

Sartre, Jean-Paul
1943. *Being and nothingness.* Translated by Hazel Barnes, 1956. New York: Philosophical Library.

Savage-Rumbaugh, E. Sue
1986. *Ape language.* New York: Columbia University Press.

Sebeok, Thomas A., and Jean Umiker-Sebeok, eds.
1980. *Speaking of apes.* New York: Plenum Press.

Strum, Shirley C.
1987. *Almost human.* New York: Random House.

Szasz, Thomas
1961. *The myth of mental illness.* New York: Hoeber-Harper.

U.S. Bureau of the Census
1991. Statistical Abstract of the United States, 1991. Washington, D.C.: U.S. Government Printing Office.

Zeitlin, Maurice
1978. Who owns America? The same old gang. *The Progressive.* Vol. 42, No. 6: 14–19.

CHAPTER 4

SOCIAL STRUCTURE AND SOCIAL INTERACTION

CHAPTER OUTLINE

LEARNING OBJECTIVES

Just as culture may be viewed as a by-product of social interaction processes, so too is social structure. Together, these three phenomena—social structure, culture, and social interaction—constitute a socially constructed reality. They encompass nearly all of what happens in social life. This chapter focuses upon social structure and social interaction. It examines the ways in which recurring patterns of social interaction become organized to create the structures of social experience and the ways in which behaviors and relationships are affected by the shape of these structures.

All human collectivities, regardless of whether they are microstructures such as families, schools, social clubs, and athletic teams, or macrostructures such as entire societies, contain the same basic components or features. An important task of this chapter is to identify these features and examine how they provide shape and boundary for recurring patterns of social life. The basic features of social structure, the forms of social interaction, and the kinds of social structures found in societies are the focus of this chapter.

After studying this chapter, you should be able to discuss answers to the following questions:

1. What is social structure, and what are its connections with culture?
2. What is the role of social interaction in the development of social structures?
3. What are the component parts of social structure, and what distinct contributions do each of these components make to the shaping of social life?
4. What are the basic forms of social interaction in societies?
5. What types of social structures are studied by sociologists, and how does each type reflect a distinctive arrangement of the basic component parts found in all social structures?

EXAMINING SOCIAL STRUCTURE

Social structure, culture, and social interaction are the three all-encompassing realms of social experience. A first step in exploring the topic of social structure is to grasp its relationships with culture and social interaction. Accordingly, this section of the chapter examines three basic questions: What, exactly is social structure? What is the relationship between social structure and culture? What is the relationship between social structures and social interaction processes?

DEFINING SOCIAL STRUCTURE

The term "social structure" embraces a wide range of human collectivities. Families, friendship cliques, universities, prisons, hospitals, and street gangs all are social structural phenomena. So, too, are entire societies, as well as such things as the United Nations and the European Common Market. What do these diverse collectivities have in common? Each is an association of people having a distinctive pattern of social organization that provides order and stability to the ways in which people within them relate to one another. Each has an underlying and enduring social structure.

Social structure

Social structures are the organized, stable patterns of human social relationships within a society. Social structure refers to the discernible shapes that are produced by the ways in which members of groups, organizations, and societies relate to one another. Sociologists often distinguish between patterns of "social structure" and processes of "social organization." *Social organization refers to the process through which the structure is produced, while social structure denotes the resulting pattern itself.* Each points to the fact that human behavior is not composed of a series of disconnected, random actions. Rather, there is both pattern and regularity (structure or organization) in social life. Sociologists study the distinctive categories or types of social structures, the processes through which they emerge and change, and the differing consequences that structural arrangements have for the persons living within them.

Social organization

CULTURE AND SOCIAL STRUCTURE

How may culture and social structure be distinguished? If culture is the accumulated social heritage produced by human interaction, social structures are the patterns which emerge from these same processes of interaction. Perhaps an analogy from the physical sciences is helpful in distinguishing between cultural and structural phenomena. In biology, the cell is the basic building block of all living things. Biologists distinguish between the content of the cell which consists of a plasmic substance, and the cell wall which gives shape and boundary to the content. Social life exhibits a certain similarity to this two-part composition in cell life. Social structure, like the cell wall in biological life, gives shape and boundary to cultural patterns which are the content of social life.

Even a cursory examination of sociological research makes this distinction between social structure and culture readily apparent. Studies of culture tend to focus upon the value systems and shared meanings that breathe life into human activities. Studies of social structure take a different focus. Here, the focus is not the meaning systems, but the shape and boundaries within which human life is enacted.

For example, studying the game of baseball from a social structural perspective entails analyzing the boundaries within which the game occurs. There is a rule system that must be obeyed by all who play the game, and penalties are assessed against those who violate the rules. There are specialized expectations for each position with some positions valued more highly than others. Pitchers, though they play less frequently than other players, generally are ranked higher. Umpires have ultimate control over the game, and managers, though they rarely step onto the field, control the strategies of the players on the field. This hierarchy is an important structural feature of the game of baseball.

From a cultural perspective, the analysis focuses upon the values, sentiments, and meanings attached to the game of baseball in American society. What is it about baseball, and indeed, other spectator sports, that commands the loyalty of a large segment of the population? Much like the larger society of which this game is a part, baseball emphasizes the importance of both winning and individual success. This concern for being "first" or the "best" may explain the almost fetish-like concentration on team and player statistics.

The point is not that baseball is wonderful and that we all should like it. Rather, the point is that the structural and cultural features of this game are distinguishable. So it is with all social life. Every pattern of human activity has both cultural and social structural properties.

SOCIAL INTERACTION AND SOCIAL STRUCTURE

We've seen that social structure and culture are two sides of social reality. When viewed from one perspective, the cultural side seems paramount. When viewed from the opposite perspective, social structures take center stage. However, it also is apparent that social interaction patterns are the common foundation from which both culture and social structures emerge. In this sense, social reality is not so much two-sided as triangular. Social interaction is the base of that triangle. This is because structural arrangements, like cultural arrangements, are humanly produced, and just as social interaction is the origin of cultural forms, so too, social interaction is the source of different categories of social structures. These relationships are depicted in Figure 4.1.

As members of collectivities interact over a period of time, they develop routine ways of relating to each other that become more and more patterned and predictable. From this patterned interaction, specific organizational properties emerge. These organizational properties exist independent of the individuals who make up the collectivity and exert constraints upon human behavior.

Once in existence, there is a relatively fixed quality to social structure that persists despite changes that occur from time to time. However, this does

FIGURE 4.1
THE TRIANGLE OF SOCIAL REALITY

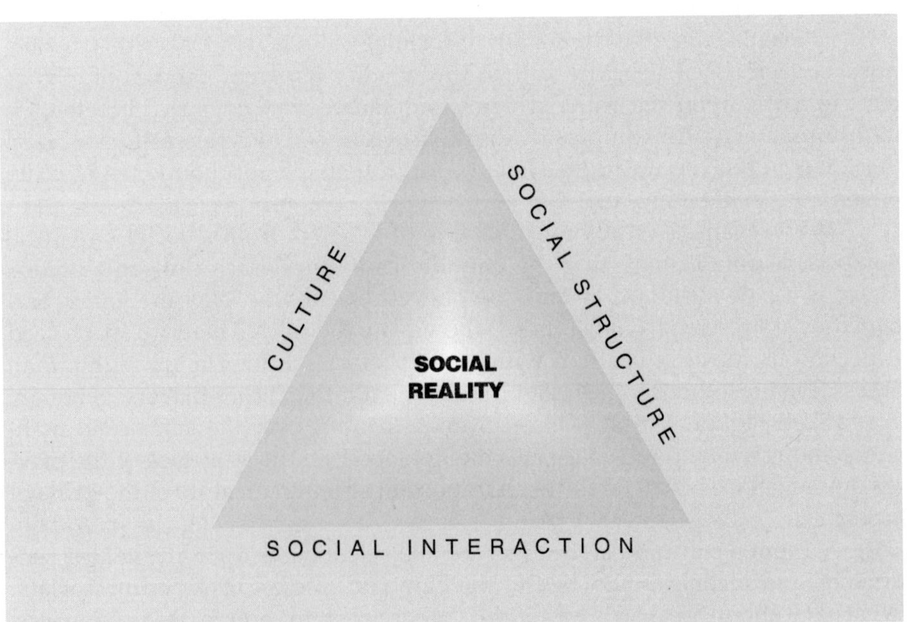

not mean that every member of a group or society must conform to social structural expectations at every moment. Social structures are stable, not static. Variation, innovation, and even deviance (see Chapter 7) can and do occur. Social structures continue to exist only as long as people's collective patterns of social interaction continue to sustain, support, and from moment to moment, re-create them.

The beginning sociology student may be confronted with a paradox. It is claimed that we invent society, but that society makes us what we are. The point here is that these claims are not quite paradoxical. Rather, these claims reflect the existence of several distinct social processes. People, in fact, do create and continuously re-create society through processes of social interaction. Similarly, patterns of social structure and culture act back upon us and make us what we are. Both claims are true.

In summary, this section of the chapter has depicted social reality as a triangular phenomenon, with culture and social structures as the sides of that triangle, and social interaction processes as its base. Social structures are the boundaries and shapes of social reality, while culture is its content. Both emerge from interaction processes, and both culture and social structure continually are affirmed and supported by routine interactions.

The Components of Social Structure

This section of the chapter provides a closer look at social structures by examining their component parts. One way to characterize and understand the nature of social structure is by comparing it to a physical structure. Let's suppose an architect has been asked to design a building. The first consideration, of course, is what type of building is required? What use will it serve, and what goals does this building fulfill? Is it to be someone's home, an office building, or a manufacturing facility? How many people will occupy it, and what types of activities will occur in it? Additionally, environmental factors impose constraints upon, and present design opportunities for, the new building. Skyscrapers don't sit well on steep hillsides, and it is unwise to have a full basement in a floodplain. While all buildings must have certain components, such as structural beams, floors, ceilings, and a roof, the specific configuration (the precise structural arrangement) will be influenced greatly by both social and environmental factors. Moreover, the ways in which the various components are linked together produce different types of buildings. Once built, a physical structure has durability and stability over a period of time and influences the kinds of activities and patterns of interaction taking place within it.

Everything said here about physical structures applies equally to social structures. All structural arrangements are influenced by both the physical and social environment. Moreover, just as certain component parts are the foundation of physical structures, all social structures are comprised of the same basic components. These are: a system of norms, a division of labor, a ranking system, and mechanisms of social control. Different configurations of these structural components produce distinctive types of social structures in the same way that the arrangement of basic parts in physical structures distinguishes one type from another. For example, consider the diversity of governments found around the world. Each of them, democracies, dictatorships, monarchies, communist systems, and others attempt to fulfill the same set of social tasks, and each establishes a system of norms, a division of labor, a system of hierarchy, and mechanisms of social control. But each creates a unique system of norms, division of labor, system of hierarchy and mechanisms of social control, and therefore, a unique pattern of governing and living.

Regardless of the specific arrangements of these component parts, once established, a social structure, like a physical structure, exhibits durability and stability and shapes the human activities occurring within it. As patterns of social organization change, they create differences in available opportunities, constraints, and requirements for daily living. Let's examine each of the four basic components of social structure.

A SYSTEM OF NORMS

Norms are a first essential ingredient in all social structures. Coordinated activities between persons cannot happen without shared rules to guide and shape behavior. These rules which people use to define what is expected of each other are called norms.

Norms

Norms are shared rules of behavior. They create shared expectations, and therefore allow people to know not only how to act, but what kinds of action to anticipate from other people. The term "norm" does not mean normal in the sense of good or bad. Rather, a norm is a socially appropriate or expected mode of conduct. Norms are the foundation stones of all structural arrangements. Several features of this normative aspect of social life deserve comment.

First, norms are variable. For example, in England, Scotland, Bermuda, and elsewhere, people drive in the left lane, not the right, as they do in the United States. Yet, in all these places orderly driving patterns result. This illustrates that specific rules are not as important as the existence of rules. Social structural arrangements are arbitrary, and emerge in different configurations. There is nothing inherent in the color red that requires stopping one's car, nor in the color green that impels going. These social arrangements are entirely conventional.

Second, not all norms enjoy the same force or importance in society, nor demand the same degree of compliance. The less important the norm, the greater people's tolerance of deviation from that norm. The American sociologist William G. Sumner (1840–1910) was one of the first writers to comment on such differences between social norms. Sumner distinguishes between *folkways* and *mores* (pronounced mor-ays) (Sumner 1906). A folkway is a norm with little moral significance. The extent of compliance with a folkway is quite flexible, and violation of a folkway typically does not elicit severe negative sanctions. Waiting your turn in line and dressing appropriately for specific occasions are folkways in American society. While it is impolite to act ahead of your turn, or arrive at a social gathering improperly dressed, there are no consistent formal sanctions for violating these norms. In contrast, mores have strong moral significance. Violation of them is culturally defined as "wrong," and elicits strong negative sanctions. A proscription against adultery is an example of a more.

Folkways

Mores

Third, in modern societies, many norms (usually mores) are formalized into laws. Laws are explicit rules of conduct that carry specific mandatory punishments or penalties for violation as designed and enforced by the state. Violations of law are criminal acts. Ultimately, however, laws must have collective support to be effective in controlling people's behavior. A law that reflects a norm to which people no longer subscribe will no longer bear the "force of law." Laws remain useful only so long as they reflect norms to which people subscribe. For example, prohibitions against gambling appear to be largely ineffective because most people do not see this as "morally" incorrect.

Fourth, while social structures consist of a complex network of norms, this does not presume that people are conscious of these norms. In fact, people constantly act according to norms about which they have no explicit awareness. Only when norms are violated does their existence and importance become readily discernible. Moreover, when the norms governing behavior are abandoned, they become clearer in their absence (Garfinkel 1967). Thus, human conduct is shaped by many norms, and this norm-bound structuring of human behavior does not rely upon a conscious awareness of those norms.

Fifth, norms are situational. That is, they derive their meaning not simply from the character of the act, but from complex connections between the act, the setting, and the players. This is one of the important teachings of the symbolic interactionist tradition in sociological thought. For example, taking the life of another human being only is viewed as murder when a particular combination of setting, players, and actions is present. Thus, in some configurations, persons suffer grievous sanctions for taking the life of another person (first-degree murder). In yet other configurations, taking the life of another is defined as legitimate behavior, and persons (police or military personnel) may even be rewarded for doing so.

A DIVISION OF LABOR

Division of labor

All social structures entail *a division of labor, an allocation of members into various positions (social statuses), having attached to them specialized activities (social roles), which define expected behaviors.* In the simplest terms then, a division of labor means specialization by tasks within a social structure. Through the allocation of different tasks to different persons, complex sets of activities may be coordinated so that the basic requirements for living are accomplished.

Social status

Social role

Each *social status is a socially recognized position in a social structure.* Each *social role is a bundle of expected behaviors for persons occupying a given status.* Social roles do not specify exact behavior, but rather, provide broad requirements within which each person must operate. Therefore, individuals may perform the same role somewhat differently, and there is a tolerance of these differences. Additionally, roles are meaningful only in relation to other roles within a given social structure (Linton 1936). For example, the role of quarterback only makes sense in relationship to the roles played by other members of a football team. Similarly, the role of teacher is only meaningful in relation to the role of student, while the role of parent only makes sense in relationship to the complementary role of child.

Ascribed status

Achieved status

Social statuses may be allocated to persons according to two very different kinds of criteria. An *ascribed status* results when social positions are assigned on the basis of criteria over which individuals have no control. Race, age, and gender are examples of ascribed criteria encountered in most societies. In contrast, an *achieved status* occurs when social positions result from the efforts and accomplishments of the individual. In modern societies, examples of achieved status are becoming a member of Phi Beta Kappa, being a husband, or being an elected official. In each of these instances, some degree of choice or effort is involved.

Master status

A related concept is that of master status. A *master status is a social status having primary significance for shaping a person's life.* Master statuses are sufficiently important to override and dominate all others, affecting almost every aspect of a person's life. Occupational statuses are especially important as master statuses in modern societies. For persons not in the labor force, age is a highly salient master status. Personal identities are shaped, and in large part defined, by statuses and accompanying role expectations. Consider that when persons meet socially for the first time, it is common to ask what he or she "does." Especially in modern societies, people tend to think of themselves and others, not so much in terms of personal traits (John is a nice person, fun, and smart), as in terms of social status (Judy is a teacher, a mother, and president of the country club). Knowing a person's social status provides expectations about how such a person should act, and in turn be treated. In this sense, social structures reach deeply into the personality or self-system and influence social relationships (see Chapter 6).

The division of labor in a social structure is shaped by a wide variety of factors. Sociologists long have recognized that changes in the size of a human group may have enormous consequences for the complexity of its division of labor. Let's consider a very simple example. If a small group of students decides to gather occasionally to go skiing there is little need for a complex division of labor. Anyone can say "let's go next weekend." However, if the group gets even as large as ten or fifteen people, this may require a formal mechanism for notifying people of the next ski trip. Of course, the minute someone is assigned this task, a first division of labor has been created. Moreover, as social structures increase in size, and as their tasks or goals increase in number, two important structural properties change. First, the division of labor becomes more fixed or permanent. Second, greater specialization of statuses and roles occurs, reflecting a more complex social structure. Our little ski group

FIGURE 4.2
Sometimes social structure is quite obvious and visible, and at other times it is not visible at all.

may, in fact, become a ski club, elect officers, establish formal duties, and hold periodic meetings. By-laws may be drafted stipulating what the officers can and cannot do. Clearly, as numbers grow, structures get more complex and formalized. Statuses and roles to accomplish those tasks proliferate.

SOCIAL CONTROL MECHANISMS

Let's recapitulate for a moment what's been said thus far about the characteristics of social structure. Each set of structural arrangements is formed by social norms (rules and expectations) and exhibits some degree of a division of labor composed of statuses persons occupy and roles they perform. But, here, a critical question emerges. How are persons kept acting according to these arrangements? Why do people conform to social norms? Why, most of the time, do people fulfill our expectations in their social performances? The answer lies, in part, in mechanisms of social control. *Social control is the application of sanctions to ensure that members abide by the rules, play their assigned roles, and coordinate their activities to achieve structural goals. Social sanctions* are rewards for appropriate conduct and punishments for inappropriate conduct.

Social control

Social sanctions

Sanctions may be either formal or informal. Smiling or saying "good job" when people act in appropriate ways, and frowning or verbally chastising them when they do not, are examples of informal sanctions. A fine for not obeying traffic laws and a ceremony honoring a "good Samaritan" are both formal sanctions. These control mechanisms allow individuals to calculate the probable social benefits of conformity, as well as the likely social costs of deviations from the norms. While anyone may sanction the actions of others, some people are empowered by the norms of the social structure to act as official norm-enforcing agents. The police within a community or state, a student judiciary board of a college, and a manger in a factory all are formal agents of social control.

Sanctions, like norms, are part of the predictive and expectation systems in all social structures. Since, as was just noted, most rules and roles allow for a range of acceptable behavior, the individuals are granted reasonable latitude in interpreting norms or performing roles. Although tolerance limits are not defined explicitly, persons learn through experience the degree of variance that will be acceptable. Viewed in this perspective, differing degrees of departure from norms do not mean that something is wrong with these norms, or that norms do not exist. Rather, it indicates that a calculation and prediction has been made about the consequences or costs of not conforming.

For instance, it is a norm for college students to attend class, and most students do so most of the time. Students who "cut" class have done so in full awareness of the consequences of doing so. Obviously, norms and sanctions are intimately connected. Both of them work most effectively when individuals internalize them, and thus self-regulate their own conduct. These processes are examined in some detail under the term "socialization" in Chapter 6, and again in Chapter 7, which focuses upon social deviance.

A SOCIAL RANKING SYSTEM

A fourth component of social structure is social ranking. *Social ranking is the evaluation and ordering of statuses into a hierarchy, placing some higher or lower than others.* Not all social positions are valued equally, nor are they all deemed to be

Social ranking

equally important or demanding. As soon as one status is evaluated as better, more desirable, or more important than others, ranking has occurred. Individuals, of course, may be ranked on the basis of personal attributes independent of the positions they hold. However, our concern here is not with individuals, but with social structural process of ranking *per se.*

Two related features of social ranking processes may be examined here, social power and social prestige. Individuals, by virtue of the ranks of the positions they occupy, are granted greater or lesser power, and accorded higher or lower prestige. *Social power is the ability of a person (or group) to control the actions of others, even in the face of resistance* (Weber 1923). Without the exercise of power, without some form of domination (even if it is temporary), without some wills being subordinated to others, no coordinated action of any type can occur. In this sense, a hierarchy of power exists in all social relationships, and accordingly, is an inherent property of all social structure.

Social power

Moreover, it is common for power relations to be transformed into rather fixed patterns that are deemed legitimate, just, and correct. When some social positions are regarded as having legitimate power, that power is transformed into authority. *Authority is the socially legitimated right to control the actions of others by virtue of a social status.* Accordingly, parents exercise authority over their children, and the tribal chief exercises authority over all members of the clan. Power may be temporary and may alternate as within marriage relationships, play groups, or friendships. In contrast, authority is a more enduring aspect of social structure, such as the authority relations in business organizations, military systems, and governments.

Authority

Prestige is an equally important consequence of social ranking. Some persons, by virtue of their social position, are accorded greater prestige than others. Once even a rudimentary division of labor is created, evaluative processes lead to the differential assignment of prestige to various positions. Prestige may be allocated to persons on a wide variety of bases. At the societal level, social ranking provides the basis for systems of stratification. These stratification processes are examined in Chapters 8 and 9.

In summary, this section of the chapter has focused upon the four basic features of all social structures; namely, a system of norms, a division of labor, mechanisms of social control, and a social ranking system. All four are present in even the most simple of structural arrangements. Moreover, as social structures increase in size, these features increase in complexity. These properties of social structure are important because they shape the social experience for individuals.

Most of this chapter focuses upon the properties of social structures and the kinds of social structural arrangements found in societies. However, before doing so, let's look a bit more closely at the forms of social interaction from which social structures emerge, and which in turn, occur within those structures.

FORMS OF SOCIAL INTERACTION

Social interaction

Social interaction is the glue that holds social structures together and the process through which structural change occurs. While social structure provides the context in which human activities occur, social interaction is the lifeblood of all structural systems. Social interaction is the moment-to-moment ebb and flow of people's life together. Social interaction patterns may assume one of four basic forms: cooperation, exchange, competition, and conflict.

While these four interaction patterns are explored here as types or categories of events, it is important to remember that they are not mutually exclusive. Rather, it is common to have shifts from one pattern to another, or even several different forms of social interaction occurring at the same time. As might be expected, some patterns of social interaction exhibit greater affinity for one another than do others. Specifically, the more socially harmonious patterns of cooperation and exchange may be contrasted with the interrelated forms of conflict and competition.

COOPERATION AND EXCHANGE

Cooperation

Cooperation exists whenever people act together to accomplish a common goal or purpose. Many 19th century writers, among them Emile Durkheim (1893), recognized cooperation as an essential social form and even speculated that society itself resulted from humankind's earliest cooperative efforts to satisfy efficiently the common needs of human life, such as food, shelter, and mutual defense. Without question, cooperation allows people to achieve goals that might not be attainable by isolated individual efforts.

Consider something as common as driving a car. Unfortunately, most of us are familiar with situations where, due to road construction or even a collision, several lanes of traffic must be squeezed into a single lane. The goal is for drivers to merge smoothly and efficiently without causing a traffic jam. If drivers cooperate, this common goal is attainable. If, however, drivers attempt to merge from one side more than the other, forcing one line to edge its way into the moving lane, traffic becomes snarled. Basic properties of social structure are involved even in this type of transient and temporary situation. A norm or rule of taking turns prevails, even if occasionally that rule is not followed. Additionally, a basic division of labor is created: one car pauses while the other drives forward and vice versa. Thus, even the temporary situation of merging lanes in traffic illustrates that basic social structural properties readily emerge from social interaction processes, in this instance cooperation.

Exchange

Exchange is a form of coordinated behavior characterized by the giving and receiving of mutual benefits. While cooperation and exchange share a number of properties (both are harmonious, coordinated, and peaceful), there are important differences between them. While cooperation involves a collaboration to achieve a commonly held value or goal, exchange presumes only mutual benefit. Beyond this, parties to an exchange need not share common values or other substantive goals. Beneficial outcomes may involve tangibles such as money or goods, or intangibles such as esteem, approval, or affection.

Exchange processes are governed by norms of reciprocity or distributive justice. A fair exchange is one in which the benefits for all parties are directly proportional to their respective investments. Violations of the rules of fair exchange may lead to tension, dissatisfaction, and both competition and conflict. While social exchange is characteristic of economic (market) activities, it also can be important in intimate relationships. Sometimes social exchanges are explicit, such as "I'll invite your friends for dinner on Saturday, if you'll wash the kitchen floor." At other times, they may be implicit, such as signs of affection and approval for a job well done. Obviously, while not based solely on exchange, intimate relationships may be seriously undermined if the costs of continuing a relationship begin to be perceived as outweighing the benefits received.

Of course, it is not always possible for individuals or groups to reach goals by processes of either cooperation or exchange. When does this occur? First, the goals of two individuals or groups may be mutually exclusive. For instance, it is not possible for both the prolife and prochoice advocates to attain their goals because they seek to promote values and activities that are diametrically opposed. Second, a scarcity of the desired material goods or social positions that different groups or individuals seek may eliminate the opportunity for cooperation or exchange. Only one person can be president of the senior class, and only one team can be the state "champs" in basketball each year. Only a limited number of students can get into a particular college or university in any one year, and not everyone can make Phi Beta Kappa. In such instances, interaction may take the form of competition or conflict.

COMPETITION AND CONFLICT

Competition

Conflict

Competition is the mutually opposed efforts of different groups or individuals to obtain the same resources or reach the same goals. Obviously, some societies value and encourage competition more than others, and, as will be seen, those that have endorsed competitive patterns historically have experienced high levels of social innovation and social change (Mannheim 1928). *Conflict is the mutually opposed efforts of different groups or individuals, in which neutralization or injury of the opposite party is a primary goal.* Just as cooperation and exchange are encountered frequently in the same social situations, so competition and conflict are closely related forms of social interaction.

There are two important conditions that precipitate conflict rather than competition. First, conflict entails a high level of awareness that one's opponent is a direct threat to achieving desired goals. Competitors may have relatively little awareness of each other, but conflict grows from an acute awareness of the "threat" posed by the other party. Second, conflict is distinguished by the undertaking of action consciously oriented toward the neutralization or injury of one's opponent rather than the attainment of the goal itself. Let's examine some consequences of these differences in greater detail.

First, unlike conflict, competition is a highly rule-bound form of social interaction. In contrast, conflict typically operates under the credo "anything goes." Said differently, nearly all competitive activities proceed under a norm of fairness. For example, most college students recognize the element of competition over grades and experience outrage if it is learned that through a stolen exam certain students gained an "unfair" competitive advantage. "Playing by the rules" is an important element of competition. It is little surprise that societies stressing competition as a valued social norm are characterized by voluntary associations, such as trade and professional groups of all sorts. These associations, among them the American Bar Association, the National Board of Realtors, and the National Association of Manufacturers, help establish normative boundaries (social structure) within which members compete.

Second, the transition from competition to conflict is marked by a decline in effective norms. When competing parties no longer play by the rules, competition becomes conflict. For instance, while it is sometimes claimed that there are "rules of war" it is difficult to find any that are consistently followed. While the Geneva Conventions outlaw the use of chemical weapons, the United States and other major world powers still produce and stockpile them. Similarly, in the Iran-Iraq War of the 1980s, at least one, if not both sides, actually used chemical weapons against civilian populations.

Third, when viewed from a macrosocial perspective, the need of competitors to innovate in order to succeed promotes a greater division of labor in the social structure. That is, as competition becomes more keen, there is a need to have specialists take charge of the process of competition. Let's consider an example. With the lowering of the birth rate in the United States, competition among colleges and universities during the 1980s for the available pool of students led to an expansion of admissions departments. No longer was it enough simply to wait for student applications. Rather, educational institutions created staffs to actively seek and recruit students.

Fourth, although there is a tendency for people to view social conflict as negative, this is not always the case. The German sociologist Georg Simmel (1908) observed that external conflict frequently serves an integrating function by providing members with an external focus for their hostility. Differences are forgotten or overcome in the interest of presenting a united front to the enemy. This can be seen quite clearly in a diversity of situations. For example, during political campaigns, both Democrats and Republicans who disagree with members of their own parties attempt to present a unified front to the voting public. Despite their internal party differences, they prefer to have their own party's members elected, rather than those of the opposition party.

In summary, there are four basic forms of social interaction; namely, cooperation, exchange, competition, and conflict. Cooperative social interactions derive from shared goals and values. In contrast, exchange relations are based upon the anticipation of mutual benefits. Competitive social interactions entail mutually opposed efforts to obtain the same goals or objects. Competi-

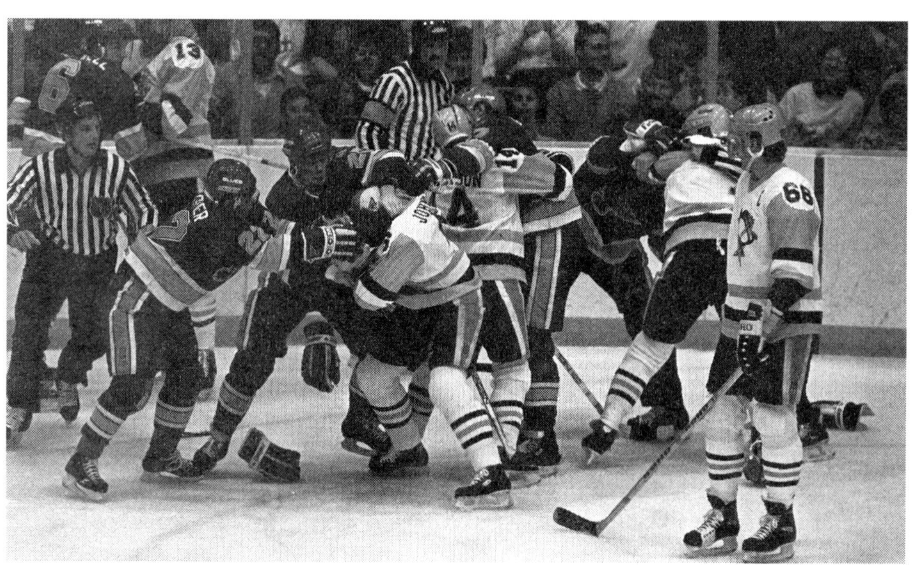

FIGURE 4.3
Forms of social interaction change rapidly. Frequently, competition becomes conflict.

tion is recognized to be a source of social innovation and typically is rule-bound. Unlike competition, social conflict is the attempt to neutralize or injure the other party in the relationship. These four forms of social interaction provide the constant flow of events and social relations in all social structures.

THE VARIETIES OF SOCIAL STRUCTURES

All sciences engage in the task of morphology, typing and classifying the phenomena studied. The following discussion provides an inventory of the types of social structural phenomena studied by sociologists. What follows here might be viewed as a sort of sociological table of the elements. Just as the chemical table of the elements provides the full array of basic phenomena which alone and in combination may be studied by chemists, so the following inventory introduces structural phenomena, ranging from small groups to entire societies, which are studied by sociologists. We've already seen that the system of norms, a division of labor, social control mechanisms, and a social ranking system are universal components of social structures. The following inventory of social structures provides an occasion for further examination of these components.

AGGREGATES, CATEGORIES, STRATA, AND GROUPS

Social group

The term "social group" is used in everyday conversation to describe almost any collection of persons. However, the term "group" has a very specific sociological meaning. *A social group is any number of persons sharing a common identity and some common goals, and who interact directly and regularly with each other on the basis of group membership.* Thus, a sense of belonging and sustained, rather than transitory, face-to-face interaction are two important criteria by which social groups are distinguished from other kinds of human collectivities. Family members, persons enrolled in this sociology course, and members of the college basketball team are but a few examples of human collectivities exhibiting these basic features of social groups.

Aggregates

Groups often are contrasted with several other types of human collectivities that do not exhibit these several important features of group life. For example, sociologists frequently study *aggregates, meaning some number of persons who share a common place, location, or situation, but who do not exhibit sustained interaction or a sense of shared identity.* Some examples of aggregates are the persons attending last night's concert, people riding a bus together, or all the shoppers at Bloomingdale's department store at a particular time. Aggregates are of interest to sociologists for several reasons. First, they have the potential for group formation. People in the same place, or in similar situations may develop an "consciousness of kind" and continue to interact on that basis. Second, aggregates may provide the foundation for several forms of collective behavior. Some classic treatises have been written on the emergence of crowd and mob behavior from aggregates (Le Bon 1895), and it has long been recognized that individuals may participate in the emergent norms of a crowd or mob in ways that contradict their usual everyday behavior.

Social category

Sociologists also study social categories. *A social category consists of individuals who share some trait or characteristics.* Some social categories are little more than statistical classifications having little or no social significance for the persons in them. For instance, all the persons who watch "Murphy Brown" on television may be an important category for sociologists studying popular culture. However, this category of viewers has little personal meaning for those so classified. On the other hand, some social categories are both socially and personally significant. That is, not only is the shared trait part of their personal identity, but they also are viewed socially as a member of that category. Typically, social ranking or stratification occurs on the basis of these shared characteristics. In other words, such categorization has meaningful consequences. *The term social strata refers to categories of persons that share a trait or characteristic having meaning both for members of the category and within society generally.* All black persons in the United States, all Roman Catholics in Canada, and blue collar workers in Arizona are examples of social strata. It is important to note that social strata are usually too large and geographically dispersed to permit the kind of regular face-to-face interaction found in social groups.

Social strata

Social categories and social strata are important bases for the formation of both groups and organizations. Many social groups such as Franco-American or Polish-American clubs have emerged from shared ethnic traits. Frequently, people who become subjectively aware of some of the consequences of being categorized organize for mutual protection and/or promotion of their interests. For example, in the United States, persons over the age of 65 are a social category. Many elderly persons experiencing discrimination on the basis of this categorization joined together to form a political action association called the Gray Panthers.

Unfortunately, even sociologists do not always use the terms group, aggregate, category, and strata with precision. For example, much sociological literature describes such strata as, Catholics, blacks, Jews, Hispanics, and women as "minority groups." Obviously, these are socially significant categories of persons, but they are not "groups" in the sociological sense of the term. Having distinguished the human group from other types of collectivities, we next examine the key distinctions between types of groups.

GROUPS: PRIMARY AND SECONDARY

Social groups have special sociological significance because of their important roles in the lives of their members, and in the societies of which they are a part. Indeed, groups are the very foundation of social life. It is through group activities that both collective and individual interests are realized. Each individual belongs to a diverse assortment of groups throughout a lifetime.

Groups vary in a number of dimensions, all having implications for their members. Groups differ in terms of size, permeability of boundaries, degrees of intimacy, degrees of social integration or cohesiveness, patterns of communication, and of course, salience for their members' identities.

For example, the size of a group determines the number and types of social interactions that may occur at any one time within it. Two-person groups (dyads) are quite different from three-person groups (triads) (Simmel 1908).

According to Simmel, the dyad is the most intimate and yet, most fragile of all human groups. Within dyads, intimacy and emotional linkages are maximized since only one relationship—that between two persons—is possible. However, it is for this very reason that dyads are more fragile than other groups. If either person leaves the relationship, the group is destroyed. Adding a third person to the group creates a more complex, yet stable group. There are now three possible dyad relationships instead of one, and coalitions of two members against the third become possible. As groups further increase in size, they change in terms of the quality of members' relationships with each other, communication processes, and the responsibilities of group members.

The most fundamental distinction between types of groups is that between primary and secondary groups. The American sociologist Charles H. Cooley (1864–1929) is credited with having distinguished these types (1909). *Primary groups are relatively small and enduring groups whose members interact informally in intimate and diffuse relationships. Secondary groups are groups of any size and permanence whose members interact in formal, instrumental, and segmented relationships.* The concept of primary and secondary groups are *ideal types. An ideal type is a mental construct used to describe and compare social phenomena in terms of their typical or common characteristics* (Weber 1904). The construct does not necessarily correspond to any one empirical observation, but rather focuses upon characteristics held in common among otherwise differing phenomena. It is useful to think of primary and secondary groups as opposite ends of a continuum with many groups falling somewhere in the middle. Let's consider some examples of primary and secondary groups.

Primary group

Secondary group

Ideal type

Both families and friendship groups are primary groups, while a college class or a work group are secondary groups. There are important structural differences between them. Interactions among members of primary groups tend to be emotion-laden and personal, encompassing the whole person in a wide variety of activities. In primary groups, expectations for the actions of members are rather nonspecific, with persons being more important than the roles they play. Thus, in families a wide latitude of actions are tolerated precisely because of the emotionally rich concern for the whole person. The division of labor in primary groups generally is implicit and flexible, although the allocation of certain tasks may become ritualized through tradition. Social control tends to be informal, and ranking is kept to a minimum.

FIGURE 4.4
In secondary groups, roles, not persons, are emphasized.

In contrast, highly specific, goal-directed modes of interaction are typical of secondary groups. In secondary groups, roles are more salient than persons. Positions are defined and allocated within a fixed division of labor, and role expectations are bounded by specific rules or norms. For example, in classrooms or in work groups, there are very specific expectations regarding what teachers and students, workers and supervisors may do, and relatively little latitude beyond those expectations is tolerated. Typically, ranks in secondary groups are more sharply and formally differentiated than in primary groups, and there is a greater reliance on formal methods of social control.

These characteristics of group structure have qualitative consequences for individuals. Primary and secondary groups typically serve different purposes and meet different needs. The primary group plays a fundamental and enduring role in human development. Within the primary group, children begin to develop a sense of self, learn appropriate ways of thinking, feeling, and behaving, and form ideas about the larger social world (see discussion in Chapter 6). The emotional bonds of early family life appear to be essential for the development of well-adjusted adults (Youniss 1980). Participation in primary groups continues to be essential throughout the life course. They provide a sense of belonging, satisfy a wide variety of interpersonal needs, and also serve as instruments of social control. Secondary groups, while less broad in their impact, satisfy a wide variety of instrumental needs. They help individuals perform activities and attain goals beyond the scope or competencies of the primary group.

FORMAL ORGANIZATIONS: VOLUNTARY AND BUREAUCRATIC

As societies modernize and become more complex, specialized limited-purpose associations called formal organizations proliferate. *Formal organizations are a type of social structure, or network of substructures, of comparatively large size created to achieve specialized goals.* Because formal organizations are purposefully designed, they tend to represent the most sophisticated level of social organization. They are the most formally and rationally patterned social structures.

Formal organizations

Formal organizations may be classified in a variety of ways, using a great number of different criteria (Scott 1982). Each typology reveals something different about formal organizations. Which typology is most useful depends upon the particular research questions being asked. The following discussion examines two such classification schemes that are encountered frequently in sociological studies.

First, formal organizations may be classified according to who benefits from the organization's existence (Blau and Scott 1962). Organizations are placed in four major categories; namely, business, mutual benefit, commonwealth, and service. Each type reflects different organizational goals, specifies why the organization exists, and identifies how the organization functions. The primary goal of *business organizations* is to make profit, and the main beneficiaries are the owners and stockholders. Although others may benefit as well, if profit does not flow to the primary beneficiaries, the organization cannot continue to exist. Examples of business organizations range from large corporations like General Motors and American Airlines, to small family-owned grocery stores.

Business organizations

Mutual benefit organizations

Mutual benefit organizations provide services to their members. Thus, the main beneficiaries of this type of organization are the members themselves. Labor unions, professional organizations and trade associations all are mutual benefit organizations. Benefiting the members is the key to the survival of such organizations. If a labor union no longer demonstrates that it is able to work in the interest of its members, the organization is weakened and its membership very likely will decline. In contrast, *service organizations* have as their main beneficiaries clients who use the services provided by the organization. Hospitals, colleges and universities, and philanthropic agencies are examples of service organizations. Finally, *commonwealth organizations* provide a service to the general public rather than to specific clients. Most government agencies are commonwealth organizations.

Service organizations

Commonwealth organizations

A second way of classifying organizations is suggested by the contemporary organizational theorist Amitai Etzioni (1961, 1964). Etzioni focuses upon three types of control structures or kinds of power used by organizations. They are coercive, remunerative, and normative. These categories correspond to people's motives for involvement in the organization, which are either alienative (I'd rather not be here, but I have to be), calculative (I have something to gain), or moral (I'm involved because I believe it is right). Etzioni calls his three types coercive (in which coercion is the major means of control over highly alienated members), utilitarian (in which remuneration is the major means of control over members who are induced by money to participate), and normative (in which members are induced to participate on the basis of their belief in the organization's tenets).

Coercive organizations

Let's consider some examples. In *coercive organizations,* people are required to join either for their own benefit or societal good. Prisons and military organizations based on compulsory draft are coercive organizations. *Utilitarian organizations* are joined because, through them, members can achieve a tangible, material benefit. Such participation is said to be calculative. Organizations from which people earn a living are examples of utilitarian organizations. Voluntary organizations, those people join of their own volition and for which they receive no financial compensation, are *normative organizations.* Examples of normative organizations are Parent-Teacher Associations, The Society for the Prevention of Cruelty to Animals, and a host of other political, religious, and recreational clubs.

Utilitarian organizations

Normative organizations

Bureaucracy

In modern societies, nearly all types of formal organizations have been subject to a general process of rationalism and *bureaucracy.* Typically, these processes involve a rigid organizational system and an over-emphasis on formal rule systems and procedures. Bureaucratization is an important theme of formal organizations and cultural trends in general, and is explored fully in Chapter 11. While groups of various types constitute the realm of microsociological events, formal organizations—be they bureaucratic or voluntary—constitute the realm of intermediate social structures.

SOCIETIES: FROM SIMPLE TO COMPLEX

Society

The study of entire societies, or social systems, is a major concern of macrosociology. *A society is a relatively self-perpetuating social structure in which persons may satisfy all the requirements of daily living. A society typically exhibits geographic contiguity, a common culture, and a sense of identification among its members.* Thus, a society is a complex social structure that integrates its members and provides guidelines for the full array of human behaviors.

Many of sociology's founding generation of scholars focused upon types of societies and macrosocial change. Many of the concepts they used remain in the sociological lexicon today. The German writer Ferdinand Toennies (1855–1936) coined the distinction between *Gemeinschaft* and *Gesellschaft*, or community and society (1887). The type he called community typically is small and possesses a homogeneous population who think and do similar things. Communal social structures are based upon norms of mutual trust, commitment, and tradition. Members are bound together by strong emotional ties. In other words, as a type, communities exhibit some of the same properties as primary groups.

Gemeinschaft

Gesellschaft

In contrast, *societies* are highly differentiated, and are characterized by contractual and utilitarian social relationships. Societies have large, heterogeneous populations and seem to promote individualism rather than shared community goals and values. Modern societies are of the *gesellschaft* type but may contain *gemeinschaft* types of social structures within them. Ethnic neighborhoods in urban areas (Gans 1962), rural villages in less populated locales (Vidich and Bensman 1958), and religious sects and cults that retreat from the surrounding host culture (Richardson *et al.* 1979) all provide examples. However, the general decline of communal type social structures remains a central feature of modern life (Stein 1964).

Emile Durkheim analyzed societies in terms of the complexity of the division of labor, or role specialization. *In simple societies role specialization (differentiation) is minimal and people are bound together by their similar ways of life. Complex societies, on the other hand, are characterized by a high degree of role specialization with social cohesion based upon the mutual exchanges of a highly differentiated population.* Durkheim described the former type as having *mechanical solidarity* because of the way norms and values are mutually reinforced by members' common experiences. In contrast, Durkheim described modern societies as having organic solidarity. Durkheim called this *organic solidarity* because these specialized roles greatly resemble the specialized parts played by organs within complex biological organisms. Both are composed of many distinct, but interdependent parts, each making a contribution to the survival of the whole. Additionally, for Durkheim, modern societies are unified by contractural norms rather than consensual ones. Consensual norms stem from agreement on basic values or goals. Small tribal societies are governed by such consensual norms. Contractural norms reflect rationally negotiated exchanges, not shared values. The two structural arrangements are quite different.

Mechanical solidarity

Organic solidarity

Modern social theorists continue to study the processes of social differentiation across societal types. As will be seen in Chapter 10, the causes of the transition from one type of social structure to the next are of paramount concern. Most writers agree with Durkheim that population size and population density are important stimulators of social structural change. Additionally, resources in the natural environment and technological development are widely recognized as factors that shape and change societal structures (Parsons 1966, 1977; Lenski 1966; Lenski and Lenski 1970). Commonly discussed types of societies are hunting and gathering, horticultural, agricultural, and industrial societies. The agricultural society is an important transitional type because it involves geographic settlement and stability, the production of surplus, the introduction of a money economy, and more complex social ranking systems. Industrial societies, of course, exhibit even more accelerated rates of social differentiation in nearly all social spheres. As one moves across types of societies, norms move from traditional to formal, the division of labor increases with greater differentiation in terms of statuses and roles, sanctions become more formal, and the stratification systems become more complex.

In summary, this section of the chapter has introduced an inventory of social structures. Groups have been distinguished from social categories, aggregates, and social strata. Primary and secondary groups differ greatly, with primary groups having very generalized expectations for the individual's conduct and less formalized structural properties. Several typologies of formal organizations have been presented, and the growth of bureaucratic organizations has been noted. Finally, we have considered differences between entire societies. Here, distinctions between mechanical and organic solidarity, *Gemeinschaft* and *Gesellschaft*, as well as differences between industrial and earlier types of societies have been examined. Throughout, it has been seen that the components of social structure—a system of norms, the division of labor, social control mechanisms, and social ranking systems—vary and change across these structural arrangements. The inventory of social structures discussed in this section of the chapter are graphically depicted in Figure 4.5

APPLICATIONS
FORMAL AND INFORMAL SOCIAL STRUCTURES

This chapter has developed the theme that societies are collections of social structures and that all social structures have certain common and readily identifiable properties. A system of social norms, a division of labor, hierarchy, and

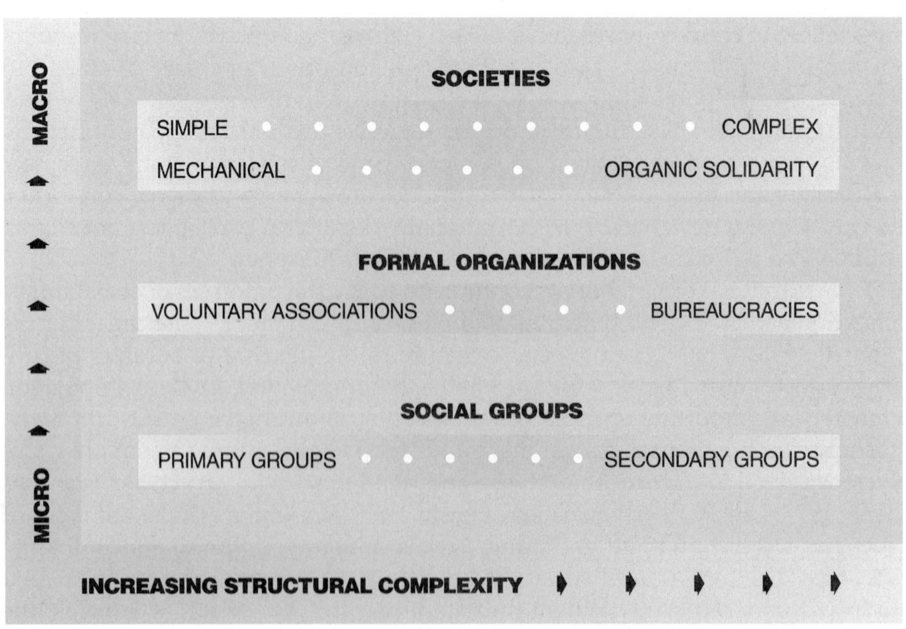

FIGURE 4.5
AN INVENTORY OF SOCIAL FORMS

social control mechanisms are the key elements of social structure examined in this chapter. However, it also is useful to distinguish between formal and informal social structures. *Formal social structures are either the officially designated or widely recognized patterns of social relations based on norms, a division of labor, social control, and social ranking.* For example, in any work situation the right of the employer or boss to decide who does what is part of the formal norm system. Most people enter a work setting knowing that someone "over" them has the authority to designate job responsibilities and to evaluate how well those duties are performed. These kinds of widely recognized social relationships are part of the formal structure.

Formal social structure

All social situations also exhibit patterns of informal social structure. *Informal social structures may be viewed as unofficial or implicit patterns of relationships that exist along side the formal structure.* Typically, the informal structure contributes to the achievement of the goals of the formal structure. For example, from time to time in most work situations, workers must "cover" for the boss. No one ever discusses who is responsible for this, how it will be accomplished, or even when "covering" for the boss will be necessary. But covering for the boss occurs frequently, and, much like the official rules at work, also exhibits a fixed pattern.

Informal social structure

At times, the goals of the informal social structure may conflict with those of the formal structure. For example, workers may develop their own norms about the typical work day, such as how many coffee breaks should occur and how long a coffee break should last. Clearly, work situations, like all social situations, have both formal and informal structural properties which may either complement each other or reflect the different concerns of various participants involved in the particular social structure.

The case study in this chapter focuses upon a social setting with which all college students are very familiar—college and university classrooms. As will be seen, there is an invisible informal structure in nearly all classrooms. This informal social structure exists along side the official or formal structure and introduces unofficial norms and goals into the classroom.

CASE

The Invisible Norms of Classrooms

The formal arrangement of norms, hierarchy, division of labor, and social control mechanisms in classrooms are in fact "news" to no one. Teachers are assigned the dominant position over students (ranking) and have the ultimate instruments of social control (examinations and grades) to induce "appropriate" student behavior. The division of labor is frightfully clear. Faculty members disseminate information, and students are expected to absorb some portion of it. So long as these norms are followed to some reasonable extent, fairly polite, orderly, and civil classroom routines occur. However, a sociological perspective reveals quite a different set of structural properties in classrooms.

First, even the hierarchical relations that govern classrooms are not quite as simple as the claim "teachers are in charge" would imply. While as a practical matter, times of classes are officially designated by the college or university administration, both faculty and students establish informal norms about the beginning and ending times for classes. Instructors designate the actual beginning of class by their time of arrival and through informal actions, such as chatting with students before beginning the day's formal proceedings. Students very quickly learn the "real" class time and gauge their arrival in class accordingly. However, students, not teachers, control the time that classes end. In both large and small classes, students begin to "pack-up," shuffle papers, close notebooks, and even become a bit noisy when they feel that the time limit has been reached. This not only is a norm, but also involves hierarchy or dominance. Only a fool would continue conducting a lecture or discussion once students have exercised the classroom norm of ending the class. This norm has less to do with the time required for getting to the next class than it does with the informal exercise of power.

Second, the routines for give-and-take, lecture and discussion in any classroom are established by informal norms and customarily are established early in the semester. Even though the course syllabus states that discussion and questions are an integral part of the course, students are highly skilled at "reading" the instructor's informal sanctions (social control) when questions are asked and discussions are initiated.

Third, research has demonstrated convincingly that in small and large classes alike, and across different academic disciplines, even when discussion is encouraged, only a small proportion of the students ask most of the questions, or speak in class at all (Karp and Yoels 1976). This fact reflects a division of labor among the students themselves. Certain students are expected to "carry" class discussions. By "allowing" these students to control the asking of questions and bulk of class discussions, other students are protected from revealing that they have not read the assigned material.

Karp and Yoels (1976) have noted that even the informal social control techniques administered by students can be fairly explicit. For example, they note that occasionally, the informally designated "talkers" in a class may begin performing like "rate busters." In factory work situations, rate busters are people who produce more completed product than other workers, and thereby raise employers' expectations about how much work should be done. In classrooms rate busters are students who lead teachers into discussions about topics beyond the interest of most students, or who raise topics that will unmask the ignorance of most students about topics in the required readings. Typically, social control is exercised by the class becoming noisy or by other students registering disinterest when rate busters begin to intrude on the approved system of norms.

Fourth, teachers participate in the informal norm that only certain students will speak in class by rarely calling upon specific students to participate. Interestingly, even though teachers distribute schedules of required weekly readings, the norm of not calling upon specific students allows a great range of individual student variation with regard to that schedule of readings. Thus, the formal norm of student participation is modified by this informal norm.

Fifth, examinations play an important role in all of this. Periodic examinations are formal social control mechanisms that insure some relative concordance between formal course schedules and informal student routines ("cramming"). However, the fact that students are tested only infrequently, and then only as announced, reduces students' responsibility for being up to date with assigned readings. This norm also illustrates the fact that most norms, both formal and informal, are well connected in a systematic way. After all, if exams were unannounced, students would need to do their assigned reading regularly, and would be more prepared and more willing to participate in class discussions.

In summary, it is clear from these observations that classrooms, like virtually all social situations, have informal structural properties that may either complement and or modify the formal social structure. It is equally clear that all participants in social structures rely upon both these formal and informal properties.

Chapter Summary

1. Social structures are the relatively stable patterns of human social relationships in societies. Social structures provide shape and boundary for patterns of culture, which in turn may be viewed as the contents within those structures.
2. Social interaction processes are the genesis of both culture and social structure. In this sense, social reality is triangular, with social interaction processes as the common base from which both social structure and culture emerge.
3. All social structures exhibit four components. They are a system of norms, a division of labor, a ranking system, and mechanisms of social control. Each of these components makes a unique contribution to the ways in which patterns of social life are shaped and bounded.
4. There are four basic types or forms of human social interaction. They are cooperation, exchange, competition, and conflict. While they exhibit very different characteristics, they often exist side by side in the same structural contexts.
5. An inventory of social structures has been examined. The human group is different from aggregates, social strata, and social categories. A social group is any number of persons who share a common identity, goals, or values, and who interact regularly. Primary groups contain intimate social relations, involve the whole person, and exhibit flexible structural components. Secondary groups exhibit more formalized and rigid structural properties.
6. Formal organizations are intermediate-sized social structures and range from voluntary associations to bureaucracies. It is useful to distinguish between business, mutual benefit, service and commonwealth organizations. Alternatively, a focus on means of control and motives for joining provides three types, coercive, utilitarian, and normative. Modern societies are characterized by the growth of bureaucratic organizations.
7. Societies, like other social structures, vary in their structural complexity. Sociologist shave distinguished between simple and complex societies, mechanical and organic solidarity, and *Gemeinschaft* (community) and *Gesellschaft* (society).

Key Concepts

achieved status
aggregates
ascribed status
authority
bureaucracy
business organizations
coercive organizations
commonwealth organizations
competition
conflict
cooperation
division of labor
exchange
folkways
formal organizations
formal social structure
Gemeinschaft
Gesellschaft
ideal type
informal social structure
master status
mechanical solidarity
mores
mutual benefit organizations
normative organizations
norms
organic solidarity
primary group
secondary group
service organizations
social category
social control
social group
social interaction
social organization
social power
social ranking
social role
social sanctions
social status
social strata
social structure
society
utilitarian organizations

Bibliography

Blau, Peter, and W. Richard Scott
1962. *Formal organizations.* San Francisco, California: Chandler Publishing Company.

Cooley, Charles Horton
1909. *Social organization.* New York: Charles Scribner.

Durkheim, Emile
1893. *The division of labor in society.* Translated by George Simpson, 1933. New York: Macmillan.

Etzioni, Amitai
1961. *A comparative analysis of complex organizations.* Rev. ed. 1975. New York: Free Press.

1964. *Complex organizations.* Englewood Cliffs, N.J.: Prentice-Hall.

Gans, Herbert
1962. *The urban villagers.* New York: Free Press.

Garfinkel, Harold
1967. *Studies in ethnomethodology.* Englewood Cliffs, N.J.: Prentice-Hall.

Karp, David A., and William C. Yoels
1976. The college classroom: Some observations on the meanings of student participation. *Sociology and Social Research,* Vol. 60, No. 4 (July): 421–39.

Le Bon, Gustave
1895. *The crowd: A study of the popular mind.* No translator identified, 1960. New York: Viking Press.

Lenski, Gerhard
1966. *Power and privilege: A theory of stratification.* New York: McGraw-Hill.

Lenski, Gerhard and Jean Lenski
1970. *Human societies: An introduction to macrosociology.* 5th ed., 1987. Englewood Cliffs, N.J.: McGraw-Hill.

Linton, Ralph
1936. *The study of man.* New York: Appleton-Century-Crofts.

Mannheim, Karl
1928. Competition as a cultural phenomena. In *Essays on the sociology of knowledge.* Edited by Paul Kecskemeti, 1952, pp. 191–229. London: Routledge & Kegan Paul, Ltd.

Parsons, Talcott
1966. *Societies: Evolutionary and comparative perspectives.* Englewood Cliffs, N.J.: Prentice-Hall.

1977. *The evolution of societies.* Englewood Cliffs, N.J.: Prentice-Hall.

Richardson, James T., Mary Stewart and Robert Simmonds
1979. *Organized miracles: A study of contemporary youth communal, fundamentalist organization.* New Brunswick, N.J.: Transaction Books.

Scott, W. Richard
1982. *Organizations: Rational, natural, and open systems.* Englewood Cliffs, N.J.: Prentice-Hall.

Simmel, Georg
1908. *Conflict and the web of group affiliations.* Translated by Kurt H. Wolff and Reinhard Bendix, 1955. New York: Free Press.

1908. *Soziologie, Untersuchungen uber die Formen der Vergesellschaftung,* Parts 2 through 5 of *The sociology of Georg Simmel.* Translated and edited by Kurt H. Wolff, 1950. New York: Free Press.

Stein, Maurice
1964. *The eclipse for community.* New York: Harper & Row.

Sumner, William Graham
1906. *Folkways: A study of the sociological importance of usages, manners, customs, mores, and morals.* 1960 Edition. New York: New American Library.

Toennies, Ferdinand
1887. *Community and society.* Translated by Charles Loomis, 1963. New York: Harper & Row.

Vidich, Arthur, and Joseph Bensman
1958. *Small town in mass society: Class, power, and religion in a rural community.* Rev. ed., 1968. Princeton, N.J.: Princeton Univ. Press.

Weber, Max
1904. Objectivity in social science and social policy. In *The methodology of the social sciences.* Translated and edited by Edward A. Shils and Henry A. Finch, 1949, pp. 50–112. New York: Free Press.

1923. *Economy and society.* Translated and edited by Guenther Roth and Claus Wittch, 1968. Totowa, N.J.: Beminster Press.

Youniss, James
1980. *Parents and peers in social development.* Chicago: Univ. of Chicago Press.

CHAPTER 5

SOCIAL INSTITUTIONS: PATTERNS IN TRANSITION

CHAPTER OUTLINE

LEARNING OBJECTIVES

It has been seen in the preceding two chapters that culture, social structures, and patterns of social interaction are the basic building blocks from which societies are constructed. This chapter examines phenomena that may be thought of as supra-structures. Social institutions are clusters of social structures, cultural values, and interaction patterns that focus upon similar tasks or purposes. These clusters of social phenomena, such as economic, medical, military, or religious institutions to name but a few, are very much like bridges. They link related social structures and patterns of human activity together. Institutions are important social phenomena because they serve powerful integrative functions in societies. Just as physical bridges keep the road system connected, and thus keep the transportation system in motion, social institutions keep the basic tasks of the social system operating.

While the most significant features of social institutions are their integrative and ordering effects, this chapter examines transitions and change within social institutions as well. Why is this so? Just as these supra-structural arrangements depict the broad outlines of life in a given society, they also provide insights into how a society is changing and where its problems and dilemmas might occur. Therefore, a dual focus on patterns of institutional stability and change has been adopted in this chapter.

Especially in complex modern societies, the sheer number of institutional arrangements available for sociological investigation is enormous. As noted in Chapter 4 (pp. 102–105), as social differentiation proceeds, more and more specialized social structures are created, and thus specialized institutional networks between these structures proliferate as well. Understandably, individual sociologists are apt to be more interested in certain institutions than in others. The field of sociology is populated by a great diversity of so-called institutional sociologies, ranging from the sociology of politics to the sociology of sports and leisure.

Obviously, many different social institutions are examined throughout this text by way of examples and illustrations. However, this chapter has some rather specific goals with regard to institutional analysis. First, it is important to recognize that certain tasks, and, therefore, certain institutions that accomplish them, are common to most, if not all, societies. Second, institutional processes may be understood most readily through a detailed analysis of one institution. The most basic of all social institutions, the family, has been selected here for that purpose.

When you've finished reading and studying this chapter you should be able to discuss answers to the following questions:

---

1. What is the sociological meaning of the term social institution?

2. Are certain institutions universally found in all societies?
3. What are the most basic or most commonly encountered institutions in human societies, and what are their tasks or functions?
4. What different forms of family institutions are found across different societies?
5. What have been the most important changes in the American family institution in the 20th century?
6. What alternative forms of family structure are emerging in contemporary American society?
7. What are some of the more important problems and dilemmas occurring in American families today?

INSTITUTIONS: BRIDGING SOCIAL STRUCTURES

The first section of this chapter addresses several basic questions about social institutions. First, exactly what is meant by the sociological term "social institution" and how does this meaning differ from the everyday uses of the term? Second, what is the place of institutional arrangements in the general scheme of human societies? Why are institutions such an important part of human societies, and what sorts of things may be learned from studying social institutions? Finally, to what extent is it useful to view certain features of social institutions as universal or omnipresent in human societies?

INSTITUTIONS DEFINED

In everyday conversation the term "institution" is used in a variety of ways. For example, the former host of NBC television's "Tonight Show," Johnny Carson, was said to have been a television institution. Because he hosted the program for some thirty years, people thought of him as a permanent feature of late night television, and of the television industry *per se.* Carson was an "institution" because it had become difficult to think of late night television without thinking of Carson. It also is common to hear people speak of colleges, hospitals, and even the United States Congress as "institutions." Used in this way, the term conveys the notion of a stable cast of persons involved in a well-coordinated set of activities, what sociologists more commonly call a formal organization (see Chapter 4, pp. 101–102). Finally, certain specific activities sometimes are called institutions, as in the expression "the institution of marriage." Here, it is being said that something has become a well-established social custom, and that participation in it is obligatory. Each of these everyday uses of the term "institution" captures some part of the sociological meaning of it, but none of these is precisely the same as its sociological use.

Social institutions

Social institutions are the relatively permanent structural configurations centered around the tasks of meeting the important material and nonmaterial requirements of a society. Typically, institutions encompass a network of social structures related to each other in terms of the particular societal requirements they satisfy, or tasks they attempt to accomplish. Institutional arrangements define what is expected and what is considered legitimate within any particular set of social structures. Accordingly, activities within any of an institution's substructures are guided by the norms and values of that institution. Let's consider an example.

In modern societies, the institution of medicine has become internally complex and specialized, encompassing hospitals, physicians, drug manufacturers, pharmacists, medical schools, private insurance companies, and because of Medicaid and Medicare, even a number of government agencies. All these social structures share in the common task of health care service and delivery. All the persons and agencies within this institution are governed by a common set of norms and values. The prevention and alleviation of pain and suffering are special goals of the medical institution.

Medicine, viewed as an institutional network, also reflects some of the basic values of the society in which it is found. American society is a capitalist society and values free enterprise. Therefore, medical practice and related health care services are sold on a fee-for-service basis. In some other modern societies, among them England, Canada, and Sweden, medical service is viewed as a right of citizenship, and the delivery of health care is seen as a public interest and responsibility. These nations have organized their medical institutions, not on a private practice basis, but on a socialized medicine model. Thus, the institution of medicine in these societies expresses a slightly different set of values and norms than is found in the United States.

Of course, in the United States today, the adequacy with which the institution of medicine accomplishes its paramount goal of health delivery has become a widely debated issue. Dramatic increases in populations that are poor, aged, and uninsured all have placed stress upon the traditional institutional arrangements of American medicine. It is entirely possible that these pressures will alter both the social structures of the medical institution in the United States and the norms and values that regulate its practitioners.

From even this brief analysis of the institution of medicine, it should be apparent that each institution in a society may be structured in a variety of ways. Each society selects one or perhaps a few of the possible options for any particular institutional realm. Once established, institutions, although somewhat adaptive to changing social circumstances, tend to change slowly because they are supported by the twin forces of custom and tradition.

CONTINUITY AND CHANGE

Social institutions are of enormous social significance for several reasons. Let's pause here to make those reasons more explicit. First, within any set of institutional structures, persons may reasonably have the expectation of stable value and normative systems. Said differently, institutions are sets of social structures in which common rules of the social game are shared. If it is useful to think of social structures as boundary systems, then institutions are like maps that show how those boundaries adjoin and connect with one another.

For example, let's examine a bit further the case of the institution of medicine. Physicians and pharmacists, though members of different professional communities, both are situated within the medical institution, and we may reasonably expect both to perform by similar institutional standards. Most persons would be shocked to find their pharmacist treating the sale of medicines the same way that automobile salespeople approach the selling of cars. The institutional contexts of car sales and medical services are different. Hopefully, one need not approach the pharmacist with the same caution employed at the used car lot.

Second, because they entail systems of shared norms, values, and expectations, institutional arrangements have powerful ordering effects in a society. This fact perhaps is not so well appreciated if we focus upon simple, undifferentiated societies. In such societies, typically, one set of institutional arrangements, the tribe or the clan, fulfills all societal requirements or needs. Social order simply does not seem to be a problem. However, in highly differentiated societies, in which institutions separate from one another, institutional linkages are extremely important. Institutions are the carriers of social values, social traditions, and social customs. In this sense, all social institutions perform social control functions in societies. Through the establishment of shared values, customs, and traditions, they define and regulate allowable conduct within each institution's network of social structures.

Third, social institutions develop and transmit the deeply held values of societies. Accordingly, such values are easily discernible in institutional arrangements. For example, the American values of independence, competition, and material accumulation are conveyed by the economic institution in the United States. American political structures reflect the values of freedom and majority rule.

Fourth, institutions are crucial indicators of social change processes in societies. Institutions change when values change, or when conditions in the society change. In the latter case, institutional change is acceptable as long as essential values continue to be reflected in the new institutional arrangement. Obviously, it is much more difficult to change the traditions and customs that permeate an entire institutional sector, than to change one structural component within it. For example, in the United States, within the institution of medicine the shift from individual practices to group practices has been an important structural change. However, this particular social structural change has occurred within the context of the prevailing institutional norms and values. Group practices operate under the same ethical norms as individual practices.

THE ISSUE OF UNIVERSALISM

Universalism

Perhaps one of the most intriguing issues about social institutions is whether or not there are universal patterns among them that exist in all societies. There is no question that while specific collective solutions to the problems of daily living differ from one society to the next, those problems are rather uniform across societies.

Human life must be provided with meaning. New generations must be born and nurtured. Children must be taught the necessary information to become functioning adult members of society. Resources and goods must be distributed according to agreed-upon methods. Techniques of mutual defense and social control must be established. To accomplish these and other tasks, human beings create and maintain institutions, sets of structural arrangements that establish how these tasks will be accomplished. Should the term "universal" be applied to these arrangements?

Consider the example of the human family. As will be seen presently, every society has some set of primary group relationships focused upon a relatively common set of tasks. Does this mean that the family is a universal institution? If it is difficult to imagine life on the planet without some set of social structures doing what family does, then yes, perhaps it is meaningful to say that "family" is a universal institution.

But, what is gained by this claim? The greater sociological insight is that the particular tasks accomplished by families are not dependent on universal structural forms. Simply stated, different societies design family institutions differently. Thus, while the needs or requirements may be encountered everywhere (universal?), the social arrangements that satisfy particular needs vary infinitely. This is true not only of the family but of all commonly encountered social institutions.

Are certain institutions universal? The answer is yes and no. The apparent community needs or requirements (the problems that must be addressed for a society to remain afloat) seem uniform across societies. They are perhaps universal. But the greater sociological interest is in the fact that different human communities solve the same problems of daily living with different expressions of these basic social institutions. The five most commonly encountered institutions in human society are family, education, religion, economy, and polity. The next section of this chapter provides a closer examination of these five institutional sectors.

In summary, social institutions are the relatively permanent structural configurations centered around the tasks of meeting the important material and nonmaterial requirements of a society. Institutions link together social structures that share common or related social tasks. Social institutions are carriers of social values, traditions and customs, and therefore are powerful stabilizing agents in any society. While the social tasks addressed by social institutions may be viewed as universal tasks, social institutions exhibit great structural variation from society to society.

Five Sectors and Their Social Tasks

This section of the chapter examines the five institutional sectors most commonly encountered in societies: family, education, religion, economy, and polity. These five do not exhaust the range either of institutions or subinstitutional networks found in societies, least of all modern societies. However, these five institutional sectors may be viewed as the primary focal points for the connections between social structures in most modern societies.

In each instance a common set of questions is asked. What are the most basic tasks addressed by this institution? Across different societies, what are some of the alternative structural arrangements or norms found in this institution? What are some of the leading features of this institution in American society, and what kinds of social changes seem to be emerging in this institution?

POLITY

A first institutional sector is the polity. *The polity is responsible for a variety of tasks, at least four of which are paramount: external defense, internal social control, government, and civic ideology.*

Polity

First, the polity is responsible for defending a society from outside encroachment. In modern societies, this task usually is addressed by the formation of a subinstitutional set of structures, the military. The extent to which military personnel are members of a distinct professional stratum and the extent of their involvement in domestic governance are important features of the polity. In most democracies, care is taken to keep the military and governance tasks of the polity separate. While some military heroes do become President (Washington, Jackson, Grant, Teddy Roosevelt, and Eisenhower), in modern times, American military heroes have not campaigned for political office in military uniform. Obviously, between societies, there is enormous variation in the separation of, or connections between, these two features of the polity.

A second task of the polity is internal social control. Ostensibly, such matters seem rather simple. The government adopts a code of laws, and a police force and criminal justice system are created to maintain order in compliance with those laws. It is rarely that simple. For example, from the very formation of the American republic there have been controversies about the relative powers of the national, state, and local polities in making laws and enforcing them. The result has been a highly complex set of legal, police, judicial, and penal systems that overlap and, at times, even contradict one another. Clearly, even fundamental social tasks in structurally complex societies become complicated.

Civic ideology

A third task of the polity is to establish and maintain a civic ideology. As was seen in Chapter 3 (pp. 79–80), every society possesses a system of values expressed in collective myths. Both political and religious institutions are involved in the creation and celebration of such myths. However, our concern for the moment is not with sacred doctrines, but with political ones. Essentially, the core values of a polity are the core values of a society. For example, in the United States, the ideas of freedom, democracy, the pursuit of happiness, and equality of opportunity all are key elements in the nation's civic ideology. The Bill of Rights and the Constitution are the texts upon which these parts of the American civic ideology are based. The polity has the responsibility of disseminating and celebrating the civic ideals in these documents. Its failure to do so can result in a weakened civic ideology and less effective internal social control.

FIGURE 5.1
There are many ways of structuring a government.

Government

No doubt, most people think of government as the primary function of the political institution. *Governments are responsible for the allocation of power and authority relations in societies.* Clearly, the means by which persons are designated as "in power" vary greatly. Generally, more traditional societies have assigned governmental authority by inheritance, essentially by family membership. In tribal societies, it is common for the son of the chief to become the next chief. In monarchies, a princess becomes a queen, and a prince becomes a king. In contrast, modern nations evidence several different means for achieving control of government. Dictatorships and military governments rule by coercion. Democracies and some socialist regimes claim to be ruled by consent of the governed.

Political parties are an essential part of the power and authority system because they implement means by which governance is created and maintained. For example, communist systems are not simply communist. They are one-party systems. Participation in the government requires good standing in the party. The American two-party system frequently is contrasted with other democratic systems requiring a coalition among multiple parties to form a government (Italy, France, England, and Israel). Many political analysts have maintained that the two-party system has provided the American polity with a uniquely high degree of governmental stability. In contrast, the multiparty systems of other Western European nations are deemed less stable because they often lack the coalition of parties required to form a government. Thus, even among democracies there are alternative institutional arrangements.

During the last half century, questions have been raised concerning the extent to which the two-party system in the United States is changing. As early as the 1960s, political analysts observed that a four-party system, composed of Presidential and Congressional Democratic and Republican Parties, was emerging. Consider that the Watergate activities that led to President Nixon's resignation were not perpetrated by the Republican Party. Rather, a special party-type organization, the Committee to Re-elect the President, was the culprit. Would such excesses as the Watergate break-in have occurred if the regular party apparatus had been in charge of the campaign?

Both low voter participation in elections throughout the 1980s and the emergence of third-party Presidential candidates (George Wallace in the 1960s and Ross Perot in the 1992 Presidential campaign) highlight the fact that the American two-party system is undergoing change. Parties no longer enlist the allegiance of large numbers of voters or "party regulars," and, at times, may fail to produce viable candidates for general elections. These trends are indications of institutional change in the polity.

RELIGION

Religion

A second and closely related institutional sector is religion. In most societies, religious institutions fulfill the task of imparting meaning and significance to social arrangements. Most sociologists use the term *religion* in a limited sense, referring to *shared patterns of belief and behavior related to a belief in the supernatural.* In most societies, religious institutions address three social tasks. Religion supplies *a meaning system*—most importantly beliefs about what is moral, right, and legitimate. Religion also provides a *community of belonging* in which individual identities may be rooted. Finally, religion provides *sacred rituals* through which moral ideals and people's identification with them may be dramatized, celebrated, and reinforced.

The first of religion's social tasks, the providing of moral authority, is of special interest because of the ways in which it may complement or compete with the task of the polity in establishing a civic ideology. Both of these institutions are involved in defining and maintaining highly inclusive value systems. Both, though in different ways, involve authority relations.

Theocracy

In the simplest societies, where a small clan or tribe is the entire social structure, religion and polity are bound together in a single institution. One individual may be both the chief of the tribe and the head shaman. Known as a *theocracy,* the situation in which earthly powers flow from the rulership of the gods represents the most forceful combination of sacred meaning systems and civil authority relations.

Separation of church and state

The separation of church and state into discrete institutions represents an important phase in the process of social differentiation. It is possible to have an *established state church,* as was once the case in most European nations. Even though church and state are institutionally separate, governance may take the form of a divine right of kings and queens. Secular government has religious significance and authority. However, *separation of church and state* tends to encourage the independent development of these institutions, and in turn, competition between them.

The blurring of the two spheres of authority, religious and secular, is a continuing problem in the United States, where it is officially maintained that the two institutions are completely separate. Is it legal for religious leaders to offer prayers and benediction at public civic events like public school graduations? Should students be permitted or required to observe a moment of prayer during the school day? If civic ideology and religious doctrines do not reinforce one another, are not both of them injured?

Religious pluralism

These issues are made even more complex by the situation of *religious pluralism.* In America, a great number of religious institutions compete with each other. Is it proper for Christmas decorations to be placed on the steps of city hall, when only a portion of the citizenry celebrate Christmas? Does this sacred competition between religious communities undermine all claims to sacred authority? We shall return to these issues in a later chapter (see discussion of secularization in Chapter 11, pp. 315–320).

While religious institutions perform certain important social tasks, there are many complex institutional arrangements for accomplishing them. Modern institutional expressions of religion, like religious pluralism and church-state separation, may impair religion's ability to perform some of its traditional roles in societies.

ECONOMY

Economy

A third institutional sector is the economy. *Economic institutions provide the means by which a society's valued resources are distributed.* In the simplest societies, the economic institution is embedded within family, religious, and polity arrangements. For example, a hunting and gathering tribe is likely to have few surplus material resources to distribute. A basic rule system for how the foodstuffs are to be allocated provides rudimentary economic norms. Often, rules of barter and exchange prevail.

In modern societies, the economic institution has become exceedingly complex and includes a number of important subsystems. For example, the invention of money introduces a great variety of economic practices (such as banking and investment) not possible in simple barter and exchange systems. Financial and investment systems, as well as occupational and employment practices, constitute important economic subsystems. The stratification arrangements in a society (see Chapter 8) are, in part, extensions of its basic economic norms and values.

Many of the economic issues in modern societies focus upon the values of capitalism, especially the norm of owning private property. Obviously, capitalism with private ownership, and socialism with public ownership and control, represent different normative frameworks upon which economic relations in a society may be based.

Social issues involving economic institutions often entail value conflicts with other institutional sectors. For example, the utility of any particular set of economic ideas and practices may be measured in terms of how well it provides gainful employment for a society's members. However, political, and even religious institutions, may pose the criteria of fairness and justice alongside the economic idea of utility. Thus, economic institutions can be evaluated not only in terms of their efficiency (do most people have jobs?), but also in terms of their ability to provide a just distribution of a society's resources (how common is poverty in the society?). A society in which everyone has a job, but in which few people can live on what their jobs pay, has serious flaws in its economic institution.

EDUCATION

Even in highly differentiated societies, some of the central social tasks are shared by several of the major institutions. As has already been seen, polity and religion both participate in authority systems, and some basic economic norms are rooted in both the polity and religious ideals. There are important reasons for viewing the *educational institution* as being a highly connective sector in most societies. The educational institution accomplishes tasks that are of consequence for most other institutional sectors.

Education

The educational institution focuses upon three primary tasks. They are cultural transmission, skill training, and occupational allocation. While *cultural transmission or socialization* is begun in the family, the older a child becomes, the more this task is accomplished by schools, rather than family. The young must learn the shared meanings and values of the culture, and in turn, use these ideas and ideals as guides for living. Educational institutions teach what it means to be a member of society, along with the concomitant roles that are expected and rules that must be followed. It is precisely because schools address these basic socialization tasks that such things as sex education and textbook content are hotly debated social issues (see discussion in Chapter 6, pp. 159–162). Of course, in less structurally complex societies, where the family is the prime educational institution, and in which a diversity of values is not encountered, these kinds of controversies do not occur.

A second task of the educational institution is *skill training*. In less complex societies, families are both economic and educational units. Trades and professions are passed from one generation to the next, and apprenticeships often are served in home-based businesses. Both agricultural and early industrial societies operate on this principle. However, in 19th century America, both the advance of industrialism and large waves of immigration signaled the need for more formal and more specialized skill training. Gradually, the basic skills of reading, writing, and arithmetic became requirements without which one could not find stable employment in American society. Today, few people will be considered "employable" without computer literacy. Clearly, technology has continued to escalate the skill requirements for labor force participation.

These trends are related to yet a third task of the educational institution, *occupational allocation*. In modern societies, schools have become the sorting mechanisms for determining which individuals and strata are channeled into which occupational categories. In this sense, educational institutions are gatekeepers for the division of labor in modern societies, and in turn, basic participants in social stratification processes.

While certainly, objective factors play a role in these selection processes, there is powerful evidence that ascribed factors such as race, gender, and social class are involved in ways that perpetuate social inequalities (Rist 1973; Brophy and Good 1974; Kozol 1991). The role of educational institutions as agents of social stratification has become an enduring social issue.

FAMILY

Family, of course, is the most basic social institution. This is true in several senses. On the one hand, in simple societies, family is *the* institution that performs a multiplicity of major social tasks. On the other hand, as societies become more structurally differentiated, as institutional sectors proliferate, the family retains certain rather unique functions. Most importantly, even in modern societies, *the family is responsible for the emotional and material support of its members; is the locus of biological reproduction; and is the agent of primary socialization.*

Family

While these three social tasks provide a theme of constancy in the family institution, it is clear that, like all other institutional spheres, family patterns have undergone important transitions. The balance of this chapter provides an in-depth examination of the family institution in American society. Two themes are developed. First, the family, like all social institutions, exhibits remarkable variation in its structural characteristics from society to society. Second, by studying historical trends in the American family institution, some of the broader social forces affecting all institutions in modern societies can be identified.

In summary, this section of the chapter has introduced five basic institutional sectors that address major tasks in most societies, especially in modern ones. While some tasks are shared between several institutional sectors it nevertheless is useful to identify social institutions by the primary tasks they accomplish. The polity assumes primary responsibility for external defense, internal social control, government, and civic ideology. Religion provides a sacred meaning system, a community of belonging and identity, and rituals through which shared symbols may be reinforced. The economic institution supplies the norms that guide resource allocation in society. This task extends to the financial, employment and stratification systems in a society. The educational institution accomplishes the goals of cultural transmission, skill training, and occupational allocation. Finally, family is the most basic institution, and in most societies accomplishes the tasks of biological reproduction, primary socialization, and the emotional and material support of its members. All of these major social institutions in American society are the locus of social issues and exhibit transitions.

FAMILY: THE MOST BASIC INSTITUTION

The next two sections of this chapter narrow the sociological lens and focus upon the most basic of all social institutions—the family. This detailed examination of family institutions surely might be justified solely on the basis of the social importance of family institutions in societies. However, this focus also is intended to illustrate some of the general themes about institutions already introduced in this chapter. What are those themes? First, human societies exhibit a remarkable diversity of specific social forms of family institutions. Second, social institutions are convenient barometers for measuring broader social change processes. Finally, even the most basic institutional arrangements in societies undergo modification and change. Accordingly, this section of the chapter concludes with an examination of some of the emerging shapes of family institutions in contemporary society.

THE FAMILY IN CROSS-CULTURAL PERSPECTIVE

Exactly what constitutes a family, who is included in it, and how relationships within a family are defined all may vary from society to society. In some societies, the *extended family* (several generations) is the basic social unit, while in others, a *nuclear family* (one generation and its offspring) is the prevailing form. In some societies, a small community is the basic family unit (such as the commune or the Israeli kibbutz); and if the society is extremely small (like a tribe or clan), the entire society is a family. When Americans think about the family, they envision a nuclear family, meaning parents and their children living in one household apart from other relatives. In fact, most industrialized nations follow this norm. However, in preindustrial societies, the dominant pattern is the extended family, with several generations of family members living near or with each other.

Extended family

Nuclear family

Let's take a closer look at the structural features of family institutions. Families are characterized by systems of norms defining patterns of residence, rules of descent, and both the mate selection processes and numbers of marriage partners. Regarding patterns of residence and descent, preindustrial families most often are *patrilocal,* with a married couple living with or near the husband's family. Less frequently they are *matrilocal,* meaning residence with or near the wife's family. However, in industrial societies the norm is *neolocal,* with couples living in a new place of residence apart from the parents of either spouse. Of course, in most societies, husbands and wives share the same household. However, this is not always the case. For example, in some Native American cultures males live in men's houses, apart from their wives and children (Bender 1967).

Patrilocal

Matrilocal

Neolocal

Patrilineal
Matrilineal
Patriarchal
Matriarchal
Bilineal

Norms of descent also vary. In preindustrial societies, the pattern is either *patrilineal,* with kinship traced through the father, or *matrilineal,* with descent traced through the mother. Ancient Israelite society was matrilineal, even though it was a *patriarchal* (male dominated) rather than a *matriarchal* (female dominated) society. In industrial societies, descent norms tend to be *bilineal,* with kinship relations established through both parents.

Polygyny
Polyandry
Monogamy

All societies provide some form of marriage, a community-sanctioned agreement specifying rights and obligations between partners. However, there are variations in both the mate selection processes and the number of partners involved. In preindustrial societies, it is common for mate selection to be a parental right. Marriages are "arranged" with such things as dowries (material possessions that go with the bride) and bride prices negotiated. In industrial societies, the norm of romantic love determines marriage partners. Regarding the number of mates persons are allowed, some societies allow men to have more than one wife *(polygyny);* and a few even allow women to have more than one husband *(polyandry).* However, in most societies one husband for one wife *(monogamy)* is the norm. Even where multiple spouses are allowed, economic considerations (it's expensive) limit the practice.

Within families, there are innumerable patterns of the division of labor. In most societies the biological father assumes financial and social responsibility for his children. Yet, in some traditional cultures, this is not so. For example, among the Nayar in India, caring for a couple's children is the responsibility of the mother's relatives (Gough 1960). Additionally, the division of labor within families appears to be universally gender-based. While there are great differences regarding which gender performs specific tasks, gender appears to be a primary criteria by which family tasks are assigned. In the United States today, even though many women work outside the home, a large array of household tasks remain "women's work."

Egalitarian

Finally, the internal ranking features of family systems also vary considerably. Patriarchal systems, meaning male authority and dominance, appear to be the most common pattern. Matriarchal systems, or female dominance, is extremely rare. While the emerging family pattern in modern societies is *egalitarian,* with authority shared by husband and wife, this is not yet a prevailing norm.

Obviously, these several features of family life only scratch the surface of the wealth of information about family systems (Collins 1988). However, two facts about the family institution are incontrovertible. First, every society has some set of structural arrangements to address the fundamental tasks of the family. Second, there is enormous variation in the specific structural features of family institutions.

AMERICAN FAMILIES IN TRANSITION

Social institutions, like all social arrangements, are shaped and reshaped by broad social trends. By examining historical developments in the American family, the effects of such trends may be discerned. The terms "modernity" and "modernization" frequently are used to describe the combination of social trends shaping societies in the 20th century (see discussion of modernity in Chapter 11, pp. 309, 317–318). Surely, industrialization and urbanization are two of the key modernization processes influencing the family and other social institutions in the United States. Let's examine the historical record.

The American family during the colonial period was characterized by several distinct norms. First, contrary to present-day popular beliefs, the colonial family was a nuclear family, not an extended family. However, both families and households were larger than they are today. In part, this was because children in an agrarian (farming) society were an economic asset. Also, nonfamily members such as farmhands, temporary boarders, and others commonly were included in the colonial household. Second, extended family systems were an important element in the structure of communities. While people lived in nuclear families, their social relations with "kin" throughout the community characterized the lifestyle.

Third, the colonial family had primary responsibility for many social tasks including procreation, physical protection, education, moral and religious training, recreation, and economic productivity. Fourth, of all these, the economic function of the family was most important. This is because in agrarian societies, all family members, children included, work to produce what they, in turn, consume. In fact, for the colonial family, economic cooperation was more important to a marriage than sexual attraction and compatibility (Shorter 1975).

By the middle of the 19th century, modernization processes, most importantly industrialization, were bringing significant changes to the family institution. Gradually, the family experienced a massive reduction of its social functions. For example, with industrialization and the emergence of the factory system, the place of work was separated from the place of residence. The family no longer was focused upon economic production. Additionally, the new industrial economy required workers with new skills, among them literacy. The educational function of the family was relinquished to formal educational institutions. School curricula were designed to create more uniform levels of reading, writing, and other basic skills in the population.

FIGURE 5.2
In agrarian societies, large families were an economic asset.

While the number of tasks performed by the family diminished, some new norms of family life gained preeminence. First, the family became centered on the emotional well-being of its individual members. The family became a place of repose and renewal, "a place to come in out of the storm" (Demos 1978). Second, families became smaller. The large families of the farming community were no longer an asset in an urban-industrial setting. Those "helping hands" on the farm became simply "more mouths to feed" in the city. Third, with fewer children in the family, a new child-centered norm began emerging. Parents placed greater emotional emphasis upon their relationships with their children. Finally, romantic love and personal fulfillment became the primary basis for marriage.

The 20th century has seen a maturing of some of these trends. Clearly, romantic love has continued to serve as the prime criterion for marriage. Ironically, this has resulted in record-high levels of divorce. Why is this so? Marriages are judged on the capability of each partner to meet the other's emotional needs at a highly intense level. A diminishing of that intensity often is experienced and interpreted as failure. However, this has not weakened America's faith in the norm of marriage. Today, in the United States, over 80 percent of all people who divorce remarry. Family analysts characterize this pattern of marriage-divorce-remarriage as *serial monogamy*. This and related trends point in the direction of new forms of the family that are emerging in American society.

Serial monogamy

SOME EMERGING FAMILY FORMS

The emerging forms of the family system in modern American life seem to point in a great many different directions. In fact, it is sociologically inaccurate to speak of "the" American family. The following discussion focuses upon only four forms that have taken a potentially enduring position in the American social structure. They are the reconstituted or blended family, the single-parent family, the dual-career family, and the voluntarily childless family.

Blended family

Reconstituted family

Blended or reconstituted families result from marriages in which children of one or both spouses from a previous marriage are included in the new family unit. Such families may be created out of two rather different circumstances. Widows and widowers who have lost a spouse may remarry. This situation has always characterized a small portion of the population. However, increasingly throughout the 20th century, remarriages of divorced persons has been the major factor creating blended families. Cherlin (1981, 29) observes that by the late 1970s, among persons remarrying 87 percent of brides and 89 percent of grooms were previously divorced rather than widowed. Moreover, considering that 5 out of 6 divorced men and 3 out of 4 divorced women will remarry, reconstituted families are an increasingly common event in American life. By 1990, approximately 15 percent of all children were living in blended or reconstituted families (Zinn and Eitzen 1990).

Reconstituted families have very special structural properties because they entail social relationships not found in traditional nuclear families. The television situation comedy "The Brady Bunch" (still on television in reruns) portrays a reconstituted family including six children (the husband and wife each had three children) in a less than real life environment. The children of this made-for-television family never had to interact with noncustodial parents, or any other extended family members. The real life situation is quite different.

Blended families involve a complexity of social relationships and boundary ambiguities. These families involve relationships not only between children and their new step-parents, but often with step-brothers and sisters, as well as step-grandparents, half-siblings, noncustodial parents, and other extended family relations. Reconstituted families must resolve the problem of redefining just who is to be included within the new nuclear family unit (Furstenberg 1984). All of these relationships may involve ambiguities and problems not because they are "unnatural," but because this society has not yet developed expectations and norms by which these new relationships are to be defined (Pasley and Ihinger-Tallman 1987). It is perhaps for these very reasons that remarriages where children are present are often more stressful than those where no children are involved.

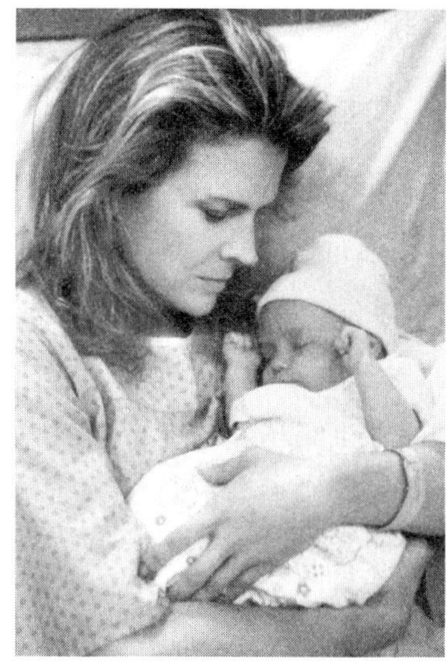

FIGURE 5.3
Art can reflect real life.

However, change is occurring. Consider the increasing availability of greeting cards for step-parents on Mother's Day and Father's Day. Clearly, these kinds of cards now are available not only because of the statistical occurrence of these relationships, but also because public recognition and acknowledgment of these social relations are in the process of becoming socially normative and legitimate.

Single-parent family

A second emerging family form is the *single-parent family,* in which *children reside in a household where only one parent, either male or female, is present.* Today, it is estimated that 61 percent of American children will spend some time in a single-parent household before reaching the age of 18 (Kutner 1991). By 1989, 24.3 percent of all families with children under the age of 18 were single-parent families. Nineteen percent of white families with children are headed by a single parent, compared to 54.5 percent of black families, and 31 percent of Hispanic families. Slightly less than 9 out of 10 such families are headed by a female, 38.1 percent of whom are divorced, 24.7 percent currently separated, 31.2 percent never married, and 6 percent widowed (U.S. Bureau of the Census 1991).

Although all types of families experience stresses and strains, single-parent households must cope with some unique problems. Single parents must play the dual roles of mother and father, making decisions that typically are shared by two persons. Additionally, a single parent must manage all the daily tasks that would be distributed between two people in two-parent families. However, the most significant problems faced by single-parent families are economic. The plight of female-headed families is particularly alarming. Half of all female-headed families live at or near the poverty level. Their economic situation results from a variety of factors. Among them are low levels of educational attainment, the inequitable division of financial resources upon divorce, the lack of affordable child care, and the low salaries paid in traditionally female jobs. Consider that even though the majority of female heads of families are in the labor force (70 percent of whites, 62 percent of blacks, and 48 percent of Hispanics), many of these employed women have incomes below the poverty level (53 percent of blacks, 52 percent of Hispanics, 28 percent of whites (National Commission on Working Women 1990).

A variation of the single-parent family are those headed by teenage mothers. More than 1 million teenage females in the United States become pregnant each year. About 400,000 of these pregnancies are aborted, some end in miscarriage, but almost half result in live births (*New York Times* 1987). Owing largely to the availability of abortion, the number of births to teenage mothers has been declining, and is at its lowest point since the 1950s (U.S. Bureau of the Census 1991). However, today, the majority of teenage mothers do not offer their children for adoption. Over 90 percent of unwed teenage mothers choose to raise their children themselves. They become female heads of households. In consequence, lasting hardships are imposed upon two generations, parent and child. In 1987, these young families cost the government 16.6 billion dollars in welfare, Medicaid, and food stamps (*New York Times* 1987). However, these mothers and their children pay the highest cost in terms of lost opportunities. Teenage mothers are less likely than their peers to complete high school, and are twice as likely to live in poverty than those women having a first child when they are in their twenties. Infants of teenage mothers have high rates of illness and mortality and tend toward educational and emotional difficulties. Additionally, many of these children will suffer some form of child abuse.

Given these problems, why is teenage pregnancy and parenting so common in the United States? When compared with other Western industrialized nations, American teenagers are no more sexually active. However, they are many times more likely to become pregnant. The United States leads all developed nations in the incidence of pregnancy among girls aged 15 to 19 (Jones 1986). What is different about the United States? In other major industrialized nations, such as Sweden, Holland, France, Canada, and Great Britain, there are liberal attitudes toward sex, free or inexpensive contraceptive services, and comprehensive sex education programs. As Jones (1986) observes, teenagers in the United States experience the worst of all possible situations. They are exposed constantly to sexuality in the media, but are given little information about contraception and the consequences of sexual activity. Although some sex education programs are available in schools, attempts to initiate comprehensive programs throughout the United States have been thwarted by conservative groups who view sex education and contraceptive information as incentives for sexual activity.

Regardless of the causes of single-parenting, much of the social criticism of single-parent families ignores the fact that most single-parenting in the United States occurs under conditions of poverty resulting in part from both gender and racial discrimination in the employment market (Mulroy 1988). Thus, it is unlikely that American society will obtain a clear view of single-parenting and its consequences until this increasingly prevalent form of the family is disentangled from its typical poverty context.

Dual-earner family

A third emerging form of the American family is the *dual-earner family*. The image of the typical American white family in which the father leaves for work each day as the mother prepares for a pleasant day of doing house chores while waiting for the children to return from school is a powerful social myth which clashes with contemporary reality. Dual-earner families are the norm rather than the exception. In this case, white families are becoming more like traditional black families in which, because of their economic marginality, both men and women had to work in order to support the household.

One of the most important changes in the American family during the past quarter of a century has been the increase in the number of married women in the labor force. In 1960 only 31.9 percent of all married women were employed, as compared with 57.8 percent in 1989. Among married women with children between the ages of 6–17, the respective statistics are 39 percent in 1960 and 73.2 percent in 1989. Even more dramatic is the increase in the labor force participation of married women with children under the age of 6, which more than tripled during this same period (from 18.6 percent in 1960 to 58.4 percent in 1989) (U.S. Bureau of the Census 1991). Today, most children live in a family in which the mother is in the labor force, at least part time. What are the social realities that underlie these increasing statistics?

The presence of married females in the American labor force is hardly a new phenomenon. However, during the decade of the 1980s, it became clear that one job no longer was sufficient to fulfill the economic needs of working-class and middle-income families. This general trend reflects a cluster of economic developments that have eroded the earning and purchasing power of American families. The loss of high-paying manufacturing jobs and the proliferation of lower paying service-sector jobs are an important part of these trends (see discussion Chapter 8, pp. 121–122).

As was noted previously, one of the key developments in 20th century American family life has been an emphasis on the role of families as emotional support mechanisms for their individual members. Work and occupation have been understood as key sources of stress and demand from which individuals seek refuge in family life (Barling 1990; Googins 1991). From this perspective, two jobs in a household greatly increase the pressures on family life. Since most families cannot afford household help, there simply is less time available for family interactions. Although realignment of the family's division of labor would aid in reducing the pressure, the majority of working women continue to bear primary responsibility for household tasks and child care. Therefore, especially for women, entrance into the labor force creates work/home conflicts (Berardo, Shehan, and Leslie 1987).

Dual-career family

A variation of the dual-earner family is the *dual-career family*, in which both adult members not only work outside the home, but also are expected to make job commitments leading to career development and advancement. Dual careers mean the addition of a second highly demanding work role to the couple's other commitments. It also creates the problem of career coordination between spouses. When children are involved, problems are magnified for both spouses. Regardless of how household tasks or child care are apportioned, this type of family confronts logistical difficulties and readily may become overextended (Hunt and Hunt 1982).

Both dual-earner families and dual-career families must withstand a substantial external demand system. However, work/home conflicts are not inevitable. A combination of family support for the mother's labor force participation, and flexible scheduling in the workplace may decrease stress and increase job satisfaction (Moen and Forest 1990; Rudd and McHenry 1986). Unfortunately, work/family stress is increased greatly by structural constraints that limit the integration of women into the occupational world and similarly limit the integration of men into the domestic sphere. Modern American society provides few structural supports that enable the dual-earner family to accomplish its tasks with ease (Hochschild 1989). Broad-scale social values and policies have enormous effects upon social institutions, including the family. Pro-family policies such as parental leave, flexible scheduling for parents of young children, and more and better daycare centers are just a few of the practices that would enable families to adapt to the economic realities of modern society.

Voluntary childlessness

A fourth emerging family form is the *voluntarily childless* family. Veevers (1980) and others have noted that *families choosing not to have children* are, in effect, selecting a lifestyle that is very much out of step with traditional American values. American culture is a pronatalist (prochildren) culture, and families without children are often viewed as less than "whole" families. Yet, a careful examination of the social characteristics of childless couples suggests that this pattern can be expected to increase.

First, the decision to remain childless increases as the age at marriage increases. Second, childless marriages increase as the level of education of the marital partners increases. Third, childlessness increases as female participation in the labor force increases (Mattessich 1979). Obviously, each of these three factors is intimately connected to general trends in American society. It has already been noted that the economic trends of the 1980s increased the need for married women to participate in work outside the home. Typically, this entails a postponement of having children, which is a first step in the process of deciding never to have children. As Veever's research has shown, the decision to have children entails the family unit's forgoing income and changing its lifestyle. It also may involve a woman leaving a career. The longer the decision is postponed, the more likely the decision will be not to become a parent.

Some professional couples who are upwardly mobile may feel that parenthood is not compatible with their career choices. Others may not be willing to assume the emotional and financial costs of raising children. This does not mean that childlessness is likely to become a norm in American society anytime soon. However, labor force patterns clearly have the effect of increasing the pool of couples that potentially may select childlessness.

In summary, an examination of family systems has demonstrated a number of basic points about social institutions in general. First, cross-cultural examples demonstrate that there are many possible institutional arrangements for accomplishing any given set of social tasks. Second, throughout American history the family institution has responded to macrosocial changes in the society itself. In this sense, while institutions provide stability and order in a society, they also are barometers of broad-scale change patterns. Finally, a number of emerging forms of family have been examined. Each exhibits realignments of traditional functions of families and roles of particular family members.

Family: The Most Violent Institution

This chapter began with the observation that social institutions provide continuity and stability for societies. In that context, it has been shown that institutional norms are altered by general processes of change in societies. This section of the chapter demonstrates that even as they persist, social institutions can be carriers of dilemmas that seriously injure members. Nothing is more opposed to the ideal of a loving and happy family than physical violence between husbands and wives or parents and children. Yet, force and violence are a part of American family life. Violence occurs among families of every social class and ethnic composition. For many persons, the family is a place where the deliberate infliction of pain and suffering are routine occurrences. Americans are more likely to be killed or injured in their own homes by members of their own families than at any other place or by any other persons (Gelles and Straus 1988). This section of the chapter examines three forms of domestic violence: spousal abuse, child abuse, and elder abuse.

SPOUSAL ABUSE

Spousal abuse

Although *spousal abuse* can take the form of violence against men by their wives, the most common and severe forms of spousal abuse are directed against women by their husbands. More than 90 percent of all physical abuse is a consequence of males aggressing against females (Kurtz 1989). It is estimated that between 10 and 20 percent of all women are physically abused by their male domestic partners (Straus and Gelles 1986).

Spousal abuse has been linked to general cultural norms that support violence. Violence is very much a part of the American way of life, and the link between violence and masculinity is glorified in the media. One need only look at the success of such films as *Rambo* and *The Terminator*. American males generally are socialized to define themselves in terms of the power they exert over others. Studies of batterers reveal that they use violence as a way to control their female partners (Yllo and Bograd 1988). Spousal abuse also has been linked to gender inequality and male dominance in the family. Marital relationships characterized by shared decision making and household responsibilities tend to be the least violent (Pedrick-Cornell and Gelles 1982).

Why do women stay in such relationships? Among the reasons are commitment to the marital relationship, economic dependency, and being raised in a family where violence was a routine occurrence. Some women in abusive relationships blame themselves for the abuse or deny its seriousness (Walker and Brown 1985). Some who have been raised in violent families, simply accept violence as part of family life. Others may want to leave but have no place to go, particularly if they have children and are without funds.

Until recently, beating one's wife was considered to be a husband's right, and wife-beating was seen as a family matter rather than a crime (Kurtz 1989). Today, police forces are more likely to intervene in what was once considered a private matter. One of the most significant expressions of increased public concern has been the emergence of community shelters as temporary havens from intrafamilial violence. Here women are given support and counseling. However, these shelters have limited resources and are unable to assist all who might request their services.

Such long standing dilemmas will not be solved quickly. However, a sociological perspective reveals that spousal abuse persists because it is supported by the larger cultural and social structural environment in which the family institution is situated.

CHILD ABUSE

Child abuse

Child abuse is a dramatic and visible aspect of the pattern of violence that characterizes the American family today (Gelles 1978). Although public awareness of child abuse is only beginning to grow, abuse of children is an ancient phenomenon. Historically, the tradition of physical punishment freely administered to children has been an accepted way of family life. Today, tens of thousands of children receive not love and support from their parents, but rage, rejection, and savage batterings. It is estimated that in 1990, 2.5 million American children suffered injury at the hands of their parents, some of whom died as a result of their injuries (U.S. House of Representatives Select Committee on Children, Youth, and Families 1992). Researchers agree that statistics on child abuse greatly underestimate its actual incidence.

Generally, the younger the child, the more likely the child will experience some form of physical violence within the family setting (Gelles and Straus 1988). Both boys and girls are equally likely to be victims of physical abuse. The effects of violence against children are long lasting. Not only are physical and emotional scars carried into adulthood, but those who experience violence are more likely as adults to be violent toward their own children (Pedrick-Cornell and Gelles 1982).

One form of child abuse, sexual abuse, is inflicted primarily against female children. It is estimated that between one-third and two-thirds of all females will experience some form of sexual abuse by the age of 18. At least half of such abuse will be perpetrated by family members (Koss 1990). The most common form of intrafamilial sexual abuse is father/daughter incest (Armstrong 1987). Violation of the parent-child relationship in this way leaves lasting psychic and emotional trauma, hindering the development of trusting relationships in adult life.

ELDER ABUSE

Elder abuse

As the numbers of persons living to old age has increased, so too has the prevalence of *elder abuse.* Modern medical and technological advances mean that a greater number of persons will spend longer periods of time in various stages of dependency, some in deteriorating physical and mental health. Since families continue to be the primary source of care for dependent elderly, these greater numbers of persons surviving to old age increase the pressures on family member serving as caretakers. Some respond to these pressures with abuse.

Because the elderly often are isolated from mainstream society, elder abuse is more hidden than other forms of family violence. It is estimated that in 1989 at least 1.5 million elderly Americans were victims of abuse. Abuse is more likely to occur among the elderly who live with a child or spouse, than among those living alone. Victims of elder abuse tend to be female and 75 years of age or older. The perpetrator of abuse typically is related to the victim, most frequently a child (30 percent) or spouse (14.8 percent) (U.S. House of Representatives Select Committee on Aging 1990).

Some researchers suggest that much elder abuse is a consequence of stress related to caring for the frail elderly. Many families are emotionally and economically ill-equipped to provide the type of day-to-day care that is required. Additionally, caregiving offspring often must cope with the problems of an aging parent just when the needs of their own nuclear families are the greatest (Stienmetz 1988). Many caregiving families have limited economic resources. The costs of providing such care on an insufficient income, combined with the inherent stress of caring for an individual who requires a great deal of assistance can sometimes be overwhelming, precipitating abuse (U.S. House Committee on Aging 1991).

In summary, this section of the chapter has examined a disturbing feature of the most basic institution—the fact that the family can be an extremely violent institution and that such violence is widespread in the American family. Spousal abuse and child abuse, particularly against females, reflect mainstream cultural values. Elder abuse often demonstrates the difficulties that basic institutional arrangements can have in adjusting to new social circumstances.

APPLICATIONS

EXPLORING MODERN FAMILY STRUCTURES

We've already seen that the contemporary family institution in the United States has been undergoing significant changes. Most importantly, there are a number of emerging forms of family that depart from the traditional model of husband, wife, and their children. These trends warrant further scrutiny. Some useful clues about them are provided by Table 5.1. The United States Census Bureau employs a very traditional definition of "family," by which it counts "two or more persons related by birth, marriage, or adoption who reside together in a household." Table 5.1 clearly demonstrates that this traditional type of family unit was not nearly so prevalent by 1989 as it was twenty years earlier. In 1970, married couples (with and without children in the household) constituted 70.5 percent of all households. Yet, by 1990, married couples represented only 56 percent of all households.

One factor in this change, of course, has been the increase in what the Census Bureau calls "Female Householder" type families, or what are popularly called female-headed households. These households represented only 8.7 percent of the total in 1970, and grew to 11.7 percent by 1990. As was noted earlier in this chapter (pp. 124–126), both out-of-wedlock births and divorce have contributed to the growth of this type of household in the United States.

A second type of household grew between 1970 and 1990 at an even more impressive rate. The Census Bureau calls them "nonfamily households" and they constituted only 18.8 percent of all households in 1970. By 1990, they

TABLE 5.1

HOUSEHOLDS BY TYPE FOR THE UNITED STATES, 1970–1990 (PRESENTED IN THOUSANDS AND PERCENTAGE OF TOTAL)

Household Types	1970		1980		1990		% Change	
	Number	%	Number	%	Number	%	1970–1980	1980–1990
Married Couples	44,728	70.5	49,112	60.8	52,317	56.0	9.8	6.5
Female-Headed	5,500	8.7	8,705	10.8	10,890	11.7	58.3	25.1
Male-Headed	1,228	2.0	1,733	2.1	2,884	3.1	41.1	66.4
Nonfamily	11,945	18.8	21,226	26.3	27,257	29.2	77.7	28.4
Total All Types	63,401	100.0	80,776	100.0	93,348	100.0	27.4	15.6

SOURCE: *Statistical Abstract of the United States,* Washington, D.C., U. S. Government Printing Office, 1991.

represented 29.2 percent of all households. Who are these so-called nonfamily households? They are of various types. Some, of course, are couples of the opposite sex who have established a stable relationship and a household but who are not married. Others are couples of the same gender, male or female, who have established homosexual rather than heterosexual relationships. Still others, especially among the aged, have established same-sex households even though they do not practice homosexuality. Consider the protagonists in the television comedy "The Golden Girls."

The point is that the official definition of "family" describes only one structural arrangement from among today's diversity of family structures. Obviously, what the Census Bureau calls a "household" most approximates what the sociological understanding of a family is. It is a primary group that exists for the well-being of its individual members. For some people this still means a traditional husband and wife relationship. But for increasing numbers of others, this is not the form of the family chosen.

Definitions of the family have important consequences for people's lives. The idea that a specific family form is most desirable influences social policies that stigmatize certain other family forms as deviant. What distinguishes families from nonfamilies? What is the irreducible basis of the concept of the family? Is it a sense of identification, a sense of obligation members feel for one another, or emotional ties? Is it some combination of these? Clearly, some emerging family forms are centered not on biological reproduction nor primary socialization of the young, but are centered on the emotional and material support of members.

The case study that follows examines the social issues that arise when members of a nontraditional family form, the homosexual couple, seek the same social and legal protections as traditional families.

CASE

The Homosexual Family

It was noted earlier that institutions are significant, in part, because they carry the full weight of tradition and custom in a society. This is a key to their integrative capabilities. Yet, periodically, institutional arrangements in societies undergo change. These bastions of tradition and custom from time to time change and adapt to new circumstances. It is common for the members of any society to experience processes of institutional change as social issues or controversies. Changing social definitions of the family have indeed been controversial in the United States in recent years.

Gay and lesbian families obviously are not the prescribed social norm in American society. Yet, with the single exception of the task of biological reproduction the gay or lesbian family meets all the defining criteria of a family. These social structures provide durable material and emotional support for their members, and no less than other adopting families, provide a supportive environment for socializing the young. Yet, gay and lesbian families have encountered mixed response in their attempts to be recognized legally and socially as families.

During 1990 and 1991, a number of American communities, among them Berkeley, San Francisco, and East Lansing, Michigan, acted to extend health and medical insurance benefits to the gay and lesbian "domestic partners" of city employees. Similarly, in 1991, New York's Montefiore Hospital became the nation's largest private sector employer to extend employment benefits to gay and lesbian spouses of its employees. Following a model law adopted in San Francisco, Minneapolis, Minnesota adopted legislation that extended to gays and lesbians the same legal protections provided to heterosexual married couples.

Yet, the record is not all one-sided. Early in 1991, Blue Cross-Blue Shield of Iowa denied family health benefits for gay and lesbian couples who claimed to be married. In the same year, a judge in Minnesota refused to grant a lesbian the legal guardianship of her live-in lover who had become brain-damaged. A "neutral third party" was granted guardianship! In Denver, Colorado in 1990, an anti-discrimination bill was changed to exclude gays and lesbians, while a year later a statewide law was adopted in Connecticut that included gays and lesbians, thus protecting them from discrimination in housing, employment, credit transactions, and public accommodations.

Clearly, the state and city laws in the United States at the present time are a "crazy patchwork quilt" of conflicting public sentiment and opinion about the social meaning of the homosexual family. Because institutional change is occurring, long-standing traditions and customs are being challenged. The process is slow, arduous, and sociologically significant.

Chapter Summary

1. Social institutions are relatively stable clusters of social structures that share a common focus on certain material and nonmaterial requirements of a society.
2. Social institutions are like bridges between social structures and are carriers of social customs and traditions. While they are powerful stabilizing and ordering phenomena, they also can be barometers of developing changes in societies as well.
3. Certain major institutional sectors tend to be found in most societies, especially in modern ones. Among them are polity, religion, economy, education, and family.
4. While institutional tasks may be shared, a particular institution may be identified with certain key social goals or functions. The polity focuses upon external defense, internal social control, governance, and the establishment of civic ideology. Religion provides a sacred meaning system, a community of belonging, and ritual practices for celebrating shared meanings and symbols. The economy accomplishes the means for distributing valued resources and includes the subinstitutional networks of financial and occupational systems. Educational systems focus upon cultural transmission, skill training, and occupational allocation. Finally, the family accomplishes biological reproduction, emotional and material support of its members, and primary socialization.
5. The most basic of all social institutions, the family, illustrates the diversity of institutional arrangements. Family systems may be either nuclear or extended. Family residence may be matrilocal, patrilocal, or neolocal. Families may be either patriarchal, matriarchal, or egalitarian, while descent and family

membership may be bilineal, matrilineal or patrilineal. Even marriage norms may differ, as between polygyny, polyandry, and monogamy.

6. Broad scale social change processes have transformed the extended kinship family system of the Colonial period into the nuclear family of the industrial age. Today, new forms of family are emerging. Among them are the dual-earner family, blended or reconstituted families, single-parent families, and the voluntarily childless family. These new family forms reflect present-day changes in the American social structure.
7. While the family is the most basic institution, it also can be the most violent institution. Spousal abuse, elder abuse, and child abuse are common occurrences in the American family. It is clear that institutions, even as they accomplish basic requirements for a society, also can maintain patterns that injure individual members.

Key Concepts

bilineal
blended family
child abuse
civic ideology
dual-career family
dual-earner family
economy
education
egalitarian
elder abuse
extended family
family
government
matriarchal
matrilineal
matrilocal
monogamy
neolocal
nuclear family
patriarchal
patrilineal
patrilocal
polity
polyandry
polygyny
reconstituted family
religion
religious pluralism
separation of church and state
serial monogamy
single-parent family
social institutions
spousal abuse
theocracy
univeralism
voluntary childlessness

Bibliography

Armstrong, L.
1987. *Kiss daddy goodnight: Ten years later.* New York: Pocket Books.

Barling, Julian
1990. *Employment, stress and family functioning.* New York: John Wiley & Sons.

Bender, D. R.
1967. A refinement of the concept of household: Families, coresidence, and domestic functions. *American Anthropologist.* Vol. 69, No. 5: 493–504.

Berardo, D. H., C. L. Shehan, and G. R. Leslie
1987. A residue of tradition: Jobs, careers, and spouses' time in housework. *Journal of Marriage and the Family.* Vol. 49, No. 2: 381–90.

Brophy, J. E. and T. L. Good
1974. *Teacher—student relationships: Causes of consequences.* New York: Holt, Rinehart & Winston.

Cherlin, Andre Paul W.
1979. Childlessness and its correlates in historical perspective. *Journal of Family History*. Vol. 4, No. 3: 299–307.

Collins, Randall
1988. *Sociology of marriage and the family*. Chicago: Nelson-Hall.

Demos, John
1978. The American family in past times. In *The changing family*, edited by J. Savells and L. J. Cross, pp. 47–65. New York: Holt, Rinehart & Winston.

Furstenberg, Frank F., Jr.
1984. The new extended family: The experience of parents and children after remarriage. Paper presented to the Changing Family Conferences XIII: The Blended Family, at University of Iowa, Iowa City.

Gelles, R. J.
1978. Violence toward children in the U.S. *The American Journal of Orthopsychiatry*. Vol. 48, No. 4: 580–92.

Gelles, R. J., and M. Straus
1988. *Intimate Violence.* New York: Simon and Schuster.

Googins, Bradley K.
1991. *Work/family conflicts: Private lives—Public responses*. Dover, Massachusetts: Auburn House Publishing Company.

Gough, K. E.
1960. Is the family universal? *Journal of Marriage and the Family* (November): 760–71.

Hochschild, A.
1989. *The second shift: Working parents and the revolution at home*. New York: Viking Press.

Hunt, J. G., and L. L. Hunt
1982. The dualities of careers and families: New integrations or new polarizations. *Social Problems*. Vol. 29, No. 5: 499–510.

Jones, E. F.
1986. *Teenage pregnancy in industrialized countries*. New Haven, CT: Yale Univ. Press.

Koss, M. P.
1990. The women's mental health research agenda: Violence against women. *American Psychologist*. Vol. 45, No. 3: 374–80.

Kozol, Jonathon
1991. *Savage inequalities*. New York: Crown.

Kurtz, Demie
1989. Social science perspectives on wife abuse: Current debates and future directions. *Gender and Society*. Vol. 3, No. 4: 489–504.

Kutner, Lawrence
1991. The new family: Breaking the stereotype of the nuclear family. *Newsweek* (November 18th): 18–19.

Mattessich, Paul W.
1979. Childlessness and its correlates in historical perspective. *Journal of Family History*. Vol. 4, No. 3: 299–307.

Moen, P., and K. B. Forest
1990. Working parents, workplace supports, and well-being: The Swedish experience. *Social Psychology Quarterly*. Vol. 53, No. 1: 117–31.

Mulroy, Elizabeth (Ed.)
1988. *Women as single parents: Confronting institutional barriers in the courts, the workplace, and the housing market.* Dover, Massachusetts: Auburn House Publishing Company.

National Commission on Working Women of Wider Opportunities for Women.
1990. *Women and work.* Washington, D.C.: National Commission on Working Women, March.

New York Times
1987. The facts of life of teen pregnancy. January 10: p. 26.

Pasley, Kay, and Marilyn Ihinger-Tallman (Eds.)
1987. *Remarriage and stepparenting: Current theory and research.* New York: Guilford Press.

Pedrick-Cornell, C., and R. J. Gelles
1982. Elder abuse: The status of current knowledge. *Family Relations.* Vol. 31, No. 3: 457–64.

Rist, Ray C.
1973. *The urban school: A factory for failure.* Cambridge, Massachusetts: M.I.T. Press.

Rudd, N. M., and P. C. McHenry
1986. Family influences on the job satisfaction of employed mothers. *Psychology of Women Quarterly.* Vol. 10, No. 10: 363–71.

Shorter, Edward
1975. *The making of the modern family.* New York: Basic Books.

Steinmetz, S. K.
1988. *Duty bound: Elder abuse and family care.* Newbury Park, CA: Sage Publications.

Straus, M., and R. J. Gelles
1986. Societal change and change in family violence from 1975–1985 as revealed by two national studies. *Journal of Marriage and the Family.* Vol. 48, No. 3: 465–79.

U.S. Bureau of the Census
1991. *Statistical abstract of the United States, 1991.* Washington, D.C.: U.S. Government Printing Office.

U.S. Congress. House Select Committee on Aging
1991. *Elder abuse: What can be done?* (Hearings, May). Washington, D.C.: U.S. Government Printing Office.

1990. *Elder abuse: Curbing a national epidemic.* (Hearings, December). Washington, D.C.: U.S. Government Printing Office.

U. S. Congress. House Select Committee on Children, Youth, and Families
1992 . *Child abuse, prevention, and treatment in the 1990s: Keeping old promises, meeting new demands* (Hearings, September 1991). Washington, D.C.: U.S. Government Printing Office.

Veevers, Joan E.
1980. *Childless by choice.* Toronto: Butterworths.

Walker, L. E. A., and A. Browne
1985. Gender and victimization by intimates. *Journal of Personality.* Vol. 53, No. 2: 179–95.

Yllo K. and Bograd, M. eds.
1988. *Feminist perspectives on wife abuse.* Newbury Park, CA: Sage Publications.

Zinn, Maxine Baca, and D. Stanley Eitzen
1990. *Diversity in families.* 2d ed. New York: Harper & Row.

CHAPTER **6**

SELVES, OTHERS, AND SOCIAL INTERACTION

CHAPTER OUTLINE

LEARNING OBJECTIVES

The study of culture and social structure are incomplete without an understanding of how culture and social structure are transmitted to living, thinking, feeling, and acting human beings. While cultures and social structures are real, in the final analysis, it is individuals who act. Understanding the relationship between the individual and the sociocultural system is the domain of social psychology. Social psychologists seek to discern the complex ways in which individuals are shaped by their social environments and to understand how the presence of others, actual, implied, or imagined, influences the development of the social self.

When you've finished studying this chapter you should be able to discuss answers to the following questions:

1. What is social psychology, and what kinds of questions does the social psychologist working within sociology wish to address?
2. What is interactionism, and what answer does it provide to the nurture-nature controversy?
3. What central ideas of Charles Cooley and George Mead form the basis of the school of thought known as symbolic interactionism?
4. What is meant by the term socialization, and what does it mean to say that socialization processes make people "human?"
5. What are the basic types or categories of things transmitted to individuals through socialization processes?
6. What are the most important contexts of socialization in most societies?
7. What are the techniques of self-presentation used by individuals in social interaction processes, and what do these techniques reveal about the self?

THE FIELD OF SOCIAL PSYCHOLOGY

Social Psychology

Understanding the relationship between society and the individual is the central goal of *social psychology*. We already have suggested that the processes of social interaction are, in a sense, the base of the triangle of social reality out of which both culture and social structures spring. Yet, ironically, the field of social psychology that examines these interactional processes has been the most recently developed component of the sociological perspective.

The first section of this chapter examines the historical emergence of the field of social psychology, as well as its place in the spectrum of sociological work. It also considers the nature-nurture controversy which is an important issue in theories of human development. The positions of biological determinism, cultural determinism, and social interactionism (which is the leading school of thought within contemporary sociological social psychology) are examined.

SOCIOLOGICAL CONCERNS

If the European scholars, Karl Marx, Max Weber, and Emile Durkheim among them, are credited with founding the field of sociology, it is equally important to note that the subfield of social psychology has been a uniquely American contribution to sociology. This is not to suggest that the Europeans were not concerned with the question of how social structure and culture are connected within individuals. Surely, they were. One need only consider Georg Simmel's essay on "The metropolis and mental life" (1902), Karl Mannheim's discussion of the "collective mind" (1950), or for that matter, Durkheim's use of the term "collective conscience" (1893). But, the European scholars of the late 19th and early 20th centuries did not develop a scientific vocabulary for discussing connections between social structure, culture, and individuals. Such concepts as the self, social roles, identity, and socialization are the contributions of 20th century American sociologists working within the field of social psychology.

Social psychology emerged as a field of study within both sociology and psychology in the first decade of the 20th century. In fact, the sociologist E. A. Ross published the first social psychological text *Social Psychology* (1908) within months of the publication of psychologist William McDougal's *Introduction to Social Psychology* (1908). While the field, in many respects, is interdisciplinary, our focus is upon those issues and processes that are of primary concern to sociologists. What are those issues, and what is distinctive about the sociological approach to the field of social psychology?

First, sociologists are concerned with the influence of social phenomena upon the individual. If research questions are conceptualized in terms of independent (causes) and dependent (effects) variables, sociologists emphasize social factors or group variables as explanatory concepts. Although sociologists are interested in the reciprocal relationship between individuals and society, the stable, persistent features of culture and social structure such as groups, organizations, norms, and values, provide the keys to understanding human development.

Second, social psychologists working within the sociological tradition focus upon the dynamics of social interaction processes. These processes are regarded by sociologists as the most basic form of social life. Not only do social interaction processes result in social structure and culture, but they are the primary vehicle for the development of human identity. Through the interactive experience of socialization, the human infant is transformed from a biological being into a socially competent member of society. Additionally, social interaction is the primary occasion for communication through which people influence each other.

FROM GENETICS TO INTERACTIONISM

The questions that are examined by social psychology inevitably entail addressing a fundamental controversy regarding human development processes. Are humans genetically programmed at birth with predispositions to think, feel, and act in specific ways; or are they shaped by their social and cultural environments? In other words, to what extent does the field of social psychology inform the age-old nature-nurture controversy?

The dominant theoretical approach to these issues within social psychology is called interactionism. Interactionism stresses the powerful role of environmental factors, without discounting completely the role of biological factors. Interactionism is best understood by examining the two opposing views to which it responds. They are biological determinism and cultural determinism. Let's examine these three views of human development.

Biological determinism

The earliest approach to understanding the dynamics of human development is *biological determinism,* which gives primacy to the individual's biological heritage. From this perspective, social patterns result from persons acting out genetically inherited (biologically determined) predispositions, or what sometimes is called "human nature." This view of human and social development gained enormous impetus from the work of Charles Darwin (1809–1892) who argued that humans, like other animals, are products of evolution through natural selection (1859). Both individuals and entire communities with the genetic makeup for adaptation tend to survive, while those without such genes perish. This view was expanded by the Social Darwinists, among them Herbert Spencer (1820–1903), to include not only the nature of individual humans and communities, but entire societies (1898).

Social Darwinism appeared in many forms, one of which was the "doctrine of instincts." Instinct theorists emphasized the biologically determined, unlearned, and unmodifiable character of human behavior. It was believed that understanding genetically given instincts was sufficient for explaining both human behavior and collective social patterns. For example, the German theorist Ludwig Gumplowitz (1838–1909) in his work *Rasse und Staat* (1875) (race and state) explained political conflicts between nations as nothing more than the acting out of genetically given instincts. Instinct theory dominated social scientific thinking in Europe from the middle of the 19th century, and was still prevalent in American scientific circles at the beginning of the 20th century. At the height of the theory's popularity, academic and popular literature contained references to over ten thousand instincts alleged to be present in human beings (Bernard 1924).

A shift in scientific thinking about human nature began emerging at the turn of the century. Cultural anthropologists, chief among them Margaret Mead (1901–1978), documented patterns of cultural diversity and variation that simply could not exist if all human societies were universally patterned alike by biology and instincts (Mead 1928, 1935). At the same time, the Russian physiologist Ivan Pavlov (1849–1936) was demonstrating that contrary to instinct theory, even so-called lower animals exhibit substantial amounts of socially learned behaviors (Pavlov 1927). However, where instinct theory erred in one direction, the reaction to it would err in the opposite direction.

Cultural determinism

The rival school of social psychological thought would become known as *cultural determinism.* Here, cultural and environmental influences were seen as all-pervasive. From this point of view, individuals are born into society as no more than flexible blobs to be shaped completely by social forces. The psychologist John B. Watson (1878–1958) best illustrates this perspective in his well known claim that if he were given a dozen healthy human infants, he could "train" any one of them to become any type of specialist he wished—regardless of that individual's "talents, penchants, tendencies, abilities, vocations, and the race of his ancestors" (Watson 1925, 104).

Clearly, cultural determinism overstated the case of the influence of social and cultural factors in the same way that biological determinism overstated the influence of genetic factors. Both views oversimplified the complex processes of the human condition. Humans are not simply motivated by either internal or external forces beyond their control. Rather, both biology and social environment contribute to the individual's development. The task of modern social psychology has been to explicate the contributions of the social environment on human development (Harris 1980).

Today, the dominant perspective within sociology that attempts this task is called *interactionism*. Here, neither biology nor society are seen as all-encompassing or all-pervasive. Rather, the individual and society are understood as inseparable units involved in a mutually interdependent and complementary relationship. Humans are both biological and social beings. The unique genetic makeup or inherited tendencies of the individual human infant are potentials to be developed and are given meaning within a framework of social structure and culture. Modern interactionism focuses upon the processes through which this shaping of biological potentials occurs.

Interactionism

In summary, the field of social psychology focuses upon the influences of the culture and social structure in shaping the individual. The earliest perspective for explaining human and social development emphasized inborn biological predispositions. In reaction to biological determinism and instinct theory, the perspective of cultural determinism emerged. Today, most sociologists subscribe to the interactionist perspective, which maintains that biological factors provide individuals with potentials that are subject to social and cultural conditioning.

Symbolic Interactionism: The Origins of the Self

The most important social psychological theory within the interactionist perspective is symbolic interactionism. *Symbolic interactionism emphasizes symbols and meanings as the basis of the self or personality.* Similarly, symbolic interactionism depicts cultural and structural systems as the results of people's actions stemming from shared symbols and meanings. This body of thought provides an insightful set of ideas about the development of the self and the relationship between the individual and society. Today, symbolic interactionism is the leading microsociological perspective.

Symbolic interactionism

An important concern in symbolic interactionism is the issue of the origin of the social self. If biology does not determine individual development, exactly how is the human personality formed? As is often the case in scientific work, a number of scholars working both in America and Europe near the end of the 19th century began to approach closure on this question simultaneously. However, the American scholars Charles Horton Cooley (1864–1929) and George Herbert Mead (1863–1931) provided the foundations for the school of thought known today as symbolic interactionism. Their ideas are of sufficient import to warrant separate treatment here. We then shall examine developments within modern symbolic interactionism.

C. H. COOLEY: HUMAN NATURE AND SOCIAL NATURE

For Charles H. Cooley, society and the individual essentially are two sides of the same coin. On the one hand, human beings are social animals. Humans acquire an identity and become "persons" through participation in social processes. On the other hand, both social structure and culture may be understood as by-products that result from human interaction processes.

Cooley's lasting contributions to the field of social psychology emerge from his answers to three basic questions. What is human nature? How is a self acquired? Where and when do basic processes of human development occur? Answers to the first two of these questions are developed in his earliest work *Human Nature and Social Order* (1902). The third question is addressed in a later work entitled *Social Organization* (1909). Let's consider Cooley's answers to each of these three questions.

Plasticity

First, what is human nature? Cooley maintains that human nature is characterized by *plasticity,* a capacity for social learning. This plasticity is the distinguishing mark of the human infant. In using the term plasticity, Cooley does not dismiss the role of biological or hereditary factors in the development of the self. Rather, the term plasticity emphasizes Cooley's insight that the human infant is capable of being socialized into any human society or culture. Thus, plasticity, meaning the capacity to be shaped and formed by environmental forces, is the essential component in human nature.

Looking-glass self

Second, given this plasticity of the human animal, how is a self acquired? Cooley's concept of *the looking-glass self* answers this question. A looking glass, of course, is the Victorian term for a mirror. The looking-glass imagery suggests that the view of one's self that emerges largely is a reflection of how we think others see us. Cooley describes these processes in the couplet "Each to each a looking-glass / Reflects the other that doth pass" (1902, 151–52).

Obviously, Cooley placed great emphasis on the mental and the subjective processes in self-development. While the social environment is the source of the self, the individual is far from a passive agent in the development of the self. According to Cooley, ideas about the self come from three sources. They are perceptions of how others see us, the assessment of how others are evaluating us, and self-feelings arising from these perceptions. Perception is the key here. We see ourselves as we think others see us, and we judge ourselves as we perceive others judging us. According to Cooley, we use others as mirrors to learn who and what we are. However, we also continue checking our social mirror, trying out new identities and revising our self image. Thus, the self is not a static entity. It is a process of development through interactions with others.

Primary group

Third, Cooley asked where and when do processes of human self-development occur? His answer is the *primary group.* Cooley called the primary group "the nursery of human nature," because through primary group participation, individuals acquire human nature itself. Cooley realized that the intimacy, cooperation, and face-to-face interaction of primary groups engender the development of self-understandings of lifelong significance.

GEORGE HERBERT MEAD: MIND, SELF, AND SOCIETY

George Herbert Mead (1863–1931) is somewhat unique for an influential thinker. During his career in philosophy at the University of Chicago, he published not a single book. His ideas are accessible today because, after his death, students and friends, relying upon classroom notes, assembled his ideas in a series of four books. Of these, the essay *Mind, Self, and Society* (1934) contains much of the thinking upon which modern symbolic interactionism is based. Let's examine Mead's ideas as they emerge from these writings.

Like Cooley, Mead believed that social interaction is necessary for the emergence of both "human nature" and society itself. Neither human beings nor social life are comprehensible apart from social interaction processes. For Mead, *social interaction* is the *reciprocally influenced behavior between two or more persons.* Why did Mead consider this element of reciprocity so important? First, because reciprocally influenced behavior (I act toward you, and you act toward me) is possible only through the assumption on the actors' parts of shared symbolic meanings. Second, because, from this perspective, both culture and social structure are entire systems of symbolic meanings, the same ones upon which interactions are based.

Social interaction

Symbolic meanings are the foundation upon which both the self and society are based. Let's examine Mead's claim that symbolic meanings are the foundation of the self, and self-development. Some of these ideas should have a familiar ring, as they were considered in the examination of culture in Chapter 3 (pp. 68–72). Mead called those symbols that reach the stage of language *significant symbols.* Symbolic meanings, as expressed in language, are both arbitrary and conventional. Symbolic meanings (words) are arbitrary because people can, and do, invent any word as a substitute stimulus for something else. For instance, a book is called a "book," but it might just as well be called a "sink." Symbolic meanings are conventional because the meanings of words derive from how we use them, not from any intrinsic meanings. Thus, we know exactly what is meant by "book," because that is how we use the term. Symbolic meanings are important because of what humans can do with them.

Symbolic meanings

Significant symbols

What special things happen to humans because of their invention, sharing, and use of the symbolic meanings of language? Humans are able to imagine things that are both abstract and invisible and are able to live not simply in the present, but in a present, a future, and even in a past. The most important thing resulting from the use of language and symbols is the human acquisition and emergence of both a self and a mind.

First, the individual is able to have a *self,* which may be defined as *one's awareness of who and what kind of person one is.* The human self is special because it is reflexive. That is, it can be an object of its own thoughts and actions. For example, I may be angry at myself for an inappropriate behavior. Second, the individual has a *mind,* defined as *the ability to learn and use significant symbols and to think in terms of these same significant symbols.* Without the acquisition of symbolic communication the human mind is not possible. This is why it is maintained that the human mind differs from that of other animals.

Self

Mind

How are the self and mind developed in the human child? Mead identified three *stages of self-development* which he called preparatory, play, and game. In the first or *preparatory stage,* the child engages in purely imitative

Preparatory stage

FIGURE 6.1
Mead's first stage

behavior. Through repeated processes of social interaction, the child begins acquiring significant symbols or language. With the acquisition of language, the child enters the *play stage,* at which time the young child learns who she/he is by pretending to be someone else, usually *significant others,* persons most important to the child. As the child assumes the role of another person, he/she acts toward things (including oneself) "as if" he/she were that person. At this stage the child begins to have an idea of self as a social object—someone who can be praised, punished, addressed verbally, or ignored.

Play stage

Significant others

Finally, a special kind of play, the *game,* ensues. To play a game requires participation in systems of reciprocal expectation. Games entail not only roles, but rules and relationships. If you think games sound a lot like society, then you've understood what Mead is saying! The child learns that she/he is expected to conform to the rules, roles, and expectations of a community of others, or society, which Mead called the "generalized other." According to Mead, at this point the child has a self, viewed as both an actor and a social object located in a social structure.

Game stage

Generalized other

Let's return to the theme with which this discussion began. Mead believed that social interaction is necessary for the emergence of both "human nature" and society itself. Now it should be clear why this is so. At some point in the complex processes of self-development, the child becomes aware not simply of specific others and their specific roles, but of the entire system of "others," what Mead called the *"generalized other,"* or what we call society.

Obviously, at some moment in the game stage, self-awareness and awareness of society happen in the same instant. They happen this way because the awareness of the self is conditioned upon the awareness of society, and vice versa. Both the self and society are products of mature, symbolic, interactional processes. Thus, at the moment the child fully perceives society as a system of rules, roles, and relationships, the child also is able to reflect upon its self in the context of these rules, roles, and relationships. From the individual's perspective, this is called self-development, while from society's perspective, it is called socialization.

I

Me

One last feature of George Mead's theory warrants comment. Mead describes the lifelong process of self-development and self-expression as involving two components—the "I" and the "me." He maintains that every act begins with an I, and ends with a me. The *"I"* refers to the impulsive, unique aspect of every self. The *"me"* refers to the requirement that to be comprehended in society, the self must be expressed in socially recognized ways. The "I-me" distinction simply is Mead's way of saying that just as all people are social

TABLE 6.1

GEORGE H. MEAD'S THEORY OF SELF-DEVELOPMENT

Stage	Child's Activity:	Child Acquires:
First	Preparation through limitation	Language and Symbols
Second	Playing at roles	Sense of self as object
Third	Games entailing roles, rules and relationships	Generalized other Self-awareness Self-concept

animals, each person is a social being in a unique and individual way. Table 6.1 summarizes the three stages in Mead's theory of human self-development.

MODERN SYMBOLIC INTERACTIONISM

The term symbolic interactionism was coined by Herbert Blumer (1900–1987) (1969). While the term "symbolic interactionism" was not used either by Charles Cooley or George Mead, their ideas were adopted under this label by later social psychologists. Since today, symbolic interactionism is the leading school of thought at the microsociological level, it will be useful to identify here the major claims of this body of sociological theory.

First, social reality consists of socially constructed meanings. These shared meanings are, at once, the basis for human interaction, the substance of culture, and the foundation for social patterns (social structures). If a macrosociologist is asked "What is the nature of social reality?," the response likely would be that social reality consists of social structures and institutions. In contrast, a symbolic interactionist would respond that social reality consists of shared meanings.

Second, meanings are the products of social interaction processes. This claim is important because it identifies interaction processes, most importantly socialization, its contents, and its contexts, as legitimate topics of sociological study. The next section of this chapter examines these topics.

Third, socially shared meanings are modified actively by persons from situation to situation. In other words, individuals are not simply passive receptacles into which culture is fed. Rather, social interaction, the definition of the situation, and the links between persons, roles, and situational settings involve dynamic processes within which meanings can be modified. These concerns identify legitimate research sites, among them the complex actions of the self. The concluding section of this chapter returns to this focus.

In summary, this section of the chapter has introduced the microsociological tradition of interactionism. Cooley emphasized the plasticity of the human animal and depicted the formation of a looking-glass self in primary group situations. Mead focused upon the centrality and uniqueness of language and the gradual emergence of mind and self through the preparatory, play, and game stages of self-development.

Modern symbolic interactionism stresses three themes. First, social reality is a constructed meaning system. Second, these meanings are produced by social interaction processes—the most important being socialization. Finally, individuals take active roles in social interaction processes. From the foregoing it is clear that socialization and the self are two major concerns of symbolic interactionist theory. The next two sections of the chapter examine these topics in detail.

SOCIALIZATION: MAKING PEOPLE HUMAN

Thus far we've seen that social psychology focuses upon the relationships between the individual and society. Human nature exhibits plasticity. Processes of social interaction are the generative source of both the self and social structures. These basic ideas set the stage for a detailed examination of the things that happen between the individual and society. To some extent, all of this chapter thus far has been but a preface to the topic of socialization. Socialization is *the* most basic interactional process.

The following discussion examines three questions about socialization: What is socialization? What are the most important contents transmitted in socialization processes? What are the major contexts of socialization in most societies?

DEFINING SOCIALIZATION

Socialization

Socialization is the process through which individuals learn the habits, beliefs, and standards of behavior that make them identifiable members of a group or society. If one were to ask how humans know what to do, how to behave, or what to think, the answer would be socialization. Socialization is how social structure and culture "get into" the individual, the way newborn infants become functioning members of society.

Socialization is necessary both for society and for the individual. From a societal perspective, new members must learn to participate in group life by internalizing some of the basic norms and values of the society, as well as those of some subgroups within society. Socialization must ensure enough similarity among the members of any given society for meaningful interaction to be possible. New members of any society must adopt the prevailing world view, perform the "expected" patterns of behavior, and learn to assume some of the "taken-for-granted" facts about reality. Children learn appropriate ways of thinking, feeling, and acting which they then use to control their own behaviors, even in the absence of others.

Of course, socialization never results in total conformity. Each individual brings different biographical and biological resources to the socialization experience, and each individual interacts with specific family and subcultural environments. Variations within acceptable tolerance limits are allowed. When too much "slippage" occurs, however, people are apt to be viewed as social deviants, a subject examined in Chapter 7. The point here, for the moment, is that socialization enables individuals to become functioning members of society.

From an individual perspective, the lack of instincts and the prolonged dependency of the human infant make socialization necessary for survival. Without a socializing experience through person-to-person interaction, the infant cannot develop the mental, physical, and social skills necessary for full participation in social life. In other words, through socialization, human animals become recognizable as "people" in their behavioral, cognitive, and emotional features. Let's pursue this observation a bit further.

We have already seen in Chapter 3 (pp. 61–63) that like all animal populations, humans exhibit certain rather fixed needs (drives); specifically, hunger, thirst, sex, and rest. However, the ways in which these drives are satisfied varies from one society to the next. Obviously, humans are not born with cultural predispositions for appropriate patterns of thought, action, and feeling. How do individuals learn their society's appropriate solutions to the problems of daily living? How do individuals learn to think, act, and feel in the ways common to his or her culture, group, or society? Socialization processes are the transmission media for these critical social learning activities. Moreover, socialization is an ongoing process and is never complete. It begins at birth and lasts throughout a lifetime.

The importance of socialization is dramatically shown in those rare cases in which biologically "normal" individuals are deprived of it. Numerous such cases have been reported. Davis (1940, 1947) writes of two individuals, Anna and Isabelle. The case of Anna emerged in the late 1930s. She was the "illegitimate" daughter of a young unmarried woman residing with her father in rural Pennsylvania. The unwanted child was caged in a single room of the farmhouse, was undernourished, and had little contact with people. Discovered by a social worker when she was in her sixth year, Anna could not walk or talk, nor feed herself. She was so devoid of "human" qualities that she erroneously was diagnosed as blind, deaf, and retarded. The extreme social isolation Anna experienced had far-ranging consequences. Even after being provided with human interaction and extensive training over a four-year period, Anna learned only a few words, could barely walk, and developed the social skills of about a two-year-old. Because Anna died in 1942, it never was possible to assess her full potential.

In the same year as Anna's discovery, a similar child, named Isabelle, was discovered in the state of Ohio. Isabelle was about six and a half years old, living a life of virtual isolation in a single room with her deaf-mute, partially blind, mother. The mother's only means of communication was through crude gestures. When found, Isabelle made strange croaking sounds, and her behavior was likened to a wild animal.

An intensive educational program was launched with Isabelle. She not only acquired language, but mastered in two years the learning that normally occurs in six years. Happily, her formal education was completed in the public school system.

A more recent case sheds even more light on the need for a socialization experience. During the 1970s, a thirteen-year-old named Genie, was discovered in California (Pines 1981). Similar to Anna and Isabelle, she had been isolated in a single room since the age of two, was undernourished (she weighed under sixty pounds), and had the mental development of a one-year-old. Regrettably, intensive educational efforts did little to enhance her social skills, and, after years of treatment, her language ability remained that of a very young child.

Similar stories of extreme isolation continue to emerge periodically. These cases demonstrate that when children are socially isolated at a very early age and are deprived of "normal" human interaction, they do not develop those qualities or traits most people call "human." Frequently, their potentials are unrealized even after attempts at social integration. There is little question, biological factors not withstanding, that socialization processes impart to individuals the qualities that are socially defined as "human."

THE CONTENTS OF SOCIALIZATION

Through socialization, a somewhat clumsy and groping animal making strange grunts and sounds (the human infant) is transformed into a graceful social being. How this magnificent social transformation occurs may be discerned by examining the contents of the socialization process. Specifically, three contents transmitted in socialization processes are examined here. They are language, self-concept, and role-taking skills.

Let's first examine the transmission of language. As was seen in Chapter 3 (pp. 69–70), language is the primary vehicle through which culture is transmitted and learned. Additionally, the cases of Anna, Isabelle, and Genie demonstrate that social isolation retards, and even cripples, language-learning potentials. Mead (1934), of course, suggested that mind is not possible without language, and quite a bit of empirical research documents the connection between language acquisition and formation of the self (Lindesmith and Strauss 1968). If language acquisition is part of what makes us human, how does language acquisition occur, and what special things are learned through language?

The most widely accepted scientific view is that human infants possess an innate capacity for learning language. However, while this innate capacity allows the child to master the structure of any language, specific cultural learning is required for the child to gain a meaning system, vocabulary, and syntax. Thus, a potential or capacity for language learning may be present at birth, but the possession of language is not. The question then is, how do infants learn the words, concepts, and meanings of a specific speech community?

Let's examine early childhood social interaction processes. Infants engage in random vocalization. Persons in the infant's social environment imbue these sounds with meaning. For example, to the proud parent looking for the development of speech, the repeated sound of "ma" becomes mama, and "da" becomes daddy. As both Cooley and Mead suggest, the infant imitates the sounds made by the adult, and, as each sound is repeated to the infant, there is greater proficiency in the development of speech skills. While the initial connections between the sounds uttered and the reactions of the adult are vague, through repeated interaction the connections between sounds and reactions become more pronounced.

The wonder of language is that what begins as meaningless sounds acquires the same common, standard meaning for the child and the adult. The process of learning language moves from the specific and concrete to the nonspecific and abstract. In the same way that children learn specific words, they also learn the meaning of abstract concepts, such as "love" and "anger," for which there are no direct concrete referents. Additionally, the child must grasp the idea that meanings can change from one context to another. Although the tasks become more difficult, the processes of interaction are the same.

What are the consequences of learning language? Language constructs the world of the child. It influences perceptions, emotions, memory, and thought processes (Foss and Hakes 1978). Through language, the child learns not only the names of things, but the appropriate attitudes to take toward that which is named. Through language, the child is able "to know" and be known. Language provides the child with motivational and interpretative schemes, differentiating its identity from that of others (Berger and Luckmann 1967). In other words, through the development of language the child is able to think about its self.

The acquisition of a self-concept is the second major content of socialization processes. Just as words are assigned meaning through social interactions with others, so too, the child acquires self-meaning through the responses of others. The child develops a self-concept as a social object, learning to identify and to define self from the perspective of others. Thus, through interaction processes, and with the help of language, the child develops a self-concept. The self-concept is the substantive dimension of the self—the individual's thoughts and feelings about the self. As Stryker (1981, 11) defines it, the *self-concept* is a *"stable set of meanings attached to the self as object."*

Self-concept

The self-concept consists of both cognitive and evaluative components. Cognitive aspects are those identities (social statuses and traits) the individual assigns to the self. For example, people think of themselves as wife, parent, company president, and member of the church, as well as tall, athletically inclined, and interested in art. The evaluative component is the person's assessment of the self within these identities and is influenced by the perceived responses of others. Of course, not all perceived responses are of equal importance. The consequences of perceived assessments for a person's self-concept depend upon several factors. First is the saliency of the identity under consideration. For example, being a good parent may be more important than being a good athlete. While performing well as an athlete may have its satisfactions, not doing so may have little consequence for one's self-concept. Second, the significance of the source of evaluation is a critical factor influencing the degree to which the perceived evaluation is accepted. Generally, the assessments of persons with whom we have strong emotional ties, and persons who control valued rewards and resources, have considerable influence upon our self-concept.

Perhaps the most important feature of the self-concept is its dual character as both a social product and a social force (Rosenberg 1981). It is a social product, because, as we have seen, the self is formed in the process of social interaction with other people. Thus, the self, in part, is a reflection of how we think others see us. However, the self-concept also is something each person actively presents back to others in the process of social interaction. How people think about themselves influences their behavior, which in turn has consequences for how others respond to them. This dual character of the self-concept is graphically depicted in Figure 6.2.

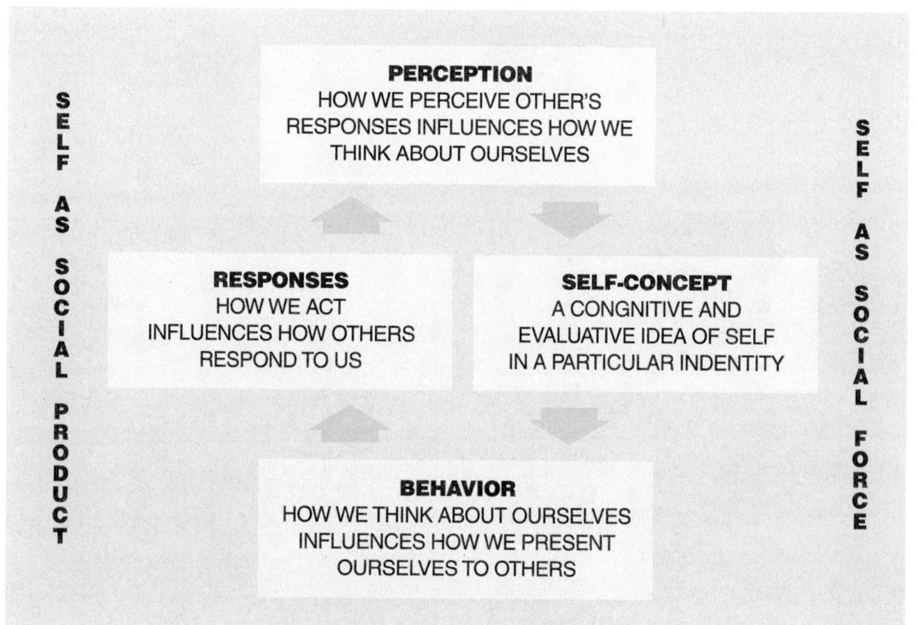

FIGURE 6.2
INTERACTION PROCESSES

The third content of socialization processes is role-taking ability. Mead, of course, described a gradual movement toward proficiency at being able to take the role of others, and consequently the ability to monitor one's own behavior. *Role-taking is an imaginative activity in which individuals attempt to see things from the perspective of other persons.* It includes being able to anticipate how others will act in particular situations and the ability to judge one's own behavior from the standpoint of others. Since roles are not rigidly defined scripts, there always is the possibility of the individual exercising a degree of control over the interaction process and how others interpret the situation. Thus, along with learning how to take the roles of others, individuals also learn skills with which to influence the viewpoints of others (Turner 1962; Hewitt 1984). This focus upon how individuals actively control role performances is a key feature of the sociological perspective known as "dramaturgical analysis," and is examined later in this chapter (pp. 155–157).

Role-taking

THE CONTEXTS OF SOCIALIZATION

Socialization is a lifelong process and, in fact, occurs in every social institution. Because of its special importance in self-development, childhood socialization is the focus of the following discussion. However, it should be remembered that significant adult socialization processes occur as well. Reference groups are an essential component of socialization contexts. A *reference group is any group whose opinions, attitudes, and values are important for individuals.* The reference groups encountered in childhood socialization have lasting effects upon self-development and may continue influencing the individual even when they are no longer situationally present. For instance, parents not only shape the young child, but also remain an influence upon the adult individual in later life situations. What, then, are the major contexts of childhood socialization in modern societies and the reference groups encountered within them?

Reference group

FIGURE 6.3
Primary socialization begins at birth and shapes the self in lasting ways.

Four socialization contexts, families, schools, peer groups, and media are examined here. Two of these, families and schools, have explicit responsibilities for socialization in modern societies. The other two, peer groups and media, are contexts for implicit socialization. That is, society does not assign responsibility for socialization to them, but much significant socialization is accomplished by them. Together, these four agents of socialization make enormous contributions to the shaping of the human animal in modern societies.

Primary socialziation

The family is of supreme importance because it is the first context of socialization and the most important setting for primary socialization. As Charles Cooley observed, *primary socialization* involves the acquisition of enduring and holistic features of the self. Therefore, its consequences are substantial for the individual (Gecas 1981). Let's pursue these themes more closely.

As the very first socialization context, the world of the family confronts the child with absoluteness. The interpersonal and situational options available to the young child are restricted severely. The infant begins life as a biological being situated in an objective social structure. The caretakers, typically parents, are the reference group for the child and the nexus of that social structure. They control the socialization experience, and accordingly, they mediate the world for the child. The child internalizes culture as interpreted by them. Whether by intent or not, the family transmits societal expectations that impinge upon the child, forming habits, setting standards, and defining roles. The child's initial view of the world and the self emerge from the ways in which these caretakers respond to the child and meet the child's needs.

Two of the most important features of primary socialization are the acquisition of a gender identity and the specific socialization contents stemming from the social class position of the family. Gender identity is the awareness and acceptance of oneself as either female or male. Much socialization in the family revolves around parental meaning of biological differences. Most parents have fairly strong ideas about the appropriate behaviors for boys and girls. These attitudes and expectations are communicated to children both directly and indirectly. The differential treatment afforded to boys and girls by their parents has enormous consequences for the development of the child's self-concept as a gendered being. Infant boys and girls start out remarkably similar in their behaviors. However, differential responses by parents and others appear to foster very different types of development (Lytton and Romney 1991).

Family socialization practices also vary by social class. Cross-cultural studies indicate that parents in different social classes socialize their children to quite different values (Kohn *et al.* 1983; Slomczynski *et al.* 1981). In the United States, parents from the middle and upper-middle classes stress the values of autonomy, self-direction, and creativity, while working class families are more likely to inculcate the values of conformity and respect for authority. According to Kohn (1983), these differences reflect the parents' occupations and their expectations about those their children will assume in the future. Working class parents experience an occupational world in which they are expected to obey unquestioningly their employers, managers, and other superiors, and they transmit this worldview to their children. Middle- and upper-class parents experience an occupational world of individual responsibility and self-direction, and so they socialize their children to these values.

Class-based differences in values are reinforced by differences in disciplinary patterns (Skolnick 1987). Typically, working-class families emphasize the overt actions of the child, what is done, rather than why the behavior occurred. The disciplinary techniques of physical punishment, threats, and scolding are implemented without justification or explanation. In contrast, the disciplinary techniques of inculcation of guilt, social isolation ("go to your room"), and withholding of love characterize middle-class families. Reasoning with the child is more common than corporal punishment (spanking). Thus, class-based values are conveyed in basic socialization practices as well as in the different kinds of disciplinary techniques used to enforce those values. In these ways social-class settings have powerful influences upon the kinds of selves that are formed.

A second major context of childhood socialization is the school. As was seen in Chapter 5 (pp. 119–120), educational institutions are formal mechanisms of socialization. Schools share with families the transfer of society's beliefs, sentiments, and patterns of behavior from one generation to the next. Similarly, both schools and families inculcate patriotism and respect for authority. However, cognitive socialization is a special responsibility of schools. Schools impart knowledge and develop mental skills and competencies. They ensure cultural reproduction in the child and thereby support the existing social order (Durkheim 1903). Let's examine some of the processes by which these things happen.

Secondary socialization

The school usually is the child's first encounter with *secondary socialization.* Secondary socialization is role-specific rather than person-centered and is more impersonal than personal. For this reason, entering school signifies a new phase in the development of the child. The young child temporarily leaves the world of the family and enters a new social world filled with new roles and expectations. Here, the adults are not family relations, and many other children populate the social environment. Clearly, this context provides increased opportunities for the development of new role-taking skills and new ideas about the self.

While families and schools share some fundamental socialization goals, there also are subtle and important differences between the socialization processes occurring within them. In schools, children advance toward adulthood by learning new norms. Dreeben (1968) identifies four of these, independence, achievement, universalism, and specificity. Independence entails accepting personal responsibility and being accountable for one's actions. According to Dreeben, schools teach this norm through definitions of what constitutes cheating and the conditions under which one must work alone or cooperatively. The second norm, achievement, denotes the ability to perform and master tasks according to standards of excellence. Obviously, test-taking and grading transmit this norm.

The third norm, universalism, entails the acceptance of uniform standards that are applicable to everyone. This norm contrasts sharply with the particularistic standards in families, where every family member is special. The child must learn that in the world outside the family "getting along" means the acceptance of uniform not special treatment. A fourth, and important norm acquired in schools is specificity. The developing child must learn that all social roles involve specific rights, duties, and obligations, and that social relationships reflect these positional elements. Thus, in teacher-student relationships, children will be treated specifically as students, and adults as teachers. The scope of involvement is not so much personal as it is positional and role-specific. This norm is reinforced by the changing of teachers from year to year, or from subject to subject. The child learns the distinction between person and role and the interchangeability of persons in roles.

In addition to teaching norms, schools also impart values. The role of schools in value socialization explains why they sometimes become the focus of intense community debates over what courses should be taught and what books should be read. This topic will be examined more closely later in this chapter (pp. 159–162).

In schools, the interactive relationships between socialization processes and the self-concept become enmeshed in the child's academic performance. The interactions between these three things are complex. On the one hand, the child enters the school on the basis of prior socialization, with a self-concept that influences his or her experience of school. If the child thinks of his or her self as competent and intelligent, school performance is likely to be compatible with that view of the self. On the other hand, schools structure learning opportunities based upon both ascribed and achieved characteristics that affect the self-concept. For example, the teacher's labeling the child "bright" or "slow" becomes part of the child's self-concept. This in turn, affects performance, and performance, in turn, further influences self-concept.

While families and schools are explicit contexts of socialization, peer groups and media represent implicit socialization contexts. They both transmit values and influence the self, even though society does not assign them these responsibilities. A *peer group consists of persons of approximately the same age and status, and frequently the same sex.* While even the preschool playgroup may be classified as a peer group, adolescent peer groups are of special importance because they are a pathway from childhood to adulthood. The adolescent peer group also is a primary mechanism through which the young person experiences separation from the family.

Peer group

Because peer groups consist of persons of similar age and status, they provide socialization contexts that differ significantly from family and school. Two aspects of peer groups make them particularly important. First, often they are linked by friendship bonds. Second, they serve as reference groups both in the normative and comparative senses. Let's explore both of these features of peer relations.

First, friendship groups, like families, are primary groups, and therefore are concerned with the entire person. However, unlike families, friendship groups consist of status equals. This explains why so much unsanctioned experimentation is allowed in friendship groups, especially in adolescence. Among equals there is less chance of the recriminations for errors so characteristic of adult-child and parent-child interactions. Accordingly, the adolescent peer group is marked by testing and mastering of role-taking skills. Here, there is latitude for experimentation with personal styles of behavior. Mistakes usually are ignored, tolerated, or corrected without much cost (Fine 1980). Peer groups provide important information about sexuality, whether correct or incorrect, not gained at home or school. They also impart the norms for cross-sex interaction.

Second, adolescent peer groups are both normative and comparative reference groups. They are a *normative reference group* because they influence the development of values, attitudes, and standards of behavior. They influence such things as the types of dress, speech, and leisure activities consid-

Normative reference group

ered appropriate (Sebald 1986). For precisely these reasons the adolescent peer group, to some extent, replaces the family as the paramount reference group. However, unlike families, peer groups also are *comparative reference groups.* Peers are used by individuals as a basis for making comparative self-evaluations to see whether they are "as good as" or "as well-dressed as" these others. Coleman (1961), for example, found that high-school students frequently compared themselves with the "in" crowd in making judgments about themselves.

Comparative reference group

This comparative function of the peer community and especially of the adolescent peer group entails some special consequences for individuals. Peer subcultures exact a tremendous amount of conformity in exchange for acceptance. Being different frequently leads to nonacceptance, and the cost of nonconformity can be quite high, ranging from ridicule to ostracism. Because adolescents have a strong desire for acceptance by their peers, they usually are willing to pay the price of conformity.

The final context of socialization to be examined here is the media. While person-to-person interaction is the most effective means of socialization, there is no question that media, meaning books, music, radio, movies, and most importantly, television, have significant socialization effects. This is hardly surprising. In the United States, the average eleven-year-old child watches more than 4 hours of television each day, and by the age of eighteen, most children have spent more time watching television than any other activity except sleeping (Liebert and Sprafkin 1988). It would be a wonder if all this media consumption had no effect.

Two of the most widely researched topics are the role of television viewing in stimulating violent behavior among children and the place of media in portraying class, ethnic, religious, and gender stereotypes. First, let's consider television and violence. Given the enormous sums of money involved in television programming, and children's programming specifically, it is understandable that there has been much controversy surrounding this research. While surely every child watching violence on "the tube" does not become violent, the research shows clearly that this kind of viewing is highly correlated with aggressive behavior in children (Ball-Rokeach, Rokeach, and Grube 1984; Liebert and Sprafkin 1988). Conversely, children who regularly view more benign programs ("Mr. Rogers," "Sesame Street," and the like) exhibit greater social control and more cooperative and sharing behaviors (Roberts and Maccoby 1985).

Second, the portrayal of racial, ethnic, religious, and gender stereotyping in media has been well documented in sociological research. The earliest work on gender stereotyping focused upon children's books (Weitzman *et al.* 1972). More recent studies demonstrate the same gender typing in television programs and movies (Garfinkle 1985; Kimball 1986; Liebert and Sprafkin 1988). Those children who watch the most television are most likely to have stereotypical views about gender and gender roles in society (Losh-Hesselbart 1987). What is the larger message of the various kinds of studies on the effects of television and other media?

Obviously, the socialization effects of media are most influential when mediated through person-to-person social interaction. It is unlikely that media alone can create violent, sexist, or racist behavior patterns, less so if such patterns are not supported by living, breathing human beings in the child's environment. However, to discount the socialization effects of media would be sociologically inept.

In summary, this section of the chapter has examined socialization processes, their contents, and contexts. Socialization is the process through which individuals acquire the habits, beliefs, and standards of behavior of the group and society. Thus, socialization is the process through which people attain their "human" qualities. Specifically, through socialization, individuals acquire a language, a self-concept, and role-taking skills. Additionally, four socialization contexts have been examined here; namely, the family, schools, peer groups, and the media. Clearly, family is the most important agency of primary socialization. Yet, throughout life, individuals are influenced by a variety of both normative and comparative reference groups. Finally, once the self is formed, its relationship with the group and society is thoroughly interactive. Just as the self is shaped by the society and the group, so it acts upon the society and the group.

THE SELF IN SOCIAL INTERACTION

Thus far this chapter has explored the origins of the self and the development of the self. The following section of the chapter examines the complex actions of the self. Specifically, we shall explore the dramaturgical framework of social psychological analysis. What are the actual techniques of social interaction employed by the self? What are the implications of dramaturgical analysis for our understanding of the human self and the role of self-esteem?

DRAMATURGICAL ANALYSIS

Dramaturgical analysis takes its name from the Shakespearian metaphor that "all the world is a stage, and all its people are players." Dramaturgical analysis focuses upon the stage of everyday life. Regardless of whether the plot is seen as tragic, comic, or something more mundane, dramaturgical analysis scrutinizes the "hows" of the performance. Dramaturgical analysis examines the moment-to-moment social performance given by each person.

It was noted previously that sociological theory explains both how and why social life proceeds as it does. *Dramaturgical analysis* focuses not so much upon why people do the things they do, but how they do the things they do. As a result, a greater appreciation of the intricate nature of human social interaction is produced. The founder of the dramaturgical perspective is the late American sociologist Erving Goffman (1922–1980), and much of our discussion of this perspective draws upon his landmark essay *The Presentation of Self in Everyday Life* (1959).

Dramaturgical analysis

Goffman's work, in many ways, extends the tradition of the Chicago School of symbolic interactionism. As will be seen, Goffman's dramaturgical analysis is a qualitative approach for examining social interaction processes. Above all else, dramaturgical analysis views the individual as an active and even manipulative participant in social interaction processes.

Impression management

The dramaturgical approach is established, in part, by renaming some of the basic concepts of symbolic interactionism. For example, the process of "social interaction" is renamed by Goffman as *impression management.* For Goffman, all social interactions, like all stage performances, are managed and controlled to make a desired impression. Thus, while symbolic interactionism defines social interaction as the conveying of shared symbolic meanings, for Goffman people engage in impression management in order to control the thoughts and actions of other people.

Teams

Audiences

Accordingly, dramaturgical analysis does not study selves and others. Rather, following the theatrical metaphor, Goffman studies *teams* and *audiences.* Team members are persons who conspire to stage a performance. Audiences are persons for whose consumption a performance is staged by a team. Both teams and audiences may be either single persons or groups of persons. For example, a teacher may be viewed as a team of one person staging a performance for an audience composed of a group of students. Parents work as a team in staging performances for their children, and so too, children are teams that stage performances for their parents. The terms team and audience are aptly applied to ordinary social interaction, which like the theater, often is planned and staged in extensive detail.

Surely, this staging is more readily apparent in some situations than in others. For instance, in dating situations, if we could see what happens in either the men's or women's dorms before the date, there would be no doubt that impression management is occurring. Similarly, upon even minimal scrutiny, it is clear that all sales situations entail a great deal of contrived impression management.

Adornment

Goffman's focus upon how impression management is staged involves studying adornment, props, and face work. *Adornment* refers to all of the things done to the human body to enhance a performance. As such, everything from the particular clothing selected to one's hairstyle, jewelry, and makeup are carefully selected aspects of impression management. Consider the time people spend selecting clothes for their wardrobes and the additional time they spend adorning (dressing and grooming) themselves. The old adage that "clothes make the man" is no longer the entire story. Today, entire fortunes have been made in producing men's hair coloring, sprays, shampoos, and jewelry. Few industries attest more to the attention to detail in adornment for the purpose of impression management than the women's shoe business. The point, then, is that there are a great variety of ways people carefully and consciously adorn the human body to manage the impression of self conveyed to others.

Props

Goffman uses the term *props* to mean any physical object employed to enhance the management of a role performance. Consider the array of desk equipment that the modern business executive has to convey the importance of his or her role. Does the fancy plaque containing the person's name and title really get "used?" Few executives open their own mail or write their own letters, but those leather desk sets complete with letter openers, pens, and calendars are impressive props. Even the fine linen napkin over the sleeve of the waiter in an expensive restaurant is a prop that does little more than enhance and dramatize the role being played. If you begin looking carefully at how people use the physical objects within their grasp to enhance their role performance, you will see that many physical objects have enhancement purposes that far outweigh their functional use in the roles being played.

Face work

Props typically are used in doing *face work,* which Goffman defines as "busy work" done solely for the purpose of seeming busy, and, therefore, seeming important. Indeed, it is unusual to enter a business office, a government agency, or even a retail store and find people doing nothing. But is the "work" people are doing really work? Is it perhaps face work that is staged to convey the impression of importance? Is the receptionist really answering a business call, or actually just chatting on the phone with a friend? Is the office manager really working on something, or just shuffling papers in order to look busy or "official?" Was the bank president really reading something urgent or just looking at that report because you were about to be ushered into the office? Was your professor really reading that essay or just doing face work because you were entering the office? After all, how many times does a retail clerk really need to rearrange the shirts on the shelf, and how often does a waiter need to arrange the table settings in his room? It is clear that a great deal of the time people engage in face work to dramatize and enhance the image they wish to convey.

Front region

Back region

Real life, just like the stage, has front and back stage areas that Goffman calls front and back regions. A *front region* is any location where a team is staging a performance for an audience. A *back region* is a location, typically in proximity to a front region, that is frequented by team (but not audience) members. The significance of this distinction is that radically different behaviors and presentations of self occur in back and front regions. In most restaurants the manner in which the food is handled in the back region (kitchen) differs greatly from how it is "served" in the front region (at your table). Most people would be mortified to see how the body is treated in the back region of the funeral home as compared to the front region (sanctuary). Automobile dealerships take great care to separate physically the front region (sales floor) from their back region (service department).

Of course, in more mundane affairs, front and back regions are not always so obvious. Students use the classroom as a back region (exchanging notes and shared complaints about the course) until the appearance of the teacher redefines the space. Of course, when the women at dinner retreat to the "powder room" together they are heading for a back region, as are the men when they say "you ladies wait here and we'll get the car." All of these situations highlight the subtle connections between settings and performances.

Critics of the dramaturgical perspective claim that it depicts an overly manipulative portrait of human beings. It is argued that some situations, especially utilitarian ones (where material gain is the goal), exhibit these traits, but that much of the rest of human social interaction does not operate in this way. It is argued that in more "personal" or primary group situations, less conscious manipulation happens. Proponents of the dramaturgical perspective see these complaints as naïveté. Obviously, the dramaturgical perspective depicts human interaction as a complex undertaking. Clearly, the usefulness or accuracy of dramaturgical theory lies in its ability to enhance our understanding of how observed events transpire.

THE IMPORTANCE OF ROLE DISTANCE

If even a minimal level of credibility is granted to the dramaturgical perspective, then it is clear that, some part of the time, individuals are quite aware that

Role distance

they are playing roles and that they are presenting a self to others. Goffman has introduced a special term that describes this fact. *Role distance* refers to *the extent of awareness an individual has that she or he is either performing a role or presenting a self to others.* The fact that persons experience role distance has a number of important implications. Two are explored here.

Presented self

Social self

First, while much effort has been expended in the field of social psychology to explain the origins of the social self, it is not the social self that other people experience in social interactions. Rather, other people experience a *"presented self."* The *social self* is the entity presenting the presented self to others in the process of social interaction.

Does this difference between the self and the presented self suggest that human beings are "phonies" and that all we see is a contrived, or even fake, self in the presented self? Such a cynical conclusion is not necessitated by the concept of role distance. However, there is little question that individuals may vary in the degree to which they wish to show others a presented self that is different from the self. The existence of role distance suggests that social interaction processes are even more complex than might have been imagined.

Second, there is reason to suspect that role distance may have important useful functions for the well-being of the self. The individual's awareness of a difference between the self and the role performed, as well as the self and the self presented, may protect the self. Life , after all, is full of "hard knocks" and "bumps in the road." In situations of criticism and failure, it is important for individuals to distinguish between the self and their role or presented self, and to realize that others are criticizing the performance not the self.

This ability to distinguish between selves and roles, as well as selves and performing selves, is a routine assumption of many child-rearing practices. The parent is cautioned to say "Johnny did a bad thing," not "Johnny is bad." There is an enormous difference. In the one instance the child's performance or role is being criticized. In the other case, the child is being criticized. The ability to make these distinctions is no less important in adult life.

THE CENTRALITY OF SELF-ESTEEM

This chapter has focused upon the ways in which humans become people. It has been suggested that symbolic interactionism provides the major microsociological approach for examining these social interaction processes. In the final analysis, how does symbolic interactionism answer the sociological question of questions—why do people do the things they do?

Self-esteem

From a microsociological perspective that question cannot be answered without reference to the important concept of self-esteem (Becker 1962, 1975). *Self-esteem* may be defined as *a person's estimation of his or her personal worth.* The human desire for self-esteem reflects the fact that most people most of the time want to feel good about themselves. Additionally, the existence of self-esteem reveals that the self-concept is much more than simply a collection of images of the self. Rather, the system of valuation called self-esteem has a structure and involves a hierarchy of concerns for the individual. It is not accidental that mental health professionals discuss the well-being and psychic health of individuals in terms of self-esteem. Obviously, there are very basic connections between how we see ourselves and how we think others see us. These connections are reflected in the individual's self-esteem.

In this context, self-esteem provides a microsociological response to the question: Why do people do the things they do? From an interactionist perspective, culture and social structure are humanly invented systems of events designed as a playing field for the satisfaction of people's self-esteem requirements. Obviously, society and culture are more than this. But, the concept of self-esteem adds yet another avenue of sociological understanding for the interpretation of social structure and culture. Both are meaning systems through which people satisfy their self-esteem requirements.

In summary, this section of the chapter has focused upon the actions of the self in social interaction processes. First, through the perspective known as "dramaturgical analysis," it has been seen that the self employs a variety of techniques to create effective impression management. Second, the concept of role distance demonstrates that the self and the presented self are, in fact, different phenomena. From this perspective social interaction is shown to be a complex process. Finally, we have explored the role of self-esteem as a microsociological response to the question: Why do people do the things they do?

APPLICATIONS

Socialization as a Public Issue

Socialization processes have been a central concern of this chapter. After all, if the basic ideas of Cooley, Mead, and others in the interactionist tradition are correct, socialization processes are more responsible for people becoming who and what they are than any other single factor. It is no surprise that social psychologists have expended considerable effort studying socialization, its contents, and contexts.

Yet, the importance of socialization processes also is widely recognized by the general public in most modern societies. It hardly is a secret that next to the family unit, school systems are powerful contexts for the socialization of children. Schools teach so much more than the "three Rs." Schools fundamentally are involved in teaching cultural values, and parents are well aware of this fact. One need only consider the large range of publicly debated issues pertaining to public school curriculum and instructional materials. In recent years, American society has witnessed heated public controversy over the role of schools in teaching in the areas of racial and gender stereotypes, sexual norms and practices, and even religious precepts.

Persons involved in these controversies struggle for control over the symbolic means by which social reality is constructed for their children. They fight for the protection and dominance of their own cultural values over competing values. Although small numbers of persons may be involved in such controversies, frequently their impact is disproportionate to their numbers. Perhaps the most enduring such controversy has been over the treatment in textbooks and teaching about evolution and creationism. Let's take a closer look.

CASE

The School Textbook Controversy

In June of 1987, the Supreme Court of the United States rendered a 7 to 2 landmark decision which overturned a Louisiana state law requiring public schools to provide equal time in the teaching of evolution and creationism. The Court based its ruling on the United States Constitution's First Amendment prohibition against the establishment of religion. Justice Antonin Scalia wrote a dissenting opinion, arguing that there was no proof that the framers of the Louisiana statute had religious motives in mind when they argued for equal time in the school curriculum for creationism. He further argued that the theory of creationism is no more or less scientific than the theory of evolution. While the theory of evolution, following Darwin, maintains that human life evolved from other life forms, the creationism theory adopts the view that all life on earth was created by God during the seven days described in the Bible. These issues are not new, nor were they settled by the 1987 Supreme Court ruling.

The conflict between evolution and creationism, and the clash of values involved in it, has been a recurring theme in 20th century American history. Basically, the issues are what kind of religious socialization, or lack of it, do Americans want their children to have, and where should that socialization occur? These are particularly difficult issues in a nation that pledges allegiance to "one nation, under God," but also maintains an official separation of church and state in the context of a religiously diverse population. What socialization mandates flow from this mixed set of historical facts?

These same issues were debated in Dayton, Tennessee in the summer of 1925 in the celebrated case known as the Scopes Monkey Trial. Young John Scopes in his first year of teaching had violated a state law by teaching the "new" and widely accepted theory of evolution to his high school class. Fundamentalist Christians objected to the evolutionary claim that humans are descended from apes rather than from Adam and Eve. Similar laws prohibiting the teaching of evolution already existed in Oklahoma and would be adopted in Florida, Mississippi, and Arkansas over the next two years. Scopes was defended by Clarence Darrow. The state's case was made by William Jennings Bryan. Although initially Scopes was found guilty of violating state law, the State Supreme Court of Tennessee later overturned the trial's findings on a technical point.

Of course, John Scopes never was the real issue. Rather, a way of life, cherished social values, and religious teachings as communicated through childhood socialization in the schools was the real issue of the Scopes trial.

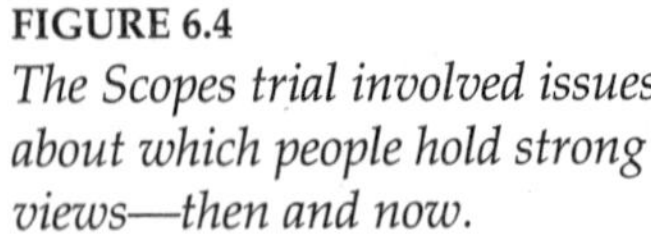

FIGURE 6.4
The Scopes trial involved issues about which people hold strong views—then and now.

Among Christian Americans, two camps had emerged, modernists and fundamentalists (Ahlstrom 1972). The modernists embraced the new scientific teachings. They supported both the separation of church and state and accepted a tolerance of religious differences, or religious pluralism. The fundamentalists, especially prevalent in the southern states, understood the "new science" as a contradiction of biblical doctrines. If modernism prevailed in the schools, it meant an erosion of their way of life and a threat to "true" Christian teachings. While these issues gradually retreated from the public limelight, they did not disappear from American life.

In 1974 the State of Texas Board of Education ruled that all textbooks used in the public school system must present the idea of evolution as a theory about the origins of life on earth rather than as proven fact. The Board's action represented a successful outcome for Mel and Norma Gabler, leaders of a conservative Christian movement of persons who were concerned about what they called the pro-Communist bias of textbooks and the erosion of Christian values. The Texas decision was important because with the third-largest state population in the nation, the Texas public school system represents millions of dollars in book purchases annually. In response to the Texas School Board decision and the continuing conflict over evolution versus creationism, many publishers of biology texts began devoting less and less space to evolutionary theory. One publisher even supplied a textbook supplement focused on the importance of religious values in American history (Guest 1987, 10). The 1974 Texas ruling providing "equal time" for creationism would stand until 1984, when a civil libertarian organization named People for the American Way was successful in having this policy reversed.

The Louisiana case decided by the Supreme Court in 1987 had its origins in a 1981 state statute requiring "balanced treatment" of evolution and creationism in public school courses. The law banned the teaching of evolution unless what it called "creation science" was taught as well. During the mid-1980s similar controversies emerged in California, Colorado, Minnesota, and Wisconsin. In all these states attempts to require the teaching of creationism were defeated. The California controversy culminated in 1985, when the California State Board of Education ruled that textbooks failing to provide adequate coverage of the theory of evolution would not be purchased. This ruling followed a complaint by the Curriculum Development Commission that 7th and 8th grade science texts minimized and distorted scientific views of evolution.

Yet, in 1987, a Tennessee judge ruled that parents could remove their children from the pubic school system if "anti-Christian" textbooks were used. In that same year in Alabama, Judge W. Brevard Hand ruled to ban from the public schools some 44 social studies textbooks because they promoted what he called the "religion of secular humanism." He based this decision on the First Amendment separation of church and state. Thus, in different states and in different court cases, when it suited their purposes, both evolutionists and creationists were claiming that the opponent was practicing religious socialization in the public school in violation of the First Amendment.

From all of this, it is clear that socialization is far from an "academic" concern. Schools often become the focus of societal disputes over values. Conflicts over school curriculum and textbooks are but a part of broader social conflicts over what kind of values and ideals should be taught to the young. The controversy between the creationists and evolutionists will not soon end. Late in 1987, an executive of the publishing firm of Harcourt, Brace, Jovanovich warned that the quality of education continues to be threatened by pressure from conservative groups and urged American publishers not to give in to proponents of creationism (*USA Today: The Magazine of the American Scene*, 1987, 11). Clearly, as long as there is a diversity of values in a society, and as long as there is a recognition that schools are in the business of socialization, there will be controversy over what should be taught.

Chapter Summary

1. While both sociology and psychology study the relationships between the individual and the group, their approaches differ. Within the field of social psychology, sociologists focus upon the influences of the group, society, and culture upon individuals.
2. Historically, the so-called nature-nurture controversy has permeated the analysis of human development. Today, an interactionist approach, which takes account of both biological and social factors, has replaced both biological determinism and cultural determinism.
3. Both Charles Cooley and George Herbert Mead are important precursors of the symbolic interactionist tradition in social psychology. Both writers stress that society, the self, and the mind are produced in social interaction. Thus, while humans have the capacity for language and culture, those capacities must be actualized in social interaction processes.
4. Symbolic interactionism is the leading microsociological approach in sociology. It stresses three themes. Social reality consists of constructed meaning systems. These meaning systems are the products of social interaction processes. Human beings are active participants in these processes.
5. Socialization is the lifelong process through which individuals acquire the appropriate patterns of thought, behavior, and feelings within their groups, society, and culture. It is the process through which people acquire human qualities. The three most important contents of socialization processes are language, a self-concept, and role-taking skills.
6. While socialization occurs in all social institutions, families, schools, peer groups, and media are among the most important socialization contexts for children in modern societies. Families accomplish primary socialization, while schools are the first agents of secondary socialization. All socialization contexts provide specific reference groups as well.
7. Dramaturgical analysis focuses upon how face-to-face interaction occurs. By studying techniques of impression management, Erving Goffman shows how individuals manage the impressions of self given to others. Individuals sometimes experience role distance, an awareness that they are playing a role and presenting a self. This concept suggests that only the "presented self" is socially available.
8. The concept of self-esteem reflects the idea that most people like to think well of themselves. If we ask why people do the things they do, self-esteem

provides a microsociological answer. Both culture and social structures may be viewed as systems through which people satisfy their self-esteem requirements.

KEY CONCEPTS

adornment
audiences
back region
biological determinism
comparative reference group
cultural determinism
dramaturgical analysis
face work
front region
game stage
generalized other
I
impression management
interactionism
looking-glass self
me
mind
normative reference group
peer group
plasticity
play stage
preparatory stage
presented self
primary group
primary socialization
props
reference group
role distance
role-taking
secondary socialization
self
self-concept
self-esteem
significant others
significant symbols
social interaction
social psychology
social role
social self
socialization
symbolic interactionism
symbolic meanings
teams

BIBLIOGRAPHY

Ahlstrom, Sydney E.
1972. *A religious history of the American people.* New Haven, Conn.: Yale Univ. Press.

Ball-Rokeach, Sandra, Milton Rokeach and Joel W. Grube
1984. *The great American values test: Influencing behavior and belief through television.* New York: Free Press.

Becker, Ernest
1962. *The birth and death of meaning: A perspective in psychiatry and anthropology.* New York: Free Press.

1975. *Escape from evil.* New York: Free Press.

Berger, Peter, and Thomas Luckmann
1967. *The social construction of reality.* Garden City, New York: Doubleday & Co.

Bernard, L. L.
1924. *Instinct.* New York: Holt, Rinehart & Winston.

Blumer, Herbert
1969. *Symbolic interactionism: Perspective and method.* Englewood Cliffs, N.J.: Prentice-Hall.

Coleman, J. S.
1961. *The adolescent society.* New York: Free Press.

Cooley, Charles Horton
1902. *Human nature and the social order.* New York: Schocken (1964).

1909. *Social organization.* New York: C. Scribner's Sons (1920).

Darwin, Charles
1859. *On the origin of the species.* Reprinted in 1927. New York: Macmillan.

Davis, Kingsley
1940. Extreme isolation of a child. *American Journal of Sociology.* Vol. 45, No. 4: 554–65.

1947. Final note on a case of extreme isolation. *American Journal of Sociology.* Vol. 52, No. 5: 432–37.

Dreeben, Robert
1968. *On what is learned in school.* Reading, Mass.: Addison-Wesley.

Durkheim, Emil
1893. *The division of labor in society.* Translated by George Simpson, 1933. New York: Free Press.

1903. *Moral education.* Translated by Everett K. Wilson and Herman Schnurer, edited by Everett K. Wilson, 1961. New York: Free Press.

Fine, Gary A.
1980. "Impression management and preadolescent behavior: Friends as socializers." In *The development of friendship.* Edited by S. Asher and J. Gottman. Cambridge: Cambridge Univ. Press.

Foss, Donald J., and David T. Hakes
1978. Psycholinguistics: An introduction to the psychology of language. Englewood Cliffs: N.J.: Prentice-Hall.

Garfinkle, Perry
1985. *In a man's world.* New York: Penguin Books.

Gecas, Viktor
1981. "Contexts of socialization." In *Social psychology: Sociological perspectives.* Edited by Morris Rosenberg and Ralph Turner, 165–99. New York: Basic Books.

Goffman, Erving
1959. *The presentation of self in everyday life.* Garden City, N.Y.: Doubleday & Co.

Guest, Ted
1987. Is 'humanism' a religion? *U.S. News & World Report,* 102 (March 16): 10.

Gumplowitz, Ludwig
1875. *Rasse und Staat* (Race and State). 1928 Edition. Innsburch Univ.: Vertag Wagner.

Harris, Marvin
1980. *Cultural materialism.* New York: Random House.

Hewitt, John
1984. *Self and society: A symbolic interactionist social psychology.* Boston: Allyn & Bacon.

Kimball, Meredith M.
1986. "Television and sex-role attitudes." In *The impact of television: A natural experiment in three communities.* Edited by Tannis M. Williams. Orlando, Florida: Academic Press.

Kohn, Melvin, with J. Miller, K. Miller, C. Schoenbach, and R. Schoenberg
1983. *Work and personality: An inquiry into the impact of social stratification.* Norwood, N.J.: Ablex.

Liebert, Robert M., and Joyce Sprafkin
1988. *The early window: Effects of television on children and youth.* New York: Pergamon Press.

Lindesmith, Alfred R., and Anselm L. Strauss
1968. *Social psychology.* New York: Holt.

Losh-Hesselbart, Susan
1987. "Development of gender roles." In *Handbook of marriage and the family.* Edited by Marvin Sussman and Suzanne Steinmetz, 535–64 (Eds)., New York: Plenum Press.

Lytton, H., and D. M. Romney
1991. Parents' differential socialization of boys and girls: A meta-analysis. *Psychological Bulletin.* Vol. 109, No. 2: 267–96.

McDougal, William
1908. *Introduction to social psychology.* New York: Barnes and Noble.

Mannheim, Karl
1950. *Freedom, power and democratic planning.* New York: Oxford Univ. Press.

Mead, George Herbert
1934. *Mind, self, and society.* Chicago: Univ. of Chicago Press.

Mead, Margaret
1928. *Coming of age in Samoa.* New York: W. Morrow & Company.

1935. *Self and temperament in three primitive societies.* New York: Mentor Books.

Pavlov, Ivan
1927. *Conditioned reflexes: An investigation of the physiological activity of the cerebral cortex.* London: Oxford Univ. Press.

Pines, Maya
1981. The civilization of Genie. *Psychology Today.* Vol. 15, No. 9 (September): 28–34.

Roberts, Donald F., and Nathan Maccoby
1985. "Effects of mass communications." In *Handbook of social psychology,* edited by G. Lindzey and E. A. Ronson, 3d ed., Vol. 2: 539–98. New York: Random House.

Rosenberg, Morris
1981. "The self-concept: Social product and social force." In *Social psychology: Sociological Perspectives.* Edited by Morris Rosenberg and Ralph Turner, 593–624. New York: Basic Books.

Ross, Edward Albion
1908. *Social psychology.* New York: Macmillan.

Sebald, Hans
1986. Adolescents shifting orientation toward parents and peers: A curvilinear trend over recent decades. *Journal of Marriage and Family.* Vol. 48, No. 1 (February): 5–13.

Simmel, Georg
1902. "The metropolis and mental life." In *The sociology of Georg Simmel.* Edited by Kurt Wolff, 1950, 409–24. New York: Free Press.

Skolnick, Arlene
1987. *The intimate environment.* 4th ed. Boston: Little Brown.

Slomczynski, Kasimierz, Joanne Miller and Melvin Kohn
1981. Stratification, work, and values: A Polish-American comparison. *American Sociological Review.* Vol. 46, No. 6: 720–44.

Spencer, Herbert
1898. *The principles of sociology.* New York: D. Appleton and Co.

Stryker, Sheldon
1981. "Symbolic interactionism: Themes and variations." In *social psychology: Sociological perspectives.* Edited by Morris Rosenberg and Ralph Turner, 3–29. New York: Basic Books.

Turner, Ralph
1962. "Role-taking: Process versus conformity." In *human nature and social processes.* Edited by Arnold M. Rose, 20–40. Boston: Houghton Mifflin.

U.S.A. Today: The Magazine of the American Scene
1987. *USA Today: The Magazine of the American Scene.* Vol. 116, No. 2511 (December).

Watson, John B.
1925. *Behaviorism.* New York: Norton.

Weitzman, L. J., D. Eifler, E. Hokada, and C. Ross
1972. Sex role socialization in picture books for pre-school children. *American Journal of Sociology.* Vol. 77, No. 6: 1128–41.

CHAPTER 7

THE PROCESSES OF SOCIAL DEVIANCE

CHAPTER OUTLINE

LEARNING OBJECTIVES

If intelligent beings from outer space land on the planet Earth tomorrow, they quickly will discover that social life on Earth is patterned and exhibits a normative order. However, as most Earth persons already know, they also will see that earthlings don't always do what is expected of them. In a word, social deviance is a prevalent feature of human societies. While surely there is a social structure "out there" with a set of rules, people deviate in varying degrees from those rules a significant part of the time. Moreover, as will be seen, deviance, like the prevailing normative order in a society, is social in nature. It is socially structured, patterned, and collective. It is little surprise that the study of deviant behavior has been a major concern of sociology throughout its history.

Exactly what is meant by the term social deviance? How does deviant behavior differ from conforming behavior? What are the characteristics that distinguish deviant persons from nondeviant persons? Ostensibly, deviance is any violation of the norms or expectations of a group or society. However, this simple definition masks a great deal of complexity surrounding the nature of social deviance.

The clearest example of deviance is crime, the violation of social norms that have been enacted into law. Yet, even here, the nature of deviance is ambiguous. Not everyone who breaks the law is treated as a deviant. For example, persons who open a package of cigarettes without also breaking the tax stamp on the package have broken the law. Similarly, drivers who turn a corner without first signaling their intention also have broken the law. However, we don't think of such persons as deviant, even if they are caught doing these illegal acts.

Moreover, deviance is not limited to criminal activity. In the United States, many people consider deviant such things as panhandling, joining a religious cult, being a "househusband," or becoming a conscientious objector. However, none of these activities is illegal. The point, then, is that social deviance is a complex phenomenon, requiring careful scrutiny and analysis. It is the purpose of this chapter to undertake this analysis.

The first section of this chapter examines alternative approaches to defining social deviance. Most importantly, it will be seen that what a society considers deviant provides fundamental clues about the ideological and institutional basis of that society's social structure. The second section of the chapter examines sociological explanations for social deviance. Why do persons deviate from what is expected of them? Under what conditions are people willing and even anxious to deviate from the prevailing conventions, and why are certain types of actions or persons considered deviant? A third section of this chapter examines some examples of deviant lifestyles. Through these examples, some of the typical social processes involved in deviant careers are analyzed. The chapter concludes with an examination of social control, the social mechanisms or strategies used to maximize conformity and minimize deviance.

After studying this chapter, you should be able to discuss answers to the following questions:

1. What is social deviance, and what kinds of behaviors are encompassed by the sociological concept of "deviance?"

2. What are the connections between social norms and social deviance? How does social deviance reveal basic features of the normative social structure?
3. How do sociological theories explain deviant behavior, and how adequate are these theories?
4. What does it mean to speak of deviance as a "career," and are there any common social processes that characterize the emergence of deviant careers and deviant identities?
5. Given the ways in which societies devalue and stigmatize deviant behavior, how does participation in such deviant subcultures as religious cults, youth gangs, or tattooing the body remain meaningful to people?
6. What are the consequences for individuals of participation in deviant groups?
7. What are the common strategies used in societies for controlling deviant behavior, and how effective are these social control techniques?

THE SOCIAL ELEMENTS OF DEVIANCE

For all scientific work one must start with clear, unambiguous definitions. It is no different with the study of deviance. It is essential to identify deviant behavior as a distinct class of social phenomena. However, this section of the chapter does much more than simply propose a definition. A sociological understanding of social deviance focuses upon not just which acts are deviant, but upon the social processes through which "deviance" is socially determined. As will be seen, an attention to these processes derives from the so-called relativist approach to studying deviance. Finally, this avenue of analysis provides an understanding of the critical relationships between basic social norms and social deviance.

Thus, we begin the examination of deviant behavior with three related questions. First, what is the sociological meaning of the term deviance? Second, what's involved in the social processes through which certain acts are defined as deviant? Third, how are basic social norms and social deviance related?

DEFINING DEVIANCE

As a starting point for obtaining a precise definition of deviance, let's consider some common, everyday meanings of the term. First, some people use the word deviance in a statistical sense. Anything that varies from an established average is referred to as deviant. However, defining deviance from a statistical perspective is not very useful. Social deviance is not equivalent to statistical rarity. People who strike it rich by winning their state lottery may be statistically rare, but certainly they are not considered deviant. How often something does or does not occur is not a sufficient criterion for making it deviant.

A second frequently encountered use of the term deviance pertains to anything "out of the ordinary." Since most people face forward when walking up stairs, we may refer laughingly to a friend who insists upon going up the stairs backwards as a "deviant." However, this use of the term is much too general. Many norms simply are not terribly important, and violation of them elicits tolerance and even indifference. This suggests yet another feature of the sociological concept of social deviance. Deviance refers to actions or attributes that are socially condemned because typically they entail a violation of significant or important norms.

Most students of deviant behavior agree that the topic may be addressed from at least two distinct approaches: the absolutist and relativist approaches (Hills 1980; Clinard and Meier 1989). Each proposes a different criterion for defining deviance and, accordingly, highlights a different aspect of the problem of defining it. Additionally, each makes different assumptions about the nature of deviance and the characteristics of persons who are deviant. Let's examine each of them.

Absolutist perspective

The absolutist perspective defines any objective norm-violation as deviance, that is, deviance is defined according to whether or not a particular activity violates written rules or shared understandings of what constitutes rule-breaking behavior. Basically, the absolutist approach asserts that in every society there are clear, widely recognized, important social norms entailing fundamental values and rules that are agreed upon by most conforming members of that society. These important norms are believed to promote the welfare of the society as a whole and to provide an unequivocal delineation of what people "ought" to do. Behaviors that depart from these standards and basic moral values constitute deviance. From this perspective, there is something inherent in a given behavior that makes it deviant, depending upon whether it conforms with, or is in violation of, important social norms.

The absolutist perspective focuses upon the question of why people become deviant. It proceeds from three assumptions. First, it assumes that people who violate socially accepted standards of behavior are essentially different from conventional or conforming people. Second, it assumes that explanations for deviant behavior can be found through an analysis of the pathological environments in which deviants are raised, or the biological and psychological disorders presumed to be characteristic of deviants (Hills 1980). Third, it assumes that there is consensus on the importance of rules. Certain categories of actions are universally seen as either "moral" or "good," and an analysis of deviance should proceed from these fixed standards.

As might be expected, the absolutist approach to defining deviance makes a great deal of sense when analyzing such acts as murder or incest, where there is clear societywide agreement that certain behaviors are wrong and should be prevented. Thus, the absolutist approach is most easily applied to those actions most persons consider heinous crimes. However, the absolutist approach is of little use in analyzing instances of changing norms, or cases where there is a lack of social consensus. As such, it is not useful in analyzing how and why new categories of deviance emerge in societies.

The absolutist approach also ignores instances in which people are treated as deviant, even though they do not engage in any objective rule-violation. For instance, the absolutist approach would not treat members of religious cults as deviant. No rules are violated by such persons. However, in the United States during the 1970s and 1980s, members of the Moonies, the Hare Krishna, and other groups commonly referred to as "cults" surely were viewed as "deviant." Precisely because it ignores the ways in which the "normal" and the "deviant" are negotiated and changeable in societies, the absolutist view is not endorsed by most sociologists.

In contrast, the *relativist approach* to deviance defines deviance in terms of societal perceptions and reactions. According to the relativist definition, *deviance is behaviors, beliefs, or attributes that elicit some form of social condemnation from others in specific situations* (Hills 1980). Clearly, while rule-breaking is an important element in analyzing deviance, the relativist approach contends that the importance of rules is not socially fixed for any definite period of time. Complex societies consist of a diverse array of groups with competing values, interests, and norms. In these social environments, definitions of "normal" and "deviant" are in a constant process of negotiation. Rather than assuming that a given act or rule-violation is socially meaningful as deviant, the sociologist must gauge people's reactions to the actions in question.

Relativist perspective

Accordingly, the relativist approach derives from the premise that there is nothing inherent in any particular social act that guarantees it being viewed as deviant. There are, in fact, no behaviors that are socially condemned in all situations and in all societies. Moreover, rule-breaking is neither a necessary nor sufficient basis for something to be considered deviant. Rather, the relativist approach maintains that all human action is situated in an arena of social settings, cultural values, specific players, and social roles. Thus, what is deviant only can be understood by examining these components within any social situation. *Deviance* is *a property assigned by specific social audiences in well-defined social environments. Thus, deviance is a matter of social definition, with the distinction between conformity and deviance being socially constructed.*

Deviance

The relativist approach asks not only why specific norm-violations occur, but also why the prevailing norms develop, and how classifications of deviance emerge with reference to those norms. Thus, where the absolutist approach examines *categories* of deviance, the relativist approach examines *processes* through which both normative and deviant acts are defined. As such, the relativist approach views deviance in society as a fluid and ever-changing set of events. The relativist approach is the more widely encountered strategy of definition among sociologists.

THE RELATIVITY OF DEVIANCE

The prevalence of the relativist approach in the sociology of deviance warrants further consideration of it. Basic definitions frequently point the researcher in the direction of particular questions and avenues of analysis. Thus, the relativist approach to deviance has embedded within it a number of important sociological insights. Let's examine four of them in greater depth.

First, the relativist approach emphasizes the highly variable nature of social deviance. What is considered deviant varies crossculturally. Even within the same culture the perception of deviance changes over time, differing in terms of the forms it takes and the degree of disapproval it elicits (Clinard and Meier 1989). Deviance can be understood only within a sociohistorical framework. What is tolerated in one society or time period may be widely condemned in another. The political terrorist may be perceived as deviant in one society, but in another is considered a "folk" hero. Similarly, within the same society, acts of terrorism may be considered politically expedient at one time, but deviant at another.

Second, the relativist perspective unmasks the highly fragile consensus over social norms in most complex societies. Since the middle of the twentieth century, in the United States there have been significant normative shifts over such things as homosexuality, premarital intercourse, and abortion. In each of these realms of human conduct, actions that previously were socially defined as either illegal or immoral, presently are legal or socially accepted.

Third, the relativist view demonstrates that not all norm-violation is behavioral. Rather, some categories of persons are assigned a deviant status without ever having engaged in an objective act of rule-violation. This is because they possess attributes or traits that are publicly disvalued. Negative reactions stem not from what these individuals do, but rather, from what they are. Consider, for example, the social treatment of physically disabled persons, or the fact that obese people often are viewed and treated as more "deviant" than certain types of criminals (Millman 1980; Deegan and Brooks 1987). As one sociologist has noted, "deviance, like beauty, is in the eyes of the beholder" (Simmons 1969, 4).

Finally, the relativist perspective reveals how the changing importance of norms is related to social power and social conflict. Frequently, definitions of deviance reflect the relative power of a group seeking to have its own norms enforced and extended to others. In this sense, social power is integral to the social processes that define who or what is deviant. For example, feminists have noted that if men could get pregnant, abortion probably would be viewed as a God-given right. In other words, the debate over the legal and moral status of abortion can be fully understood by examining the historical position of females in male-dominated societies.

DEVIANCE AS A CLUE TO THE SOCIAL STRUCTURE

Why do conceptions of deviance vary so widely from one society to another? Clearly, there is no single explanation that accounts for the condemnation of certain persons and behaviors as deviant. However, examining what a society punishes most severely may reveal essential features of the ideological basis of its social structure. What are the underlying values and beliefs in a society? Which institutions are the most important? What is its hierarchical structure? The variability of public reactions to certain types of deviance reflects an implied threat to the dominant moral codes of the society. The types of things a society punishes most severely also reveals the sorts of things it values most.

In the 1890s, Emile Durkheim (1893) observed that actions do not offend society because they are deviant. Rather, actions are defined as deviant because they offend society. From the perspective of conventional persons, the condemnation and punishment of deviants stem from the fact that they are dangerous and threaten the physical well-being of others. While certainly this is true of some types of deviants (e.g., rapists, muggers, and terrorists), many others considered deviant represent no physical threat at all. Rather, they threaten the "taken-for-granted" nature of the social order by challenging extant definitions of social reality and the moral order upon which such definitions are based.

What does society do about such persons? Typically, they must be annihilated, punished, or undergo therapy. These "treatments" validate society's institutionalized worldview (Berger and Luckmann 1967). Thus, threats to whatever seems most important in creating social solidarity will be the most widely condemned and punished as deviant. Of course, what is highly valued differs from one society to the next. The foundation of the social order may be politics in one society, religion in another, and family traditions in yet another. Where religious values dominate, religious heresy will be severely punished. Even apparently minor transgressions against religious beliefs may be viewed as a threat to the social order, and, therefore, deviant. For example, a visitor to an Islamic nation who treats religious codes as voluntary would be making a serious error. Also, in the past, communist societies gave high moral priority to the political institution, and, accordingly, political subversion was treated severely. Punishment ranged from being confined to a mental institution to physical extermination.

A society's legal and moral system also reflects the interests of those in power. Those with a vested interest in maintaining the existing system will view seriously, and accordingly, will punish acts that represent a challenge to the existing hierarchical structure. Those dominating the key positions in the major institutions, the elite of a society, are in the best position to legitimate their versions of morality and immorality and to enact laws supporting their conceptions of right and wrong.

This relationship between deviance and the social structure is illuminated by a typology developed by Joseph Gusfield (1967). He categorizes deviants in terms of their symbolic threat to, or affirmation of, the dominant social order. Deviants are classified either as enemy, sick, repentant, or cynical deviants. According to Gusfield, those representing the greatest symbolic threat to the legitimacy of the normative order are treated the harshest. Let's consider his types.

Enemy deviants

Enemy deviants, such as political activists who openly challenge the legitimacy of the normative order, represent a substantial threat. Accordingly, they elicit severe sanctioning. For instance, in the United States during the 1960s, civil rights militants like the Black Panther party, as well as other black power advocates, represented enemy deviance. Consequently, even after the government's own Kerner Commission Report (1968) declared that most of the riots in American cities during that period were, in effect, "police riots" against blacks, few people objected. This is because black power was defined by the American public as enemy deviance, an unmasked threat to the legitimacy of the American system as they knew it. The treatment of political espionage in all historical periods illustrates the same point.

Sick deviants

A second category examined by Gusfield is *sick deviants.* While undoubtedly, there are some instances of social deviance that justify the label "mental illness," Szasz (1961) and others focus upon the use of the "sick" label as a sanctioning mechanism. In other words, one way to defeat those deviants who would criticize or even threaten implicity the social order is to declare them "sick." This can be a powerful political tool used by governments to discredit certain behaviors that threaten to undermine the social order. Moreover, classifying deviance as illness frequently justifies using repressive methods of social control, such as incarceration.

Repentant deviants

In contrast, *repentant deviants* actually affirm the social order by admitting publicly the wrongness of their actions. In the American criminal justice system, repentant deviants who confess their guilt typically are treated more leniently than unrepentant deviants. Consider, for instance, the repentant drug user who is sentenced to performing community service, such as participation in drug education programs in local schools. Similarly, persons who declare their guilt, throwing themselves upon the mercy of the court, generally are given lighter sentences than those who steadfastly maintain their innocence in the face of overwhelming evidence to the contrary.

Cynical deviants

Finally, *cynical deviants,* those who engage in self-serving actions such as theft and burglary, represent the least symbolic threat to the dominant social order. Their cases are the routine stuff of the justice system, and their crimes rarely elicit public attention. These are "common criminals" who are seen as a threat only if they become repeat offenders launching criminal careers.

In summary, this section of the chapter has explored a number of basic issues concerning social deviance. Most sociologists endorse a relativist, rather than an absolutist approach, with deviance being defined as those activities or social characteristics eliciting social disapproval and condemnation in specific situations. The relativist approach demonstrates that what is defined as deviant exhibits enormous social variability. The forms of deviance a society punishes most severely provides clues to that society's most cherished values. The distinctions between enemy, sick, repentant, and cynical deviants are useful for studying societal reactions to the different kinds of things defined as deviant.

Explaining Social Deviance: Four Theory Traditions

Having arrived at some conceptual boundaries—that deviance is behavior, beliefs, or attributes that elicit social condemnation in specific social contexts—we turn next to the origins of social deviance. There is no question that order and continuity permeate social life. Yet, at the same time, in ways both small and large, deviance also is an enduring feature of human societies. What are the social conditions that give rise to deviance? By what social mechanisms are patterns of deviance supported, sustained, and even institutionalized in human communities? Why are some behaviors and categories of individuals defined as deviant, while others are not?

These questions have been addressed by four different avenues of sociological theory about social deviance. The various theories converge and diverge in many ways. Obviously, since what constitutes deviance is extremely diverse, no single theory explains all types of deviance. The following discussion identifies four streams of theory about social deviance: namely, anomie, socialization, conflict, and labeling theories. These four theoretical approaches differ, in part, because they ask slightly different questions about social deviance, and thus, each contributes uniquely to the sociological understanding of social deviance.

ANOMIE, SOCIAL DISORGANIZATION, AND SOCIAL STRAIN

The term anomie (from the Greek *nomos,* meaning order) was first introduced into sociology by Emile Durkheim (1858–1917) in his study *Suicide* (1897). Durkheim described *anomie* as *a social condition in which the norms governing social behavior are weak, conflicting, or absent, creating normative confusion.* Under these conditions, social sanctions are ineffective, and existing rules and values fail to control people's behavior. People either do not know what the norms are, or they are not motivated to obey them even if the norms are understood. Durkheim argued that suicide, viewed as one form of deviant behavior, would increase in proportion to the increase in anomie or a weakened state of normative order in society. In present-day vernacular, anomie theory explains social deviance as the inevitable "slippage" in the social system.

Anomie

Similar to Durkheim's work in France, an American version of the anomie theory of deviance known as *social disorganization theory* was developed by the Chicago School sociologists early in the 20th century (Cooley 1918; Thomas and Znaniecki 1919). While the social disorganization theory of deviance is not widely supported by sociologists today, it did prepare the intellectual stage for subsequent theorizing. Let's briefly examine it.

Social disorganization theory

The theory maintains that social organization depends upon a widespread consensus about fundamental values and norms within a society. When the consensus weakens, and those values and norms no longer effectively control behavior, social disorganization, as expressed in deviant behavior, results. In Chicago during the first quarter of this century, rapid social changes associated with immigration and urbanization were viewed by sociologists as evidence of growing social disorganization. Thus, the sociologists at Chicago and elsewhere focused their research upon street gangs, mental illness, prostitution, juvenile delinquency, and other urban problems. All of these were viewed as "social disorganization" resulting from a decline of normative values.

Many of the early studies done at Chicago are viewed today as sociological "classics," and there is no question that the proponents of social disorganization theory moved the field well beyond the then-popular view that deviance resulted from flawed personality types. The social disorganization theorists revealed the social conditioning of deviant behavior. However, social disorganization theory had at least three major flaws which led to its demise.

First, because the Chicago sociologists focused mainly upon lower-class populations in the inner city, deviance in other social strata was ignored. This resulted in the biased notion that deviance is a lower-class phenomenon. Second, the Chicago sociologists did not distinguish clearly between social disorganization and social change. For example, would a trend toward increasing numbers of single-parent households be understood as "disorganization," or change in the family structure? In other words, they failed to recognize new and emerging forms of social organization. Finally, they did not see that some of what they called "social disorganization" was actually a highly organized system of competing norms and values. The social structures of street gangs, organized crime syndicates, and prostitution rings cannot be described accurately as "disorganized." Today, sociologists surely would not label such things as the Medellin Drug Cartel, the social networks of The Bloods, or the complex social structure of the prostitution business that was run by New York socialite Sidney Biddle Barrows (Barrows and Novak 1986) as "disorganized." Later theories of social deviance would take their cue from these early pitfalls.

Strain theory

Yet another theory of deviance within the general framework of anomie theorizing was formulated by Robert Merton (1938). His approach, frequently called *strain theory,* explicitly follows Durkheim by focusing upon conflicts inherent within society's prevailing norms. According to Merton, some rules of society are contradictory, and some goals set by society are impossible to achieve. Both situations result in a state of anomie. Merton suggests that in every society there is an emphasis upon the attainment of certain culturally shared goals. Anomie occurs when there is a discrepancy between the emphasis placed on the attainment of culturally valued goals and opportunities for the achievement of these goals through institutionalized means (socially acceptable ways). Under such conditions, strong pressures are exerted upon individuals to attain these goals through illegitimate (deviant) means.

For example, in modern industrialized societies, anomie results from an overemphasis on success-oriented goals (attaining wealth, living the "good life," and having "nice things"), and the failure of the social structure to provide equal opportunities for attaining these goals through legitimate means (getting a college degree or obtaining a good-paying job). Consequently, some persons resort to illegitimate means. Merton argues that the highest rates of deviance (especially crime) are to be found at those points in society where the goals/means disjuncture is the greatest—among the poor and the lower classes. Moreover, in this theoretical context, deviance is a rational response to social structural conditions. The more a goal is socially emphasized, and the more the legitimate means for attaining that goal are unequally available, the greater the tendency for deviance to represent an adaptive response.

Merton developed a typology based on the various ways in which persons adapt to the goals/means disjunction. These modes of adaptation depend on the acceptance or rejection of cultural goals and adherence to or violation of accepted means. They are conformity, innovation, ritualism, retreatism, and rebellion. Let's briefly examine them.

Conformity

The most common mode of adaptation, according to Merton, is *conformity,* pursuing culturally approved goals through legitimate means. Regardless of whether or not a person objectively has an opportunity to achieve culturally approved goals through legitimate means, most individuals continue to accept the goals and abide by the rules of attainment.

Ritualism

A second response is *ritualism,* a mode of adaptation in which a person accepts the legitimacy of socially prescribed means, but has "given up" or rejected achieving the goals. This is the person who appears to be most concerned with overconforming to the rules, like that of the bureaucrat just doing her/his job. Although Merton describes this response as a deviant adaptation, such behavior is not likely to be recognized and socially defined as deviant.

Innovation

Innovation results when persons accept the socially prescribed goals (I want a job with a good salary) but reject legitimate means that are not available to them (I can't afford to go to college, and without a degree I won't get a good job). Under these conditions, Merton argues, there is a tendency to "innovate"—to succeed by illegitimate means. For example, the con artist attempts to obtain the "good life," (a legitimate goal) but does so through deception and misrepresentation (an innovative, but illegal method of adaptation). Similarly, women who see their chances of economic success limited by poorly paid jobs may resort to prostitution as a means of getting ahead—an innovative mode of adaptation.

Retreatism

Another deviant mode of adaptation is simply to "drop out" from both the culturally shared goals and institutionalized means. This is called *retreatism.* Here, a wide assortment of behaviors commonly viewed as deviant are encountered. Drug addicts, skid row alcoholics, and some persons joining religious communes would be classified as retreatists. Clearly, during the 1970s many persons who joined Hare Krishna, or followed the late Bhagwan Shree Rajneesh had given up on American society and were viewed as deviant.

Rebellion

Finally, Merton considers the pattern of *rebellion.* Here, both socially prescribed goals and means are rejected in favor of overt attempts to change the social system by substituting new goals in place of existing ones and by restructuring the means of attaining them. For example, revolutionaries and terrorists seek to change the social order through overtly dramatic means.

Although Merton's theory of anomie offers a perspective for understanding the occurrence of a broad range of certain forms of deviance, it excludes from consideration many others. As Clinard and Meier observe (1989), Merton's version of anomie theory has been debated widely. Here are three of the major criticisms of Merton's approach.

First, Merton's view that deviance is a response to structural strains resulting from poor means-ends alignment, just like social disorganization theory, overemphasizes lower-class deviance. It is argued that poor people become deviant because of blocked opportunity structures. Anomie theory does not focus on deviance in other strata where the means-ends disjuncture is not present and, thus, does not explain deviance in these social strata. For example, the banking crisis in the late 1980s and early 1990s was created, in part, by wealthy persons who had special access to lending institutions and loan officers. Their deviant and fraudulent actions were facilitated by unique access to means, not deprivation of means. The same may be said of persons who engaged in stock market manipulation and illegal junk bond dealings during this same period.

Second, the theory also oversimplifies the reasons for deviance. It fails to recognize that what is considered deviant may have very different meanings

TABLE 7.1

DEVIANCE AS MODES OF ADAPTATION

Adaptation Modes:	Cultural Goals:	Prescribed Means:
Conformity	+	+
Innovation	+	–
Ritualism	–	+
Retreatism	–	–
Rebellion	+/–	+/–

SOURCE: *Adapted from Robert Merton, "Social structure and anomie" (1938).*

for those so defined. For example, drugs may be used for kicks or as part of a religious ritual (as in the case for the Rastifarians) rather than as a retreat from society.

Finally, the role of deviant subcultures or groups in influencing and supporting certain activities is not considered. For example, the middle-class college student who cheats on exams is behaving in an innovative way, but surely not because legitimate means are unavailable. It's not quite that simple. The college student surely is deviant and innovative, but does not suffer the strain of a blocked opportunity structure. From the student's perspective, cheating may be a very rational and efficient strategy of test-taking. The student relies upon a student culture and a support group in opting for this sort of deviant behavior.

Perhaps another way of stating the problems inherent in anomie theories of deviance is to note that they leave unanswered the question of *how* situations conducive to deviance get translated into action. What are the links between social structural conditions and a deviant response? In other words, what processes lead persons to choose deviance over conformity as a mode of adaptation to structural strains? A scrutiny of these factors is not central to anomie theory. They are, however, key elements in socialization theories of deviance.

SOCIALIZATION AND DIFFERENTIAL ASSOCIATION

The socialization theories of deviance, alternately known as learning theories, apply much of what is known about socialization in normative cultural settings (Chapter 6) to the study of deviance. As we've already noted, the primary mode of adaptation to a goals-means disjuncture is not deviance, but conformity. Relatively few persons whose chances for success are blocked become thieves. Additionally, not all persons who engage in deviant behavior have blocked opportunity structures. The idea behind socialization theories is that people learn deviance in the same way they learn normative behavior—through interaction with other people. Thus, for deviance to occur, people must learn ideas that favor deviant actions.

Socialization theories

Socialization theories maintain that like normative behavior, deviance is something taught and learned in primary group settings, as well as through secondary agents of socialization like schools, peer and work groups, and the media. Moreover, not only is deviant behavior taught and learned, but the justifications and rationalizations for these nonconforming actions are learned as well. Cheating may be "O.K." because "no one gets hurt," and robbery is acceptable because "society is not fair anyway." Taking drugs is reasonable because "I'm the only one who might get hurt," and stealing stationary supplies at the office is fine because "everyone does it." Similarly, joining a street gang or a controversial religious cult simply is an exercise of freedom of choice. "It doesn't involve anyone else."

Differential association

The idea that socialization processes may explain deviant conduct initially was formulated by Edwin Sutherland, who argued that deviance, like conformity, is learned through association with others. His *theory of differential association* (1939) *emphasized the importance of the social structure and interactional processes involved in the learning of any behavior, deviant as well as conforming.* Sutherland observed that during the course of a lifetime, people are exposed to values, attitudes, and beliefs both favorable and unfavorable to violation of the law. If our patterns of association favor conformity to conventional norms, then we will likely be conformists. If, on the other hand, our patterns of association are with those who deviate from conventional norms, there is a greater likelihood for engaging in deviant activities.

Thus, one learns to be a thief or a drug dealer in the same way one learns to be a lawyer or a teacher. When an individual's patterns of association with persons who engage in deviant behavior outweigh the influence of associations with persons who abide by the norms, there is a greater tendency for deviance. Whether the person internalizes norms emphasizing conformity or deviance depends upon the significance that associations and social relationships have for the individual. Significant others (see discussion Chapter 6, pp. 143–144) provide the individual with motivation and support for their violating or obeying socially acceptable norms.

Although Sutherland's theory was developed primarily as a way of understanding criminal behavior, it is equally useful for understanding noncriminal deviance (Akers 1985). Later in this chapter, we shall examine studies in which socialization theory explains why some persons join exotic religious cults, and why others cover their bodies with tattoos. Both are nonconforming, though not criminal, deviant careers that involve strong socialization and subcultural support systems.

Socialization theory emphasizes that what is conforming from the perspective of one group may be nonconforming from the perspective of another. It also helps explain why some "recovering deviants" fall back into their old behaviors after rejoining those primary groups from whom they receive support for their deviant activities. However, the theory is not without its limitations. For example, it fails to explain why some persons, despite their primary association with others who are deviant, fail to become deviants themselves. For example, many children raised in high-crime areas never become criminals. It also fails to address the question of why certain noncriminal activities are defined as deviant in the first place. Like all theories, it is better equipped to answer some questions than others.

CONFLICT, POWER, AND POLITICS

The conflict approach to deviance focuses more upon the categories of deviance itself than upon why people engage in deviant activity (Clinard and Meier 1989). Of particular interest to conflict theorists is the origin of norms that define certain acts as deviant. Major questions addressed by conflict theorists are, why are the norms of only some groups made into laws, and why are the laws enforced more against some than others (Liska 1981)?

Many of the ideas of the conflict perspective are grounded in Marxist theory. Karl Marx viewed society as being composed primarily of two competing strata with incompatible economic interests. These two strata, the bourgeoisie (capitalists) and the proletariat (workers), differ in terms of power and resources. According to *conflict theorists, societal definitions and the treatment of deviance, particularly crime, are a consequence of these social inequalities.* Indeed, some criminologists argue that most of what constitutes crime and the penalties for criminal action, are consequences of certain segments of society having greater power to shape criminal policy than others (Quinney 1977).

Conflict theory

Those in power, for example, are likely to define street crime as more reprehensible than corporate crime. Thus, the person who robs someone in the street of a few dollars is more likely to go to prison than the corporate executives at Eastern Airlines who, during the early 1990s, falsified maintenance records in order to enhance profits. What becomes defined as the most serious crimes is a reflection of social class distinctions. Deviance is behavior that conflicts with the interests of those having the greatest power and the greatest resources to shape public opinion and public policy. From this perspective, the legal system is a tool by which those who rule are able to exercise power over those who are ruled (Beirne and Quinney 1982).

Conflict theorists argue that officially recorded crime rates, which are highest among the lower classes, obscure the amount of crime committed by those in the upper classes. Quinney (1975) relates this both to differences in the distribution of opportunities to engage in types of deviance, and to differences in the ability to control ideas about what constitutes deviance. Specifically, powerless persons have more opportunity to engage in *high consensus deviance.* These so-called street crimes are viewed by the majority of conforming people as deviant. Conversely, powerful people have more opportunity to engage in *low-consensus deviance,* so-called elite deviance, about which there is far less agreement. The reason for the low consensus, according to conflict theorists, is the greater ability of those in power to shape public opinion. For example, deliberate manufacturing of faulty automobiles is likely to be seen as less deviant than a mugging in the street, even though the potential for violent death is greater in the first instance than the second.

High consensus deviance

Low consensus deviance

Additionally, conflict theorists observe that even when powerful persons are caught, their punishment is likely to be less severe than that of powerless persons. Poor persons and socially powerless ethnic or racial communities receive the harshest treatment in the American criminal justice system. Persons committing conventional crimes (robbery, prostitution, or vagrancy) are much more likely to be arrested, convicted, and sentenced to long prison terms than persons committing white-collar and corporate crimes (Reiman 1984). For instance, during the 1980s the brokerage firm of E. F. Hutton perpetrated a complex check floating scheme, in which they wrote checks against insufficient funds (an illegal activity). The scheme allowed the firm to use money it never had by maximizing "the float," the time between check writing and check cashing through the banking system. The United States Justice Department under the Reagan administration simply agreed not to prosecute E. F. Hutton, a favor for the powerful by the powerful. Yet, there are persons serving time in prison today for this very activity, and involving far less money.

Conflict theory makes a useful contribution to the study of deviance by emphasizing the inconsistencies and contradictions in the making and enforcement of rules. It also prompts an examination of different types of deviance common to different social classes. It shows the ability of the powerful to influence what is considered deviant. However, it does not attempt to explain why individuals engage in nonconforming activity in the first place.

LABELING THEORY

Labeling theory

The fourth, and final, theoretical approach to be examined here is labeling theory. *Labeling theory* maintains that the key feature of deviance in society is the actual act by which some people label others as deviant. From this perspective, *deviants are those to whom a label has been applied successfully* (Becker 1963). The labeling approach is the most recently formulated theory of deviant behavior and borrows many of its basic ideas from both conflict theory and the general theory of symbolic interactionism. It focuses upon how definitions of deviance arise through social interaction processes. Thus, it is not simply the act, but also the social situation, and the reaction of a social audience that shape definitions of deviance. Some important questions are addressed by labeling theorists. Why do certain people and acts become labeled deviant while others do not? Who has the power to attach labels? What are the consequences of being labeled deviant for the future behavior and self-concept of persons so labeled?

Labeling theory takes its initial cues from an important fact already noted in our discussion of other theories. Although the deviant label frequently is related to specific norm-violating behavior, there are also many instances when the application of the label "deviant" has no direct connection to deviant activity. Some persons, for reasons quite apart from norm-violating behavior, are labeled as deviant. In these cases, certain cues, attributes of the actors, or features of the situation, lead to the defining of persons as deviant.

Consider, for the moment, two such cases. First, teenagers with severe cases of acne, obesity, or other variations from prevailing standards of beauty may be shunned by their peers, rejected for employment, and generally relegated to the role of outsiders (Millman 1980). Such persons, in common parlance, are shunned because they are fat, or perceived as ugly, not because of their willful behaviors. Second, being seen with a drug dealer, even if one does not use or sell drugs, may be sufficient to result in the application of a deviant label. Here "guilt by association" emphasizes the situational factors that generate the social perception of a deviant status.

The successful application of a deviant label has far-reaching consequences. Once a deviant label has been applied, it stigmatizes persons, and places them in a socially devalued category. According to Goffman (1963), a stigma represents a "spoiled identity," and is based upon a characteristic that others find unusual, unpleasant, or morally offensive. The term *stigma refers to any attribute that is deeply discrediting, thus making persons different from others, and of a less desirable kind.* The individual is diminished from a whole person to one who is tainted and discounted—that is, persons are treated primarily in terms of their presumed membership in the devalued category, not as individuals.

Stigma

Additionally, generalizations, however erroneous, are made about the character of persons labeled as deviant. For example, drug addicts may be perceived as thieves as well. Fat people are alleged to exhibit unpleasant personality traits. Political deviants, as we've already noted, may be viewed as mentally deranged (sick). Devalued categorization is a way of socially creating we-they distinctions. It justifies placing as much social distance as possible between so-called normals and deviants (Adam 1978).

Labeling theorists distinguish between *primary deviance* and *secondary deviance* (Lemert 1967). This distinction hinges on the question of the importance of the deviant status for the identity and lifestyle of persons so labeled. *The primary deviant is one who commits deviant acts, while continuing to occupy a conventional status and role. The secondary deviant is someone who has become labeled as a deviant, and through a series of individual adaptations made in response to this label, adopts a deviant identity and role.* Let's examine both types.

Primary deviance

Secondary deviance

Any person may steal, engage in some form of sexual deviance, cheat, use drugs, or commit any number of specific actions understood as socially deviant. In fact, many "average citizens" commit isolated deviant acts from time to time. However, this does not make them "deviants." For instance, many people frequently drive over the legal speed limit, smoke in places where "no smoking" signs are posted, or drop small pieces of litter on the ground. These isolated acts are both deviant and illegal. Moreover, most persons at some time have engaged in even more serious norm-violations. Consider for instance, the number of persons, who at least once, have engaged in shoplifting. Such behavior may remain undetected, or even may be excused both by one's self and others. To the extent that these deviant acts remain incidental to one's life situation, and do not affect one's self-concept, they remain primary deviance.

In a compelling study of adolescent boys, sociologist Albert Reiss (1961) has demonstrated exactly how primary deviance operates. These youngsters participated in homosexual acts but rationalized and justified their actions in ways that did not disturb their identities as heterosexuals. Similarly, it is not uncommon for business persons in the United States convicted of tax evasion to escape the stigma of being labeled deviant. They seem to have been operating according to socially acceptable standards. The crime lies in getting caught, not in the deed itself. Financial fines and possible imprisonment notwithstanding, the deviant activity has few consequences for the perpetrator's self-image as a conforming member of society. This too is primary deviance.

In contrast, in secondary deviance, the status of being deviant is reinforced because the relationship between the person and the larger community centers on the deviant label. In such cases, a self-fulfilling prophecy may emerge. Persons modify their self-concept and future behavior in accordance with the deviant label. Moreover, as opportunities for socially legitimate actions decrease, such persons may embark upon deviant careers. A *deviant career* exists *when an individual's involvement in and identity with a deviant subculture becomes a predominant focus of her/his lifestyle.* Persons may gravitate toward others similarly defined and may participate in deviant subcultures that offer social support for the deviant role.

Deviant career

Frequently, the very sanctioning and social control techniques that are intended to deter deviance have the effect of stabilizing the deviant role. For example, not only are prison systems efficient crime schools, places where those who have been assigned a criminal identity can learn further criminal skills, but the stigma attached to being an ex-felon frequently precludes integration back into conforming society. There are many sociological studies of persons who adopt deviant identities and develop deviant careers, including studies of con men (Maurer 1949), hustlers (Polsky 1967), drug users (Becker 1963), racketeers (Gardiner 1970), religious cultists (Lofland 1966), hit men (Levi 1981), drug traffikers (Adler and Adler 1983), and graffiti artists (Lachmann 1988).

A related focus of labeling theory is the question of who is most likely to be successfully labeled? Along with conflict theory, labeling theory examines how social inequalities influence the assignment of deviant labels. Labeling theory focuses upon the significant role played by social control and social power in determining who and what is deviant, who creates the rules for defining deviance, and how certain individuals and groups are targeted for labeling.

As we've already seen, ultimately, who is defined as deviant is a question of social, political, and economic power. As Schur maintains (1980, 1984), powerful persons are better able to deflect the deviant label. The overrepresentation of powerless groups in deviant categories reflects this fact. For instance, Scott (1969) identifies a variety of negative social patterns, having nothing to do with the inability to see, that are imposed upon blind persons. The result is the adoption of a deviant career centered around the societal definition of blindness.

From these several avenues of analysis it should be clear that secondary rather than primary deviance has absorbed the attention and concern of labeling theorists. The concentration of labeling theory upon secondary deviance derives from the focus upon the interactive processes through which social deviance occurs.

BRINGING THEORIES TOGETHER: AN ASSESSMENT

This section of the chapter has examined some central themes in and critiques of four different avenues of sociological theorizing on social deviance. Obviously, each of these theories asks slightly different questions, and therefore, provides a different body of information about social deviance.

Why is there deviance in societies? Three of these theory traditions provide related answers. First, anomie theories suggest that under various conditions social norms do not supply the degree of social cohesion they might. Nonconforming behaviors result. From a different perspective, both labeling theory and conflict theory suggest that in any society, powerful interests will suppress and stigmatize persons whose values, conduct, or very existence in some manner threaten the interests of the dominant classes.

Of course, the question "why is there deviance?" if asked a bit differently, might yield a different answer. Why do individuals select either criminal or nonconforming conduct? If the question is asked in this manner, both socialization theories and labeling theory are especially useful. The more individuals can justify, rationalize, and find social support for departing from normative patterns, the more likely they are to do so. Patterns of differential association, subcultural socialization, and even deviant careers and lifestyles are entirely explainable.

Each of the four theoretical traditions examined in this section of the chapter sheds a different light on patterns of social deviance. The major theories of social deviance, their respective explanations of why deviance occurs, and the types of deviance upon which they focus are summarized in Table 7.2. Together these theories provide an assortment of empirically testable claims about both criminal and nonconforming forms of deviance. To be sure, no single theory explains all forms of social deviance. Perhaps it is unrealistic to expect them to do so. After all, we've seen that there are very significant and meaningful differences between types of social deviance. Why should all types be explained by a single theory?

In summary, there are four major theory traditions used in the sociological study of deviance. Anomie theories, including social disorganization and social strain theories are important because they locate the causes of social deviance not within the individual, but within the prevailing social structural conditions. Socialization theories, including the theory of differential associa-

TABLE 7.2

SOCIOLOGICAL THEORIES OF DEVIANCE COMPARED

Theory:	Deviance Results From:	Types of Deviance Best Explained:
ANOMIE	Weakened social norms	Lower-class deviance
STRAIN THEORY	Means-ends disjunctures	Lower-class deviance
SOCIALIZATION	Learning alternative values and roles	Criminal behavior Delinquent gangs Deviant subcultures
CONFLICT	Structured inequalities in societies	High-concensus deviance Political crime
LABELING	Societal definitions and reactions to them	Secondary deviance Deviant careers

tion, contribute the notion that patterns of deviance are socially produced through the very same processes of social interaction that result in social conformity.

The social conflict theory of deviance focuses upon the extent to which social power and political forces are involved in defining who and what is "deviant" in a society. Finally, the labeling theory examines not simply who is "deviant," but how the label "deviant" is socially assigned, and how those so labeled react to that assignment. Together these four major avenues of theory provide a substantial body of explanatory information about social deviance.

EXPLORING DEVIANT CAREERS AND PROCESSES

Subculture

The following section of this chapter explores three case examples of deviant subcultures. They are religious cults, juvenile street gangs, and people who tattoo their bodies. A *subculture* exists when *persons routinely act upon beliefs, values, and a lifestyle that differ in socially significant respects from that of the dominant culture.* Most modern societies contain many different types of subcultures: religious, occupational, ethnic, political, and others. Obviously, our concern here is with deviant subcultures, those that are focused upon beliefs, values, or lifestyles that are the objects of some degree of condemnation by the dominant culture.

Social enclosure

The three deviant subcultures examined here, the religious cult, the street gang, and the subculture of tattooing, exhibit different degrees of social enclosure. The term *social enclosure* refers to *the degree of separateness of the social structures in which the subculture is found.* The religious cult, for instance, often constructs a completely separate social community that lives apart from the host society. As a sort of minisociety within society, the religious cult represents a very high degree of social enclosure. Street gangs, of course, have criteria for membership, and even rituals of initiation. However, while members do spend significant time together, usually they do not engage in communal living the way cult members do. Their social structures provide less social enclosure than do communal religious cults. Of the three deviant subcultures examined here, the tattooing subculture exhibits the least degree of social enclosure. The only requirement for subculture membership is the possession of a tattoo. While members may spend substantial time together at meetings and other social gatherings, most of their daily activities are spent in a nontattooed society.

Why is the degree of social enclosure an important sociological issue? The very social mechanisms that provide social enclosure at the collective level may be analyzed in terms of a deviant career at the individual level. As we've already noted, the term deviant career refers to the individual's progressive involvement in and identity with, the deviant subculture. A deviant career involves the individual's progressive self-identification with, for example, The Bloods, The Moonies, The Jesus People, or members of the tattoo subculture. The sociological concepts of social enclosure and a deviant career will prove useful as we focus upon several key questions about these deviant subcultures.

For each of these three deviant subcultures some key sociological questions are asked. Who joins? Why do these people engage in deviant behavior? Through what social processes do they begin their deviant careers, and what does this kind of social involvement mean to them? Finally, what are the consequences of these deviant careers for the individuals involved?

RELIGIOUS CULTS: HIGH SOCIAL ENCLOSURE

Most Americans claim a preference for, or an affiliation with, some type of religious organization. The 1992 *Yearbook of American and Canadian Churches* claims over 145,000,000 adult "believers" in mainstream denominations (Protestants, Catholics, and Jews) in the United States (National Council of Churches of Christ 1992). Yet, deviant religious communities and religious cults also have flourished from time to time in American history. During the 19th century, a large number of religious communes formed a variety of socioreligious experiments, many of them attempting to create the ideal communist or socialist society (Kanter 1972). Some of these, like the Oneida community in New York State and the Amana and Zoar communities in Ohio and elsewhere were long-lived. Many of them, like Mother Ann Lee's Shaker community were persecuted for their social and religious deviance. During the 20th century, there have been at least two distinct periods of high cult activity, the 1920s and the 1970s. We shall focus here upon the rich sociological information derived from the latter.

The cult movements of the 1970s drew upon two distinct theological resources. Some, like the Meher Baba, Hare Krishna, the Bhagwan movement of Shree Rajneesh, and followers of Reverend Sun Myung Moon's Unification Church drew upon the ideas of Eastern religious traditions. Others, among them the Children of God, The Jesus Movement, the Alamo Foundation, and The Way International, claimed to be re-Christianizing America. In either case, whether they were "Jesus freaks" or Moonies, these movements were seen as deviant.

The labeling of these religious cults as deviant was clearly demonstrated in a series of legal battles in which parents claimed that their children had been brainwashed into joining these cults. You may recognize this as an instance of "sick deviance" (Gusfield 1967). It shows that these cults were viewed as quite a threat to the host culture. Some of these court cases involved so-called deprogramming instances in which parents kidnapped their own children so they could be deprogrammed (brainwashed back into being normal) (Robbins 1988).

Who were these deviant religious "zealots" of the 1970s, and how were they initiated into their deviant religious careers? The religious cultists of the 1970s were primarily, though not exclusively, young, white, and from middle- to upper-middle class family backgrounds. Indeed, college campuses became fertile recruiting grounds for the various "new religions." These followers of culturally deviant cults were the sons and daughters of middle America (Wright 1987).

In explaining the emergence of these cults, sociologists argue that Watergate and other events of the 1960s and 1970s produced a general weakening of the normative power of traditional American institutions, traditional religion included. The anomie theory of social deviance is relevant because those joining the cults were seeking an ordered universe of events not readily found in a society damaged by Watergate, Vietnam syndrome, racism, a failed war on poverty, and the corporate pollution of places like Love Canal. Consistent with Merton's (1938) strain theory of deviance, it might be argued that the cult members of the 1970s were seeking the American dream of an ordered, moral, and in many cases "Christian" life. However, they chose deviant means for attaining this goal (innovation).

How did these Moonies and Jesus freaks begin their deviant careers? In the first instance, those who joined cults were "seekers" (Robbins 1988), individuals searching for answers to some of life's confusing questions. However, most cult members joined because they "liked the members" or "had friends who joined," not because they instantaneously discovered religious truth. Socialization theories and especially the theory of differential association provide an understanding of how supposedly "normal" youngsters become followers in deviant cults.

Cult participation provides a clear illustration of how a deviant career and a deviant identity develop gradually, typically after the initial act of joining. Identification with the cult grows from participation and involvement in it. Here, social enclosure is critically important because many of the cults of the 1970s not only required living in geographically removed communes, but also required members to discontinue associating with people in their "past" lives, most importantly parents, siblings, and former close friends. These groups created nearly total social enclosure. In some of these religious communities, members had constant contact only with other cult members, and thus, were exposed only to the cult's definitions of reality.

Correspondingly, cults seemed to be quite successful in achieving identity transformations, in which members gradually adopted new definitions of the self as they embarked upon deviant careers. The cults provide dramatic lessons in basic socialization theory. The force of these resocialization experiences is what generated the label of "brainwashing" by parents and other family members.

What are the meanings and consequences of such intense deviant religious careers? Clearly, it is difficult for any small community to sustain a meaningful, totally deviant social reality for an indefinite period of time. Consider that Kanter studied the materials describing some 91 American religious communes that appeared between 1790 and 1860. Only eleven of them were deemed to have been "successful!" It is too soon to know how many cults that emerged in the United States in late 20th century will either survive or succeed. However, we do know that individuals remain members of these cults for relatively short periods of time, on average only two years.

Studies of those who leave cults (Jacobs 1984; Wright 1987) indicate that most people who voluntarily leave will insist that the cult experience was, on the whole, a positive one. Thus, it cannot be assumed that because persons adopt deviant careers and deviant identities, that they somehow are injured by having embraced a deviant label. While cult ex-members may no longer see the outside world as "evil" and "sinful," they maintain that the closed deviant world of the cult provided something positive they needed at the time of their membership.

On balance then, the total social enclosure of the deviant religious life is meaningful, but fragile. Because everything about the lifestyle is so intimately connected, a small doubt created in one aspect of the life of the community can lead the member to doubt all. In fact, "deconversion" tends to happen in just that way. Poor ethical conduct by a leader or key member of the cult, the imposition of new rules or regulations that somehow don't make sense, or the decision of a close friend to leave may lead to an unraveling of the entire way of life for the individual.

JUVENILE STREET GANGS: MODERATE SOCIAL ENCLOSURE

Juvenile street gangs represent yet another form of social deviance. Here, the extent of social enclosure is not quite as great as in the religious cult. Yet, there is a distinct subculture, typically requiring behavior that is strongly disapproved by the host society.

There are many varieties of adolescent gangs in America, and as might be expected, they have been the focus of much sociological attention. This is not only because they are socially distinct, but also because they frequently engage in unlawful (criminal) behavior. The study of juvenile delinquency is an important subfield within the sociology of deviant behavior. Here the focus is upon the subculture of urban lower-class delinquent boys' gangs. Typically, members are drawn from neighborhoods characterized by high unemployment and high crime rates. These are the streetwise children of the American inner city who were portrayed romantically in Leonard Bernstein's *West Side Story* and who tragically make the evening news broadcasts as both victims and perpetrators of much violent crime.

Why do inner-city kids become gang members? In his ground-breaking study *Delinquent Boys* (1955), Albert Cohen suggests that joining a delinquent gang is a way for these youngsters to solve the problem of status deprivation. Cohen explains that juveniles from lower-class backgrounds are not well prepared to compete for success in the middle-class world. This problem becomes particularly acute in the school systems, where rewards are bestowed on the

FIGURE 7.1
Deviant patterns may be every bit as long-lived as normative ones.

basis of middle-class standards, such as verbal and social skills and academic success (Cohen 1955; Kelly and Pink 1982). In such an environment, lower-class children are faced with a dilemma. They have internalized middle-class goals, but do not have the culturally transmitted skills for achieving them.

According to Cohen, one solution to this dilemma entails gravitating toward other children who share these problems. Within this peer group environment, lower-class youth may establish new norms and criteria of status attainment that "define as meritorious the characteristics they *do* possess, the kinds of conduct of which they *are* capable" (1955, 66). Within the social enclosure of the juvenile gang, subcultural norms are instituted, and through these norms, the gang members' self-worth may be validated. Typically, the street gang values physical strength, street smarts, and defiance of authority. Middle-class values and middle-class people often become "the enemy." Wanton destruction of property and vandalism, which defy middle-class values, are prescribed subcultural behaviors (Cohen 1955; Bordua 1961). Thus, destructive and violent behaviors that seem crazy or stupid from a middle-class perspective, actually "make sense" for juvenile gang members.

By now it should be obvious that several theories of deviance provide an understanding of the emergence of juvenile street gangs. First, Merton's anomie theory is helpful in explaining why participation in street gangs is found most often among lower-class youths. Denied legitimate avenues to success and status, these boys choose illegitimate means of status-seeking within a deviant subculture (Cohen 1955). Following the deviant code of the gang is, in fact, an innovative strategy for gaining the respect that is unavailable to these lower-class kids in the middle-class world.

Second, Sutherland's theory of differential association also provides important insights into how young people become gang members. They become delinquent because most of their significant social attachments are to other youngsters who engage in and approve of delinquent acts (Kaplan, Johnson, and Baily 1987). Those with whom the boys associate reward deviant behavior and condemn conventional behavior. Becoming a gang member involves a socialization process with appropriate rituals of entry, rites of passage, and, of course, mechanisms of status approval within the gang. Through these activities a deviant career is launched and a deviant identity is sustained and reinforced.

As was noted at the outset, there are many different kinds of juvenile gangs. Some are focused on collective violence and turf wars, while others restrict their deviance to robbery and theft. During the 1980s and 1990s, the American public became most aware of those specializing in drug trafficking. What determines these sorts of differences in gang subcultures?

Cloward and Ohlin (1960) suggest that illegitimate opportunities (types of deviance) are socially structured in very much the same way as legitimate opportunities (normative behaviors) are. Thus, the type of juvenile gang that emerges depends upon the opportunities, role models, and resources in the environmental setting. For example, recent studies of street gangs in American cities demonstrate that gangs no longer are strictly youth organizations from which inner city youngsters "graduate" into more normative adult-life patterns. Rather, given the limited opportunities available, especially for racial minorities in America's cities, gangs have become important economic organizations through which individuals make an early entrance into the underground (criminal) economy (Hagedorn 1988, 1991).

If it is granted that deviance says much about the nature of the society in which it is produced, then the extent of criminally oriented gang violence (most of it drug related) in the United States in recent decades is cause for alarm. It suggests that American society possesses an enormous criminal opportunity structure, and that the criminal opportunity structure far outweighs the socially legitimate opportunity structure for the less-privileged classes in American society. In other words, the prevalence of this kind of social deviance suggests that we ought to examine how well and for whom the American system of opportunity does or does not work.

TATTOOING THE HUMAN BODY: LOW SOCIAL ENCLOSURE

Although tattooing, as an acceptable form of body art, has been used extensively in ancient and tribal cultures, throughout most of American history, tattooing of the human body has been defined culturally as a deviant activity. One need only consider that in modern times, tattooed people have been essential exhibits in circus and carnival "freak shows." They are categorized with the two-headed man, fire-eaters, and snake charmers. Tattooing, its practitioners, and clients have been considered both disreputable and unsavory. Such images have been reinforced by scientific studies of tattooing which assume pathology (mental disorder, or sick deviance) and focus primarily on institutionalized populations such as prison inmates (Taylor 1970). Despite the fact that both practitioners and clients have changed dramatically during the last several decades, the definition of tattooing as deviant and its connection to socially marginal groups remain firmly entrenched in the public mind.

Why is tattooing a deviant act? Getting a tattoo violates strongly held norms of physical appearance. The degree of stigma attached to appearance norms reflects the extent to which persons are blamed or held responsible for their own condition (Goffman 1963). Those who voluntarily modify their bodies in socially unacceptable ways, such as obtaining a punk haircut, being tattooed (Sanders 1989), or becoming excessively fat (Millman 1980), risk being defined as socially or morally inferior. Tattoos are especially discrediting, since tattooees (persons having tattoos) are viewed as being responsible for their own deviant condition (Jones *et al.* 1984).

Why, then, do persons alter their bodies in socially disvalued ways and risk being labeled deviant? Although much of the underlying appeal of tattooing entails the flaunting of conventional norms, Sanders (1989) identifies at least three reasons for obtaining tattoos. First, many persons acquire tattoos as a sign of affiliation with or commitment to other persons or groups. Thus, the modern youth gang member wears a tattoo of the gang's insignia, just as in tribal societies people wear the mark of their tribe or clan. Second, tattoos are a means of signifying uniqueness through the use of a creative, innovative design. While such persons wear tattoos for their uniqueness, over time they find social support among like-minded persons in the subculture of tattooing. Third, people tattoo their bodies to commemorate significant life transitions, or to take control of their own bodies (Sanders 1989). The more private such acts are, the more likely they are to represent primary rather than secondary deviance. In other words, persons in this last category, like a husband or wife getting an anniversary tattoo in a rather private location on the body, exemplify primary deviance and are not likely to develop deviant careers.

Who are these people that are so willing to mark their bodies permanently? During the 1970s and 1980s the once homogeneous social characteristics of the clientele obtaining tattoos has undergone considerable change. At one time, clientele were predominantly working-class youth for whom tattoos were marks of social membership. However, the newer clients tend to come from a higher socioeconomic background than traditional clients, have more disposable income, and place greater emphasis on the aesthetic and decorative significance of tattoos (Sanders 1989).

What are the social processes through which the decision to become tattooed is made? Despite the public image of this as an impulsive act, the process of decision usually extends over a substantial period of time. At first, the individual mentally "tries on" the new identity. What will it mean to be a tattooed person? Once the individual can think of him or herself as a tattooed person, the decision to obtain the desired mark can be undertaken. Within the context of this decisional process, the act of being tattooed for the first time is impulsive. It requires having "extra" cash and being in proximity to a tattoo establishment. Most importantly, it typically involves the active social support of friends, who not accidentally already have tattoos (Sanders 1989).

From a sociological viewpoint, tattooing is interesting because it reveals the social process of deviant identity formation and the management of a deviant label by the tattooee. Many first-time tattooees choose a relatively small, inexpensive mark placed on a body location easily exposed or hidden according to one's definition of the situation. This minimizes the social and economic costs of the initial commitment to become tattooed. With relatively small, inconspicuously placed marks, the novice tattooee may select those persons to whom the mark will be revealed, and thus, may control the likelihood of becoming the object of a deviant label or stigma.

As Sanders (1989) observes, it is possible through such concealment of the tattoo, for the individual to live in two worlds. Societies exhibit a precarious balance between norms of individuality and norms of social acceptance. Tattooed persons straddle these two norms with more daring than most. They participate in the dominant culture as part of the normative mainstream, while at the same time maintaining an identity with the tattoo subculture. Obviously, the relatively low level of social enclosure of this deviant subculture allows this dual lifestyle. However, once the tattoo is revealed publicly, or if the placement of the tattoo makes it readily observable, the response frequently is negative, and a stigma is assigned.

Labeling theory, of course, emphasizes that social deviance emerges both from the assignment of the label "deviant," as well as the ways in which the persons so labeled react to it. The tattooee may respond to a deviant label in several different ways, each revealing information about his or her deviant identity and deviant career.

First, the tattooee may reject stigmatization by disvaluing those who assign the label. Ultimately, this will lead to a greater involvement in the tattoo subculture, where support for tattooing rather than stigma, is obtained. Obviously, involvement in and identity with the subculture will reinforce each other. A second response to stigma is to conceal the tattoo in future interactions. The individual pursues both a conventional and a deviant career and, therefore, is at the same time deviant, without accepting a "spoiled identity." Third, one may accept society's definition of the tattooed person as deviant, attempt to obliterate the tattoo, and thereby regain a nondeviant identity. In such instances, the act of obtaining a tattoo may be understood as primary deviance. Consistent with labeling theory, both obtaining and publicly exposing tattoos are expressions of identity decisions. The individual's involvement in secondary deviance, or a deviant career, emerges from the label assigned and the reactions to that label.

What are the consequences of becoming tattooed and being labeled as such? Interestingly, most tattooees express a great deal of satisfaction with their decision to mark their bodies in this way. Where dissatisfaction is encountered, it frequently results from the aesthetic quality of the tattoo rather than regret about having been tattooed (Sanders 1989). Therefore, it is not surprising that today, tattooees are attempting to change negative definitions of tattooing as deviant. Organized groups, such as the National Tattoo Association, have attained some limited success in having tattooing defined as a culturally legitimate art form (Sanders 1989). However, at the present time, the general public continues to view marking the human body with a tattoo as a deviant practice.

In summary, this section of the chapter has examined three very different cases of social deviance. Each exhibits a different level of social enclosure, or degree of separateness in the social structures in which the deviant subculture is located. These three cases also provide illustrations of the utility of the theories discussed in this chapter.

Religious cults exhibit high levels of social enclosure, and the individuals within them adopt rather complete deviant identities and deviant careers. The theories of anomie and social strain both explain why people join these kinds of religious communities. Both the socialization and differential association theories reveal much about recruitment processes and why a deviant identity remains meaningful to those who join. Moderate levels of social enclosure characterize juvenile street gangs. Here, too, anomie and differential association theories explain why people join. The retreatist and conflict-orientation of these groups are keys to understanding how deviant careers nurture the self-esteem of gang members. Finally, the subculture of tattooing exhibits a relatively low level of social enclosure. Consistent with labeling theory, a public display of tattoos typically results in stigma. Responses to that stigma reflect different levels of secondary deviance and deviant careers.

Crime and Social Control

This chapter has examined social deviance in a variety of its forms and manifestations. Clearly, all societies, especially modern ones, are engaged in maintaining a delicate balance between social conformity and social deviance. In order for any society to exist, the majority of its members must conform to its basic rules and values, and thus, the level of social deviance must be restricted. All societies invent *social control* strategies, that is, *techniques that obtain conformity and minimize deviance from the society's prescribed norms and values.* What kinds of social control techniques are employed in most societies? As Durkheim first observed (1895), there are two types of social control strategies, *socialization* and *coercion.* Let's consider each of them.

Social control

A first route to effective social control is socialization, through which the members of a society internalize the prescribed norms and values of that society. We've already examined socialization processes (Chapter 6) in some detail. In essence, people conform because they've been socialized to believe that the socially expected behaviors are correct. To the extent that socialization is successful, people internalize normative guidelines for behavior. They believe that the society's norms should be obeyed.

However, socialization is imperfect and incomplete. It never guarantees total conformity. Moreover, as the several theories of social deviance explored earlier in this chapter make clear, there are many conditions under which deviance becomes both rational and meaningful to people. Prescribed norms and goals may be viewed as unjust, inappropriate, or even unattainable. Under these conditions, socialization no longer sufficiently controls behavior for some persons, and external sanctions become necessary.

Coercion takes many forms in societies, and in modern industrial societies, laws are the most important form of coercive social control. In essence, a formal rule system is established, violation of which exposes the individual to physical coercion by the ultimate source of coercive force—the state. All of this sounds somewhat threatening, and, in fact, it is just that. When serious violations of the law occur, the offenders are subject to formal sanctions by agents of the state. A complex array of formal agents of social control become involved; namely, the police, the courts, and correctional facilities. Collectively, these agents of social control represent the criminal justice system, and through this system's use of sanctions (ranging from financial fines to the death penalty), it is claimed that justice is dispensed and criminal deviance is deterred.

Exactly how effective are justice systems? Under what conditions are techniques of deterrence effective? Turning first to the effectiveness of the American criminal justice system, we discover that it is not very effective. The United States has one of the highest crime rates and rates of recidivism (crimes committed by persons previously convicted of crime) in the Western world. It is estimated that a serious crime (a felony) is committed about every two seconds, and a violent crime every 21 seconds (Federal Bureau of Investigation 1987). A government study of former prison inmates reveals that 63 percent were rearrested within three years of their release from prison, and 41 percent would return to prison (U.S. Bureau of Justice Statistics 1989).

Deterrence is best achieved through informal communal sanctions. When these mechanisms fail, the effectiveness of the criminal justice system in deterring crime is, at best, limited (Currie 1990). Interestingly, Wood (1974) suggests that the most coercive social control techniques are at once, the most expensive and the least effective. Why is this so? Coercive (force), rather than consensual (socialization and community control) techniques are most required when dealing with deviants who are alienated from the system and seem to have little investment in it. Thus, enormous sums of money are spent apprehending (police and courts), punishing (prisons), and monitoring (parole systems) the behavior of these persons who are least convinced of the legitimacy of all this control.

While most American citizens believe that criminals are treated too leniently, the United States has the highest imprisonment rate among Western industrialized nations. In 1989, the most recent year for which statistics are available, there were nearly 700,000 persons in state and federal prisons (U.S. Bureau of the Census 1991). Moreover, as we've already noted, America's crime and recidivism rates also are the highest among the Western industrialized nations. These facts suggest that presently in the United States punishment is not an effective deterrent. It does not induce people to refrain from criminal behavior. Why is this so, and what could change this remarkably inefficient relationship between punishment and future crime?

Isadore Chein (1975) suggests that in any society, for punishment to deter crime effectively, several conditions must be met. Let's examine them.

First, punishment must be certain. The punishment of crimes cannot be a matter of chance, luck, or courtroom technicalities. If crimes go undetected, or known criminals go unpunished, the deterrent effect of punishment is greatly diminished. Second, the probability of suffering punishment must be much greater for the guilty than for the innocent. When innocent persons are as likely to become enmeshed in the criminal justice system as guilty persons, punishment no longer serves as a deterrent.

Third, punishment, like justice, must not be significantly delayed. Such delays lessen the deterrent effect of punishment. Fourth, punishment must fit the crime. Plea bargaining may be an efficient way of moving cases in a clogged court system, but it is not an efficient means for making punishments deter crimes.

Fifth, punishment must be dictated by the specific offense, not by the desire of the authorities to "get a conviction," or to convict a specific individual in any way possible. Convicting a "drug lord" on a tax evasion charge surely makes him or her serve time, but no certain message is sent about the surety of punishment for drug trafficking. Sixth, justice must be blind. Punishment cannot be more likely for persons of specific class, race, ethnic, or gender categories. If corporate theft is treated less harshly than street crime, and imprisonment is more likely for blacks and Hispanics than whites (for the same crimes), there is no justice.

Seventh, the suffering and shame of punishment and imprisonment are meaningful only so long as normal life on the "outside" is free of these things. Where poverty, homelessness, and desperation are widespread, the threat of "punishment" has little consequence. Finally, punishment cannot deter crime in the absence of a moral climate. Criminals who fear only punishment will plan more sophisticated crimes more carefully. They'll believe that the error lies in being caught, not in the commission of crimes. Only when there is a strong normative context—that crime is wrong—does punishment become meaningful. In other words, coercive social control has optimal value in the context of normative control.

Chein's analysis illuminates the problem of social control from a societal perspective. Debates over the effectiveness of punishment, including the death penalty, too often occur in a vacuum. These debates fail to examine, as Chein has done, the societal context in which crimes and punishment occur. Social policies involving deviance, or anything else, derive their meaning from the social context in which they occur.

In summary, social control refers to all techniques intended to maximize social conformity and minimize social deviance. Consensual techniques, primarily socialization, are more effective and less expensive than coercive techniques. Ironically, the United States has an extremely expensive coercive system of criminal justice which, when compared with those of other societies, is largely ineffective. However, this ineffectiveness clearly is related to the social environment in which crime is punished in the United States. The uncertainty of punishment, the practice of plea bargaining, the delay of justice, and the very existence of widespread inequalities in society, all undermine the meaning of punishment as a deterrent of crime.

APPLICATIONS

In Sickness and Health

This chapter has shown that the term "deviant" may be socially assigned to a remarkably wide range of human behaviors, beliefs, and appearances. Many physical disabilities, and even illnesses, have been regarded as deviant, resulting in stigma and discrimination. Few instances of this are more disturbing than those involving persons who have become afflicted by a disease over which they have no control. Consider the social treatment of those who have contracted leprosy. Leprosy, also known as Hansen's disease, actually is an ailment of the skin and nerve endings. The disease, while carried by bacteria, is extremely difficult to contract. Yet, it does produce disfigurement of the skin, especially the face, arms, and legs. Even though it rarely, if ever, is fatal, throughout history, leprosy has been feared and lepers have been treated as deviants. They have been severely stigmatized, and have experienced much discrimination.

Until the 1940s, when drug treatments for the disease became available, social containment and segregation were practiced widely, a sad fact considering that the disease is far more prevalent in children than adults. Historically, in both Europe and Asia, leper colonies were dreaded places where few "normal" persons would go voluntarily. It would be comforting to believe that modern societies are not capable of producing this type of stigma out of fear and ignorance. However, this is not so. No disease in recent history has aroused more prejudice against the afflicted than the Acquired Immune Deficiency Syndrome (AIDS). Like the lepers of earlier times, today's victims of AIDS, are the objects of stigmatization.

FIGURE 7.2
Ryan White, who died in 1990 at the age of 18, contracted AIDS from a blood transfusion.

CASE

AIDS Victims as Deviants

In 1984, a then twelve-year-old boy named Ryan White was as "middle American" as any child could have been. A resident of Kokomo, Indiana, young Ryan was different from his classmates and playmates in only one unapparent regard. Ryan had hemophilia, a disease of the blood which retards blood clotting. Hemophiliacs are at risk of bleeding to death, even from minor injuries, and are treated routinely with clotting agents drawn from whole blood. However, in 1984, Ryan also was diagnosed as having AIDS-related pneumonia. This diagnosis not only was the beginning of the process of dying for Ryan, it also began a process of social stigmatization—the treatment of Ryan as a member of a devalued social category.

In 1985, despite repeated assurances by health professionals that Ryan posed no risk to the health of other students, public school officials in Kokomo decided that Ryan's presence in the classroom did represent a threat to his classmates. Invoking a 1949 Indiana statute barring from the classroom students with communicable diseases, they expelled Ryan from school. Out of fear, ignorance, and misconceptions about how the disease is transmitted, Ryan was socially ostracized. While it was clear that Ryan had contracted AIDS from a transfusion of a blood-clotting agent, not from casual social contact, Ryan had become stigmatized and successfully labeled as deviant.

In 1985, Ryan and his mother Jeanne initiated what would become a six-month-long court battle to regain Ryan's right to attend public school. In 1986, the courts ruled in Ryan's favor, but not without mandating certain stigmatizing procedures. Even though one cannot contract AIDS through casual contact such as sharing bathrooms, dishes, and towels, the court ruled that Ryan would use a separate bathroom, use only disposable eating utensils in the school cafeteria, and would be exempt from taking gym. Thus, while Ryan could go to school again, these precautions would insure the continued myth that he was a danger to other people. By this time some of Ryan's former classmates, in order to avoid contact with him, were attending privately organized alternate schools. Ryan's family moved to Cicero, Indiana, where he re-entered the public school system, and was treated more humanely. Early in 1990, eighteen-year-old Ryan White died of AIDS complications at Indianapolis' Riley Hospital for Children.

There is little question that AIDS is a deadly disease. However, it is difficult to contract. AIDS is readily communicable only through the exchange of bodily fluids, such as semen and blood. Considerable misinformation exists about how AIDS is transmitted. While the disease is potentially the most serious epidemic of modern times, stigmatizing the victims of AIDS won't prevent its spread. Still, a study conducted in 1989 revealed that one out of three Americans favors tattooing individuals who test HIV-positive (Whitman 1990). HIV (human immunodeficiency virus) is the precursor of AIDS. The virus attaches itself to white blood cells which are the basis of the immune system through which the body protects itself against infection, rendering the immune system incapable of fighting off common infections.

The treatment of AIDS victims as deviant is, in part, a result of the social characteristics of the earliest known victims of the illness in American society—homosexual males, a socially devalued population. Although in other countries AIDS victims primarily are heterosexual, in this country, the initial diagnosis among homosexual males led to AIDS being viewed as a gay men's disease. During the 1980s, AIDS was heavily concentrated among homosexual males and intravenous drug users. Since these victims were seen as responsible for their own illness, there was little public response to the disease. Some people even suggested that AIDS constitutes divine retribution against those ("sinners") who deserved their fate. In retrospect, it is clear that the dual social stigma attached to both AIDS and its victims led both politicians and health professionals to underestimate the pervasiveness of the disease and its dangers to the general population.

Since that time, this has begun to change. Many more persons not associated with previously stigmatized categories have contracted the disease. The discovery that AIDS is not exclusively a disease affecting those with "deviant" lifestyles has led to increased research funds, although to some extent ignorance and unfounded fears still transform victims of this deadly disease into social outcasts. In the face of this ignorance and fear, victims of AIDS, like Ryan White, suffer both medically and socially. However, the announcement in November of 1991 by the popular former NBA star Earvin "Magic" Johnson that he had contracted the HIV virus from "normal" heterosexual contact, may help remove some of the social stigma attached to AIDS victims. Johnson's actions in becoming "a spokesman for AIDS" has greatly increased AIDS awareness among the general public and is helping to educate the public about the disease and its potential impact on everyone. Hopefully, Ryan's example and the efforts of "Magic" will help remove the social stigma attached to all who contract AIDS, be they heterosexual, homosexual, men, women, young, or old.

Chapter Summary

1. The absolutist approach to studying social deviance defines deviance as norm-violating behavior. However, most sociologists endorse a relativist approach to definition, in which deviance is understood as behaviors, beliefs, and social attributes that elicit social condemnation.

2. Social norms and social deviance are intimately related. The ultimate values of a society often are revealed in the kinds of social deviance it most punishes. Both social norms and social deviance are highly variable and socially fragile.

3. Social deviance is explained by four distinct traditions of theorizing: namely, anomie theory, socialization theory, conflict theory, and labeling theory. Each theory tradition makes a useful contribution to the sociological understanding of why and how people engage in deviant behavior.

4. Anomie theories, including the social disorganization and social strain theories, depict social deviance as a meaningful response to situations of weak or confused social norms. These theories are most useful in explaining how lower-class deviance may be understood as an innovative social response.

5. Socialization theories, including the theory of differential association, focus upon the ways in which deviance, like normative behavior, is socially learned in both primary and secondary group contexts. It is a useful perspective for explaining how persons become involved in both criminal and noncriminal forms of social deviance.

6. Conflict theory focuses upon the political and power processes involved in social definitions of deviance. The theory hinges on the fact that much social effort is expended punishing high-consensus deviance, which, in effect, is lower-class deviance. In contrast, deviance by elite populations is less frequently and less severely punished.

7. Labeling theory focuses upon the social processes through which deviant status is assigned. By focusing on both the act of labeling persons deviant, and upon persons' responses to that label, it shows how deviant identities are formed, and how deviant careers are adopted.

8. Deviant subcultures exhibit varying degrees of social enclosure as well as the processes through which deviant careers and deviant identities are formed. Religious cults, juvenile street gangs, and the subculture of tattooing have been examined in this chapter to illustrate these processes.

9. Social control refers to all techniques used to maximize social conformity and minimize social deviance. Socialization and social coercion are the two basic categories of social control techniques. Social coercion techniques of control, like the punishment of criminals, are most effective when a moral climate (the result of socialization techniques) exists.

Key Concepts

absolutist perspective
anomie
conflict theory
conformity
cynical deviants
deviance
deviant career
differential association
enemy deviants
high-consensus deviance
innovation
labeling theory
low-consensus deviance
primary deviance
rebellion
relativist perspective
repentant deviants
retreatism
ritualism
secondary deviance
sick deviants
social control
social disorganization theory
social enclosure
socialization theories
stigma
strain theory
subculture

BIBLIOGRAPHY

Adam, Barry D.
1978. *The survival of domination.* New York: Elsivier.

Adler, Patricia A., and Peter Adler
1983. Shifts and oscillations in deviant careers: The case of upper-level drug dealers and smugglers. *Social Problems.* Vol. 31, No. 2: 195–207.

Akers, Ronald
1985. *Deviant behavior: A social learning approach.* Belmont, California: Wadsworth.

Barrows, Sidney Biddle, and William Novak
1986. *Mayflower madam: The secret life of Sidney Biddle Barrows.* New York: Morrow.

Becker, Howard S.
1963. *The outsiders: Studies in the sociology of deviance.* New York: Free Press.

Beirne, Piers, and Richard Quinney
1982. *Marxism and law.* New York: Wiley.

Berger, Peter L., and Thomas Luckmann
1967. *The social construction of reality.* New York: Doubleday & Co.

Bordua, David
1961. Delinquent subcultures: Sociological interpretations of gang delinquency. *Annals of the American Academy of Political and Social Science.* Vol. 388, No. 1 (November): 119–36.

Chein, Isadore
1975. There ought to be a law: But why? *Journal of Social Issues.* Vol. 31, No. 4: 221–44.

Clinard, Marshall B., and Robert F. Meier
1989. *Sociology of deviant behavior.* 7th ed. Chicago: Holt, Rinehart & Winston.

Cloward, Richard A. and Lloyd E. Ohlin
1960. *Delinquency and opportunity.* New York: Free Press.

Cohen, Albert K.
1955. *Delinquent boys: The culture of the gang.* New York: Free Press.

Cooley, Charles H.
1918. *Social process.* New York: Scribner.

Currie, Elliot P.
1990. "The limits of imprisonment." In *Criminal behavior,* Edited by Delos H. Kelly. 497–509. New York: St. Martin's Press.

Deegan, Mary Jo., and Nancy Brooks, eds.
1987. *Women and disability: The double handicap.* New Brunswick, N.J.: Transaction Books.

Durkheim, Emile
1893. *The division of labor in society.* Translated by George Simpson, 1933. New York: Macmillan.

1895. *The rules of sociological method.* Translated by Sarah Solovay and John H. Mueller; New York: Free Press. Edited by George E. G. Catlin, 1933.

1897. *Suicide.* Translated by John A. Spaulding and George Simpson. Glencoe, Illinois: Free Press.

Federal Bureau of Investigation
1987. *Uniform Crime Reports: Crime in the United States, 1986.* Washington, D.C.: U.S. Government Printing Office.

Gardiner, John A.
1970. *The politics of corruption: Organized crime on an American city.* New York: Russell Sage Foundation.

Goffman, Erving
1963. *Stigma.* Englewood Cliffs, N.J.: Prentice-Hall.

Gusfield, Joseph
1967. Moral passage: The symbolic process in public designations of deviance. *Social Problems.* Vol. 15, No. 2 (Fall): 175–88.

Hagedorn, John M.
1988. *People and folks: Gangs, crime and the underclass in a rustbelt city.* Chicago, Illinois: Lake View Press.

1991. Gangs, neighborhoods, and public policy. *Social problems.* Vol. 38, No. 4 (November): 529–542.

Hills, Stuart L.
1980. *Demystifying social deviance.* New York: McGraw-Hill.

Jacobs, Janet L.
1984. The economy of love in religious commitment: The deconversion of women from non-traditional religious movements. *Journal for the Scientific Study of Religion.* Vol. 23, No. 2: 155–71.

Jones, Edward, Amerigo Farina, Albert Hastorf, Hazael Markus, Dale Miller, and Robert Scott.
1984. *Social stigma: The psychology of marked relationships.* New York: Freeman.

Kanter, Rosabeth Moss
1972. *Commitment and community: Communes and utopias in sociological perspective.* Cambridge, Massachusetts: Harvard Univ. Press.

Kaplan, Howard B., Robert J. Johnson, and Carol A. Bailey
1987. Deviant peers and deviant behavior: Further elaborations of a model. *Social Psychology Quarterly.* Vol. 50, No. 4: 227–52.

Kelly, Delos H., and William T. Pink
1982. Crime and individual responsibility: The perpetuation of a myth? *Urban Review.* Vol. 14, No. 1: 47–63.

Kerner, Otto, *et al.*
1968. Report of the National Advisory Commission on Civil Disorders. New York: Bantam.

Lachmann, Richard
1988. Graffiti as career and ideology. *American Journal of Sociology.* Vol. 94, No. 2: 229–50.

Lemert, Edwin M.
1967. *Human deviance, social problems and social control.* Englewood Cliffs, N.J.: Prentice-Hall.

Levi, Ken
1981. Becoming a hit man: Neutralization in a very deviant career. *Urban Life.* Vol. 10, No. 1: 47–63.

Liska, Allen E.
1981. *Perspectives in deviance.* Englewood Cliffs, N.J.: Prentice-Hall.

Lofland, John
1966. *Doomsday cult: A study of conversion, proselytization and maintenance of faith.* Englewood Cliffs, N.J.: Prentice-Hall.

Maurer, David W.
1949. *The big con: The story of the confidence man and the confidence game.* Indianapolis, Indiana: Bobbs-Merrill.

Merton, Robert
1938. Social structure and anomie. *American Sociological Review.* Vol. 3, No. 5: 672–82.

Millman, Marcia
1980. *Such a pretty face: Being fat in America.* New York: W. W. Norton.

National Council of Churches of Christ
1992. *Yearbook of American and Canadian Churches.* New York: National Council of Churches of Christ.

Polsky, Ned
1967. *Hustlers, beats, and others.* Rev. ed., 1969. New York: Doubleday, Anchor Books. Chicago: Aldine Publishing Company.

Quinney, Richard
1975. *Criminology.* Boston, Massachusetts: Little, Brown & Co.

1977. *Class, state and crime.* 2d ed., 1980. New York: Longman. David McKay.

Reiman, Jeffrey H.
1984. *The rich get richer and the poor get prison.* 2d ed. New York: Wiley.

Reiss, Albert J., Jr.
1961. The social integration of queers and peers. *Social Problems.* Vol. 9, No. 2 (Fall): 102–120.

Robbins, Thomas
1988. *Cults, converts and charisma.* Beverly Hills, California: Sage Publications.

Sanders, Clinton K.
1989. *Customizing the body: The art and culture of tattooing.* Philadelphia: Temple Univ. Press.

Schur, Edwin M.
1980. *The politics of deviance: Stigma contests and the uses of power.* Englewood Cliffs, N.J.: Prentice-Hall.

1984. *Labeling women deviant: Gender, stigma and social control.* New York: Random House.

Scott, Richard A.
1969. *The making of blind men.* New York: Russell Sage Foundation.

Simmons, J. L.
1969. *Deviants.* Berkeley, California: Glendassary.

Sutherland, Edwin H.
1939. *Principles of criminology.* (Later editions entitled *Criminology*). Chicago: Univ. of Chicago Press.

Szasz, Thomas
1961. *The myth of mental illness.* Rev. ed., 1974, Harper & Row. New York: Hoeber-Harper.

Taylor, A. J. W.
1970. Tattooing among male and female offenders of different ages in different types of institutions. *Genetic Psychology Monographs.* Vol. 81: 81–119.

Thomas, W. I., and Florian Znaniecki
1919. *The Polish peasant in Europe and America.* New York: Alfred Knopf.

U.S. Bureau of Justice Statistics
1989. *Recidivism of Prisoners Released in 1983.* Washington, D.C.: Government Printing Office.

U.S. Bureau of the Census
1991. *Statistical Abstract of the United States.* Washington, D.C.: Government Printing Office.

Whitman, David
1990. To a poster child dying young. *U.S. News & World Report.* Vol. 108, No. 15 (April 16): 8.

Wood, Arthur L.
1974. *Deviant behavior and control strategies.* Lexington, Massachusetts: Lexington Books.

Wright, Stuart
1987. *Leaving cults: The dynamics of defection.* (*Monograph Series,* no. 7). Storrs, Connecticut: Society for the Scientific Study of Religion.

CHAPTER **8**

SOCIAL STRATIFICATION: STRUCTURES OF INEQUALITY

CHAPTER OUTLINE

LEARNING OBJECTIVES

Stratification is a basic component of all social structures. This chapter examines the ways in which social ranking operates to produce entire systems of social inequality. American society has a complex system of stratification in which women are paid less than men, even for the same work; and people with college degrees are paid more than those with only a high school diploma, even if the latter work harder and longer hours. On any given day, while some people are vacationing in the Caribbean, others stand in lines waiting for food in soup kitchens in cities across the nation. American society is not unique in this regard. In South Africa, whites enjoy all the riches of "the good life," while blacks, working underground in the diamond mines, earn barely enough to feed their families. In Mexico, abandoned children, whose families could not feed them, roam the streets, while the wealthy relax on the beaches of Cancun. These different life situations all demonstrate that in most societies, inequality tends to be the norm. Regardless of whether one examines democracies or dictatorships, capitalist, socialist, or communist societies, inequality prevails.

Inequality is both a cause and a consequence of stratification. Inequality emerges from processes of social differentiation and social evaluation. Some types of people and activities are evaluated and ranked more highly than others, and these differences in social worth, in turn, are translated into socially structured inequalities of living conditions and social opportunities. This chapter examines types of stratification systems and the processes through which these systems are created, sustained, and changed. Specifically, this chapter addresses the following questions about social stratification.

1. What is stratification, and what are the bases for ranking in all stratification systems?
2. What types of stratification systems are found in different societies, and how do they either promote or restrict people's opportunities?
3. What general trends are revealed in studies of social stratification in the United States and other modern societies? To what extent do "open" societies really provide opportunities for advancement of groups and individuals?
4. What is the overall shape of the American stratification system, and what kinds of social classes or strata do societies like the United States have?
5. What are the most recent trends affecting the American stratification system? Are people's opportunities for a better life increasing or decreasing?
6. Why is there stratification in societies? Are social inequalities necessary or inevitable?

THE ELEMENTS OF STRATIFICATION

Stratification

There are few aspects of social life that have a greater impact upon people's lives and life chances than social stratification. In the simplest terms, *stratification means ranking. Persons are ranked in terms of their possession of, and access to, those things valued by their society.* Those possessing more of whatever is valued by a society are ranked higher. This translates into inequality of opportunity for gaining access to, and control over, those things perceived as valuable. What are the things which, through patterns of unequal access and distribution, create unequal ranks or strata? The student of social stratification wants to know who gets what, how, and why. Inequalities of all sorts, domination and subordination, wealth and deprivation, privilege and social stigma, illustrate the extremes of social stratification patterns. Why such inequalities exist and how they are socially constructed and sustained are the focus of the sociological understanding of stratification processes.

Max Weber (1865–1920) observed that all societies are involved in the distribution of three distinct stratification resources: namely, class, status, and power (Weber 1923). A person's position in a society's stratification system is measured by how much of each of these three interrelated variables one possesses. How did Weber distinguish these three phenomena? First, class means material wealth. Those who share basically the same economic position in a society are referred to as a class. Second, status refers to honor, prestige, or privilege. Third, power is the ability to control the actions of others despite their wishes or resistance.

These three stratification variables over which people and groups compete and conflict are variously referred to as rewards and resources. Class, status, and power are rewards both given and received in exchange for valued characteristics, activities, or services. They also are resources that, once possessed, may be used, spent, or invested.

The idea that class, status, and power are social rewards is derived from the view that much of the game of life involves acts of acquisition in which the players attempt to maximize their share. As a "Yuppie" quip of the 1980s put matters, "Whoever dies with the most toys, wins." Obviously, the specific toys for which one plays the game are, in part, a function of one's relative social position. Some adult players are seeking such toys as houses, cars, boats, jewelry, and warm vacations in the cold winter months. Others would settle for three square meals per day. The contrasting notion, that class, status, and power are social resources, stems from the sociological understanding that how much of them individuals or collectivities have at the outset of the game strongly influences their life chances or conditions of living.

While class, status, and power are intimately connected in all societies, they are conceptually and empirically different, and they exhibit some very different characteristics and properties. Simply because the rich often are powerful, does not mean that wealth and power are the same. Just because better-paying occupations (wealth) are usually more respected (prestige), does not mean that wealth and prestige are the same. Additionally, as Weber observed, different types of societies place greater emphasis on one or another of these stratification variables. These issues require examination in greater detail.

CLASS

Class refers to any stratum of persons sharing a similar economic position in a society. Basically, class means material wealth. Of course, societies define and measure wealth differently, and even in the same society, it may take different forms. In Saudi Arabia, a man's wealth is measured by the number of wives he can support, while in most industrialized nations, the key forms of wealth are ownership in companies (stocks and bonds), real estate, and precious gems. In most societies, demonstrating that one has surplus material goods to be disposed of in an ostentatious manner, what Thorstein Veblin (1857–1929) called "conspicuous consumption" (1899), is a measure of material wealth. For example, in some tribal societies offering sumptuous feasts (obviously, one's surplus food) to the gods is a way of demonstrating one's wealth. The contributing of large sums of money to a charity by a millionaire in a modern society is not so different from the tribesman offering his surplus food to the gods. All such acts demonstrate that one has excess wealth. As a television advertisement of the 1980s proclaimed, "If you have it, flaunt it."

Class

Of course, for most persons, wealth means money. Yet, money is not wealth. Rather, money is only an exchange system for wealth. Not all societies have money, and even among those that do, there are different systems of money or exchange. Various Native American tribes used beads, shells (wampum), and other scarce objects as systems of wealth exchange. Each society, depending upon its particular cultural values and traditions, will define material wealth and well-being differently. This does not change the fact that in all societies class refers to the wealth or economic position of persons or groups. According to Weber, class assumes its greatest importance as a stratification variable in newly industrialized societies, since the process of industrialization generates increased economic differences throughout the population.

What are the distinguishing characteristics of class or wealth resources? First, wealth resources are more easily acquired than either status or power. However, this does not mean that it is easy to become rich. In most capitalist societies, and even in many socialist ones, income is the primary mechanism for the accumulation of wealth resources. Class position derives mainly from money received for the performance of occupational roles. Money is paid on an hourly basis for human labor and services of all sorts and varieties. Thus, income, though not always enough upon which to live, let alone become rich, is an extremely fluid resource. However, the relative ease of this kind of minimal income production is related to the second characteristic of wealth. The use or disposition of wealth depletes it. Spend it, and it's gone.

There is a difference between spending and investing material wealth. Investment is a way of changing the form of wealth, with, of course, the expectation of a relationship between risk and wealth increase. Historically, the less liquid (i.e. the less easily exchanged) forms of wealth, such as gems, real estate, and even collectibles, seem to increase in value most impressively. Conversely, those forms of wealth having the most liquidity, such as money, grow at modest rates. After all, the interest (rent for the use of money) that banks pay on saving accounts rarely allows the value of that money to keep pace with inflation. The essential difference between investing and spending is demonstrated by the fact that the consumer commodities for which people spend their income rarely can be exchanged for their original value. Unlike stocks and bonds, these consumer goods like cars, stereos, and designer clothing are sold as "used." Clearly, spending and investing are different activities with very different social consequences. Moreover, the ability to invest or spend is unequally distributed in society. The greater one's accrued wealth (the higher one's class position), the more likely one is to have a surplus for investing. Those with little wealth are most likely to deplete their supply through spending. This is the meaning of the old adage "The rich get richer, while the poor get poorer."

A third aspect of wealth resources is their primacy as objects of conflict between individuals and groups. Because material wealth resources are the channel through which persons obtain the basic necessities of life, they are the first objects of conflict.

STATUS

Status

Status refers to the honor, prestige, and privilege associated with different positions in a society or with categories of persons in a society. While class resources are the very first things over which groups and individuals engage in overt conflict, prestige distinctions tend to be the very first stratification designations made. Said differently, designations of status are the first forms of inequality that occur.

The criteria upon which status assignments are made are indeed varied. They may be physical, such as skin color, gender, or even stature. They may be cognitive, as in political ideology or religion, or behavioral, as in sexual preference. The criteria are as varied as human physical and cultural variation itself. Status assignments flow from arbitrary cultural designations that impart meanings to differences in human physical, cognitive, and behavioral patterns. In American society these criteria include such things as educational level, nationality, gender, and race. By using various criteria to separate themselves from others some members of collectivities are able to monopolize status resources that bring them high esteem.

Like class and power, status exhibits a number of distinctive characteristics. First, of the three stratification variables, status is the most stable, and, therefore, the most resistant to change. For example, in the United States, in spite of a significant body of anti-discrimination laws passed, certain status distinctions (blacks and whites, males and females, heterosexuals and homosexuals) remain part of the culture. Blacks who achieve professional status as doctors and lawyers, and who accumulate substantial wealth doing so, still are objects of racism in America. These same processes are apparent in gender relationships. For example, the prestige of any occupational role (doctor, nurse, lawyer, or secretary) is strongly influenced by whether that occupation is predominantly occupied by men or women. On the other hand, the prestige associated with being from an "old moneyed" family, tends to remain long after the money is gone. It is clear that status designations, although not static, do not change quickly.

Second, unlike wealth, which depletes when spent, social status neither increases nor decreases through use. For example, if Judge Smith arrives at "the club" without a reservation, he probably will be seated for lunch without much waiting because of his honored position in the community. If the Judge does this on Monday, he also can do so again on any given day. Judge Smith probably will receive similar treatment in other restaurants in the community. The degree of prestige does not change because it is used frequently. However, the privileges stemming from status designations do not increase if they are not used. Unlike wealth, one cannot "save" or accumulate honor and prestige in order to have more of it for use at a later time.

Third, social status exhibits a high degree of institutional specificity. The further one moves away from the institution that defines and confers a particular position with prestige, the more the social impact of that prestige decreases. For example, the prestige associated with being a physician in American society is remarkably high. Yet, the privileges of being a doctor are greatest in the setting of the medical profession itself, in hospitals, clinics, and private offices. Typically, once outside the medical setting, physicians no longer can make the rules of the game quite so easily. Similarly, while General Gunblast enjoys substantial privilege on the military base, in civil society he must follow the same rules as all other citizens. This aspect of status differs from wealth. It is said that "money talks" and speaks with equal loudness in all settings. The mechanisms of social status speak most loudly closest to their points of origin.

POWER

Power

Power is the ability to control the actions of others, regardless of their will. Just as wealth and status, though measured differently in different societies, are constant features of all social structures, so social power is an ever-present feature of social life. Power, understood as the ability of a person, group, or society to dominate over another for the purpose of causing some course of action or lack of it, is part of every social relationship. Just as wealth is distributed through the specialized institution of the economy in society, so power, in its institutional expressions, is distributed through political processes. Power is the ability to control, and thus, is an extremely important stratification variable. Moreover, those with power have the means to control access to, and distribution of, other stratification resources.

There are several distinctive characteristics of social power. First, social power tends to emerge as a later rather than an earlier object of explicit conflict in societies. As Weber observed (1923), as the wealth positions of different groups in a social system become equalized, or more alike, conflict will focus increasingly upon status and power. The actions of various ethnic communities in American society, whose economic ascendancy has been followed by subsequent movement into the political arena, illustrate Weber's proposition. Thus, stratification processes between competing groups in more complex societies follow a typical life cycle. Following the initial status assignments, competition for wealth resources soon ensues. The onset of power struggles in political institutions is very likely a signal that some degree of upward economic mobility has already occurred. Status designations, having a special tenacity, mark the last realm of intergroup struggle. These processes are examined in Chapter 9.

Second, power, if used effectively will increase and be used again with greater ease. Conversely, power, if used ineffectively, diminishes and becomes more difficult to use again. In the simplest case, consider the schoolyard bully who is forced to "back down." He is not likely to make the same move again. Yet, the bully whose threats produce results can impose his will on others more easily the next time. The forces of intimidation accruing with the effective use of power work in quite the same manner on both the individual and collective levels. Considered from this perspective, the ability to have others comply with one's requests while expending minimal effort is the goal of all "power plays."

In summary, class, status, and power are the three resources by which individuals and groups are ranked and for which individuals and groups compete and conflict in all societies. While different societies may quantify these phenomena a bit differently, they are, nonetheless, in the abstract, the same in all societies. Class resources, meaning material wealth in whatever form, are highly volatile. They are the most easily obtained, but also diminish when spent. Class position typically is the first resource over which groups are likely to openly compete with one another. Social status, meaning honor, prestige, and privilege, is the first form of ranking that occurs between groups and individuals in any social relationship. Status ranking is extremely stable, and thus, is the most difficult stratification resource to alter. Finally, power, the ability to control the actions of others, is a feature of all social relationships. Power, when used effectively, grows. When it is used ineffectively, it diminishes.

Types of Stratification Systems

Having considered some basic features of the class, status, and power resources found in all societies, one must next ask: What are the different types of stratification systems that emerge in human societies? What sorts of arrangements have human beings designed for distributing these three resources?

Even a cursory examination of some different societies reveals that not all societies play the stratification game by the same rules. The chances that a particular player will collect a significant share of these resources varies from one society to the next. Moreover, stratification resources may accrue not only for what people do, but also for certain desirable attributes or traits they possess. In this regard, it is useful to distinguish between ascription and achievement processes. *All stratification may be either ascribed, that is, assigned at birth, or achieved, granted because of something the person has done or accomplished.* These two stratification processes are not mutually exclusive. Both may occur in the same society.

Ascribed

Achieved

Social mobility

Social mobility is the process by which social groups and individuals alter their share of the status, class, and power resources that are allocated to them at birth. The opportunities for upward social mobility available to groups and individuals vary considerably, depending upon whether a society emphasizes ascribed or achieved stratification processes. All societies, even those that proclaim equal opportunity, engage in ascriptive status ranking. The important question is how and why do some societies allow more opportunities for upward social mobility than others? The answer lies in the ways that different stratification systems are imbued with norms of either ascription or achievement.

Closed system

Social stratification systems may be classified into two categories, open and closed systems. The first of these, variously called *closed or ascriptive stratification systems are those in which upward social mobility either is not possible or when it happens, represents a variation from established norms.* The term ascription means that stratification resources are allocated at birth, rather than being based upon anything the individual does to alter these resources. Both caste systems and estate systems are examples of ascriptive stratification systems.

Open system

At the opposite end of the spectrum are *open mobility or achievement systems in which upward social mobility or change in relative stratification position is the norm.* In these systems persons have significant opportunities to move beyond the position ascribed at birth. Social class systems that prevail in many Western nations are examples of open mobility systems.

CASTE AND STIGMA

Caste

A caste is a category of persons whose stratification position is determined by unchangeable status norms, and who are powerless to alter either those defining norms or the resulting resource positions they create. A caste is a stratification category characterized by rigidity. While ascriptive status allocations occur among groups in virtually all societies, caste systems are those in which such status designations entirely determine and control the distribution of resources among people. Caste systems provide rigid, indelible categories of persons, some of whom are given permanent and greatly deficient shares of class, status, and power.

The criteria upon which such caste systems are based are varied. Perhaps the most severe instances of caste stratification were the slave systems of antiquity. Tribal, ethnic, and religious differences were just a few of the specific criteria used to create castes. A more recent example is the system of castes that has prevailed among the Hindus of India for approximately 2,000 years. Given the Hindu belief in reincarnation, this earthly caste system seems to make sense for those in the highest (Brahmin) and lowest (Harijan or untouchable) castes alike. The Hindu religion explains that caste position is part of the great order of the universe and is changed only as a person returns to this world in another life. In a sense, it simply means that individuals are taking turns at being greatly privileged or disadvantaged.

Not all caste systems are based upon the degree of theological elegance encountered in the case of Hinduism. The system of apartheid in South Africa has been a state-enforced caste system based upon variations in skin color, or alleged racial differences. This is a system in which virtually all routes of social mobility open to whites have been closed legally to blacks. The system is justified by a rather thin veneer of racial supremacy doctrines, for which some of the Christian churches in South Africa (most importantly the Dutch Reformed Church) claim a biblical foundation. These different examples of caste systems have in common the nearly complete inability of those without privilege to obtain upward social mobility. In fact, mobility, even by a small portion of the lowest caste in such a system, is a signal that the system is undergoing transition to some other form of social stratification. This has already happened in India, where, in the cities, untouchables are able to "pass" as members of higher strata, and where a class system of stratification slowly has been replacing the caste system.

A number of sociologists, among them John Dollard in his study *Caste and Class in a Southern Town* (1937) and Gerald Berreman (1960) have argued that different forms of stratification may exist side by side within the same society. Both of these writers, though in different periods (the 1930s and 1960s), have claimed that the position of blacks in American society, at least prior to the Civil Rights Act of 1964, fits all the criteria by which one would identify a caste. Castes usually are characterized by several features. Among them are endogamy, meaning marriage only within the caste; ascriptive membership at birth and for life; and, strict avoidance of members of other strata. Additionally, caste ranking also typically includes stigma (van den Berghe 1981).

Stigma

Stigma refers to any human attribute that is deeply discrediting, thus making persons different from others, and of a less desirable kind. Stigma prevents caste members from escaping or "passing" as something different from what society says they are. While skin color is defined as a physical stigma in many societies, physical stigma may be socially fabricated if such markings do not occur biologically. Under Nazism, since Jews had no such physical markings, they were required by law to wear identifying arm bands and emblems on their clothing. Such marks guarantee that "proper" relationships between castes are maintained. If Dollard, Berreman, and others are correct in arguing that in the not so distant past American blacks represented a caste, today it is equally clear that there has been substantial movement away from that status. During the 1970s and 1980s, while the economic position of American blacks still lagged behind that of whites, some blacks entered professional, occupational, and business fields that would have remained entirely closed to them in a caste system. Whether the term caste should be used to refer to a type of system overall or also to types of collective statuses within various systems is an empirically open issue.

ESTATE: LIMITED OPENINGS

Estate system

Estate systems of stratification are those in which groups and individuals are ranked relative to the ownership of land. While family, and even birth order within family, frequently determines land ownership in such systems, it is, nonetheless, land ownership or its absence that defines social rank. The estate system was a significant phase in the development of Western societies. It prevailed in most Western European nations throughout the Middle Ages, and even survived in North America until the early 19th century. Moreover, many analysts of social stratification systems, among them Karl Marx in his work *Capital* (1867), view the emergence of estate systems as a major step in the gradual movement toward stratification by class (with rank based on all forms of wealth, not just land). Two features of estate systems support this interpretation. First, land is a form of material wealth, and accordingly, estate systems may be viewed as opening the door to stratification by all forms of material wealth (class). Second, while estate systems are relatively closed, there are some opportunities for upward social mobility within them.

The estate system, in its medieval European form, consisted of three social strata. The highest stratum, or nobility, owned land. In the case of royalty, such as the kings and queens of European nations, both the privilege of land ownership and the resulting powers of rulership were claimed to be divinely given (the divine right of kings). The lowest stratum in these systems were the peasants, most of whom were agricultural workers. Finally, the clergy constituted a middle stratum, serving the interests of the nobility and the crown. Social mobility was possible, though not common, through several routes. First, peasants who migrated into the church either as monks, or as friars working among the commoners, enjoyed a far better life than they would have had as peasants. Second, women, for whom marriage was but a form of servitude, could join a nunnery as a way of escaping into a better life. Third, men who were valiant in battle could earn that special privilege—land ownership—which normally had to be inherited. Lancelot, the hero of King Arthur's Knights of the Round Table, was a commoner made noble through just such a process. Finally, a peasant woman might marry royalty, and through that union be transported into a completely different social position.

THE CLASS SYSTEM: MARX'S ANALYSIS

Today, there is little question that the historical transition from an estate system to a class system marked the emergence of more open stratification processes. Yet, ironically, the scholar who first documented this transition, Karl Marx, doubted that greater openness would be the immediate result. *The class system of stratification ranks groups and individuals according to their possession of material wealth.* Class systems are characterized by an achievement ethos, in which individuals are encouraged to attain social rewards beyond those ascribed at birth. Historically, much of the debate about class systems has stemmed form Karl Marx's analysis in his *magnum opus Capital* (1867). Accordingly, we too, shall begin with Marx.

Class system

In *Capital* Marx described the enormous social transformation from rural-agricultural to urban-industrial society. Convinced that economic forces shape social structures, he searched for the economic changes that were carrying much of mid-19th century Western Europe, as well as North America, into the urban-industrial era. For Marx, capitalism was that force. Society was no longer organized according to patterns of land ownership (estates). Rather, social structures were becoming organized according to people's relationships to productive capital (material wealth of all types). While Marx saw a diversity of social classes emerging, he believed that in the long run, society would become divided between two classes: a small class of owners of capital (the *bourgeoisie*), and a large class of impoverished workers (the *proletariat*). This prediction about the ultimate shape of the social structure was based on Marx's economic theory of industrial-capitalism.

Bourgeoisie

Proletariat

According to Marx, all capitalist systems are built upon the exploitation and oppression of the working class. By underpaying workers for their labor, and by overcharging consumers for products, capitalists create profits. However, since these underpaid workers also play the role of consumers who must purchase overpriced goods, in time, the system will self-destruct. Eventually, the poverty-stricken workers will lack enough money to purchase the bare essentials of life. Inventories that no one can afford to purchase will accumulate. With capital overinvested in factories and inventories, the economic system will collapse. In the *Communist Manifesto* (1848) and other writings, Marx and his co-author Frederich Engels (1820–1895) had already suggested that this economic crisis would precipitate a social revolution establishing the communist (classless) state.

Marx accurately described the historical transition into industrial-capitalist society. He also was correct about the economic forces that would precipitate a crisis in this system. However, today, industrial capitalist societies in both North America and Western Europe do not appear divided into rigid two-class systems of capitalists and workers. Rather, in the 20th century, a diverse assortment of upper, middle, and lower classes has emerged. In the

United States, the middle (not the lower) stratum became the largest segment of the population. Moreover, as indicated by the growth of the middle stratum, many persons have experienced substantial upward social mobility. How can it be possible that Marx's view of capitalist society was correct, but today these societies do not appear as he predicted they would?

First, Marx was correct in his understanding of the workings of capitalism and capitalist exploitation of the working class. His prediction of an economic crisis that would afflict an uncontrolled capitalist economic system also was correct. Ironically, while he anticipated a first economic collapse in the more advanced capitalist systems of Germany and England, the crisis happened in the United States in 1929. The economic conditions of the Great Depression were a textbook example of what Marx had predicted for free-market capitalism. The stock market crash was only the proverbial "tip of the iceberg," the precipitating event that toppled an unsound economic system.

Second, in the wake of the Great Depression, a new form of state-controlled capitalism was designed. Government entered the economy as an employer and spender in ways that could not have been anticipated by Marx and his contemporaries. Today, through monetary and fiscal policies, government controls the supply of capital in the system, stimulates new jobs in periods of recession, and even creates unemployment to cool the system in the periods of inflation. Even prior to the economic crisis of the late 1920s, an organized labor movement was emerging that would moderate the relations between capital and labor. Thus, the system after the Depression was no longer a "free" capitalist system like the one Marx had analyzed in the middle of the 19th century.

Today, it is clear that the early capitalist system, even with its abuses of the working classes, was a powerful economic and social mechanism that was producing a new multi-strata system. The modifications of that system introduced in response to the Great Depression continued the process of erecting a multi-class social system. Most importantly, that system produced substantial amounts of upward social mobility.

SOCIOECONOMIC STATUS

It was noted at the outset of this chapter that modern sociology, consistent with Max Weber's analysis, views all three elements—class, status, and power—as important components in the stratification systems of modern societies. Today, the terms social class and *socioeconomic status* (also called SES) frequently are used interchangeably when referring to *stratification systems based on a mixture of wealth, status, and power.* Moreover, the concept of SES reflects the Weberian idea that these types of stratification systems generally are characteristic of societies with a high degree of openness and social mobility.

Socioeconomic status

How is SES actually measured? Socioeconomic status is a composite measure that usually includes occupational prestige, income, and educational attainment (Duncan 1961). The statistical measure of SES assigns numerical values to levels of these three variables. Each of these three variables contains a diversity of information. For example, occupational categories such as professional, managerial, and manual labor reflect not only probable earning levels, but also prestige and on-the-job autonomy, which is one form of power. Similarly, one's level of educational attainment reflects both a relative income position and potential level of occupational prestige because in modern societies, education is the pathway to upward social mobility for many persons. Even the measurement of income involves more than just salary or earned wages. It must be remembered that, like human work, investments yield income. The point then, is that modern stratification systems rank individuals, groups, and entire strata in terms of combinations of wealth, prestige, and power. The concept of socioeconomic status reflects these complexities.

In summary, social stratification systems may be divided into two types: closed systems based on ascription, and open systems based on an achievement ethos. Caste and estate are both examples of systems in which little or no social mobility occurs. Class systems in which social position is based upon wealth exhibit substantial mobility. Marx believed that under capitalism a relatively closed class system eventually would be produced. However, in contrast to a two-class system based solely upon economic factors as predicted by Marx, a complex system of socioeconomic status ranking based on wealth, status, and power has emerged. Moreover, it is claimed that considerable upward social mobility and wealth redistribution occur in these SES systems.

The Limits to Social Mobility

Thus far, it has been seen that societies may be very different from one another in either preventing or allowing persons to change their share of social resources and rewards. Most sociologists would agree that the socioeconomic status systems of modern societies provide more upward social mobility than do other types of systems, especially those organized according to caste or estate. However, at this juncture, a critically important question must be asked. Exactly how much upward social mobility occurs in these kinds of systems? Precisely how open are these "open" stratification systems?

Sociological research on stratification in the United States and other highly industrialized nations provides several different answers to this question. In part, different impressions of these stratification systems result from different angles of vision. Some studies reveal impressive amounts of internal change and upward social mobility. Yet, other kinds of research document substantial degrees of stability, not mobility.

Two, somewhat complementary, bodies of analysis focus upon aspects of modern stratification systems that reflect stability and permanence, not change. They focus upon populations located at the extreme ends of the social structure. These are the firmly entrenched elites, what some have called the super rich, and the underclasses, those living in poverty. The very rich and the very poor both convey the image of a highly closed stratification system in which little genuine social mobility occurs. Two other bodies of research focusing upon yet different aspects of the stratification system highlight the processes of upward social mobility and change. The first of these consists of studies of intergenerational mobility indicating substantial upward movement within the middle strata in the United States and other nations. A related tradition of research attempts to identify the overall shape of modern socioeconomic status systems. These studies address several related concerns. They focus upon the degree of mobility between strata, and the characteristics of persons within each stratum. After examining what the various studies reveal about established patterns of stratification, we shall examine the most recent trends, some of which suggest that the established patterns are changing.

THE RICH AND THE POOR

The Marxian view, of course, suggests that in any capitalist system, a relatively small elite stratum will control the forces of production and wealth in society. In modern parlance, they are the "super rich." Does the United States have such a class of persons? Sociologist Maurice Zeitlin (1978) observes that in 1860, on the eve of the Civil War, 24 percent of the nation's wealth was owned by only 1 percent of all families. A full century later, in 1960, that same 1 percent owned just a bit more, 24.9 percent, of the nation's wealth. Given the remarkable changes that occurred in American society over that one-hundred-year period, this is very little change in the distribution of wealth.

The concentration of wealth in American society has been the focus of a number of government studies. A survey conducted by the Federal Reserve Board in 1983 examined wealth distribution in the United States over the twenty-year-period 1963–1983 (U.S. Congress Joint Economic Committee 1986). When measured in constant dollars, the wealth of the top 5 percent of households increased during these years from 3.9 to 10.6 trillion dollars. By 1983 the top 5 percent of households owned 29.6 percent of the nation's wealth, and by the mid-1980s, the average net worth of individuals in the top 5 percent of households was 8.9 million dollars per person (*Facts on File* 1986, 622). Statistics provided by the U.S. Internal Revenue Service (1990) show that the top 5 percent of families accounted for 15.5 percent of all income in 1980, and 17.9 percent of income in 1989. While there is some debate about the precise size of this stratum—some writers claim 1 percent, others say 3 percent, and many government publications focus on the top 5 percent—there is no questioning that American society has a relatively stable elite stratum.

Who are America's "super rich" (Lundberg 1968), persons who, by any measure, appear to control a disproportionate share of the nation's wealth? According to sociologist E. Digby Baltzell (1958, 1964), this elite is predominantly White-Anglo-Saxon-Protestant males. It is a highly exclusive group in which family background is as important as money. In other words, this is inherited wealth. Moreover, in his study *The Power Elite* (1956), the late C. Wright Mills argued that this same wealthy, high-status stratum controls key positions in government, business, and industry. Having experienced similar class backgrounds and socialization, these people act in ways that maintain the existing stratification system. Although Mills recognized that occasionally some new wealth, such as celebrities and exceptional business entrepreneurs, enter this upper-class grouping, on the whole Mills saw this as a relatively closed stratum. These same themes are echoed in William Domhoff's work *Who Rules America Now? A View for the '80s* (1983).

In terms of composition, this elite stratum is a bit more heterogeneous today than it was several decades ago. For example, data collected by the Federal Reserve Board in 1983 show some increase in the proportion of the fortunes of the very rich and super rich that are based upon accumulated earnings rather than inherited wealth (U.S. Congress Joint Economic Committee 1986). But, on balance, the upper stratum remains relatively closed. Few white ethnic minorities, virtually no people of color or women have entered elite positions in the top-ranked public and private organizations in the United States (Dye 1986). Clearly, being born into an elite family is still the best predictor of whether an individual will enter America's elite stratum.

At the other end of the spectrum, abject poverty remains a constant feature of American life. In 1991, the median (half are higher and half are lower) household income in the United States was $30,126.00. Yet, in that same year over 35 million persons were living at or below the poverty level, defined as an income of $13,924.00 for an urban family of four. These persons represented 14.2 percent of the American population in 1991 (U.S. Bureau of the Census 1992).

The tenacity of poverty in the United States is dramatically revealed in the patterns of these sorts of income statistics over time. Government figures on poverty have been reported regularly since the late 1950s. Figure 8.1 shows both the poverty rate and the actual number of persons in poverty for the quarter of a century between 1960–1991. Perhaps there is some consolation in the fact that the rate of poverty (as a percent of the population) has declined very substantially since the early 1960s, when over one in every five Americans (22.2 percent) lived in poverty. However, it also is clear that by 1970, the government had lost the "War on Poverty." From that year onward, the actual number of

FIGURE 8.1
PERCENT AND NUMBER OF PERSONS IN POVERTY IN THE UNITED STATES 1960–1991

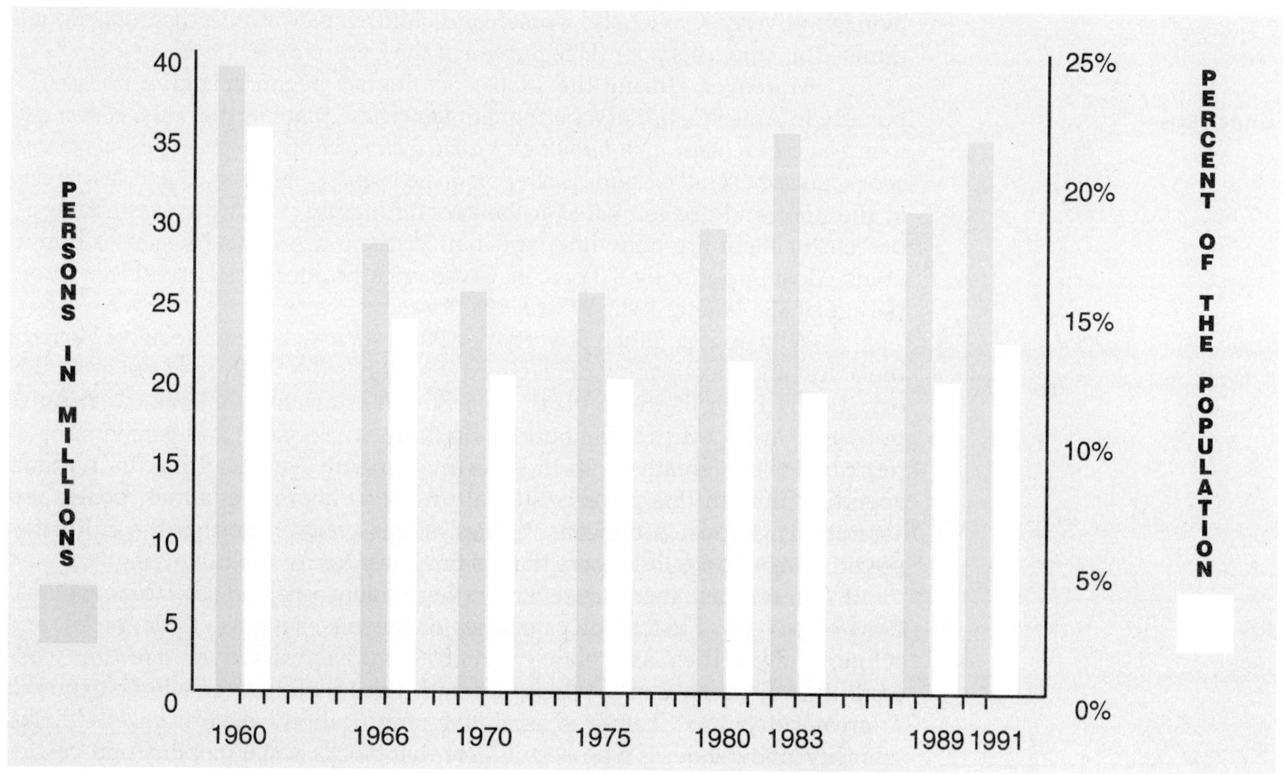

SOURCE: Statistical Abstract of the United States, 1992. Washington, D.C. Bureau of the Census.

persons who were poor steadily increased. By 1983, American society had almost as many persons in poverty (35.3 million) as a quarter of a century earlier (39.9 million in 1960). While the number decreases during the 1980s, there still were 35.7 million persons living in poverty in 1991. These figures do not include the "near poor," people living slightly above the poverty level. In 1989, those living at or near poverty (defined as an income at or below $15,844.00 for a family of four) accounted for 42.7 million persons or 17.3 percent of the American population (U.S. Bureau of the Census 1991). These statistics only begin to show the dramatic rise in poverty associated with the economic recession of the early 1990s. Who are these people living in poverty, and why does such an affluent nation have so much poverty?

Of the 31.5 million persons living in poverty in 1989, 66 percent were white. Thus, the common complaint that minorities, among them blacks and Hispanics, are a disproportionate part of those who "don't make it" in modern society is simply not true. Most poor people are drawn from the white majority. However, a person's chances of being poor surely varies by so-called race. In 1991, 11.3 percent of whites, 28.7 percent of Hispanics, and 32.7 percent of blacks were poor. Shockingly, nearly one out of every five (19 percent) American children (under age 18) was living in poverty in 1989. Among whites 14 percent of children were among the poor, among Hispanics 36 percent, and among blacks 43 percent. In recent years, the number of aged (over age 65) persons in poverty has declined, with only 11.4 percent of them in poverty in 1989. However, there has been a distinct "feminization of poverty." The 1970s and the 1980s saw a dramatic increase in the number of impoverished households headed by women. In 1989, 45 percent of all female-headed households with children were living in poverty. Obviously, women and children constitute a disproportionate number of America's poor (U.S. Bureau of the Census 1991, 1992).

Underclass

Moreover, during the 1980s sociologists began speaking not just of poverty in America, but of a permanent *underclass, meaning a stratum of poor persons who are excluded from meaningful participation in the economy and thus experience no upward social mobility*. Such persons comprise between 33 and 45 percent of the poor and are estimated to be predominantly urban dwellers. Some 70 percent of them are nonwhite, and half of them are female heads of households. Most importantly, 70 percent of America's underclass are children under the age of 18 (Auletta 1982; Wilson 1987).

Why does so much poverty persist in such an affluent society? Perhaps the oldest and most widely debated explanation is the "culture of poverty" theory (Lewis 1959; Banfield 1974). Basically, it is argued that the situation of poverty spawns a distinctive outlook on life, a world view, and behavioral patterns that differ greatly from those of mainstream American life. Individuals spending time in this poverty subculture don't share the values, goals, and aspirations of most Americans. Critics of this view argue that the culture of poverty theory does little more than blame the poor for their own plight.

In contrast, there are several rather widely accepted structural explanations of poverty. First, some categories of persons, such as ethnic, racial, and religious minorities, as well as women, have been disadvantaged by well-institutionalized patterns of prejudice and discrimination. As will be explored in greater detail in Chapter 9, ascriptive stratification based on race, religion, ethnicity, and gender is a powerful force that blocks social mobility and creates poverty.

Second, in certain ways, the presence of poor people has been built into modern economic systems, especially in capitalist societies (Gans 1971; Wright 1978). Most societies contain some undesirable jobs that no one really wants to perform. It becomes socially useful to maintain a stratum of persons (the poor) who must perform such tasks because they have little choice. Some dramatic statistical evidence supports this theory. In 1989, over 50 percent of all heads of families (officially called "householders") living in poverty reported having some kind of gainful employment for some time during that year, and 21 percent of the poor held continuous full-time jobs throughout the year (U.S. Bureau of the Census 1991). Moreover, many who are poor often must settle for part-time work because they cannot find full-time jobs (Pear 1986). In other words, many persons are poor because the work they do does not support them or because they cannot find full-time work. They are not poor because they don't want to work.

Yet a third structural view explains poverty as a consequence of both government policies and specific economic trends. Regarding the former, there is no question that the cutting of social welfare programs by the Reagan administration during the 1980s had severe consequences for the working poor and the near poor (Duncan *et al.* 1984). Additionally, macrosocial economic trends play a role in the incidence of poverty. For example, most job growth during the 1980s was either in dead-end, low-paying jobs or in "high-tech" jobs for which only well-educated persons qualify.

On balance, the extremes of the system do not support the claim that the American stratification system has undergone much change. Government statistics do not indicate a redistribution of wealth. In fact, the super rich today are a bit richer than in past times. Poverty, while variable, is not disappearing from the system. By 1991, nearly as many Americans lived in poverty as a quarter of a century earlier.

FIGURE 8.2
Poverty and wealth are permanent features of the same society and exist side by side.

PATTERNS OF MOBILITY

Is there evidence, then, in support of the view that the United States and other industrialized nations promote upward social mobility? While comprehensive studies of social mobility in large populations are not conducted frequently, there have been two major intergenerational studies of the American population, as well as several attempts to examine comparative data for the United States and Eastern and Western Europe. Let's first consider the American case.

In 1962, and again in 1973, the U.S. Census Bureau administered large (20,000 and 30,000 persons respectively) sample surveys aimed at determining the intergenerational social mobility between fathers and their sons (Blau and Duncan 1967; Featherman and Hauser 1978). These studies indicate that the period between 1930 and 1970 was characterized by high rates of upward social mobility. For example, in comparing a father's occupation with his son's present job, Featherman and Hauser (1978) found upward social mobility occurred in five out of ten cases, while downward mobility occurred in only two out of ten cases. However, because these studies only focus upon fathers and sons, rather than upon the occupational careers of both males and females, it has been argued that they overestimate the degree of social mobility. Even given this flaw in measuring mobility, it is widely accepted that a general trend toward upward social mobility was prevalent during this period. How can these trends be explained?

First, in the years covered by these particular studies, the United States underwent the late phases of a transition from farm employment to industrial employment. This transition was marked by a period of economic growth and industrial expansion. Industrialism meant an increase in the number of upper-status positions available, making some upward mobility inevitable. The proportion of professional and managerial positions almost doubled, with a corresponding increase in the number of white-collar service jobs (U.S. Bureau of the Census 1975). During the period 1945 to 1965 alone, there was a shift of approximately 30 percent from manual to nonmanual occupations (Lenski 1966). While this transition meant genuine improvement in living standards for many Americans, mobility rates were affected more by structural factors than any characteristics of individuals themselves. Social mobility for individuals always is affected by the number and type of occupational positions available to be filled in the society. If more openings exist at the top for the present generation than existed for the previous generation, some children of lower-status parents must move up into higher occupational positions. The reverse also is true. If fewer openings exist at the top for the present generation than previously, then some children of higher-status parents will experience downward mobility. As will be seen, comparative studies of other countries also support the notion that industrialism creates economic opportunities for people.

However, it is also significant that social mobility occurs in small steps, rather than in great leaps. It is rare for the son of a janitor to become a Supreme Court justice. Thus, in Blau and Duncan's study, only one out of ten sons of manual workers were represented in professional categories, as compared with seven out of ten sons of professionals. Still, for the period 1930–1970, chances were 50/50 that a father who spent his working life in a factory would see his son employed in a white-collar job and enjoying a more comfortable lifestyle. Is the United States unique in this regard?

Even given the difficulties of obtaining comparable statistics across different nations with different political and monetary systems, there is a consistent pattern. From the benchmark study of Lipset and Bendix (1959) to more recent studies done in the 1970s and 1980s (Tyree *et al.* 1979; Gruskey and Hauser 1984; Kerckhoff *et al.* 1985; Kaelble 1986), social mobility consistently is associated with industrialism. Mobility from blue-collar to white-collar occupations between fathers and sons varies in different countries from 27 to 31 percent, with the United States being in the upper-middle part of this range. Both Western and Eastern European nations exhibit a persistent relationship between industrialism and upward social mobility. When compared to other industrialized nations, regardless of the political system, the United States does not appear to be more open.

Thus, in spite of the persistence of both elite and poor strata, industrialized nations do promote upward social mobility. In the United States, some mobility has resulted in a large middle class population comprising anywhere from 40 to 65 percent of the entire society, depending of course, upon how one defines "middle class."

THE SHAPE OF MODERN STRATIFICATION SYSTEMS

Given the diversity of information about modern stratification systems, exactly what is known about the distribution of different social strata in these societies? How many strata are there in modern societies, and what are the social characteristics of those strata?

Studies of community life have been a rich source of information about social stratification systems. In American sociology, an important tradition of such studies beginning with the Lynds' studies of *Middletown* (1929, 1937) and the *Yankee City Series* of Lloyd Warner and his associates (Warner *et al.* 1949a, 1949b) has depicted as few as six social classes (Warner and Lunt 1941) and as many as fifteen distinct strata (Davis *et al.* 1941). More recent sociological studies seem to depict from three basic strata (upper, middle, and lower) to six (showing upper and lower divisions in each of these three major categories). Warner's work is deemed important because he and others in his research group used both wealth (class) and prestige (status) factors in depicting the American stratification system. In this sense, their work is a precursor of the more statistical approaches of Duncan's SES Index (1961) and Blau and Duncan's studies of the occupational prestige rankings (1967). Differences not withstanding, nearly all such studies depict the "middle class" as the largest single stratum. Additionally, it is argued that this large middle stratum has resulted from significant upward social mobility trends, typically propelled by industrial growth.

Inevitably, the number of classes or strata one sees is partially a matter of how social class is measured. The so-called *objective method* focuses upon easily quantifiable (i.e., statistical) measures such as income levels. Government reports, for example, commonly plot income distributions in relation to the median (middle) or mean (average) income. Critics of this approach argue that statistical measures don't convey the important cultural or lifestyle components in class groupings. This problem is solved by the *self-placement method,* in which people are asked to provide their own subjective view of their class posi-

Objective method

Self-placement method

Reputational method

tion. A more common approach is the *reputational method,* in which persons are asked to identify the class positions of other persons. Warner and other community sociologists used this method widely in the 1930s and 1940s. It is an effective tool in smaller communities, where people have substantial personal knowledge about their neighbors. It is not suitable for studying large populations or samples. Some researchers (Coleman and Rainwater 1978) have combined several of these ways of measuring class. Clearly, the two subjective ways of measuring class reveal social distinctions not included in strictly statistical approaches. The interesting distinction between "old family" wealth and "new rich" encountered by Warner (1949b) would not be reflected in a purely statistical approach. Obviously, stratification involves both structural and cultural components.

Gilbert and Kahl (1982) have attempted to distill the information from many different kinds of studies of modern stratification systems. The schema they offer consists of six classes or strata (see Table 8.1). First, they agree with

TABLE 8.1

A MODEL OF THE AMERICAN CLASS STRUCTURE

% of the Population and Class		Education Level	Occupation	Income	Budget Level
1 % Capitalists		Prestige university	Executives Investors Heirs	$540,000 from assets	Very high
14% Upper middle		College and Graduate study	Professionals Upper management Some businessmen	$54,000 or more	High
65%	Middle	High school Some college or Apprentice	Managers, sales Semi-professions Nonretail crafts Foremen	about $36,000	Intermediate
	Working	High school	Operatives Crafts Clerical Retail sales	about $27,600	Intermediate to low
20%	Working poor	Some high school	Service work Laborers Low operatives	below $18,400	Under low budget
	Under-class	Primary school	Unemployed Part-timers Welfare clients	below $12,880	Under poverty line

SOURCE: *The American Class Structure: A New Synthesis,* by Dennis Gilbert and Joseph A. Kahl, Copyright 1982 by Dennis Gilbert and Joseph A. Kahl. Reprinted by permission of Wadsworth Inc. Note: the 1978 income statistics in the original have been adjusted (Consumer Price Index) to reflect comparable 1989 dollar values. For comparison, the Bureau of the Census (1991) defines the poverty line in 1989 at $12,675. and median income at $28,906.

the literature on an elite stratum (Mills 1956; Domhoff 1967; Zeitlin 1978) by suggesting that there is a traditional capitalist class consisting of about 1 percent of the population. Second, their upper-middle stratum, about 14 percent of the population, looks very much like the technocrats and managerial elite that various writers have described. While the older capitalist elite (1 percent) represents old-family money, this larger managerial elite (14 percent) contains newly arrived persons, especially those "moving up" through educational attainment. Next, Gilbert and Kahl place some 65 percent of the population in the middle and working (lower-middle) strata. This departs from some of the more purely statistical approaches that depict the "middle class" as being 40–45 percent of the population.

Obviously, Gilbert and Kahl are arguing that the middle and working strata are similar because of common values and lifestyles. This approach stresses the cultural elements in social class groupings. This 65 percent of the population fuels the consumer economy by working toward home ownership and sending their children to college. Finally, most sociologists would agree with the identification of the two lower strata, the working poor and the underclass. This seems to be the same 20 percent of the population that is consistently depicted by various studies, including Census Bureau statistics, as being at or near the poverty level.

This six-class schema offers a reasonable overview of the large body of research about the stratification system of American society and other industrialized nations. Several clear patterns emerge from this schema and others similar to it. First, the class structure is internally diverse. This diversity stems not simply from different life chances (wealth), but also from different lifestyles (family background, occupational choice, etc.). Second, for the greater part of the 20th century, most Americans were situated neither among the extremely rich nor among the extremely poor. Rather, the largest number of persons occupied a middle position in the stratification system and thus constitute a central trend (65 percent). Within these middle strata, there appear to be relatively few barriers to movement across substrata boundaries, for example, from upper-blue collar to lower-white collar, or from clerical to managerial levels. As such, the presence of these strata provides support for the claim that substantial amounts of upward social mobility have occurred.

ASSESSING RECENT TRENDS

What clues about future trends are available? What do the most recent studies of social stratification indicate about this system as the dawn of the 21st century approaches? By the time of the 1960 United States Census, it was becoming clear that America's period of industrialism was waning. Census materials collected in that year showed that over half of all persons in the workforce were employed in service occupations. That trend has prevailed sufficiently to justify the label "post-industrial" (Bell 1973) when describing the American economy. Better paying industrial jobs that once were the underpinning of the American working class have fallen prey to two factors. First, technology has simply eliminated many such jobs. Second, as other nations have industrialized, many of these jobs have gone "off shore."

The de-industrialization of American society would not be a problem if the new service occupations offered incomes similar to those of the dying industrial economy. They do not. Several researchers have provided evidence of a dual or split labor market (Wilson 1980; Beck *et al.* 1978, 1980). They find the wealthy and the poor growing in numbers, and the middle class shrinking. It is predicted that those persons attaining higher levels of education will occupy high-paying positions in the growing techno-service economy. Conversely, those without educational training will fill the lower-paying jobs of the service economy. Employment patterns during the 1980s provided chilling support for these views. While Americans enjoyed nearly full employment and saw record-setting new job creation, most of these were lower-paying service jobs. Additionally, the two-job household (with both adults working to support the family) became a norm. Some studies reveal that specific populations, among them racial minorities and women, are being recruited and "trained" for low-echelon employment (Wilson 1980; Scott 1985).

Whether the trends of the 1980s represent a temporary shift in the pattern of stratification in industrialized nations or the beginning of a new post-industrial era that will be marked by fundamental realignments of the stratification system is not yet clear. These trends and questions, no doubt, will remain high among the issues concerning sociologists in the twilight of the 20th century. We've noted at several junctures that social mobility for individuals must in part be understood as a consequence of the society's "opportunity structure." During the late 1980s the opportunity structure in American society began to shrink.

In summary, this section of the chapter has examined several complex patterns of stratification in the United States and other modern societies. For most of this century, American society has exhibited a well-entrenched elite socioeconomic stratum, a capitalist stratum not unlike that described by Marx. However, poverty has also been a constant feature of the American stratification system. Between these two extremes there is a large middle strata within which upward social mobility has been prevalent. Of the six different social classes described by Gilbert and Kahl (1982), the working and middle strata together comprise 65 percent of the population. However, trends in the 1980s suggest that important changes are occurring that will reduce the size of these middle strata in a post-industrial economy.

EXPLAINING SOCIAL STRATIFICATION

A final concern of this chapter is the question, why do social stratification systems exist in societies? Especially for persons living in societies which, like the United States, stress equality of opportunity in their public doctrines, the near universality of inequality is a puzzling phenomena. As was seen earlier in this chapter, even the more open stratification systems contain substantial elements of inequality. While the nature of ascriptive inequalities will be explored in Chapter 9, the task here is to explain the occurrence of stratification in general.

Three different theories of stratification are examined, compared, and evaluated. They are structural-functionalism, social conflict theory, and self-esteem theory. Each theory offers different reasons for the emergence of stratification, and each focuses upon certain features of social stratification while underplaying other aspects of these systems. A balanced understanding of social stratification should be based upon the relevant elements in each of these theories.

STRUCTURAL-FUNCTIONAL THEORY

Structural-functional theory

Structural-functional theory focuses upon the structural arrangements in societies and attempts to discern the functions or tasks that are accomplished for the society by various social structures and institutions. The theory assumes that every social structure yields some benefit and fulfills some need for the social system as a whole and that this function is the reason and explanation for the existence of that social structural or institutional component (Parsons 1951).

This general perspective as applied to stratification systems in society produces the following scenario. First, all societies, in order to maintain themselves, must have certain tasks accomplished. Second, some tasks require more diligence and training than others. Third, in order to insure that these more important tasks will attract appropriate personnel, societies offer substantial rewards to induce persons to fulfill such tasks. Thus, persons are rewarded unequally because the tasks they accomplish for the society are not of equal importance. Those people doing the more important jobs get rewarded more than others. The entire system of unequal rewards insures that the most talented and hard-working people will be recruited for the most important tasks. In this way, social stratification, a system of unequal rewards, functions to maintain the social system.

Functionalists argue that the tasks performed by persons in certain professions, such as medicine, dentistry, law, and corporate leadership are socially important tasks. The skillful accomplishment of such tasks is necessary for the orderly functioning of the society. Therefore, persons performing these social roles are highly rewarded in terms of both income and prestige. Typically, these occupational positions require high levels of educational training. In simple terms, the most important jobs, and those requiring the greatest skill and training, are rewarded with the highest "perks." Jobs requiring much less preparation, dedication, and skill, and for which there is a much larger pool of possible candidates, such as retail clerks, secretaries, and manual laborers, do not offer such attractive rewards. Moreover, as was seen earlier, some analysts extend this view to the explanation of poverty. That is, it is functional for society to maintain a stratum of poor persons who must perform the most undesirable tasks.

To what extent do these mechanisms of societal needs and occupational recruitment actually explain the stratification system and the inequalities encountered in societies? Criticisms of functional theory are of two types, those challenging the assumptions underlying the theory and those disputing that empirical events in societies actually "fit" the theory (Davis and Moore 1945).

Turning first to the more general assumptions of structural-functionalism, the idea that all social institutions yield functions that contribute to the stability or maintenance of society is far from accepted by all sociologists. For instance, critics of the theory observe that in the United States, high school drop-out rates indicate a serious malfunctioning of the educational system. If schools are doing such a good job why don't they produce more graduates? Similarly, high levels of family violence and divorce demonstrate disruptive, rather than functional, consequences of family patterns in the United States. Thus, the assumption that all institutions yield positive functions for the society is challenged. Some social arrangements may be more dysfunctional than functional. Additionally, it is argued that there are no established criteria by which one may say what *the* most important function of a specific institution may be. How is it decided which tasks, jobs, or professions are most important? For instance, garbage collectors surely don't earn what lawyers do, but a lapse in garbage collection would threaten the stability of the social system much more quickly than a lawyer's strike! These criticisms suggest that there are some complex conceptual issues involved in applying the ideas of structural-functionalism to stratification systems.

Perhaps even more telling are criticisms of the degree of "fit" between functional explanations of social arrangements and actual happenings in societies. For instance, some of the highest-paid people in American society, such as movie stars, rock musicians, professional athletes, and television personalities, don't seem to reflect the functionalist claim that rewards will be proportional to the importance of the task performed, or the extent of educational preparation required for the job. It is difficult to argue that the members of the Minnesota Twins or the Washington Redskins, the cast of the television show "L.A. Law," or such rock music idols as Michael Jackson, Bruce Springsteen, and Madonna are so highly rewarded because they perform tasks that are essential for the stability of American society. Clearly, much of stratification processes bear little relationship to basic societal needs and functions. Conversely, in the United States, persons with college degrees, in the aggregate, earn substantially more than do those with only high school diplomas; and for most persons, education is a path to higher salaries and more prestigious occupational positions. Thus, while there seems to be a general relationship between the qualifications and training required for a job and the salary, prestige, and career opportunities offered, there are sufficient exceptions to this relationship to raise questions about the accuracy of the functional theory of stratification.

A second instance of poor empirical fit between the theory and actual events involves patterns of prejudice and discrimination. These forms of ascriptive stratification prevent talented and diligent persons from obtaining stratification resources. For instance, in 1989, on average, women in the United States earned only 63.1 cents for every dollar earned by men (U.S. Bureau of the Census 1991). This discrepancy persists even at comparable levels of attained education (i.e., all college graduates and all high school graduates). Occupational categories traditionally dominated by females, such as nursing and secretarial work, suffer very low prestige, and, considering the importance of the work performed, relatively low wages.

This differential reward system conflicts greatly with the claims of functional theory. For reasons of religion, ethnic background, age, gender, and so called race, persons routinely are prevented from obtaining social rewards that surely are within their range of competence and ability. Discrimination deprives society of the talents and abilities of untold numbers of persons. Racism, ageism, anti-Semitism, sexism, and ethnic prejudice in the United States, just like apartheid in South Africa, and anti-Catholicism in Northern Ireland, all contradict the basic claims of functional theory. Even if everyone could agree upon which social tasks are the most important, in many societies entire categories of persons still would be ascriptively stratified in ways that are neither socially functional nor just. The structural-functional theory does not explain these occurrences.

SOCIAL CONFLICT THEORY

The assumptions that underlie social conflict theories are very different from those giving rise to functional theory. What are the basic elements of social conflict theory? First, social conflict theorists claim that most people, most of the time, wish to maintain and increase their social resources, class, status, and power. Second, persons view these resources as scarce, and thus, see each other as competitive threats. People act as though "your gain is my loss." Third, this perception gives rise to both individual and collective strategies of competition and even conflict between different individuals, groups, and strata.

Social conflict theory

According to conflict theory, social stratification and inequality may be understood as the result of these competitive struggles and conflicts between individuals and strata. Even prejudice and discrimination may be seen as techniques by which one party neutralizes the competitive efforts of others (see discussion Chapter 9, pp. 239–243). In this sense inequalities in the social structure are a living history of who is winning and losing the stratification contests in society. When asked, "Why is there stratification?" the conflict theorist replies that stratification is simply the social structural by-product of people's attempts to maximize their shares of the social resource system.

What are the benefits and shortcomings involved in viewing the stratification system from a conflict perspective? On the positive side, social conflict theories explain certain important facts that seem to escape notice in functional theory. While functionalism may explain why there is inequality, it does not explain why some inequalities are so great. For example, while one might expect physicians to be paid more than sales clerks or construction workers, the difference in these salaries is rather large. Similarly, American corporate executives often are paid salaries hundreds of times greater than the average workers in their companies. Such differences in income are the results of dominance and control, not incentive. Such magnitudes of income difference result from the disproportionate ability of some persons to control the game, not from the societal need to induce better qualified persons to take more difficult positions.

On the other hand, social conflict theories, which view most social relationships in terms of competition, somewhat underestimate the extent of cooperation even between apparent adversaries such as management and labor in the industrial setting. The conflict perspective also seems to ignore the extent to which people do things for reasons other than personal gain. There is much that people do that does not entail the struggle for society's "goodies."

Social conflict theories offer a powerful explanation for instances where distributive justice does not prevail, where inequalities seem to exceed functional need, and where deprivation of certain groups and individuals simply contradicts a rational incentive model. It is apparent that many people do not "get ahead" because the social structure conspires against them, and the conflict perspective focuses upon the processes involved in these struggles.

SELF-ESTEEM THEORY

Yet a different explanation of social stratification processes is offered by the micro-social perspective of symbolic interactionism, especially in the writings of the late Ernest Becker (1962, 1975). Following the social psychological theories of Charles Cooley and George Mead (see Chapter 6), Becker argues that the human personality is extremely flexible, capable of responding to the social and physical environment in innumerable ways. The human animal is characterized by plasticity. However, Becker does see the innate need or drive for self-esteem as a constant feature of the human condition. How do humans satisfy the need to feel good about themselves? For Becker, it is here that stratification enters the picture.

Stratification rewards are understood as self-esteem mechanisms. People develop feelings of self-worth by comparison with other persons. Becker argues that by valuing and rewarding our own characteristics, and disvaluing those of other persons—their race, religious beliefs, ethnic origins, or gender—we satisfy the craving for self-esteem. Thus, *self-esteem theories interpret much of culture and social structure as self-esteem maintenance systems.*

Self-esteem theory

There is little question that the stratification processes in societies, in addition to being an allocation system, also entail the construction of symbolic meaning systems. These meaning systems explain who and what we are, and are not. Surely, especially in capitalist cultures, persons measure some part of their self-worth by the share of class, status, and power they have. However, most sociologists would argue that to discover the meanings of events is different from discovering their causes. Thus the microsocial perspective of Becker and other symbolic interactionists adds a dimension to the understanding of why stratification exists that complements the more structural explanations of conflict and functional theories.

In summary, this section of the chapter has examined three different theoretical views of social stratification systems: namely, structural-functionalism, social conflict, and self-esteem. Functionalism stresses the ways in which differential reward systems encourage individuals to seek higher levels of accomplishment. However, the tendency to reward hard work and diligence is not quite so pervasive as functionlism suggests. Rather, as conflict theories demonstrate, there is much ascriptive ranking even in the most achievement-oriented societies. Much inequality is the result of struggle and competition. Finally, a symbolic interactionist view shows that inequality in society also involves symbolic meaning systems. For those persons who enjoy greater rather than lesser rewards, these inequalities "make sense." Indeed, in societies that stress the ideology of personal achievement and individual accomplishment, even the disprivileged may come to adopt the prevailing view that large social inequalities "make sense."

APPLICATIONS
STRATIFICATION AS LIFESTYLE

Travis Williams, in the words of a well-known song, had "the world on a string." As the star punt returner for the Green Bay Packers, he established a record-setting 41.1 yards per return in 1967 and was a key special teams player in the 1968 Super Bowl II, when the Packers took the championship by defeating the Oakland Raiders 33–14. Through football greatness, Williams had arrived at what C. Wright Mills (1956) calls the "celebrity" component of the American upper class. Most of the real wealth in the United States consists of "old money." However, as Mills observes, through the entertainment business and related fields (like professional sports) some "newcomers" also arrive in the American upper class.

Unfortunately, for Travis Williams, the good life was short-lived. A football injury ended his career in 1972, and the road downhill was steep. On February 17, 1991, Williams ran what a *Sports Illustrated* obituary poetically labeled his "last return" (Newman 1991). He died destitute, having battled depression and alcoholism in the years following his injury. Yet, tragic as the events of Travis Williams' life are, they are not typical. Few people will experience in the space of one lifetime the lifestyles of superstardom and abject poverty. As we've already seen (pp. 218–221) social mobility, both upward and downward, tends to happen in small steps. However, in at least one regard, Williams was like thousands of other Americans—homeless; and his tragedy calls attention to what is perhaps the fastest growing social stratum in the American stratification system.

Homelessness is not a new phenomenon in the Untied States. However, the number of homeless as a distinct social stratum in the 1980s and 1990s is virtually without precedent. In Colonial times, most communities cared for their own "settled poor," leaving a rather small transient population that was shuttled from one community to the next. Populations of tramps, bums, and hoboes emerged after the Civil War, and, for a time, were a significant part of the seasonal labor force. By the turn of the century such populations were concentrated in "skid row" sections of American cities (Rossi 1989).

Prior to the 1980s, the Great Depression of the 1930s is the only period in American history characterized by a distinct and socially diverse homeless population. In 1933, the Federal Emergency Relief Administration housed 125,000 persons in transient camps, and in 1934, a nationwide survey of some 700 communities estimated the homeless at 200,000 persons (Landers 1990). Today, it is estimated that there are over half a million homeless people in the United States. What has caused the emergence of a new homeless stratum in American society? and exactly how extensive is the problem of homelessness?

CASE
HOMELESSNESS

A precise accounting of homelessness is not easily obtained. Most studies of population characteristics track people by their place of residence, and the homeless have no place of residence. A survey conducted by the U.S. Department of Housing and Urban Development (HUD) in 1988 found that between 1984 and 1988 the number of shelters for the homeless nearly tripled, increasing from 1,900 to 5,400. During this same period, shelter bed capacity increased from 100,000 to 275,000 (U.S. Department of Housing and Urban Development 1989). In 1989, sociologist Peter Rossi, after reviewing a diversity of estimates, determined America's homeless population to be at least 300,000 persons, and more likely 500,000 persons on any given night (Rossi 1989).

Who are America's homeless? The 1988 HUD study found that unattached males accounted for 66 percent of the homeless in 1984 but were only 45 percent of the homeless by 1988. In contrast, families accounted for only 21 percent of the homeless in 1984 but were 40 percent of America's homeless by

1988. In 1988, single parents and their children accounted for 30 percent of homeless Americans. Other surveys have shown that the aged are only 6 percent of homeless persons and that contrary to the stereotype of homeless women as elderly "bag ladies," the average homeless woman is only 28.4 years of age (Sullivan and Damrosch 1987, 89). Thus, the time-tested image of the homeless as down-and-out elderly people is not accurate. Today's homeless are disproportionately young, female, parents, unemployed, black, and Hispanic (Institute of Medicine 1988).

Why is homelessness in the United States such a fast-growing phenomenon? At least four social factors are involved in these trends. First, during the late 1970s and early 1980s, there was a concerted government policy aimed at the deinstitutionalization of persons with varying degrees of mental illness. The idea of treating "minimally disabled" persons in more humane community-based settings was well-intentioned. However, sufficient funding for community treatment programs, half-way houses, and group homes never materialized. Several studies (Dear and Wolch 1987; U.S. Department of Housing and Urban Development 1989; Institute of Medicine 1988) indicate that persons with chronic mental and physical disabilities (schizophrenia, alcoholism, drug abuse, and AIDS) and victims of domestic violence are strongly represented among the homeless. However, they alone are not the entire story.

Second, the shortage of affordable housing has been an undeniable force in creating homelessness. Several related trends are involved in this pattern. First, during the years of the Reagan presidency (1980–1988), federal housing subsidy programs were reduced by some 70 percent (Palen 1992). Thus, programs that made housing affordable for low-income families were decreased and sometimes eliminated. Poor families were displaced into the streets. Second, the supply of SRO (single-room occupancy) housing in American cities decreased dramatically (Wright 1989). Through urban renewal and related programs, this type of housing, typically frequented by the inner city poor who were not part of family units, was destroyed and nothing was provided to replace it, leaving former tenants with nowhere to go.

Third, homelessness increases because poverty increases. To understand increasing levels of homelessness, the structure of the economic system must be examined. Jonathan Kozol (1988) observes that since 1980, the American economy has been losing two million traditional industrial jobs per year. As noted earlier in this chapter (see discussion pp. 221–222), these high paying industrial jobs typically are replaced by minimum-wage service jobs. These observations have been echoed by analysts throughout the economic recession of the late 1980s and early 1990s. Unemployment and underemployment reflect long-term structural trends affecting not only the poor and uneducated (a typical recessionary trend), but the middle classes as well. In this sense, just like the figures for those "near poverty," there are millions of "near homeless." Many individuals and families drift in and out of poverty, and at least one survey shows that persons drift in and out of homelessness on average for periods of about 21.9 months (Rossi 1989). Many persons on the streets are there simply because they are poor.

Finally, homelessness has become a consequence of America's drug epidemic. Because of drug abuse, untold numbers of persons have been rendered socially dysfunctional. They are either physically unable to sustain meaningful employment, or psychically unable to spend their funds on anything (including housing) other than drugs. In this sense, some extent of homelessness is but a reflection of the wider problem of drug abuse that afflicts the American social structure.

By the early 1990s the homeless were emerging as a distinct social stratum in American society. Today they are too numerous to be "invisible." If it is correct that the homeless reflect structural factors in the American economy, then, unless a concerned social policy is instituted to alleviate their plight, they will not soon disappear from the American social landscape.

Chapter Summary

1. Social stratification, or ranking, is a process through which class (wealth), status (prestige), and power (control) resources are distributed to groups and individuals in societies.

2. The three social resources, class, status, and power have different properties. Class or wealth is the most easily obtained, but is depleted when used. Status, meaning honor, prestige, and privilege is very stable and neither increases nor diminishes with use. Power, the ability to control one's own actions as well as those of others, grows when used effectively, but decreases when used ineffectively.

3. Social stratification systems may be either closed (ascriptive) or open (achievement-oriented). Closed systems, such as caste and estate allow little or no social mobility. Open systems, such as those based on socioeconomic status, encourage upward social mobility.

4. Karl Marx analyzed the change from agricultural to industrial society. While he correctly depicted the faults of capitalism, he did not anticipate modifications of the capitalist system that would produce much internal social mobility.

5. Sociological research indicates that the United States possesses an elite upper stratum as well as a relatively stable poverty stratum, or underclass. Both of these trends appear to persist over long periods of time, and both trends conflict with the idea that modern SES systems promote social mobility and wealth redistribution.

6. Studies of the United States and other industrialized nations support the claim that substantial upward social mobility has occurred throughout much of the 20th century. Measures of socioeconomic status (occupational prestige, income, and educational attainment) demonstrate that the middle stratum is the largest single component (65 percent) of modern industrial societies.

7. Stratification trends during the 1980s suggest certain limits to these earlier patterns. The emergence of a post-industrial service economy has been accompanied by a shrinking middle stratum. The number of women, children, and minority populations in poverty seem to reflect a split labor market. The general impression is that during the 1980s the American opportunity structure changed direction.

8. Structural-functionalism, social conflict theory, and symbolic interactionism provide three different views of why stratification occurs. Functionalism claims that differential rewards insure the recruitment of qualified persons to important jobs. Conflict theories see inequality as the result of status ascription and social competition. Symbolic interactionism suggests that social inequalities entail meaning systems that satisfy people's self-esteem needs. Each theory contributes something useful to the sociological understanding of stratification.

Key Concepts

achieved
ascribed
bourgeoisie
caste
class
class system
closed system
estate systems
objective method
open system
power
proletariat
reputational method
self-esteem theory
self-placement method
social conflict theory
social mobility
socioeconomic status (SES)
status
stigma
stratification
structural-functional theory
underclass

Bibliography

Auletta, Ken
1982. *The underclass.* New York: Vintage.

Baltzell, E. Digby
1958. *Philadelphia gentlemen: The making of a national upper class.* Glencoe, Illinois: Free Press.

1964. *The protestant establishment: Aristocracy and caste in America.* New York: Random House.

Banfield, Edward C.
1974. *The unheavenly city revisited.* Boston: Little, Brown & Co.

Beck, E. M., Patrick Horan and Charles Tolbert
1978. Stratification in a dual economy: A structural model of income determination. *American Sociological Review.* Vol. 43, No. 4: 704–20.

1980. Social stratification in industrial society: Further evidence for a structural alternative. *American Sociological Review.* Vol. 45, No. 1: 712–19.

Becker, Ernest
1962. *The birth and death of meaning.* New York: Free Press.

1975. *Escape from evil.* New York: Free Press.

Bell, Daniel
1973. *The coming of post-industrial society: A venture in social forecasting.* New York: Basic Books.

Berreman, Gerald
1960. Caste in India and the United States. *American Journal of Sociology.* Vol. 66, No. 1: 120–27.

Blau, Peter, and Otis Dudley Duncan
1967. *The America occupational structure.* New York: John Wiley and Sons.

Coleman, James S., and Lee Rainwater
1978. *Social standing in America.* New York: Basic Books.

Davis, Allison, Burleigh Gardner and Mary Gardner
1941. *Deep South: A social-anthropological study of caste and class.* Chicago: Univ. of Chicago Press.

Davis, Kingsley, and Wilbert Moore
1945. Some principles of stratification. *American Sociological Review.* Vol. 10, No. 2: 242–49.

Dear, Michael J., and Jennifer R. Wolch
1987. *Landscapes of despair: From deinstitutionalization to homelessness.* Oxford, England: Polity Press.

Dollard, John
1937. *Caste and class in a southern town.* New Haven, Conn.: Yale Univ. Press.

Domhoff, G. William
1967. *Who rules America?* Englewood Cliffs, N.J.: Prentice-Hall.

1983. *Who rules America now? A view for the 80s.* Englewood Cliffs, N.J.: Prentice-Hall.

Duncan, Greg J., with Richad D. Coe, Mary E. Corcoran, Martha S. Hill, Saul D. Hoffman, and James N. Morgan
1984. *Years of poverty, years of plenty: The changing economic fortunes of American workers and families.* Ann Arbor, Michigan: Institute for Social Research.

Duncan, Otis Dudley
1961. Properties and characteristics of the socio-economic index. In *Occupations and social status,* edited by Albert Reiss. Glencoe, Illinois: Free Press.

Dye, Thomas
1986. *Who's running America? The conservative years.* 4th ed. Englewood Cliffs, N.J.: Prentice-Hall.

Facts on File
1986. *Facts on file.* Chicago, Illinois: Rand McNally and Company (August 1), p. 622, Column 2.

Featherman, David L., and Robert M. Hauser
1978. *Opportunity and change.* New York: Academic Press.

Gans, Herbert J.
1971. The uses of poverty: The poor pay all. *Social Policy* 2: 20–24.

Gilbert, Dennis, and Joseph A. Kahl
1982. *The American class structure.* Homewood, Illinois: The Dorsey Press.

Grusky, David, and Robert M. Hauser
1984. Comparative social mobility revisited: Models of convergence and divergence in 16 countries. *American Sociological Review* 49: 19–38.

Institute of Medicine
1988. *Homelessness, health and human needs.* Washington, D.C.: National Academy Press.

Kaelble, Hartmut
1986. *Social mobility in the 19th and 20th centuries: Europe and America in comparative perspective.* New York: St. Martin's Press.

Kerckhoff, Alan C., Richard T. Campbell, and Idee Winfield
1985. Social mobility in Great Britain and the United States. *American Journal of Sociology* 91: 281–308.

Kozol, Jonathan
1988. Distancing the homeless. *The Yale Review.* Vol. 77, No. 2 (Winter): 153–67.

Landers, Robert K.
1990. "Why homeless need more than shelter." In *Editorial Research Reports.* Vol. 1, No. 12. Washington, D.C.: Congressional Quarterly Inc.

Lenski, Gerhard
1966. *Power and privilege: A theory of social stratification.* New York: McGraw-Hill.

Lewis, Oscar
1959. *Five families: Mexican case studies in the culture of poverty.* New York: Basic Books.

Lipset, Seymour Martin, and Reinhard Bendix
1959. *Social mobility in industrial society.* Berkeley, California: Univ. of California Press.

Lundberg, Ferdinand
1968. *The rich and the super-rich.* New York: L. Stuart.

Lynd, Robert S., and Helen Merrill Lynd
1929. *Middletown.* New York: Harcourt Brace Jovanovich.

1937. *Middletown in transition.* New York: Harcourt Brace Jovanovich.

Marx, Karl
1867. *Capital.* Translated by Samuel Moore and Edward Aveling, 3 vols., 1967. New York: International Publishers.

Marx, Karl, and Friedrich Engles
1848. *The Communist Manifesto.* Translated by Samuel Moore, 1969. Chicago: Regnery.

Mills, C. Wright
1956. *The power elite.* New York: Oxford Univ. Press.

Newman, Bruce
1991. The last return. *Sports Illustrated* 74 (March 11th): 38–42.

Palen, John J.
1992. *The urban world.* 4th ed. New York: McGraw-Hill.

Parsons, Talcott
1951. *The social system.* Glencoe, Illinois: Free Press.

Pear, Robert
1986. "Millions bypassed as economy soars," *New York Times.* March 16: A-12.

Rossi, Peter
1989. *Down and out in America: The origins of homelessness.* Chicago: Univ. of Chicago Press.

Scott, Hilda
1985. *Working your way to the bottom: The feminization of poverty.* London: Routledge & Kegan Paul.

Sullivan, Patricia A., and Shirley P. Damrosch
1987. "Homeless women and children." *The homeless in contemporary society*. Edited by Richard D. Bingham *et al.*, 82–98. Beverly Hills, California: Sage Publications.

Tyree, Andrea, Moshe Semyonov, and Robert W. Hodge
1979. Gaps and glissandos: Inequality, economic development and social mobility. *American Sociological Review*. Vol. 44, No. 3: 410–24.

U.S. Bureau of the Census
1975. *Statistical Abstract of the United States*. Washington, D.C.: U.S. Government Printing Office.

1991. *Statistical Abstract of the United States*. Washington, D.C.: U.S. Government Printing Office.

1992. Annual Report on Income and Poverty. Washington, D.C.: U.S. Government Printing Office.

U.S. Congress. Joint Economic Committee
1986. *The Concentration of Wealth in the United States*. (July) Washington, D.C.: U.S. Congress Joint Economic Committee (CIS number J842–21.0).

U.S. Department of Housing and Urban Development
1989. *A Report on the 1988 National Survey of Shelters of the Homeless*. Washington, D.C.: HUD Office of Policy Development and Research (March) (Publication number HUD-1212-PDR).

U.S. Internal Revenue Service
1990. *Statistics of Income Bulletin*. Washington, D.C.: U.S. Government Printing Office.

van den Berghe, Pierre L.
1981. *The ethnic phenomenon*. New York: Elsevier.

Veblin, Thorstein
1899. *The theory of the leisure class*. Modern Library Edition, 1934. New York: The Macmillan Company.

Warner, Lloyd, Marchia Meeker and Kenneth Gells
1949a. *Social class in America*. Chicago: The Science Research Association.

1949b. *Democracy in Jonesville*. New York: Harper & Row.

Warner, Lloyd, and Paul S. Lunt
1941. *The social life of a modern community*. New Haven, Connecticut: Yale Univ. Press.

Weber, Max
1923. *Economy and society*. Translated and edited by Guenther Roth and Claus Wittich, 3 vols., 1968. Totowa, N.J.: Bedminster Press.

Wilson, William Julius
1980. *The declining significance of race*. Chicago: Univ. of Chicago Press.

1987. *The truly disadvantaged: The inner city, the underclass, and public policy*. Chicago: Univ. of Chicago Press.

Wright, Erik Olin
1978. *Class, crisis, and the state*. New York: Schocken Books.

Zeitlin, Maurice
1978. Who owns America? The same old gang. *The Progressive*. Vol. 42, No. 6: 14–19.

CHAPTER **9**

STATUS RELATIONS: BARRIERS TO EQUALITY

CHAPTER OUTLINE

LEARNING OBJECTIVES

One summer's evening during the mid-1980s in a place called Howard Beach, a working-class white neighborhood in New York City, a small group of white men noticed two black men passing in front of a pizza parlor. One of the black men was chased onto a nearby highway where he was struck and killed instantly by a passing car. The second black man was beaten mercilessly until an off-duty police officer brought the unprovoked attack to a halt. The purpose of this chapter is to provide a sociological understanding of the unfortunate events at Howard Beach, and, in a larger sense, an understanding of the social processes, cultural values, and social structures that provide the context for events like the Howard Beach incident.

Unfortunately, in the aftermath of incidents like Howard Beach, one is mistakenly left with the impression, and the comforting rationalization that such events are unique. Such events, it is maintained, represent uncommon and bizarre happenings in an otherwise calm and rational social order. A central theme of this chapter is that they are not. Ugly as events like Howard Beach may be, they "make sense" against the backdrop of prevailing cultural and structural conditions in this and other societies. Obviously, by "make sense" we do not mean that such events are justified, reasonable, or "O.K." Rather, we mean that it is possible to understand how and why they occur. Dramatic social inequalities, racial and ethnic stereotypes, and a diversity of generally unpleasant social realities lie just beneath the surface of apparently harmonious social arrangements. A sociological view suggests that social structural arrangements and cultural traditions are the nexus from which these sorts of happenings spring.

When you've completed reading and studying this chapter you should be able to discuss answers to the following questions:

1. What is meant by the terms status community and minority group?
2. How are status distinctions formed in societies, and what kinds of social factors influence the extent of negative status assignment that occurs?
3. What kinds of human traits are most commonly the basis of status assignments in the United States and other societies?
4. How may patterns of prejudice and discrimination be understood as the consequences of status relations between dominant and subordinate communities?
5. How do the relationships between majority and minority communities illustrate the basic social processes of cooperation, exchange, competition, and conflict?

6. What have been the historical experiences of the major status communities in the United States, and to what extent have they overcome their negative status assignments?

STATUS ASSIGNMENTS: THE ROLE OF SOCIAL STRUCTURE

This chapter examines processes of resource ascription and resource deprivation. Here, the question is not so much to what extent people get ahead, but what factors prevent people from changing their social positions? In what ways are upward social mobility patterns thwarted? Even in highly open or mobility-oriented societies, ascriptive processes restrict people's social mobility. Patterns of status ascription determine that people enter the social game with unequal shares of social resources, and therefore unequal opportunities for changing their shares of those resources. To understand these processes one must examine the status assignments that occur in nearly all societies.

The first section of this chapter examines the nature of status assignments, the ways in which they emerge in societies, the kinds of human characteristics around which status distinctions occur, and the prejudicial and discriminatory consequences of those distinctions.

STATUS COMMUNITIES DEFINED

Much sociological and even nonscientific writing about status ascription processes centers upon the concept of "minority groups." The term is commonly used with reference to a great diversity of communities: among them, Italians, Poles, Russians, Irish, Hungarians, Greeks, Hispanics, Asians, Native Americans, blacks, Jews, women, and even the aged. What are the underlying sociological notions that allow one term to be used with reference to such diverse social strata?

Minority group

The definition of the term *minority group* proposed by Louis Wirth (1891–1952) has been used widely by sociologists. Wirth defines a minority as "a group of people who, because of their physical or cultural characteristics, are singled out from the others in the society in which they live for differential and unequal treatment, and who therefore regard themselves as objects of collective discrimination" (1945, 347). For Wirth, the key is that particular collective traits become the basis for social evaluation, status rankings. Discrimination against the minority and collective awareness within the minority are consequences of the basic assignment of a negative social rank.

Status community

Obviously, most of these social strata—blacks, women, Italians, Jews, and others—are much too large in size to be called "groups" (see the definition in Chapter 4, pp. 98–99). To avoid confusion, in this text, the terms minority community and status community are used interchangeably. *A status community is some number of persons exhibiting a distinctive physical, behavioral, or cultural trait or combination of such traits, that becomes the basis of a relatively stable ascriptive status assignment, either positive or negative, in a society.* From this perspective, most, if not all societies, consist of a diversity of status communities that ascriptively either are awarded or deprived of honor, prestige, and privilege. When positive status is assigned, social dominance results. Such high-status communities typically occupy the *majority* position in majority-minority relations. Negative status communities or minorities typically occupy a diversity of low-status positions in modern societies. Moreover, status ascription involves indigenous populations within a society, such as age and gender strata, as well as new migrants into a society, such as ethnic, racial, and religious communities. This assignment of unequal status occurs nearly universally in societies, and is the basis of other forms of social inequality, such as class and power inequalities.

THE ORIGINS OF STATUS RELATIONS

If it is asked why Jews have been disdained in Christian cultures, the answer is because they are Jews. If one asks why women are oppressed in male-dominated societies, the answer is because they are women. Blacks are discriminated against in America because they are black, and the aged are deprived of social power because they are old. In each of these cases a negative status assignment has been made (deprivation of honor, prestige and privilege), and from that assignment further deprivation of class and power resources generally follow. What is the social origin of these kinds of social distinctions?

Let's return momentarily to that hypothetical first human society, that small hunting and gathering tribe we visited briefly in Chapter 3 (pp. 65–66). There are no distinctions of religious, ethnic, tribal, racial, or other traits around which status distinctions may cluster. Will there be status distinctions? Will there be different ranks of honor, prestige, or privilege?

A rudimentary division of labor is an essential feature of all social structures. Just as a division of labor emerges, so a status-ranking system emerges differentially evaluating people performing certain tasks from those performing others (Chapter 4, pp. 93–94). It is entirely possible, for instance, that status distinctions initially emerge in relation to individual accomplishments. Individuals excelling at certain skills, such as warfare or hunting, may be awarded honored status. However, inevitably such distinctions become collectively assigned. Lenski (1966) maintains that such processes begin in agrarian societies dwelling in geographically permanent locations. Family systems become key mechanisms through which status distinctions are collectively shared and passed from one generation to the next. Gradually, the family name is associated with its special function and position in the community. Royalty represents the highest expression of this type of status distinction. Thus, rulership, kings and queens, are established through inherited family status.

The importance of social roles and functions in creating unequal social status is a widely debated feature of gender stratification. It is argued that in most societies, the connection of women to birth, nursing, and child-rearing has relegated females to "home and hearth" social roles, giving males the more socially powerful "public roles," even in simple societies. Put simply, a gendered division of labor may have produced gendered status ranks. Critics of this interpretation note that in more developed horticultural societies, women take their babies into the fields with them, thus accomplishing important private tasks (child nurturing) as well as important public tasks (food acquisition)

(Collins 1988). Therefore, it is questionable that the negative social ranking of females is a consequence solely of their reproductive or child-rearing tasks.

An alternative approach suggests that status assignments of varying degrees are based on the low-status community's difference from the norms of high-status community. For example, regardless of how a division of labor initially is invented, the physical differences between males and females provide a constantly available reference marker for status differentiation. This same principle of "difference from the high-status norm" clearly operates when different communities first have contact with one another and explains why the apparent physical difference of skin color creates such rigid status distinctions. Additionally, the extent to which a dominant community defines the minority's "differences" as threatening to its values or material resources also influences the severity of status deprivation. The answer to the question "Will status ranks emerge?" is yes. While sociologists are not of one mind on why this happens, the "hows" are readily apparent. Moreover, there is little disagreement that once status rankings are created, they become embodied in a society's social structures and cultural traditions.

Physical minorities

Cognitive minorities

Behavioral minorities

The principle of "difference from high-status norms" operates across the entire range of human physical, cognitive, and behavioral characteristics (Newman 1973). *Physical minorities* may include such characteristics as skin color, age, gender, and even body type (consider the differences between the small-statured Pygmies and the taller Hottentots in Africa). *Cognitive minorities* may be formed around such traits as religious or political beliefs. *Behavioral minorities* may be formed on the basis of cultural traditions such as ethnicity, tribe, dialect or language, and regional differences.

What determines social dominance in situations of initial contact between different physical, cognitive, or behavioral strata? It has long been recognized that both military superiority and technological sophistication have been prime factors in determining who is ranked as dominant and who becomes subordinate. However, sociologists have placed considerable emphasis on the social structural conditions governing migration. Schermerhorn (1970) has distinguished four such conditions: forced labor, contracted labor, displaced persons or refugees, and voluntary migration.

Forced labor

Forced labor is the most disadvantageous form of population movement because a migrating population that must work without economic compensation has virtually no means of establishing autonomy in the new host social structure. Some writers have argued that this condition of migration (slavery) was a key element distinguishing the situation of African-Americans from that of most white ethnic communities in the United States. While forced migration some 250 years ago does not explain contemporary patterns of black-white race relations, the situation of forced labor surely became a context from which subsequent forms of social and economic disenfranchisement of blacks developed (Wilson 1980, 1987).

Contracted labor

Contracted labor is a fundamentally different situation from forced labor. During the colonial period in American history, many Irish immigrants arrived in British households as indentured servants. When their terms of servitude were completed, they were able to expand their economic roles in the society (Greeley 1981). Similarly, during the mid-19th century, many Chinese migrated to the Western territories as contracted laborers and were a significant portion of the labor force that completed the transcontinental railroad.

They, too, were able to expand their economic roles in American society (Lyman 1974).

Typically, contracted laborers immigrate with their own cultural system intact. Forced laborers rarely enjoy this advantage. Thus, the Jewish slaves in the cultures of antiquity were punished severely if they practiced their "strange" religion. It has been argued convincingly that slave owners in the American South viewed the indigenous cultures of Africans as something to be demolished (Frazier 1963). In contrast, the Church of the American-Irish became a source of community solidarity, just as the traditional cultural practices of Chinese-Americans became a powerful economic asset (Light 1972).

These observations about differences between the economic and cultural situations of contracted and forced laborers should not lead to the view that contracted laborers have an "easy time of it." During the 1980s, shocking information emerged concerning the treatment of contracted Mexican farm laborers in the Southwestern states. Contracted migrant workers have no permanent place of residence, and thus, are deprived of even the most basic services and protections. With only minimal wages and few social services, such as food stamps and medical care, their lot often is hardly better than that of slaves (Burawoy 1976). Once over the border, they are truly a "captive" population.

Displaced persons

Displaced persons may result from economic disruption, political oppression, or warfare. The United States often has been a point of destination for refugees fleeing from all three kinds of situations. While refugees move under conditions of duress, they are more likely than slaves or contracted laborers to bring cultural and material resources with them. The First (1820–1860) and Second (1870–1930) "Great Waves" of European immigration to the United States illustrate these processes. The Irish, Italians, Germans, Russians, Greeks, and many others fled to America with their families and cultural systems in strongly supportive roles (Jones 1960). The experience of Asian populations from the nations of Indo-China, as well as refugees from South America during the 1970s and 1980s, reveal similar conditions.

Voluntary migration

Obviously, *voluntary migration* represents the most advantageous form of population movement. The resettlement of large numbers of Cubans in the State of Florida represents a case falling somewhere between voluntary migration and refugee status. Fleeing the political policies of the then-new Castro government in the late 1950s and early 1960s, economically established middle- and upper-class populations predominated in the move. These conditions of migration do much to explain the speed with which the Cuban community in southern Florida obtained a high degree of both political and economic autonomy (Hispanic Policy Development Project 1984). Regardless of the specific patterns of contact between different communities, once status assignments are created, ultimately they become institutionalized in patterns of culture and social structure. Precisely how does this happen?

PREJUDICE AND DISCRIMINATION

Prejudice and discrimination are critically important mechanisms in these processes. From a sociological perspective, especially one that is cross-cultural, prejudice and discrimination are normative. They are more likely to be encountered than not. This does not mean that prejudice and discrimination are acceptable because they are common. An elementary sociological lesson about prejudice and discrimination is that they are fairly constant and frequent occurrences in most societies.

Prejudice

The first step toward understanding these two social phenomena is to discern their differences and the empirical relationships between them. *Prejudice is any set of ideas or beliefs that negatively prejudge individuals, groups, communities, or strata on the basis of real or alleged collective traits or characteristics.* This definition stresses several important components of prejudice. First, prejudice is cognitive. It is not something that people do. It is something that people know, think, or believe.

Second, prejudice is something believed about collections of persons, not individuals. It is for this reason that the roots of prejudice, like all other collectively held ideas, values, and traditions lie in culture. Prejudice involves culturally transmitted notions about the various communities within a social structure and the respective places they occupy within it. All human communities exhibit some degree of ethnocentrism (see Chapter 3, pp. 77–78), a belief that their own culture or "type" of person (physical, cognitive, or behavioral) is preferable, if not superior, to others. The difference between this minimal ethnocentrism and highly negative stereotypes about the "outgroup" is one of degree. Ingroup ethnocentrism is a powerful cognitive base upon which prejudices may be constructed. As we have just seen, social patterns emerging from the division of labor, social perceptions of "differences from the norm," and real or alleged threats that these differences symbolize for the dominant stratum's values or material resources all may be translated into prejudices. Once created, negative claims about outgroups become a social resource to be used by the dominant community.

A third feature of prejudice is that once it is established, it persists as a component of the culture and may even be openly expressed in the society. For example, "We can't admit you into our club, but it is nothing personal" (we simply don't admit blacks, Jews, Hispanics, etc.). Consider the claim frequently heard in private settings that he or she "is just like the rest of them" (i.e., I really have nothing against Mr. Chan personally, it's just that he is like all Chinese).

Stereotypes

Inevitably, prejudice involves stereotypes. *Stereotypes are negative sets of characteristics attributed to an entire category of persons in a generalized manner.* Stereotypes are socially significant because, as broadly shared parts of a culture, they shape the ways in which minority populations are perceived. Social experiences that provide discrepancies from anticipated stereotypes are rationalized in ways that leave the stereotypes in place. Thus, if Mr. Chan seems to be a fine person, it is because he is the exception from an assumed stereotype in which all of "his kind" exhibit socially undesirable behavior.

Prejudice must be recognized as part of the cultural stock of knowledge or information that is transmitted from generation to generation within a society. But prejudice, while surely part of the context for discrimination, should not be equated with the act of discrimination. Prejudice is cognitive, and discrimination is behavioral.

Discrimination

Discrimination is any act of differential treatment of persons that creates a social disadvantage and is based upon the perception of persons as members of a group, community, or stratum. The concept of discrimination is important for an understanding of status relations because, in varying degrees, discrimination translates status assignments into socially structured inequalities. Discrimination, minority awareness of it, and responses to it, are the wellspring out of which patterns of status relationships emerge.

Robert Merton (1949) has observed that prejudice and discrimination must be understood as social phenomena that may vary either together or independently. Thus, it is an error to view discrimination solely as the acting out of prejudice, or to view prejudice as merely the ideological justification for discriminatory actions. Rather, once prejudice and discrimination become incorporated into the cultural and structural arrangements of a society they become parts of the normative pattern of events, and need not be contingent upon one another. At the individual level, these two social variables may prevail in four ideal-typical relationships: the bigot (prejudice with discrimination), the timid bigot (prejudice in the absence of discrimination), the fair-weather liberal (discrimination in the absence of prejudice), and the all-weather liberal (neither prejudice nor discrimination occur).

Bigot

As seen in Table 9.1, the *bigot* is the one instance where discrimination occurs and is justified by the open expression of prejudice. This is the white supremacist who marches in the streets claiming that blacks and Jews are ruining the American dream. It's the white college student who says to his fraternity brothers, "We don't want any Chinese or Koreans here because none of those 'gooks' are any good." Such cases are far from the majority of instances in which either prejudice or discrimination occur. *The timid bigot* is the prejudiced individual who does not discriminate because discrimination is not supported by the cultural environment. For example, much anti-Semitism exists in American society (Glock and Stark 1966), but these prejudiced views do not result in large amounts of overt discrimination. This is because such actions are not consistent with the prevailing norms of the social structure or the established cultural traditions. Thus, prejudice is not always accompanied by discrimination.

Timid bigot

The reverse situation, in which persons who are not prejudiced do discriminate, also is quite common. Consider the bank executive who fails to promote a female employee because he knows there are no other women at a particular job level. He is conforming to a systematic pattern of discrimination even though he may not be prejudiced against females. Discrimination occurs in the absence of prejudice on the part of the individual acting in a discrimina-

TABLE 9.1

PREJUDICE AND DISCRIMINATION: FOUR RELATIONSHIPS

	Prejudice	Discrimination
Bigot	+	+
Timid bigot	+	–
Fair-weather liberal	–	+
All-weather liberal	–	–

SOURCE: Adapted from Robert Merton "Discrimination and the American Creed," in Robert MacIver *Discrimination and National Welfare.* Copyright 1949 by the Institute for Religious and Social Studies, reprinted by permission of Harper Collins Publishers.

Fair-weather liberal

All-weather liberal

tory way. Such persons are *fair-weather liberals* because they do not act on their liberal views when the prevailing social structure or cultural values do not support those views. Finally, the person who is neither prejudiced nor discriminates, the *all-weather liberal,* seems rare because few persons are entirely free of some ethnocentrism or prejudice.

Institutional discrimination

Of these four types of relationships between prejudice and discrimination, one has special significance for understanding the transmission of collective patterns of discrimination. The term *institutional discrimination* refers to situations in which *discriminatory practices have become routine parts of a cultural tradition and, thus, are ingrained in social structural arrangements,* regardless of whether the persons involved in those patterns are prejudiced. Institutional discrimination is significant because it consists of patterns of conduct that are not just individual but are collective. Even if individual prejudices and discrimination were to be eliminated from society, they would survive in institutional practices. For example, exclusion of many minorities from certain occupations in the past means that today they are the most recently hired. During times of economic recession, when businesses must cut back on their personnel, the policy of "last hired-first fired" means that the first to go are minorities.

Direct institutional discrimination

Indirect institutional discrimination

It is useful to distinguish between *direct institutional discrimination* and *indirect institutional discrimination* (Marger 1991; Feagin 1989). Direct institutional discrimination refers to patterns of differential treatment that have been incorporated into the formal norms of a society. Thus, failure to comply with those norms elicits sanctions from the formal agents of social control. So-called Jim Crow laws in the American South and the entire system of apartheid in South Africa are instances of direct institutional discrimination. Indirect institutional discrimination refers to patterns of differential treatment that rely upon voluntary rather than mandatory compliance. Such norms are enforced by informal rather than formal mechanisms of social control. This form of discrimination is a matter of custom not law, and punishment entails social condemnation, not the wrath of the criminal justice system.

Indirect institutional discrimination is of particular concern for a number of reasons. First, in many ways, indirect institutional discrimination is less readily changed than direct institutional discrimination. In its direct form, discrimination is explicitly known and recognized in a society, and in modern societies is expressed in systems of laws. The key tasks involved in changing the system are political: gathering support for a change in the formal, legal system. In contrast, to change indirect discriminatory patterns, people must first recognize these patterns, and their complicity in sustaining them.

This points to a second feature of indirect institutional discrimination. It is subtle to the extent that the discriminators are not likely to recognize the consequences of their actions. Consider the example of prevailing inequalities in the United States between racial communities in terms of housing and public school facilities. Few whites view these patterns as their fault, and many refuse to concede that a white-controlled society and its cultural traditions have created these unequal patterns.

Because discrimination is so ingrained in social structures, concerted social intervention is required to produce change. Inevitably, policies designed to remedy these patterns result in social controversy. The debate in the United States over compensatory hiring and affirmative action policies illustrates these processes. Whites maintain that these programs are "reverse discrimina-

FIGURE 9.1
Have they already been stereotyped?

tion" precisely because they experience neither guilt nor blame for discriminatory patterns they, personally, did not create. Yet, members of minority status communities, be they black, Hispanic, female or other, argue that discriminatory patterns are real and are real in their social consequences.

BLAMING THE VICTIMS

Blaming the victim

William Ryan has discussed these tendencies involved in indirect institutional discrimination as "blaming the victim" (1971). Specifically, *blaming the victim entails blaming subordinate communities for the very negative circumstances that have been imposed upon them by discriminatory practices.* Let's explore this theme with regard to several major status communities in American society.

Patterns of discrimination against women in the employment market have been documented widely (Pear 1987). Yet, the often-heard scenario is that the absence of women in "high places" demonstrates their inability to perform executive-level work. It is said that women are "too emotional" for high-level corporate positions. Rather than acknowledging patterns of discrimination, society promotes the popular cultural theme that women are at fault. Thus, the victims, in this case females, are blamed for employment patterns that have been imposed upon them.

The same technique of blaming the victim has been used against most ethnic and religious minority communities in the United States and elsewhere. For example, most white ethnic communities that immigrated to the United States late in the 19th century and early in the 20th century were forced into segregated ethnic ghettos. Initially, most of them, Greeks, Italians, Polish-Catholics, Jews, and others also were excluded from many Anglo-Protestant controlled institutions, such as banks, colleges, and the corporate business community. Because of exclusionary practices most of these minorities were forced to rely upon the resources of their own ethnic and religious communities. The claim, of course, was that these people are "clannish." They tend to stick together too much, and this prevents them from getting more involved in the dominant society. Thus, patterns of ghettoization and exclusion imposed by the host society are depicted as negative practices that the victims invented!

The worst patterns of discrimination have been inflicted upon communities of color. These communities, native Americans and Mexican-Americans in the Southwest, Hispanics and blacks in the Northeast and Midwest, and recently South Americans and Asians in the South and far West, experience substandard housing conditions. Again it is easy to blame the victim. "Look how they live. They are dirty and unclean." "If they wanted better, they would have better!"

The practice of blaming the victim exposes yet a related feature of intergroup relations. Typically, the presence of one type of status characteristic leads the dominant community to allege others. Thus, Jews, a cognitive minority, are alleged to be a physical minority (race). Blacks, a physical minority, are alleged to be a cognitive minority (intellectually inferior). Early in this century, ethnic groups like Italians, Poles, and Greeks (behavioral minorities) actually were called races (physical minorities). Women, a physical minority, often are treated as a cognitive minority (too emotional and not rational).

In summary, minorities are social strata that have been assigned negative social status, are the objects of discrimination, and have developed an awareness of these facts. The entire range of human physical, cognitive, and behavioral traits may become the foci of such status communities. Status distinctions may originate from the division of labor in societies, the perception of differences from a norm, and the perception of threat to the dominant stratum's values and material resources. The conditions of initial contact between communities often influence the relative degree of minority deprivation. Prejudice and discrimination are important mechanisms through which patterns of minority deprivation are transmitted from generation to generation. Most importantly, institutional discrimination, both direct and indirect, becomes established and compounded by the tendency to blame the victims.

Status Relations as Interaction Processes

Given that the emergence of ascriptive status relations is an ongoing feature of human societies, what are the typical processes of social interaction that characterize these relationships? It will be recalled (Chapter 4, pp. 94–98) that there are four basic types of social interaction processes: cooperation, exchange, competition, and conflict. The following discussion examines the variety of status relations as specific cases of these four basic types.

Cooperative interactions include assimilation, amalgamation, and some forms of cultural pluralism. Conflict among status communities takes the form of genocide, slavery, colonialism, and split labor markets. Exchange processes are apparent in the formation of so-called middleman minorities and ethnic enclaves. Finally, competitive processes are inherent in the formation of parallel social structures, among them political, educational, and economic institutions.

COOPERATION: ASSIMILATION, AMALGAMATION, AND PLURALISM

Cooperation

Cooperation is any social process in which different groups or communities coordinate their efforts to accomplish a shared goal, purpose, or value. Much of the sociological study of intergroup relations has focused upon three cooperative processes: assimilation, amalgamation, and cultural pluralism (Newman 1973). Let's examine each of them.

Assimilation

The idea of *assimilation* has been a powerful element in the history of American intergroup relations. Expressed *in the formula A+B+C=A, where A is a dominant stratum, and B and C represent subordinate communities, assimilation means that over time, subordinate status populations will become more and more like the dominant community and eventually will be absorbed into it* (Newman 1973). There is, of course, substantial irony here. During much of American history minority populations, especially so-called white ethnic groups, have been urged to "become more like us," while at the same time they were excluded from mainstream institutions and told that they were "different."

Cultural assimilation

Structural assimilation

Just as the idea of assimilation prevailed in American society for many generations, so too it dominated the research interests of American sociologists for many years. Sociologist Milton Gordon (1964) distinguishes between structural assimilation and cultural assimilation. *Cultural assimilation refers to the ways in which subordinate status communities adopt the values and lifestyle of the dominant community.* Matters of language, dress, and everyday social norms are of prime importance here. In contrast, *structural assimilation refers to the entrance of minority individuals into dominant community-controlled institutions.* In Gordon's view, the emergence of structural assimilation will precipitate complete absorption of the minority or subordinate community into the dominant status community. Gordon proposes five different measures of assimilation processes: identificational assimilation, the absence of prejudice, the absence of discrimination, the absence of power or value conflicts between strata, and most importantly, the emergence of intermarriage patterns (Gordon 1964).

To what extent do these assimilation processes describe what actually happens between dominant and subordinate status communities? To what extent do the various forms of assimilation occur, and what conditions seem to foster assimilation processes between strata? Some level of cultural assimilation appears to be a minimal requirement for most subordinate status communities entering a new host culture. Cultural assimilation advances with the passing of generations, but rarely to the point where the minority subculture is entirely lost. Thus, first generation Italian-Americans rapidly become as much American as Italian; and sixth-generation Italian-Americans still are likely to value distinctively ethnic foods and customs, even though they are American-born. The formation of distinctive hyphenated American subcultures (for example, Polish-, German-, Irish-, Jewish-, Greek-, African-, and Hispanic-American) is a compelling part of the American mosaic of diverse peoples. As Glazer and Moynihan observe, "the ethnic group in American society became not a survival from the age of mass immigration, but a new social form" (1963, 16).

It must be remembered that intergroup relations are, first and foremost, stratification relationships. Accordingly, assimilation processes are tied to changes in the status assignments given to the various communities. While immigrant populations experience varying levels of cultural assimilation, the most advanced level of structural assimilation seems to be accepted only grudgingly by the dominant status community. In contemporary American society, Protestant-Jewish intermarriages or Polish-Irish intermarriages are accepted with difficulty by the respective status communities, as are black-white or Hispanic-Anglo intermarriages. As might be expected, assimilative processes have been least in evidence where physical minorities, especially racial communities, are involved.

Amalgamation

A second historically powerful idea about intergroup processes is the notion of *amalgamation*, which was popularly expressed at the turn of the century in the myth of the "melting pot" (Zangwill 1909). *Expressed by the formula A+B+C=D, amalgamation means that different status communities will intermarry and mix both biologically and culturally so that a new cultural amalgam is formed.* There is substantial empirical evidence (Lazerwitz 1971; Goldstein and Goldschneider 1968; Greeley 1964) showing that in American society high levels of interethnic, religious, and even racial intermarriage occur. While it may be argued that some extent of biological amalgamation occurs, it is less clear that cultural amalgamations result. Rather, studies of intermarriage have shown that such "mixed" couples have a propensity to select the status identity of the male member of the pair, or to identify with the higher-status community (Simpson and Yinger 1972, 502–16; Simpson and Yinger 1985, 296–307). Perhaps most revealing are studies of the offspring of mixed race couples. These children of black-white, Asian-white, and Indian-white parents constitute 3 percent of births in the United States (100,000 births in 1987) and seem to face enormous identity problems, often welcomed in neither parental ethnic community (Barringer 1989). Thus, in modern societies at least, cultural amalgamation between high and low-status communities is neither statistically prevalent nor culturally fashionable.

There are exceptions to this general pattern. First, as in the case of Spanish-Harlem, some extent of cultural amalgamation may occur if the biological unions are between members of relatively equal-status communities. Second, the comparative cases of South America and the Caribbean show that amalgams do result if one of the two uniting populations is completely without a choice of mates from within their own community of origin. The Spanish Conquistadores arriving in South America in the 18th century with no Spanish females did, in fact, amalgamate with native populations. However, these Mestizo populations became ranked as low- rather than high-status communities in their respective societies. A very similar process resulted from the American, military presence in Vietnam during the 1960s and 1970s. These "Amerasian" offspring became a pariah stratum in their own Asian homelands.

FIGURE 9.2
Even after many generations, ethnic pride continues. Is this pluralism or assimilation?

Perhaps more "successful" instances of amalgamation occurred on the European continent in earlier times. For example, the nation of Belgium emerged from an amalgamation of French and German peoples, and today it is a distinct ethnic community having a homeland. However, amalgams in the modern world in which high- and low-status communities transcend existing stratification differences to form an idyllic melting pot are not likely happenings.

Cultural pluralism

A third view of intergroup relations is the notion of social or *cultural pluralism*. Pluralist visions have taken several forms. Early in the 20th century, pluralism, meaning a peaceful coexistence of diverse populations, was a popular idea (Kallen 1924), though not as widely endorsed as the doctrine of assimilation. Surely, a more realistic sociological view of pluralism is offered by Glazer and Moynihan in their modern classic *Beyond the Melting Pot* (1963). *Expressed in the formula A+B+C=A1+B1+C1, where A is the dominant community and B and C are minority communities, the modern pluralist view recognizes that immigrant populations are changed through a process of cultural assimilation, but that they remain, nonetheless, culturally distinct from one another and from the host or high-status community.* In the simplest empirical terms, Italian-Americans are different from Italians (in Italy) but also remain distinct from Anglo-Americans, Jewish-Americans, Greek-Americans and other hyphenated American populations. The pattern is one of pluralism, a diversity of groups that retain elements of their cultures of origin, but also share in the common host culture. However, social pluralism is not automatically a peaceful relationship between communities. Rather, various forms of conflict, competition, and exchange also emerge in pluralistic societies.

CONFLICT: GENOCIDE, SLAVERY, COLONIALISM, AND SPLIT LABOR MARKETS

Conflict

Social conflict is the mutually opposed efforts of different individuals, groups, or communities, in which injury or neutralization of the opposite party is a primary goal. Among status communities, social conflict may appear in a variety of specific forms that vary in their degree of severity. Four of these are examined here: genocide, slavery, colonialism, and split labor markets. Since all of these entail the injury or neutralization of the minority community, they fit well into the definition of discrimination (pp. 240–243). Prejudice and discrimination both are techniques or weapons of social conflict.

Genocide

Genocide is the systematic killing of the members of a status community with the intent of annihilating the entire community. The 1951 United Nations Convention on Genocide also identifies other activities, such as involuntary sterilization, as genocide. Genocide occurs when a dominant status community defines the very existence of a subordinate community as a threat to its values or domestic tranquility, or when a dominant community desires all the material social resources of a subordinate community. Typically, members of the subordinate status community are viewed as a discrete biological population (such as a race) that offers no redeeming value or purpose in the society.

Instances of genocide are shockingly frequent in human affairs, even in modern times. In the late 19th century, systematic genocide was perpetrated against the native American tribes until the policy was abandoned in favor of a policy of spatial containment (reservations) (Howton 1971). The German Third Reich murdered over twelve million citizens. While half of these were Jews, the balance were an assortment of status communities thought to be "unpure" and injurious to the Reich, such as Gypsies, homosexuals, certain categories of Christian sects, and others. Similar policies resulted in the murder of thousands upon thousands of Armenians under Islamic rule in Turkey at the beginning of the 20th century (Dadrian 1975). These are but a few of the many cases of genocide in recent history (Horowitz 1976).

Slavery

Slavery, colonialism, and split labor markets are forms of subjugation through which dominant communities attempt to exploit the labor and other resources of subordinate communities. *Slavery is a system of forced labor in which members of a subordinate community are treated as property.* It is at least analytically important to recognize that slavery and genocide have rather contrary purposes. Genocide, systematic murdering, is not consistent with slavery, a system that attributes a labor value to the oppressed. In some slave systems, persons literally have been "worked to death." However, it is more common for slave populations to be viewed as "breeding" populations, capable of producing more slaves. Working them to death has negative economic consequences, and therefore, typically is not done.

Substantial controversy emerged around these issues during the 1970s in response to Fogel and Engerman's book *Time on the Cross* (1974), in which a concept of "mitigated slavery" was introduced. These authors claim that economic rationality mandated that slave owners in the American South would treat their slaves well, keep them healthy, and maintain strong family systems because such behavior insured maximum labor value and maximum reproductive value. At best, Fogel and Engerman's research ignores what slavery means to the slaves and overestimates the role of rational conduct in guiding the treatment of slaves. Slavery is a totally debasing system of subjugation. To understand these points one only need examine present-day systems based not upon slavery but on colonialism.

Colonialism

Colonialism is any system in which a population or community is subjugated through economic dependency and, thus, is controlled and exploited by another community or population. In classical Marxian analysis, capitalist nations are seen as exploiters of "colonies" through such dependency. While the term "colonialism" describes the relationship between two societies, this kind of relationship between two communities within the same society is described by the term *internal colonialism.*

Internal colonialism

Both forms of colonialism abound in the contemporary world. Apartheid in South Africa is the most stark example of internal colonialism. A small European high-status community exploits both the labor and natural resources of native Africans. Mexican farm laborers in the United States also experience this sort of exploitative economic relationship. Many politically independent nations in the Caribbean continue to be in colonial relationships to their former homelands (England, France, and the Netherlands). Obviously, the U.S. Virgin Islands and Puerto Rico are colonies, even though they officially are called "possessions."

It was fashionable in the early 1960s to depict African-Americans as an "internal colony" (Carmichael and Hamilton 1967). This use of the term may be questioned because prejudice and discrimination against American blacks is, in fact, economically disadvantageous to the host society. There is economic loss for the host society through the costs of public assistance programs and the loss of economic productivity by the black community in these forms of "internal colonialism."

Recent analyses of American society have suggested yet another way of viewing these economic relationships between dominant and subordinate status communities. The key idea is that of "split labor markets." A split labor market is a form of economic exploitation, which, though not as rigid and all-encompassing as a colonial system, still effectively restricts economic opportunities for low-status communities. Specifically, *a split labor market exists when low-status and high-status community members are allocated to different economic segments of the employment marketplace.* Bonacich (1972) argues that most persons of color, and especially American blacks, have been relegated systematically to

Split labor market

the lower end of the employment marketplace in the United States. The same interpretation applies to the place of women in the employment market. Obviously, whenever a split labor market is discernible, it indicates that certain strata have been losing the battle of economic conflict.

COMPETITION: MIDDLEMEN, ETHNIC ENCLAVES, AND PARALLELISM

Competition

While competition is closely related to conflict, its character and consequences are rather different. *Competition refers to situations in which different communities exhibit mutually opposed efforts to obtain the same resources or goals.* Unlike conflict, neutralization of the opposing parties is not a characteristic of competition. Three competitive patterns are examined here: middleman minorities, ethnic enclaves, and parallelism.

Middleman minorities

The term "middleman minorities" has been used to describe the tendency for some low-status communities to occupy economic positions that are literally in the middle, between capitalists and workers, between producers and consumers (Bonacich 1973). Control of some part of an economic niche, accompanied by opportunities for self-employment, is characteristic of the middleman position. By occupying middling positions that yield a function for the economic system, status communities are able to compete effectively for upward social class mobility.

American history is replete with examples. In the post-World War II period, Italian-Americans gained prominence in the construction industry, just as Jewish-Americans took a similar position in retailing, and later in some segments of manufacturing. First generation Japanese-Americans also predominated in retailing, but on the West Coast. Presently, Korean-Americans have become a predominant community in the green-grocery industry in the United States. In each of these instances, the subordinate status community plays a

FIGURE 9.3
Economic issues can be important aspects of ethnic community life.

specialized role or function in the economic system. In a certain sense, the ethnic community captures and controls a segment of the economic system.

Ethnic enclaves

The term *ethnic enclaves* also is used to describe this phenomenon. Again, the central notion is that some part of an industry or segment of the economy is dominated by a particular status community. In some instances this extends to the formation of an enclave in which members of the status community render services primarily to their own members and only secondarily to members of the dominant community. The "little Italys" and "Chinatowns" of major American cities exemplify this pattern. More recently, the formation of the Korean section in Los Angeles, and the Cuban community in Miami fit an "enclave" pattern. In the latter two instances, immigration entailed the movement of persons with substantial skills and resources who, therefore, were able to attain quickly a substantial degree of economic autonomy. In cases like these, the residential and even economic segregation of the minority community represents not a form of dominant-enforced deprivation, but a voluntary option that symbolizes the subordinate community's autonomy.

Parallel institutions

A related aspect of these patterns is the growth of "parallel institutions" within the subordinate status community. *The term parallel institutions refers to instances in which status communities create their own self-controlled social structures that address the same community needs as those found in the dominant community* (Newman 1973). The growth of ethnic and religioethnic educational institutions in the United States illustrates this pattern.

Even during the colonial period, different branches of Protestantism established their own colleges and universities in the United States. Thus, Princeton (Presbyterian), Trinity (Episcopal), and Brown (Baptist) all reflected different Protestant denominational cultures. This continued into the 19th century when German Lutherans (Concordia) and Methodists (Southern Methodist University, Syracuse University, and American University) also established their own higher educational institutions. The same pattern characterized the immigration of sizeable Catholic (Holy Cross, Notre Dame, and Boston College) and Jewish (Brandeis and Einstein Medical School) communities. Among African-Americans, the formation of Grambling and Howard University represents the same pattern. Failing to gain entrance into dominant institutions, the subordinate community created parallel institutional structures which, over time existed as a matter of preference.

In Canada, where there are no public schools and colleges, this parallelism was formally adopted in the system of religiously separate schools. This official parallelism between the Protestant and Catholic communities extends to how the government keeps immigration and birth records in Canada. Overall, it is common for subordinate-status communities to create parallel institutions in response to discrimination, and for those institutions to prevail at a later time as a matter of preference.

EXCHANGE AND COALITION

Exchange

Social exchange represents a fourth kind of interaction process. *Exchange exists when communities and groups cooperate, not out of shared values and goals, but from a recognition of mutual benefit.* This phenomenon, cooperation between communities that do not agree on even the most basic values, is the source of the observation that "history makes strange bedfellows." Communities that are strongly opposed to one another in many ways may form a coalition based on the expectation of mutual benefit. This does not prevent their being in competition or conflict at other times.

This ability of communities to alternate between being allies and opponents surely has characterized the relations between blacks and Jews in the United States. Jewish-Americans have been prominent in the fight against racism, prejudice, and discriminatory practices affecting blacks. This coalition was particularly apparent during the Civil Rights crusades of the 1960s. This coalition was predicated upon the understanding that a common defense yields mutual benefits.

Yet, at the same time, Jews and blacks have been in competitive and even conflictual economic stances toward one another, with blacks seeing Jewish businesses in the ghetto as just another form of white oppression. Clearly, such perceptions were a major factor in New York City in 1989, when a black mayoral candidate (David Dinkins) defeated the incumbent Jewish mayor, Ed Koch in the Democratic party primary election. Of course, after the primary election, the Jewish democrat Koch supported the black democrat Dinkins in his electoral victory over the white Republican (Italian) candidate Rudolph Guliani.

Similar patterns have existed in the relations between blacks and Puerto Ricans, especially in the Northeastern states. Both communities have seen the real enemy as whites, and, on occasion, have formed coalitions to combat a common enemy. At the same time, African-Americans and Puerto Ricans have competed for the same jobs, housing, and educational opportunities in the inner cities of the Northeast.

This tendency for opponents to become allies also is apparent in the recent history of the Ku Klux Klan. For many years, the white-Protestant dominated Ku Klux Klan perpetrated discrimination and violence against all who were "different," especially blacks, Jews, and Catholics. Yet, when the Klan moved North during the 1970s and entered New England where a plurality of the population in several states (Connecticut, Rhode Island, and Massachusetts) is Catholic, the Klan dropped its long-standing anti-Catholic rhetoric. Suddenly, the formerly "white Protestant race" the clan sought to protect became a "white Christian race" (including Catholics). Social expediency can make unusual coalitions.

In summary, cooperation, conflict, competition, and exchange are four basic forms of social interaction. Among status communities, assimilation, amalgamation, and cultural pluralism represent cooperative processes. In sharp contrast, genocide, slavery, colonialism, and split labor markets characterize conflict relations between status communities. Competitive social relations include the emergence of enclaves, middleman minorities, and parallel institutions. Finally, exchange relations are expressed in coalitions, especially in political affairs. These social processes are summarized in Table 9.2.

Exploring the American Mosaic

It is often noted that American society is a rich mosaic of peoples. This section of the chapter examines the historical experiences of a number of major status

TABLE 9.2

STATUS RELATIONS AS SOCIAL PROCESSES

Social Process:	Status Relations:	Defined as:
Cooperation: Mutually shared goals and values	Assimilation:	Subordinate community adopts dominant culture and lifestyle.
	Amalgamation:	Subordinate community absorbed biologically into dominant community.
	Pluralism:	Subordinate and dominant communities co-exist.
Social Conflict: Neutralize and/or injure the other party	Genocide:	Mass extermination.
	Slavery:	Subordinate community treated as property.
	Colonialism:	Exploitation of subordinate community resources.
	Split Labor Market:	Economic opportunities of subordinate community systematically restricted.
Competition: Mutually opposed effort to obtain the same objects or resources	Enclaves:	Subordinate community control of economic function/market.
	Economic Middlemen:	Subordinate community secures a "middle position" in some economic sector.
	Parallel Institutions:	Subordinate community creates self-controlled institutions in response to exclusion.
Exchange: Coordinated action under anticipated mutual benefit	Coalitions:	Coordinated effort through political associations and voluntary social movements.

communities in the United States. What internal ranking processes, social contact or immigration circumstances have affected the social status of these minorities? What kinds of interactions with the dominant community have evolved? What is the relative social standing of each of these status communities today?

While the communities examined here are not exhaustive of those in the United States, they do provide a representative range of the various physical, cognitive, and behavioral minorities in the nation. In that regard, some number of them are commonly viewed as "racial" minorities, and a cautionary word is in order. There is no scientific agreement about the criteria by which different so-called races may be distinguished, nor about how many races there are or ever were. Obviously, the social definition of race focuses upon skin color communities: black, white, and yellow. Some alleged racial communities, Australian aborigines and American Indians, don't fit into any of these three categories. Thus, the term race is used here with reluctance and with the understanding that it refers only to socially defined skin color communities. Nothing more is intended by the term. The term "race" is a social but not a scientific idea, and thus, no scientific specification for it is given here.

NATIVE AMERICANS

Native American tribal societies thrived in North America prior to the arrival of Europeans. Estimates range from as few as a million to over ten million native Americans in North America during the 1600s (Dobyns 1960). The so-called Indian Wars, genocidal treatment by whites, and eventual relocation, diminished American Indian populations to a low of perhaps only 200,000 to 300,000 by the early 20th century. According to the Bureau of the Census (1991), by 1989 there were upwards of 1.7 million native Americans in the United States, and perhaps four times that number claiming some Indian ancestry. The Bureau of Indian Affairs recognizes 493 different tribes and over 300 separate language communities. Today, most native American populations are housed on some 267 reservations (Wax 1971).

The brutal treatment of native Americans by whites has focused on all three types of minority status traits: cognitive, behavioral, and physical. Indians were disdained as "unChristian" (a cognitive trait) and were viewed as having heathen ways of life (behavioral traits). Yet, unquestionably, the physical trait of race governed the treatment of native Americans. They were labeled a "savage race" and genocidal policies allowed their indiscriminate slaughter. In time, native Americans became a segregated population in what once had been their own land.

Conflict has been the dominant pattern, resulting in what may be viewed either as colonialism (exploitation of native American resources) or concentration camps (the reservation system was forced). Most historians recognize the Dawes Act of 1887 as a critically damaging blow to the remaining tribal populations. It allotted small portions of tribal land to individual native Americans and allowed whites to purchase "left over" land. By the 1930s, native Americans had lost over 150 million acres of "left over" land, and possessed only 50 million acres (U.S. Bureau of Indian Affairs 1975).

A gradual reversal of government policy began during the New Deal period. Tribal governments re-emerged, and modest gains toward economic development for native Americans were made. During the 1960s the emergence of a "red power" movement and a number of intra-tribal associations marked a changed consciousness among native American communities. However, unemployment, low levels of educational attainment, and alcoholism remain chronic problems of reservation life. These patterns are not difficult to understand. Native Americans dwell within the United States, but really are not part of the United States. Retaining what little property they have means continuing a highly segregated lifestyle. In part, native Americans are caught in the dilemma of wanting to preserve with dignity their unique cultural traditions, but also wanting to become full economic participants in American society. It is clear that racism has extracted a terrible toll from the first Americans.

HISPANIC-AMERICANS

Hispanic-Americans represent a rapidly growing minority community, with a population of over 20 million persons in 1989 (U.S. Bureau of the Census 1991). Even though Hispanics are viewed by Anglos as a single racial community, they are in fact, internally diverse. In addition to persons from Spain, Hispanic-Americans include Mexicans, Puerto Ricans, Cubans, and immigrants from numerous South and Central American nations. The latter have experienced biological mixing between Spanish Conquistadores, native Americans, and Africans. What they share most is a Spanish language and cultural tradition.

Mexican-Americans account for approximately two-thirds of the Hispanic-American population, and, owing to continued immigration across the Mexican-American border, constitute the single largest immigrant community in the United States. Like native Americans, Mexicans point to a history of colonization and exploitation. Texas was initially part of Mexico, and its annexation by the United States led to the Mexican-American War of 1848. By the war's end, not only Texas, but most of what would become the states of California, Colorado, New Mexico, Nevada, Utah, and Arizona were transferred from Mexican to American control. Although the Treaty of Guadalupe Hidalgo legally granted citizenship to Mexicans remaining in these lands, in practice, it made them a minority-status community (McWilliams 1948).

Throughout both the 19th and 20th centuries, Mexican immigration has followed the ebb and flow of economic trends and labor force requirements in the American Southwest. By official estimates, in 1989, Mexican-Americans numbered upwards of 12 million persons (U.S. Bureau of the Census 1991). Today, the constant stream of undocumented migrants crossing the Mexican-American border complicates the task of estimating the exact size of the Mexican-American population. The lack of economic opportunity in Mexico drives immigrant labor across the border. Yet, once in America, Mexican workers become trapped in low-income occupations in both the agricultural and industrial employment sectors (Barrera 1979). While today much Mexican immigration is voluntary, once in the United States, Mexicans suffer the consequences of a split labor market. The jobs they are offered provide little real social class advancement. Racial discrimination, language and cultural barriers all combine to block social mobility.

Puerto Ricans account for approximately 13 percent of the Hispanic-American population and in 1989 numbered almost 1.5 million persons (U.S. Bureau of the Census 1991). The island of Puerto Rico was a Spanish colony that became an American possession in 1899 as a result of the Spanish-American War. Significant migration to the American mainland did not begin until the 1950s when a rapidly growing island population and a lack of economic opportunity combined to push Puerto Ricans toward the mainland.

Since the 1950s, cross-migration patterns between the island of Puerto Rico and the American mainland have been complex. The possession of United States citizenship, and relatively inexpensive air transportation have facilitated movement back and forth between Puerto Rico and major East Coast mainland cities, especially New York City. Consequently, nearly half of all Puerto Ricans were born on the mainland, and about a third of Puerto Ricans live on the mainland (Fitzpatrick 1971).

From a sociological perspective, Puerto Rico is a case of colonialism. Economic opportunities on the island never have kept pace with population growth among Puerto Ricans, a primarily Catholic population with large families. If it is true that racial minorities are the most oppressed in America, Puerto Ricans validate that claim. Yet, it also must be remembered that distinctive cultural traits, including a language difference, have hindered the Puerto Rican quest for opportunity in America.

Cuban-Americans constitute less than 6 percent of the Hispanic-American population. While some Cuban migration to the United States occurred in the late 19th and early 20th centuries, a distinct enclave of Cuban-Americans developed in Miami, Florida, during the 1960s. Substantial numbers of financially established Cubans arrived in the United States fleeing the communist revolution of Fidel Castro. These were refugees in the classic sense of the term. While their migration was to a degree forced, they migrated with substantial personal resources and with family systems intact. Moreover, initially, America welcomed them as political victims of an evil communist insurgent government.

Today, a Cuban-American community of over half a million persons enjoys a level of economic autonomy that is relatively unique for an American racial minority (Jafee, Cullen, and Boswell 1980). No doubt, the small size of the Cuban community and the compactness of its settlement have been factors in its well-being. To a large degree, this is an ethnic enclave, exhibiting substantial economic parallelism.

The balance of the American-Hispanic community, consisting of approximately 4 million persons, contains a diversity of migrants from various South and Central American nations and from Spain. Here again, in spite of the tendency for these persons to be viewed as racially Hispanic, there is enormous ethnic and cultural diversity among them. Perhaps the one thing uniting all Hispanics in the United States is the extent of racial discrimination against them.

ASIAN-AMERICANS

Asian-Americans, like Hispanic-Americans, are an internally diverse population. Asian migration to the United States has occurred in two very different and widely separated historical periods. The first period stretches from the mid-19th century to early in the 20th, when the National Origins Quota Act of 1924 effectively excluded all but Northern and Western Europeans. During this first period, substantial numbers of Chinese, Japanese, Korean, and Filipino nationals immigrated. Most became unskilled agricultural and industrial laborers on the West Coast.

A second and much more diverse era of Asian migration, including that from Vietnam, followed the comprehensive overhaul of American immigration laws in 1965. The more recent period of Asian immigration also has included populations from the Asian subcontinent, most importantly from India, Pakistan and Bangladesh. The influx of Asians has been so great that today, with the exception of Japanese-Americans, most Asian-Americans are foreign-born. While the diversity of these communities prohibits discussing all of them here, we shall examine the historical experiences of the Chinese, Japanese, Filipino, Korean, and Vietnamese communities in America.

Chinese-Americans are estimated to number nearly a million persons, representing nearly 20 percent of the Asian-American population (U.S. Commission on Civil Rights 1988). By the mid-19th century, social and economic disruptions in China had propelled Chinese immigrants across the globe. Thus, their initial contact with America as voluntary migrants changed. Under more difficult circumstances, they became political refugees experiencing forced migration. In America, the California gold rush seemed to provide opportunity, and the building of a transcontinental railroad surely provided employment. Fueled by labor conflicts with whites, racial stereotyping (the "yellow peril") became vicious.

Between 1882 and 1907, a series of Chinese Exclusion Acts made the Chinese the first specific immigrant community to be barred by law from entering the United States. Throughout this period, the Chinese-American population declined from perhaps 125,000 persons to approximately 70,000 persons. An important factor was the predominantly male composition of the early immigration. Clearly, many of the early Chinese immigrants hoped to make their fortunes in America, and then return to their homeland using their newfound wealth to enjoy a better, though traditional, life. Moreover, for a substantial time, interracial marriage between Chinese and whites was illegal in California. The Exclusion Acts, coupled with little interracial mating, created a population decrease (Lyman 1974). Assimilation was not a theme in the Chinese-American experience. Asians were viewed as racially, culturally, and religiously different.

Following the reform of American immigration regulations in 1965, Chinese immigration from Hong Kong, Taiwan, and Vietnam, where there are many Chinese nationals, increased substantially. In spite of continued racial prejudice, today, Chinese-Americans can boast of higher median family incomes than most other ethnic communities, including the culturally dominant white population. Why is this so? There is little question that Chinese, Korean, and Vietnamese immigrants have evidenced a strong work ethic. Strong traditional family systems have been a resource. Light (1972) has shown that among both Chinese and Koreans, parallel structures in the form of ethnic banking systems have been a powerful factor translating into social class mobility in the United States.

Korean and Vietnamese populations in America number slightly less than a million persons each, with each accounting for approximately 10 percent of the total Asian-American community. Their histories in America are quite similar to the extent that significant immigration was stimulated by American involvements in wars in their countries of origin. Korean immigration began in the late 1950s, and as a result of the new immigration laws (1965), the Korean-American population increased between 1970 and 1980 by a factor of five, resulting in a resident population of a third of a million (Light and Bonacich 1988).

Vietnamese immigration was slight (20,000 persons) prior to the fall of the American supported South Vietnamese government in 1975. Between 1975 and 1984 nearly three-quarters of a million Vietnamese migrated. Included were several hundred thousand "boat people" who emigrated from Vietnam, Cambodia, and Laos in 1979 and 1980. The earlier Vietnamese immigrants were well educated and thus were more prepared for adjustment to the United States than the most recent immigrants. The latter have arrived in large numbers in a short period of time, most of them coming from rural agricultural environments where few of the skills required for urban-industrial living are acquired. It is not surprising that Vietnamese-Americans occupy a lower economic position than most other Asian-American populations (U.S. Commission on Civil Rights 1988). They are war refugees, not voluntary migrants. They have relocated to America without material resources and with few language and cultural skills that would help in adjusting to America. Still, only the first chapter of the Vietnamese-American story has been written.

Japanese-Americans accounted for approximately 12 percent of the Asian-American population in 1989. This population of just over 850,000 persons is not growing at the same rate as most other Asian-American populations. Obviously, different historical circumstances are involved. During the late 19th century, the Chinese Exclusion Acts allowed continued immigration from Japan, and racism against Chinese-Americans quickly was redirected against Japanese-Americans. The Oriental Exclusion Act of 1924 effectively ended Japanese immigration to the United States.

Ironically, on the eve of the Second World War, when Japanese-Americans were summarily relocated into what amounted to concentration camps for the duration of the war, two-thirds of these "Japanese" were American-born citizens. Few of them regained the personal property they lost during the "relocation" program (Kitano and Daniels 1988). In 1988, the United States Congress officially apologized for the treatment of Japanese-Americans during the 1940s and granted nominal financial reparations for survivors of the Japanese internment.

Today, Japanese-Americans are a community of relatively stable size and possess an economic profile well above that of the American white population. Some have argued that culturally the Shinto ethic is quite like the Protestant ethic and that traditional Japanese family and religious life emphasize values consistent with economic advancement in America.

Filipinos form the largest Asian-American population, numbering 1.5 million persons and constituting approximately 20 percent of the Asian-American population. The residents of the Philippine Islands differ from other Asians, being both Hispanic (as former colonials under Spain) and Roman Catholic. Because the Philippines, prior to becoming independent in 1935, were a United States territory, its residents were considered American nationals even though they did not have United States citizenship.

During the late 19th and much of the 20th century, Filipino immigration to the American mainland has been relatively slight (less than 30,000 by the early 1930s), and like the Chinese of the period, supplied inexpensive agricultural labor for the State of California. In contrast, immigrants from the Philippine Islands since the 1960s have been relatively well-educated and upwardly mobile. Today, they are a growing Asian-American community with an economic and occupational profile similar to that of Chinese-Americans (Carino 1987).

AFRICAN-AMERICANS

African-Americans in 1989 numbered over 30 million persons, accounting for approximately 14 percent of the United States population (U.S. Bureau of the Census 1991). Over a third of America's black population lives at or below the poverty level. Even though blacks are but one of a number of racial minorities in American society, much of the discussion of race relations focuses upon black-white relations.

Blacks first arrived in North America in the early 1600s, and along with others, including whites, were indentured servants who were able to earn a free status in the new land. However, by the middle of the 17th century that situation changed. A distinctly racial slave system emerged and was codified in laws throughout the Southern colonies. Slave status most distinguishes the African-American experience from that of all other minority communities.

Africans not only were physically distinct from the dominant white population, but also practiced their own "heathen" (unChristian) religions (a cognitive trait). However, unlike native Americans, who also exhibited both traits, blacks could not easily escape into nearby familiar physical and cultural surroundings. Moreover, unlike slave systems in other times and places, the racial slave system practiced in colonial America deprived the slaves of all family and property rights (Elkins 1959). Slavery was uniquely destructive for the cultural and social traditions of African-Americans.

As we've noted previously (Chapter 8, pp. 209–210), it has been argued that with the abolition of slavery, African-Americans became a socially and economically restricted caste in the midst of a class system of stratification. By the end of the 19th century, 90 percent of blacks still were dwelling in the rural South, outside the mainstream of what was becoming an increasingly urban-industrial society. However, several important changes were soon to occur.

Beginning in the 1940s, unprecedented internal migration of blacks from the rural South to urbanized areas of the North and West occurred. This transition marked the entrance of African-Americans into the mainstream industrial economy. Perhaps for the first time in American history, black laborers were entering into a competitive stance with their white counterparts. Not surprisingly, the 1950s and 1960s were marked by racial conflict. The 1954 Supreme Court decision in *Brown v. Board of Education* (school desegregation) and the Civil Rights Acts that accompanied Lyndon Johnson's Great Society program of the mid-1960s were watershed advances in American race relations.

As William Wilson observes (1987), today, the great majority of black Americans have not obtained equality of opportunity nor economic parity with white Americans. While there is far greater occupational and income diversity among African-Americans today than at any previous time, the effects of racism still are much in evidence. To some observers the slow pace of black economic mobility is a puzzle. To the sociological eye, certain facts are unavoidable. Segregated schools, segregated housing, and split labor markets have restricted most black Americans to a social experience that is both separate and unequal. While equal rights legislation since the 1960s has made a difference for a small number of African-Americans, firmly entrenched patterns of socially structured inequality still are a reality.

WHITE ETHNIC CATHOLICS

Of the 3.2 million Americans estimated by the first census conducted in 1790, fully 75 percent were of British origin (LeMay 1987). While small numbers of Dutch, French, Spanish, German, and other ethnic communities were present, these white, Anglo-Saxon Protestants (WASPs) were numerically and culturally dominant.

In the 1840s, massive immigration by four European national communities began: Germans, Irish, Scandinavians, and, of course, more British. The German and Scandinavian "newcomers" were mostly Protestants and, therefore, were "acceptable" even though the various brands of Lutheranism and Calvinism they practiced differed from the established branches of Anglo-

Calvinism (Episcopal, Presbyterian, Congregational, Unitarian, Methodist, and Baptist). Geographic disperson surely helped the situation, for large numbers of Scandinavian and German immigrants moved westward to previously unsettled locales. However, the American reaction to Irish-Catholics was quite another matter.

By the 1880s, a wholly new pattern of European immigration had ensued. The new arrivals were Southern and Eastern Europeans, not Northern and Western Europeans (Hansen 1940; Higham 1955). These were Italian and Polish-Catholics, Russians, Greeks, and Jews of various nationalities. Ultimately, the Quota Act of 1924 ended the ethnically and religiously diverse stream of immigration. It provided for an annual quota of 150,000 immigrants, 82 percent of them to come from Northern and Western Europe (i.e., Anglo and Germanic Protestants) (Bouvier and Gardner 1986). America's restrictive immigration policies would only begin to change with the comprehensive Reform Act of 1965. Still, by the 1920s, the European migration already had created an entirely new mix of white religio-ethnic communities.

Today, American Catholics number upwards of 60 million persons and account for roughly 40 percent of the Christian population of the United States (Jaquet 1990). In addition to the Hispanic Catholics already discussed here, white ethnic Catholics are a diverse population, including Russians, Greeks, Poles, Irish, Italians, Germans and French-Canadians. Two of these communities, Irish-Catholics and Italian-Catholics are examined here.

Irish-Catholics were the earliest sizeable non-Protestant community to immigrate to the new American nation. As many as half a million arrived even before 1820, and 1.6 million immigrated between 1841 and 1860. They were the object of both violent and politically well-organized anti-Catholic sentiment in the form of the American Nativist Movement of the 1830s and 1840s and the "American" or "Know Nothing" party of the 1850s. The Irish were viewed as troublemaking Papists. Help-wanted ads frequently stated "No Irish need apply." Undoubtedly, anti-Catholic and anti-Irish prejudice were fueled by the fact that instead of moving westward, the Irish-Catholics "invaded" previously settled areas, most importantly Massachusetts, New York, New Jersey, and Pennsylvania (Jones 1960). While Irish-Catholic immigration was voluntary, one should not underestimate the degree to which they were pushed from their homeland by the potato famine and a stagnant economy (Greeley 1981).

Irish-Catholic social class mobility in the United States has been associated both with the labor movement and the political party system. The Irish possessed experiences that readily could be applied in American urban political affairs: a knowledge of the workings of political bureaucracy, preference for informal over formal institutions, and pride from working in an ordered chain of command, which in America meant the political patronage system (Glazer and Moynihan 1963). By the early 1900s, the Irish had become politically dominant and had populated the civil service occupations in the Northeastern cities. While the earliest generations of Irish-Catholics populated the lower economic strata, today they are located in the middle stratum.

The relatively slow pace of Irish economic mobility surely is related to the fact that much of the early immigration was by females. These young women initially became domestic servants and later became factory workers. In short, they did "women's work." Irish-Catholic social mobility in traditionally male occupational categories would not occur until well into the 20th century. Interestingly, as other white ethnics entered at the bottom of the occupational ladder, the Irish gradually moved upward above them and were perceived as part of the power structure by those coming after them. After all, the Irish were more ethnically similar to the Anglos (British Isles), than were the later Eastern and Southern European immigrants.

Italian-Catholic immigration to the United States was slight for most of the 19th century. However, between 1880 and 1930, over 5 million Italians immigrated, most settling in the new "little Italys" in the major cities in the Northeast. Like the Irish before them, Italians encountered both ethnic and religious prejudice. The influx of not just Italians, but other Catholic ethnic communities, heightened the level of anti-Papalism in the United States. Italian-Catholics bore the brunt of much of this prejudice. In the industrial North, where they competed with both the Irish and Anglos for factory work, they were viciously attacked as strike breakers. In the South, since they entered the bottom of the work force along side blacks, Southern whites treated them in the same manner as they did blacks.

Italians were suspect for their alleged radical political and criminal tendencies. As a result, they often received less than equal treatment from the justice system. The trial and execution in Massachusetts in 1927 of two Italian immigrants, Nicola Sacco and Bartolomeo Vanzetti, would later symbolize the extent of prejudice in the treatment of Italian-Americans. Sacco and Vanzetti were "railroaded" with flimsy evidence in a biased court system. Their conviction and execution served to appease the negative public sentiment toward Italian-Catholics (Gambino 1975; Lopreato 1970).

Throughout the 20th century, Italian-Catholics have played predominant roles in the building trades and industrial unions of the nation. Today, Italian-Catholics have experienced substantial economic mobility, with a greater percentage of Italians employed in white-collar occupations than in the population as a whole. Italian-Catholics have been voluntary migrants. Bringing to America supportive family systems, they have emulated the American norms of private entrepreneurship and mobility through educational attainment (Alba 1985).

Both Irish-Catholics and Italian-Catholics illustrate the mixed character of assimilation and pluralism for many American white ethnic minorities. Both communities encountered aggressive patterns of prejudice and discrimination over long periods of time. Both have retained their religious and ethnic distinctiveness (pluralism) while entering the mainstream of American life through social class ascendancy (assimilation).

JEWISH-AMERICANS

Jewish migration to North America has been in several distinct phases. Spanish Jews fleeing persecution by the Catholic monarchy arrived in the 16th and 17th centuries. Throughout the 19th century, German Jews fled to America as Jewish persecution in Europe escalated. There were as many as a quarter of a million Jews in the United States by the early 1880s when the massive Southern and Eastern European immigration began. By 1927, the number of Jewish-Americans had risen to approximately 4 million. Most of them immigrated in refugee status, fleeing from pogroms in Russia, Poland, and the Austro-Hungarian Empire. In spite of the ethnic differences among them, all Jews would become viewed as a cognitive and physical minority (alleged racial group) and would experience anti-Semitism in the United States (Sklare 1971).

Today, Jewish-Americans of various ethnic backgrounds constitute approximately 3 percent of the American population and number about 6 million persons. While nearly half of that population resides in the Northeast, especially the New York metropolitan area, in recent decades, there has been a greater dispersal of the American Jewish population into major metropolitan centers throughout the nation (Goldstein 1981; Newman and Halvorson 1990). This trend, coupled with impressive upward social mobility, seems to reflect substantial assimilation into American culture within the larger framework of religious pluralism.

Jewish social mobility in the United States has been viewed as the result of several related social factors. First, unlike other Eastern and Southern European immigrants arriving early in this century, Jews were religious refugees and knew well that they would not return to their "homelands" where they were being persecuted. Thus, the motive to adapt to the new world was strong. In contrast, it is estimated that nearly a quarter of the non-Jewish Southern and Eastern European immigrants arriving in the late 19th and early 20th centuries returned to their homelands. Second, in much of Europe and Eurasia, Jews had been ghettoized and subject to a split labor market. Economic mobility and physical mobility were greatly restricted. In America, there was prejudice and discrimination but not legal restrictions. When compared to the European situation, this truly was a "land of opportunity." Finally, it has been argued that religious and family values stressed individual achievement, especially through educational attainment. These several factors then, depict American Jewish social mobility as an understandable response to the social circumstances encountered here.

A significant aspect of the Jewish-American story has been the creation of parallel institutions. The latter, it will be recalled (pp. 249–250) are subordinate-group controlled institutions that provide the minority access and opportunity denied them in the surrounding society. For Jewish-Americans, parallel institutions were created in numerous social and economic realms. Included were separate business institutions, colleges and universities, country clubs, and vacation resorts, all of which were responses to anti-Semitic exclusionary practices in the United States. These institutions effectively neutralized discriminatory practices against Jews and provided pathways to social mobility.

Today, most American Jews are American-born. The only departure from this pattern is the large scale immigration of Russian Jews that is now occurring. It is too soon to know if the Russian Jews of the 1990s will follow the path of assimilation and social mobility that was traveled by the Russian, Polish, and other immigrant Jews of the 1890s.

WOMEN

In 1989, women comprised 51.2 percent of the population of the United States (U.S. Bureau of the Census 1991). Although women are a numerical majority, they also socially are a minority stratum. This is because like blacks and Jews, Hispanics and Asians, women are the objects of stereotyping and discrimination.

It is important to distinguish between sex and gender. The terms female and male refer to a person's biological sex, while gender (feminine or masculine) is a socially constructed category. The physical trait, sex, is a primary basis for status ascription leading to gender stratification. On the basis of physical differences between men and women, cognitive and emotional differences are alleged. Thus, women are a physical minority to whom both cognitive and behavioral characteristics have been attributed. Women differ not only in their lack of the high-status male physique, but also in their allegedly different values, beliefs, and ways of being. For example, women are thought to be less rational and more emotional; less self-reliant and less mechanically skilled; and, of course, less aggressive and more easily influenced than men. Those women not exhibiting these traits are, by definition, less "feminine."

Gender differences are created and supported by socialization experiences. All of the major agencies of socialization, parents, peers, schools, and the mass media (see Chapter 6, pp. 150–155) reinforce a subordinate position for women as compared to men. Although social class, racial, and ethnic differences among women give some women advantages denied to others, women in comparison to men of the same social status (race, ethnicity, and class) typically are in a subordinate position. The term gender inequality describes differences between the sexes in the distribution of status assignment (Mason 1986).

The elaborate social and intellectual processes through which women have been denigrated have been widely documented (Daly 1968). Historically, gender inequality has been maintained by tying women to the domestic sphere and especially to their reproductive functions. Labor in the domestic sphere has been undervalued, while labor in the public sphere has been rewarded with money, prestige, and power (Daniels 1987). So long as women assume primary responsibility for children and the home, they cannot compete in the public sphere on an equal basis with males. This particularly is true of those occupational positions requiring high investments of time and energy.

Female participation in the American occupational structure clearly reflects a split labor market at best, and more probably colonization. For example, one measure of social class mobility for females is provided by calculating women's incomes as a percentage of men's incomes. For the entire period between 1945 and 1988, American women never have earned greater than 66.1 percent of men's incomes. The high-income watermark for women, the year in which the percentage actually hit 66.1 percent, was 1945! This is because in the period immediately following World War Two, many women were yet to be displaced from the previously male-dominated occupations they had acquired during the war. As the servicemen came home, more traditional gender stratification patterns in the workplace were reinstituted, and women's incomes fell. In spite of the dramatic changes in the American economy during the forty-three years between 1945 and 1988, on average, the income gap between males and females did not improve.

Specific labor market trends further confirm the reality of a split labor market. Certain occupational categories are culturally defined as "women's work." At the beginning of the 20th century, the American garment industry centered in the Northeast thrived on low-wage-earning immigrant females. It is no accident that the premier labor union in this industry became the International *Ladies* Garment Workers Union. Even today, semiskilled factory work in American industry is a primarily female employment field. Of course, even in the white-collar world, a split market prevails, with nurses, secretaries, and retail sales clerks being disproportionately female. Some sociologists, stressing the gender difference, have termed these "pink collar" occupations.

Obviously, the emergence of a women's movement is a direct response to a collective awareness of patterns of differential treatment, an important criterion in Wirth's (1945) definition of a "minority." Historians point to three distinct phases of feminist activism in American history (Chafetz and Dworkin 1986). In its earliest phase (1820–1850), the new women's movement focused upon such issues as slavery and peace. This phase of the movement is significant for several reasons. First, it constituted an initial venturing into the public realms of American society by women. Previously, women generally were confined to the domicile, a practice that might be labeled segregation or even colonialism, for in the home, women spent the entire day working. Second, as evidenced by the first women's rights conference held at Seneca Falls, New York, in 1848, concern for the rights of slaves quickly lead to a heightened consciousness about the lack of female rights in a male dominated society.

The second phase of the movement (1890–1920) entailed a freeing of American women from the oppressive moral standards of Victorian culture, including the "double standard" (different rules for men than women) in sexual mores. Some of the issues raised at the time, such as women's control over their own bodies and women's right to reproductive choice (the right to use contraception), remain controversial issues today. Of course, this phase of the movement resulted in the passing in 1919 of the 19th Amendment to the Constitution of the United States, giving females the right to vote.

The modern period of the movement dates from around 1965 to the present and surely is linked to other minority rights movements, most importantly the Civil Rights movement. The women's movement has splintered into a great diversity of special issue organizations, each focusing on particular causes. Organizations like the National Organization of Women (NOW) have provided leadership in the political arena, and, of course, there is a women's caucus in the United States Congress. The National Planned Parenthood Association has become the premier agency for defending women's reproductive rights.

Clearly, during the 1970s and 1980s, women's rights organizations placed special emphasis on the social mobility routes within American society, education, and jobs. In this sense, women have followed the same strategy as religious, racial, and ethnic communities seeking to combat status ascription. As Travis and Wade (1984) observe, this phase of the movement has witnessed many occupational "firsts" for American women. Included have been the first woman in space, the first female Episcopal priests, the first female Justice of the Supreme Court of the United States, and other important "firsts." Yet, even where women have entered traditionally male occupations and professions, they continue to face many barriers to full participation and mobility.

THE AGED

Age is a significant characteristic for status ascription in human societies. The status of the elderly depends upon many variables, especially their perceived utility to the community. In societies where conditions of living are harsh and resources scarce, such as hunting and gathering societies, the status of the elderly typically is low. In more traditional societies, such as agrarian societies, aging garners high social status. Elders are seen as advisors. Knowledge gained through experience gives them special economic, familial, and cultural roles. Similarly, it is common for elders to have control over valued community property and resources (Simmons 1960; Press and McKool 1972).

As societies modernize, the esteem accorded to elderly members changes, and they become less valued than persons in other age categories. Today, it is common sociological practice to view older Americans as a minority community. Three primary factors associated with modernization are involved in the devaluing of the elderly: modern health technology, technological innovation, and urbanization (Cowgill 1972, 1986).

First, modern health technology dramatically lowers both birth and death rates, leading to the "aging of the population." Lower death rates reduce the need for replacement of the labor force, and intergenerational competition over jobs emerges. Mandatory retirement becomes a social institution. For example, in the United States, as the "baby boomers" (the unusually large birth cohort of the 1950s) entered the job market, they found large numbers of older Americans not yet ready to retire. Consider that between 1920 and 1990 the average life expectancy in the United States increased from 54.8 to 80.4 for females and from 53.6 to 73.5 for males. In those same years, the percentage of the population aged 65 and older increased from 4.7 percent to 12.7 percent (U.S. Bureau of the Census 1991). The enactment of mandatory retirement laws that accompanied the "greying of America" in the 1970s must be viewed as a status-community conflict in which older Americans' access to valued social resources (employment) was damaged. According to Cowgill, modernization typically is characterized by a strong work ethic, thereby diminishing the status of the retirement role.

A second work-related factor associated with modernization which greatly undermines the social position of the elderly is technological innovation in the workplace. Many of the work skills and much of the knowledge gained by older Americans no longer translate into economic success. Today, younger workers with higher levels of formal education and computer-related skills dominate the workplace. Such differences have led younger Americans to view their elders as "over-the-hill" and "not with it." These same attitudes frequently lead employers not to invest resources in retraining older persons.

FIGURE 9.4
For America's elderly, social activism has produced results.

Third, long-term urbanization trends surely have weakened traditional extended-family patterns in the United States. Career opportunities have moved younger Americans to major urban centers, away from the traditional influence of parents and the extended family system. As younger people follow their jobs, many of the traditional relationships between generations are lost. Most especially the authority position of elders is weakened.

Interestingly, the greatest forms of deprivation for America's elderly have been status rather than economic deprivations. Government entitlement programs ranging from Social Security benefits to Medicaid and Medicare, have provided a more impressive level of well-being for the present generation of elderly than for any previous generation. However, this fact should not be taken to mean that most elderly are without financial concern or that there are not many elderly poor in the United States. Neither of these things is true.

The term *ageism* (Butler 1975; Levin and Levin 1980) has been coined to describe prejudice and discrimination against the elderly. We've seen earlier in this chapter (p. 244) that whenever a particular physical, cognitive, or behavioral trait becomes the focus of status deprivation, other traits are alleged. Accordingly, the physical trait of age has been accompanied by the social definition of the aged as mentally slow and incompetent. Frequently, in daily face-to-face relationships, the aged are treated as though they were children or

RACIAL COMMUNITIES	NUMBER
WHITE	179.4
BLACK	30.3
HISPANIC	20.7
ASIAN	6.6
NATIVE AMER.	1.7
OTHERS	7.1

EUROPEAN ETHNIC COMMUNITIES	NUMBER
ENGLISH	49.5
GERMAN	49.2
IRISH	40.1
FRENCH	12.8
ITALIAN	12.1
SCOTTISH	10.0
POLISH	8.2
DUTCH	6.3

RELIGIOUS COMMUNITIES	NUMBER
PROTESTANTS	79.3
ROMAN CATHOLIC	54.9
EASTERN CATHOLIC	4.0
JEWS	5.9
BUDDIST	0.1
OTHERS	0.2

HISPANIC-AMERICAN COMMUNITIES	NUMBER
MEXICAN	13.7
PUERTO RICAN	2.6
CUBAN	1.2
ALL OTHERS	3.2

ASIAN-AMERICAN COMMUNITIES	NUMBER
CHINESE	1.3
KOREAN	0.6
VIETNAMESE	0.6
JAPANESE	0.9
PHILLIPINES	1.5

IN 1990 THERE WERE 249 MILLION AMERICANS

FIGURE 9.5
THE AMERICAN MOSAIC: A STATISTICAL PROFILE (in millions of persons)

SOURCE: Religious statistics are taken from the National Council of Churches' publication *Yearbook of American and Canadian Churches* (Jaquet 1990). All other statistics are for the year 1989 as published in the *Statistical Abstract of the United States* (U.S. Bureau of the Census 1991), except the statistics for European Ethnic Communities, for which the most recent estimates are from the publication *1980 Census of the Population, Supplementary Report,* series PC80-S1-10.

senile. They are viewed as unintelligent and even asexual (Comfort 1976). Shockingly, as the elderly population has increased, so too, have reports of physical abuse of the elderly.

In response to these disturbing social trends, political activism by the elderly has been extensive. Several writers (Pratt 1977; Ward 1984) maintain that the 1950s were a watershed period for activism by senior citizens. The American Association of Retired Persons, the National Retired Teachers Association, and the National Council of Senior Citizens all emerged during those years. The 1971 White House Conference on Aging marked the beginning of the government's response to the problems of America's aged. The enactment of a series of Social Security amendments and Medicare, periodic White House Conferences on Aging, and the creation of the National Institute on Aging and the Federal Administration on Aging all must be seen as the results of effective and sustained political activism.

On balance, it may be argued that just as the treatment of the aged resembles that of racial, religious, and ethnic status communities, so the organized self-defense activities of the elderly provides a useful model for other status communities to emulate.

In summary, this section of the chapter has examined the historical experiences of a number of American status communities: native Americans, Hispanics, Asians, blacks, Catholic ethnic communities, Jews, the aged, and women. Similar initial contacts or immigration circumstances often produce similar outcomes. This is illustrated by the colonization of native Americans and Mexican Americans. Internal community resources and the establishment of parallel institutional structures can be important factors in social mobility. The situations of Cubans, European Jews, and several Asian communities illustrate these processes. While each case is historically unique, all subordinate communities, women, blacks, Hispanics, and others share a common task in overcoming the consequences of minority status. Figure 9.5 provides a statistical profile of the American mosaic of status communities.

APPLICATIONS

ECONOMIC PARALLELISM

It has been seen in this chapter that throughout American history, a great many status communities have been the objects of prejudice and discrimination and have encountered roadblocks to their social mobility. Of course, the precise ways in which minority communities may combat and overcome such treatment depends upon a number of factors.

The conditions of migration, ranging from forced migration (such as slavery) to voluntary migration surely affect the kinds of resources, both cultural and material, that a given status community may have. However, it should not be assumed that the simple act of acquiring resources leads to economic prosperity. Institutional discrimination does not change quickly.

In the midst of the American banking crisis of the early 1990s, the only black-owned banking institution in the nation, New York City's Freedom National Bank fell under the scrutiny of the Federal Deposit Insurance Corporation. When the FDIC moved to close Freedom National, a consortium of financial backers in the black community announced that they had the capital to stabilize the bank and asked for the weekend to do so. The FDIC refused the request and closed the bank with dire financial consequences for its shareholders from the black community. Freedom National Bank is an example of a parallel economic institution, a phenomenon discussed earlier in this chapter (pp. 249–250). Other examples include the system of Catholic colleges and universities in the United States, Greek-American predominance in some parts of the food industry, Irish control of municipal service employment in certain Northeastern urban centers, and even Mormon control of much of what happens in the State of Utah. None of these cases of ethnic enterprise happens without a struggle. One such struggle, still occurring, is the entrance of native Americans into the gaming industry.

CASE

THE NATIVE AMERICAN GAMBLING ENTERPRISE

The containment of native Americans on segregated reservations has been a double-edged sword. On the one hand, the preservation of so-called Indian lands has protected native Americans from the kind of land-grabbing by non-Indians that occurred under the Dawes Act (see discussion p. 253). Yet, confined to the reservations, native Americans have encountered few avenues for social and economic well-being.

A potentially momentous change in this situation occurred in 1982 when a federal appellate court ruled that Indian lands are exempt from state gaming regulations. By 1985, over 80 different tribes across the United States had entered the bingo industry. What once had been a modest weekly fund-raiser for the local Catholic Church or VFW was being transformed into "High Stakes Bingo" by the Mashantucket Pequots in Connecticut, the Mohawks in New York, the Otoe Missouria in Oklahoma, the Winnebagos in Wisconsin, and many other tribes. Moreover, by the late 1980s, dozens of tribes from California to Connecticut had either implemented or were making plans to implement full-scale casino operations.

From a sociological perspective, these native Americans are doing little more than what many immigrant minority communities have done previously. They are creating a parallel economic institution. They are building an "ethnic" economic niche, one that can yield remarkable social and economic service to their communities. By one report, casino gambling administered by native Americans in 1991 was a 400 million dollar business (Gruson 1991). Additionally, one Minnesota tribe earns sufficient proceeds from its casino operations to write a dividend check for $2,000.00 per month for each member of the tribe.

Yet, these native American economic enterprises do not emerge without conflict. Court battles, raids upon tribal casinos, and the seizure of gambling equipment by state authorities have been common. Why have state governments so aggressively opposed these Indian gambling operations? Beginning in the early 1970s, state governments entered the gambling business to cover increasing shortfalls in tax revenues. State lotteries have become a big business in the United States, and many states that once outlawed all gambling activities now allow casinos, dog and horse tracks, jai alai frontons, teletracks, and even off-track parimutuel betting. Americans no longer need travel to Las Vegas to place a bet.

The Indian gaming enterprises illustrate the processes of dominant-subordinate competition and even conflict. To the dismay of many state governments, in 1988 the United States Congress passed the Indian Gambling Control Act which authorizes native American tribes to offer any kind of gambling on Indian lands that already is available elsewhere in a state. This Act created an equal playing field. In California, for example, where county sheriffs had been conducting raids on Indian gambling enterprises and confiscating valuable gaming equipment, the tribes invoked the 1988 federal statute (Lieberman 1991).

Yet another illustration of this is provided by the Mashantucket Pequot tribe in Connecticut. Based on the success of their High Stakes Bingo enterprise, the Connecticut Pequots petitioned the state for full casino operations. Their request, following the federal Indian Gambling Control Act, noted that under Connecticut law, various nonprofit organizations already were conducting games of chance like blackjack and roulette. State officials maintained that a gambling casino in the state would open Connecticut to organized crime elements. The Mashantucket Pequots observed that this concern did not prevent Connecticut from allowing dog racing, jai alai, and off-track betting, all gambling activities that could be exploited by organized crime, but from which the state receives part of the profit margin. The federal courts found that Connecticut's Las Vegas Night statute, which allows charity groups to raise money by gambling, essentially established casino activities regardless of the sponsors (Ravo 1991). On this basis, a native American casino enterprise was launched in 1992.

It is clear that ethnic enterprise can be an arduous undertaking. For the Mashantucket Pequots it has involved difficult and expensive legal undertakings and tough negotiations with state government. For a time, conflict was turned to exchange and perhaps even cooperation, for the state government recognized the new casino as a significant source of non-tribal employment in that region of the state. However, competition has not disappeared. In the Spring of 1992, Connecticut's legislature debated authorizing other casino operations that would compete with the Mashantuckets. Time will reveal if the Connecticut process sets the pattern for what will happen in other states and if casino gambling becomes the long-needed parallel economic structure that will end the poverty that has afflicted so many native American communities.

Chapter Summary

1. Minorities are status communities that, because of distinctive physical, behavioral, or cognitive traits, are the objects of discrimnation and regard themselves a such. There are no apparent limits to the kinds of human traits that are the focus of negative social status assignments.
2. Status relations may originate in connection with the division of labor in societies and frequently attach to such differences as gender, family, and age. Technology and military force affect the creation of dominant-subordinate patterns between different societies.
3. For immigrating populations, the apparent differences from the host society's physical, cognitive, and behavioral high-status norms influence the extent of negative status ascription. The conditions of migration also are important, with four types being distinguished: forced labor, contracted labor, displaced persons, and voluntary migration.
4. Prejudice consists of ideas or beliefs that negatively prejudge individuals, groups, communities, or strata, on the basis of real or alleged collective traits. Discrimination consists of any act of differential treatment based upon the perception of persons as members of a group, community, or stratum. Both of these phenomena along with stereotypes are essential mechanisms that institutionalize status relations in societies.
5. Institutionalized discrimination in its direct and indirect forms creates rigid barriers for minorities. Direct institutional discrimination is incorporated into the formal norms of a society, while indirect institutional discrimination is a matter of custom not law.
6. The four basic forms of social interaction—cooperation, conflict, competition, and exchange—are expressed in specific intergroup patterns.
7. Cooperative processes include assimilation, amalgamation, and pluralism. Amalgamation is the least probable of these. The diverse processes of both assimilation and pluralism seem to characterize the American experience.
8. Conflict processes include genocide, slavery, colonialism, and split labor markets. All of these constitute discrimination as they are intended to injure

and/or neutralize minority communities. In contrast, competitive processes include the formation of ethnic enclaves, parallel institutions, and middleman minorities. Exchange relations between dominant and subordinate communities often take the form of political coalitions.

9. American society contains a great number of minority communities that are distinguished by skin color, ethnicity, religion, gender, and age differences, as well as by various combinations of these traits. Immigration laws in the Untied States have been an important element in the histories of many of these communities. Each community exhibits a unique combination of variables influencing its response to negative status ascription in America.

Key Concepts

all-weather liberal
amalgamation
assimilation
behavioral minorities
bigot
blaming the victim
cognitive minorities
colonialism
competition
conflict
contracted labor
cooperation
cultural assimilation
cultural pluralism
direct institutional discrimination
discrimination
displaced persons
ethnic enclaves
exchange
fair-weather liberal
forced labor
genocide
indirect institutional discrimination
institutional discrimination
internal colonialism
middleman minorities
minority group
parallel institutions
physical minorities
prejudice
slavery
split labor market
status community
stereotypes
structural assimilation
timid bigot
voluntary migration

Bibliography

Alba, Richard
1985. *Italian Americans.* Englewood Cliffs: N.J.: Prentice-Hall.

Barrera, Mario
1979. *Race and class in the southwest: A theory of racial inequality.* South Bend, Indiana: Univ. of Notre Dame Press.

Barringer, Felicity
1989. "Mixed-race generation emerges but is not sure where it fits." *New York Times,* September 24: 22.

Bonacich, Edna
1972. A theory of ethnic antagonism: The split labor market. *American Sociological Review.* Vol. 37, No. 5 (October): 547–59.

1973. A theory of middleman minorities, *American Sociological Review.* Vol. 38, No. 5 (October): 583–94.

Bouvier, Leon F., and Robert W. Gardner
1986. *Immigration to the U.S.: The unfinished story. Population Bulletin.* Vol. 41, No. 4 (November).

Burawoy, Michael
1976. The function and reproduction of migrant labor: Comparative material from Southern Africa and the United States. *American Journal of Sociology.* Vol. 81, No. 5 (March): 1050–86.

Butler, Robert
1975. *Why survive? Being old in America.* New York: Harper & Row.

Carino, Benjamin V.
1987. "The Philippines and Southeast Asia: Historical roots and contemporary linkages." In *Pacific bridges: The new immigration from Asia and the Pacific Islands,* edited by James T. Fawcett and Benjamin V. Carino, 305–25. Staten Island, New York: Center for Migration Studies.

Carmichael, Stokely, and Charles Hamilton
1967. *Black power.* New York: Random House.

Chafetz, Janet Saltzman, and Anthony Gary Dworkin
1986. *Female revolt: Women's movements in world and historical perspective.* Totowa, N.J.: Rowman and Allanheld.

Collins, Randall
1988. *Sociology of marriage and the family.* 2d ed. Chicago, Illinois: Nelson-Hall.

Comfort, Alex
1976. *A good age.* New York: Crown Publishing Company.

Cowgill, Donald O.
1972. "A theory of Aging in Cross-cultural Perspective." In *Aging and modernization,* edited by Donald O. Cowgill and Lowell Holmes, 1–14. New York: Appleton-Century-Crofts.

1986. *Aging around the world.* Belmont, California: Wadsworth Publishing Company.

Dadrian, Vahakn N.
1975. "The Common Features of the Armenian and Jewish Cases of Genocide: A Comparative Victimology Perspective." In *Victimology: a new focus. Vol. 4. Violence and its victims,* edited by Israel Drapkin and Emilio Viano, 99–120. D.C. Heath.

Daly, Mary
1968. *The church and the second sex.* New York: Harper & Row.

Daniels, Arlene Kaplan
1987. Invisible work. *Social Problems.* Vol. 34, No. 5: 403–15.

Dobyns, Henry F.
1960. Estimating aboriginal American populations. *Current Anthropology.* Vol. 7, No. 4 (October): 395–416.

Elkins, Stanley
1959. *Slavery: A problem in American institutional and intellectual history.* 3d ed., 1976. Chicago: Univ. of Chicago Press.

Feagin, Joe R.
1989. *Racial and ethnic relations.* 3d ed. Englewood Cliffs, N.J.: Prentice-Hall.

Fitzpatrick, Joseph P.
1971. *Puerto Rican Americans: The meaning of migration to the mainland.* 2d ed., 1987. Englewood Cliffs, N.J.: Prentice-Hall.

Fogel, Robert, and Stanley Engerman
1974. *Time on the cross.* 2 vols. Boston: Little, Brown & Co.

Frazier, E. Franklin
1963. *The negro church in America.* New York: Schocken Books.

Gambino, Richard
1975. *Blood of my blood.* Garden City, New York: Doubleday Books.

Glazer, Nathan, and Daniel Patrick Moynihan
1963. *Beyond the melting pot.* Rev. ed., 1970. Cambridge, Mass.: M.I.T. Press.

Glock, Charles, and Rodney Stark
1966. *Christian beliefs and anti-Semitism.* New York: Harper & Row.

Goldstein, Sidney
1981. "Jews in the United States: Perspectives from Demography." In *American Jewish yearbook, 1981,* 3–59. New York: American Jewish Committee.

Goldstein, Sidney, and Calvin Goldschneider
1968. *Jewish Americans.* Englewood Cliffs, N.J.: Prentice-Hall.

Gordon, Milton
1964. *Assimilation in American life.* New York: Oxford Univ. Press.

Greeley, Andrew
1964. "Mixed Marriages in the United States." Mimeograph. Chicago: National Opinion Research Center.

1981. *The Irish Americans.* New York: Harper & Row.

Gruson, Lindsey
1991. "U.S. approves Indian casino in Connecticut." *New York Times,* May 25: 26.

Hansen, Marcus Lee
1940. *The Atlantic migration, 1607–1860.* Harper Torchbook edition, 1961 New York: Harper & Row.

Higham, John
1955. *Strangers in the land: Patterns of American nativism, 1860–1925.* Paperback ed., 1963. New York: Atheneum. New Brunswick, N.J.: The Trustees of Rutgers College in New Jersey.

Hispanic Policy Development Project
1984. *The Hispanic Almanac.* Washington, D.C.: Hispanic Policy Development Project.

Horowitz, Irving L.
1976. *Genocide: State power and mass murder.* New Brunswick, N.J.: Transaction Books.

Howton, Louise G.
1971. "Genocide and the American Indians." In *Mass society in crisis,* 2d ed., edited by Bernard Rosenberg, Israel Gerver, and William Howton, 144–50. New York: Macmillan.

Jaffee, A. J., Ruth M. Cullen, and Thomas D. Boswell
1980. *The changing demography of Spanish Americans.* New York: Academic Press.

Jaquet, Constant, ed.
1990. *Yearbook of American and Canadian churches, 1990.* Nashville, Tennessee: Abingdon Press.

Jones, Maldwyn Allen
1960. *American immigration.* Chicago: Univ. of Chicago Press.

Kallen, Horace
1924. *Culture and democracy in the United States.* New York: Liveright.

Kitano, Harry, and Roger Daniels
1988. *Asian Americans: Emerging minorities.* Englewood Cliffs, N.J.: Prentice-Hall.

Lazerwitz, Bernard
1971. Intermarriage and conversion: A guide for future research. *Jewish Journal of Sociology.* Vol. 13, No. 1: 41–63.

LeMay, Michael C.
1987. *From open door to Dutch door: An analysis of U.S. immigration policy since 1820.* New York: Praeger.

Lenski, Gerhard
1966. *Power and privilege: A theory of social stratification.* New York: McGraw-Hill.

Levin, Jack, and William C. Levin
1980. *Ageism: Prejudice and discrimination against the elderly.* Belmont, California: Wadsworth Publishing Company.

Lieberman, Paul
1991. "Indians warn Lungren against crackdown." *Los Angeles Times,* (Sunday), October 13: 4.

Light, Ivan
1972. *Ethnic enterprise in America.* Berkeley, California: Univ. of California Press.

Light, Ivan, and Edna Bonacich
1988. *Immigrant entrepreneurs: Koreans in Los Angeles, 1965–1982.* Berkeley, California: Univ. of California Press.

Lopreato, Joseph
1970. *Italian Americans.* New York: Random House.

Lyman, Stanford
1974. *Chinese Americans.* New York: Random House.

Marger, Martin
1991. *Race and ethnic relations: American and global perspectives.* 2d ed. Belmont, California: Wadsworth Publishing Company.

Mason, Karen Oppenheim
1986. The status of women: Conception and methodological issues in demographic studies. *Sociological Forum.* Vol. 1: 284–300.

McWilliams, Carey
1948. *North from Mexico: The Spanish speaking people of the United States.* 1968 ed. New York: Greenwood Press.

Merton, Robert
1949. "Discrimination and the American Creed." In *Discrimination and national welfare,* edited by Robert MacIver. New York: Harper & Row.

Newman, William M.
1973. *American pluralism: A study of minority groups and social theory.* New York: Harper & Row.

Newman, William M., and Peter L. Halvorson
1990. An American Diaspora: Patterns of Jewish population change 1971–1980. *Review of Religious Research.* Vol. 31, No. 3: 259–67.

Park, Robert E., and Ernest W. Burgess
1924. *Introduction to the science of sociology.* Chicago: Univ. of Chicago Press.

Pear, Robert
1987. "Women reduce lag in earnings, but disparities with men remain." *New York Times,* September 4: 1, 7.

Pratt, Henry J.
1977. *The grey lobby.* Chicago, Illinois: Univ. of Chicago Press.

Press, I., and M. McKool Jr.
1972. Social structure and status of the aged: Toward some valid cross-cultural generalizations. *Aging and Human Development.* Vol. 3, 297–306.

Ravo, Nick
1991. "How a tribe in Connecticut is taking on Atlantic City." *New York Times,* April 14: 6.

Ryan, William
1971. *Blaming the victim.* New York: Vintage Books.

Schermerhorn, Richard
1970. *Comparative ethnic relations.* New York: Random House.

Simmons, Leo
1960. "Aging in Preindustrial Societies." In *Handbook of social gerontology,* edited by Clark Tibbitts, 62–91. Chicago, Illinois: Univ. of Chicago Press.

Simpson, George Eaton, and J. Milton Yinger
1972. *Racial and cultural minorities: An analysis of prejudice and discrimination.* 4th ed. New York: Harper & Row, (Fourth Edition).

1985. *Racial and cultural minorities: An analysis of prejudice and discrimination.* 5th ed. New York: Plenum Press.

Sklare, Marshall
1971. *America's Jews.* New York: Random House.

Travis, Carol, and Carole Wade
1984. *The longest war: Sex differences in perspective.* 2d ed. New York: Harcourt Brace Jovanovich.

U.S. Bureau of the Census
1991. *Statistical Abstract of the United States, 1991.* Washington, D.C.: U.S. Government Printing Office.

U.S. Bureau of Indian Affairs
1975. *Federal Indian Policies.* Washington, D.C.: U.S. Government Printing Office.

U.S. Commission on Civil Rights
1988. *The Economic Status of Americans of Asian Descent: An Exploratory Investigation.* Washington, D.C.: Clearinghouse Publication.

Ward, Russell A.
1984. *The aging experience: An introduction to gerontology.* 2d ed. New York: Harper & Row.

Wax, Murray L.
1971. *American Indians: Unity and diversity.* Englewood Cliffs, N.J.:Prentice-Hall.

Wilson, William J.
1980. *The declining significance of race.* Chicago: Univ. of Chicago Press.

1987. *The truly disadvantaged: The inner city, the underclass, and public policy.* Chicago: Univ. of Chicago Press.

Wirth, Louis
1945. "The problem of minority groups." In *the science of man in the world crisis,* edited by Ralph Linton. New York: Columbia Univ. Press.

Zangwill, Israel
1909. *The melting pot.* New York: Macmillan.

CHAPTER **10**

SOCIAL CHANGE: MACROSOCIOLOGY

CHAPTER OUTLINE

LEARNING OBJECTIVES

A well-known French proverb claims that "the more things change, the more they stay the same." If this proverb is taken to mean that the dilemmas of the human condition seem to be timeless, even as the surrounding cultures and social structures exhibit continual change, then there is no arguing with this claim. A more skeptical American view of the human condition states that "some problems don't get solved, they just get older." Of course, if the matter were that simple, there would be little purpose in studying societies, the ways they change, and the consequences of those changes.

As was seen in Chapter 1, the emergence of sociology was, in part, a response to social change. In both Europe and America, the 19th century founders of sociology recognized that, in their day, the processes of social change had altered fundamentally the structures of societies, both quantitatively and qualitatively. From a quantitative standpoint, from the 19th century to the present, social change has proceeded at a dizzying pace. From a qualitative perspective, sociology's classic tradition demonstrated that life in modern societies is different from what preceded it.

If it is true that people feel "at home" when they are surrounded by the familiar, then it is fair to say that the extraordinary pace of change in modern societies results in a certain degree of human discomfort. In their book *The Homeless Mind,* sociologists Brigitte Berger, Peter L. Berger, and Hansfried Kellner (1973) suggest that living with modernity requires some special skills of adjustment precisely because of the rapid pace of social and cultural change. In a widely read treatment of this subject, Alvin Toffler (1970) describes this as "future shock," by which he means the repeating discovery in modern life that things, once again, have changed. Indeed, there is even a group called the World Future Society, which, since the late 1960s, has published the journal *The Futurist.* Futurists take as their mission the forecasting of relatively short-range change trends. There is little question, the French proverb not withstanding that things do change, and that rapidly changing social structures are a fact of modern social life.

This chapter examines social change processes. The first section of the chapter explores some differences between the scientific study of social change and the political doctrine of social progress. Next, the specific kinds of variables or forces that trigger and instigate social change processes in societies are examined. Finally, this chapter examines general theories of social change.

After studying this chapter you should be able to discuss answers to the following questions:

1. What is meant by social change and how can it be distinguished from progress? What are some common "pitfalls" involved in studying social change?

2. What are the major categories of intended change in human societies?
3. How successful are such intended change agents as government planning or voluntary social movements?
4. What are the major factors that cause unintended change in societies?
5. What kinds of general theories have been used to study social change?
6. How useful are these general social change theories for studying social change processes?

THE SOCIOLOGICAL CONTEXT

The first section of this chapter focuses upon two critical issues that inevitably are raised in the study of social change. First, what is the relationship between social change and social progress? In the normal course of events, people rarely discuss social change without also evaluating the changes confronting them. The questions "Do we like these changes?" and "Are these things good or bad?" are inescapable. Yet, from a scientific standpoint, it is essential that the distinction between scientific (descriptive, explanatory, and predictive) and evaluative (good, bad, helpful, or harmful) be maintained. Second, there always is a tendency to look for relatively simple answers to complex questions. Yet, processes of social change are exceedingly complex and rarely are explained adequately by focusing upon a single cause. Thus, the idea of multicausality must be examined.

CHANGE AND PROGRESS

Social change

Exactly what is meant by the term "social change"? The idea of social change hinges on the sociological understanding of social reality as structural. Social structures, of course, are the shapes or patterns in which human activities are packaged in societies. Frequently, repeated patterns of human activity are said to be institutionalized. They exhibit repeatability and predictability. It will be recalled (Chapter 4) that social structures always exhibit four characteristics; namely, norms, a division of labor, social controls, and hierarchy. Accordingly, *social change is the process through which alterations are created in social norms, the division of labor, social controls, and hierarchy.* In the simplest terms, social change means that the patterns of life in a society are becoming different from what they were. Some sociologists maintain a sharp distinction between social change, as it has been defined here, and cultural change. While the definition proposed here focuses upon structural features of societies, the term "social change" is used to encompass both structural and cultural change. Let's examine an example of social change, labor market trends in the United States in the second half of the 20th century.

Since midcentury, labor market patterns in the United States have undergone remarkable transformations. One feature of these trends has been the creation of new educational requirements for labor market participation. Whether it be in the form of a college or university degree, technical school training, or attendance at career institutes, it is clear that the rules for getting and keeping employment and for advancing in the world of work have changed.

These new rules are reflected in new educational norms in the American population. Consider that in 1940 only 16 percent of Americans in the 18 to 24-year-old age category attended college. By the mid-1980s 39 percent would do so (U.S. Bureau of the Census 1991). The median school years completed by the American adult population provides yet another statistical measure of these changed norms. In 1940, half of all adults attained only a junior high school education (8.4 years), while by 1987, half of all Americans would attain some schooling beyond a high school diploma (12.7 years) (U.S. Bureau of the Census 1991). There is no question that education norms have changed.

These new norms have been accompanied by significant changes in the division of labor. Both in the employment market itself and in the educational institutions that service that market, extensive specialization has occurred. At all levels of the college and university system, programs of study have become highly specialized. Students wishing to change schools within the university or major areas within the college frequently have substantial requirements and prerequisites to "make up." In the employment markets, the old pattern of starting at the bottom, learning the system, and "moving up" through the company by advancing through different job levels is indeed rare. The new division of labor more frequently requires individuals to change companies in order to advance.

These new rules for labor force participation, the new educational norms, and the increasing complexity in the division of labor, have been accompanied by a number of hierarchical changes as well. First, in American society before 1950, being a college graduate was a mark of high social honor. Today, men and women with baccalaureate degrees are not rare. Obtaining a college degree does not produce the prestige it once did. Indeed, whenever something becomes a prerequisite, the prestige attached to it decreases. Today, want ads in newspapers are more likely than not to specify "B.A. degree required."

Finally, whenever social change occurs, patterns of social control are altered. In the American social structure of the first half of the 20th century, college graduation reflected broader aspects of the social ranking system. Only the "upper crust" could afford to attend college, and college entrance reflected not what the person was to become, but who the person already was! Colleges were not mobility mechanisms for members of the general public so much as they were elite institutions attended by the already rich and powerful. All of this has changed. As more and more people attain higher levels of education, and as educational requirements escalate, educational institutions have become powerful agents of social control.

Educational credentials, certified levels of educational attainment, and types of specialized training received, have become vehicles for channeling people into the social structure (see discussion in Chapter 5, pp. 119–120). These processes begin in the primary school grades as children are divided into ability levels and later into types of programs (such as vocational education and college preparatory). College and university admissions offices, as well as the entrance exams upon which they so often rely (SAT), are mechanisms of social control. The quip so often heard on college campuses is sociologically astute. "The hard part is getting in. Once you're in, graduating is easy." This may not seem so apparent to the first-year college student struggling to pass all his or her courses. However, persons who do not get "selected" for admission to a college or university, or who cannot afford to attend have been dealt a severe blow having enormous consequences. Whatever else they may be, educational institutions have become systems of reward allocation and agents of social control.

Clearly, the rules and norms, the division of labor, hierarchical patterns, and social control mechanisms surrounding labor-force participation for Americans have undergone substantial modification during the second half of the twentieth century. Based on these alterations in basic features of the social structure it can be said that social change has occurred.

What is the difference between social change and social progress? After all, the idea of progress has been part of social thought in the West since ancient times (Nisbet 1980). Sociologists study social change not simply to describe what's happening but also to explain how and why the apparent changes are occurring and to predict the probable consequences of these new patterns of human conduct. However, it is difficult for most persons to confront changes in an accustomed way of life without asking whether such changes are desirable. Are they good or bad?

Progress

Progress is an evaluative concept. To say that a particular social trend is progressing means not only that something has become different but that somehow it is better. But, who decides what constitutes progress? To answer this question one needs to know who benefits from the observed changes in social institutions. Obviously, the decision about what constitutes progress (whether something is good or bad) is a social issue, which, in part, is decided through political decisions in most modern societies. In the language of the contemporary consumer movement, people vote with their feet and their pocketbooks. In other words, there are several distinct ways (voting, joining, participating, spending, and supporting) in which citizens in modern cultures indicate their judgments regarding what is good, and what represents progress. Basic sciences are not in the business of assessing progress. Rather, as was noted previously (Chapter 1, pp. 2–3), understanding and explanation are the goals of basic sociological science.

The doctrine of progress, however, does enter the realm of sociological discourse in one important regard. Applied sociologists like social workers, city planners, family counselors, and clinical sociologists focus their efforts upon social problems and their remedies. Such tasks presume a social determination about what is good or desirable. These professions specialize in applying scientific knowledge for social betterment and progress. The city planner makes progress when old buildings are renovated and given new uses, or when new buildings are brought into a formerly blighted downtown area. The social worker makes progress when child abuse and drug addiction are abated. The family counselor makes progress when family members derive a sense of well-being and personal fulfillment from their participation in the family unit.

There are some social problems, which, if eliminated, likely would represent progress to all persons. Poverty, hunger, homelessness, war, prejudice, and discrimination are but a few of the evils that seem to afflict the modern world. One hopes that all persons would rejoice in their elimination. However, beyond the eradication of these rather widespread social ills, it becomes difficult to reach agreement about exactly what constitutes social progress. For our present purposes, the key idea is that what constitutes social progress is a political, not a scientific, question.

Sociological analysis does include interpreting the meanings of new structural arrangements. This act of interpretation entails discerning consequences of emerging social structures, and of explaining how new social patterns embody new norms and ways of living, even if people don't intend them to do so. But, the question of progress is not circumscribed within these tasks. The idea of progress is a political, not a scientific, concept.

MULTICAUSALITY AND TYPES OF CAUSES

Perhaps one of the more difficult problems for the analyst of social change processes is the extent to which the social forces that produce social change are interconnected. In fact, the more complex and differentiated the social system being studied, the greater the likelihood that change processes will entail multiple interrelated causes. Let's return for a moment to the case of labor market trends discussed earlier.

The relationship between educational requirements and employment practices developed from a number of related causes. Changes in the economy stimulated changes in the occupational structure, which in turn precipitated new educational requirements. The shift in the American economy from manufacturing to a service orientation and the rapid increase in professional and technical occupations were of prime significance. The development of large-scale organizations and the expansion of white-collar occupations in the early decades of the 20th century created a need for workers with more than an elementary school education. Today's service workers, be they sales managers, computer engineers, or telephone repair personnel, require skills beyond those acquired in high school. Obviously, technology, and most importantly the computer, has played a central role in these developments. Thus, changes in the character and complexity of work demand more and different kinds of schooling. Skills that once were acquired "on the job" no longer suffice. However, the changed structure of education cannot be understood without also considering the role of political factors. When that small Russian spacecraft named Sputnik became the first vehicle to escape the earth's atmosphere, American political leaders made a conscious decision to change the social role of education in the United States. In the political context of this Russian "first," American educational institutions were viewed as a national resource, and those who were willing to apply their talents in certain higher education fields were highly rewarded for doing so.

The entire story of how a concern for advanced educational training developed in American society cannot be told here. However, the point should be clear. A multiplicity of factors, political, economic, and technological are involved in these changes (Trow 1961). No single-variable explanation does justice to these complex chains of events.

Modern statistical techniques such as multiple regression analysis and path analysis (Duncan 1975) provide quantitative methods for assessing the relative contributions of different causal factors. However, our concern here is not so much statistical as conceptual. While the next section of this chapter focuses in a serial manner on individual change factors, one should not lose sight of the fact that in everyday life, social change tends to be multicausal. Thus, ultimately, the analysis of social change requires a scrutiny of how individual change factors combine with one another from one situation to the next.

Moreover, two distinct types of change factors may be distinguished. They are motivated change and unintended change. Motivated change is social change that in some manner results from the intentions and efforts of people to create change. Motivated change may be either planned and guided by official agencies such as governments, or it may result from the efforts of people who organize voluntarily to bring about change. Sociologists call these collective efforts "social movements." In contrast, unintended change refers to changes that result from social forces that are neither intended nor controlled by people. Four such factors will be examined here: namely, demographic or population factors, technology, the physical environment, and cultural diffusion.

In summary, social change consists of processes through which alterations are created in basic features of social structures: norms, the division of labor, patterns of hierarchy, and social control. The scientific concept of change should not be confused with the idea of progress, which is an evaluative concept referring not simply to change but to betterment. Most social change processes are multicausal. The next two sections of this chapter examine two kinds of change factors, motivated change and unintended change.

Motivated Change

Motivated change

Motivated or intentional change refers to social change processes that result from the efforts and intentions of persons to change a society. The term "intended" should not be taken to mean that all attempts to produce social change result in the desired effects. In fact, there is much evidence that specific intended changes are rather difficult to produce. This is true, in part, because most social processes entail unforeseen or unintended consequences that were not envisioned by those attempting to induce change. However, it remains useful to distinguish between those changes that somehow flow from human efforts and those that emerge from unintended social forces.

The following discussion explores two very different kinds of motivated social change agents. The first, planned or guided change, refers to rationally calculated programs for social change. By its nature, such guided or planned change is most often implemented by official governmental agencies. This is because only government (especially in modern societies) possesses sufficient control over the political and economic institutions through which social change may be induced, legitimized, or coerced. Voluntary associations without official sanctions constitute a second change agent. There has been substantial sociological research focused on these social movements. A social movement is a voluntary gathering of persons created for the purpose of promoting some form of structural or cultural change in a society. Both guided change and social movements are powerful sources of social change in modern societies. Let's examine each of them.

PLANNED AND GUIDED CHANGE

Planned change

Planned change is the rational coordination of human energies and material resources to bring about desired effects in the social and physical environment. The idea that sociological knowledge can be used to design a "better" world was a guiding precept for the first generation of American sociologists at the beginning of the 20th century. However, with the development of a basic science focus within sociology, applied concerns (including the notion of social planning) were left to other related social science disciplines. Today, within academia, the planning curriculum typically is located in such departments as public administration, business administration, and occasionally, in a separate planning department.

The rational planning of social change is a powerful tool, and no examination of social change processes would be complete without some consideration of it. The concept of planning carries with it an implied notion of effective control or authority to implement the plans formulated. This is why planning usually is done either by a governmental unit with a clear jurisdiction, such as federal, state, county, or local community agencies, or within a private organizational framework where planners have an official "mission" to solve certain problems identified by the owners or managers of the firm.

Within both public and private settings, planning strategies are most successfully implemented in smaller rather than larger social units. The reasons for this are twofold. First, as social units grow in size it becomes more difficult to identify and assess the various factors that may influence them. For example, the operational problems in a small work group are more easily diagnosed that those of a large corporation. Similarly, it is easier to plan the work program for one city agency than for the entire state. There simply are fewer variables that must be considered in formulating and implementing a plan. The second, and perhaps more important reason is that effective control of events is more readily accomplished in smaller rather than larger social units. Let's examine some cases of both public and private planning.

The use of planning techniques in private organizational settings has been a major feature of business management strategies in the United States since the 1950s. The technique known as management by objectives (MBO) (Drucker 1954) is based on the premise that business organizations can be more efficient and successful if they rationally plan tangible goals within the company rather than simply reacting to events in their external environment. The concept of *MBO* involves upper-level planning of objectives and translation of those objectives into specific goals and tasks at lower levels of the organizational structure. A substantial body of research suggests that the rational planning techniques of MBO are reasonably effective.

MBO

A more recent extension of this approach is represented by the so-called Theory Z management techniques (Ouchi 1981). Popularly attributed to the style of management in Japanese companies, *Theory Z* maintains that rational planning must occur at all levels of an organization. Applied in the Japanese automotive industry, this has meant the use of quality circles in which planning sessions and a process of problem-solving take place on the manufacturing floor of the factory. Whether it be MBO or Theory Z, it is clear that in the

Theory Z

social setting of the single company, organization, or factory, rational planning of daily goals and activities does work.

Surely, a major advantage of the business organization in using such planning techniques is that for employees, these companies are what Etzioni (1961, 1964) calls utilitarian organizations (see Chapter 4, pp. 101–102). The company has the authority to implement change. Salary increases and promotions in rank are used as inducements for getting people to comply with the desired planned goals. The withholding of raises and career advancements are powerful sanctions for those persons who do not become good team players in implementing the organization's plan.

Rational planning techniques also are a major feature of how modern governmental agencies accomplish long-range goals. In the United States, at the state level, the formation of state-sponsored higher educational institutions illustrates the implementation of long-range planning strategies. From the technical colleges and community colleges to the major state colleges and universities, comprehensive educational systems have been created where previously only a fledgling assortment of state land-grant and teacher's colleges once existed.

Similarly, the formation of the National Defense Highway System, popularly known as "the interstate highway system," was a result of federal governmental planning and incentives to states implemented after the Second World War. The more recent creation of the Bay Area Rapid Transit System (BART) in San Francisco, California, provides an interesting case in metropolitan planning in the United States. Designed as a technique for reducing both highway congestion and the air pollution that automobiles produce, the BART facility was met with skepticism and opposition in the planning phases. Raising funds to finance the system was also a significant political hurdle. Yet, once it was created people used it.

Social change at the national level frequently involves both legislation and administrative policies. Obviously, in democratic societies, political and electoral processes can either promote or retard social change. In the United States, the election of a new federal government (which happens every four years) often means termination of projects planned by the former administration. One need only look at the vacillating federal enforcement of such things as affirmative action laws and occupational health and safety standards. Additionally, the actions of planners and elected officials cannot be implemented unless funding—often dependent upon local bonding and public referenda—can be obtained.

Ironically, since planned change requires control of the social systems being changed, dictatorships may be more efficient agents of change than democracies. For instance, it is claimed that under Joseph Stalin's rule, the Soviet Union accomplished a level of industrialism in several decades equal to that which took the United States nearly the entire 19th century to accomplish! However, few people would want to have lived under Stalinism. The point then, is that in democracies quite a lot of planned change occurs, but it also occurs within a certain political context. That context, fortunately, minimizes the coercion of persons by their government.

SOCIAL MOVEMENTS AS CHANGE AGENTS

Social movements

Social movements represent a second category of motivated change forces within societies. *A social movement is a voluntary association of persons, formed for the purpose of promoting or resisting some form of structural and/or cultural goal in a society.* The key difference between movement-generated change, and what here has been called guided change, is that social movements do not enjoy the legitimate authority of government office. In this sense the study of social movements offers a "bottom-up" rather than a "top-down" view of social change processes. The French social analyst Alexis de Toqueville (1805–1859) observed that voluntary movements of all types were a uniquely prominent feature of American culture (1835–40). This remains true today, with voluntary movements in this society focused upon such things as civil rights, gay rights, and even animal rights. There are movements for prolife, prochoice, and euthanasia. There are social movements that are antiwar, antinuclear, and antipoverty. Social movements are a diverse subject area for sociological study.

Social movement organizations

There are a variety of sociological approaches to analyzing such movements. Some sociologists distinguish between *social movement organizations* (called SMOs) (i.e., formal organizations) and the broader "social movements" from which these formal organizations spring. For example, the National Organization of Women, because it is a formal organization, would be viewed as an SMO that is part of the movement known as the Women's Movement. This distinction is useful because it demonstrates that within many social movements there are diverse formal organizations representing different versions of the movement's goals, and often using different tactics and strategies for obtaining social change. For instance, in the civil rights struggles of the 1960s, organizations adopting a "Black Power" stance endorsed very different tactics than those of traditional civil rights organizations like the Student Non-Violent Coordinating Committee.

Yet another conceptual issue pertains to the nature of the goals of social movements. Much of the literature on social movements argues that the term "social movements," by definition, refers to collectivities that are seeking to change society in some manner. However, it is important to recognize that many social movements emerge to support the *status quo.* The emergence of such groups often is a reaction to the perceived threat of change, and as such,

FIGURE 10.1
Social movements express motivated change goals.

these antichange movements play significant roles in change processes. Our inclination is to include in the term social movements all voluntary associations (i.e., all those not enjoying the support of government sponsorship) regardless of whether their social program attempts to support old social practices or foster new ones. Accordingly, both the prochoice movement (presently the law of the land) and the prolife movement are social movements. Several key issues about social movements are examined here. First, how may the emergence of social movements be explained? Why do they emerge when they do? Second, how are they similar to or different from one another? What types are there? Third, to what degree are social movements successful in accomplishing their goals?

Resource mobilization theory

The perspective known as *resource mobilization theory* provides an answer to the first of these questions (McAdam, McCarthy, and Zald 1988; McCarthy and Zald 1977). Obviously, in any society, at any time, there are many persons concerned about how the society could be different. What brings such persons together into a social movement? Resource mobilization theory focuses upon the processes through which three critical resources are mobilized: potential participants, networks for recruiting them, and leaders. The theory also focuses upon the tactics that social movements employ to neutralize agents of social control. Resource mobilization theory has been applied in studies of the United Farm Workers movement in the 1970s (Jenkins 1985), historical trends in the civil rights movement (Killian 1984) and many others.

What types of movements are there? A frequently encountered approach to classifying social movements and SMOs focuses on the nature of their goals. Four types are distinguished. *Reform movements* typically accept the normative social framework but seek certain limited goals within it. Reform movements attempt to "fine tune" existing social structures, and normally will do so through socially legitimate mechanisms, such as the established legal and political institutions.

Reform movements

Revolutionary movements

Revolutionary movements seek changes that strongly conflict with the existing normative structural and cultural system, and accordingly, will more readily adopt noninstitutionalized tactics. While terrorism represents an extreme instance of this, violence and "noninstitutionalized" tactics should not be equated. Indeed, in the 1950s nonviolent tactics like sit-ins and boycotts were extremely noninstitutionalized and extremely effective civil rights tactics. Neither involved the use of violence by the SMOs involved. More recently, members of the environmental movement known as Greenpeace have staged what amounts to sit-ins on the high seas. While Greenpeace activities use rather non-normative tactics, they are not violent. However, frequently they are the targets of violent practices used against them. In one dramatic incident in 1985, a Greenpeace ship, the Rainbow Warrier, was bombed by French agents using terrorist tactics at the instigation of the French government. The Greenpeace activists were protesting the testing of nuclear devices in the South Pacific by the French government. Similarly, in the 1980s, a United States Naval vessel rammed a Greenpeace boat, inflicting substantial damage.

Resistance movements

Resistance movements, also called restoration movements either seek to preserve aspects of the social structure that are waning, or re-establish earlier practices. In common political parlance, reform and revolutionary movements occupy the "left" side of the sociopolitical spectrum, while resistance movements spring from the more conservative or "right" side of the spectrum. For example, during the 1980s an SMO known as the Moral Majority, led by the

Reverend Jerry Falwell, endorsed a wide range of conservative social policies, including an anti-abortion stance, a defense of "traditional family values," and a criticism of "evolutionism" and "liberalism." The Moral Majority became a resistance movement opposing what it considered recent or impending social changes.

Utopian movements

Finally, *utopian movements* seek highly idealistic social goals. Such movements are interesting because they frequently retreat from the broader social structure into self-contained, communal, social structures. By doing so, they make much less of a direct impact on societal change processes than do other types of movements. A variety of religious utopias, including the Amish communities in Pennsylvania, and the Bruderhoff Community in Connecticut illustrate the processes by which Utopian communities insulate their members from the surrounding society. In contrast, such movement organizations as SANE (Society Against Nuclear Energy) adopt an aggressive stance in promoting their views throughout the society.

How successful are social movements in altering social structures and cultural practices, and what determines their degrees of success? Sociologist Gary Marx suggests a variety of factors based on his scrutiny of the Civil Rights movements of the 1960s (Marx 1971). Social movements focusing upon specific goals that are consistent with widely endorsed social values, and thus, gaining the support of influential third parties, have a good chance of success. These traits are characteristic of reform movements, rather than revolutionary movements. However, Marx also notes that movements adopting new tactics with which authorities have had little experience coping stand a good chance of getting public attention, especially in the media. Successful movements are innovative in ways that spread their message.

Alternatively, it may be argued that the more radical movements, by entering at an extreme end of the social spectrum, have the effect of making some existing movements seem more mainstream or middle of the road. While such extreme movements may not see their own goals enacted, they do promote the acceptance of other, apparently less radical, movement objectives. The Black Power movement of the 1960s had just such an effect upon the acceptance of the goals of the Civil Rights movement (Killian 1975). Thus, a social movement need not accomplish its own goals to have an impact upon the social structure.

In summary, this section of the chapter has examined two types of motivated change. First, planning processes have been examined in both private and government settings. Techniques such as MBO and Theory Z work well in private settings, in part, because of the ability of planners and executives to control people's behaviors through utilitarian incentives. Although democratic governments have the force of law to implement change, this is mediated by changing administrations and the need for economic resources. The second type of motivated change involves social movements. Resource mobilization theory focuses on recruitment of potential movement participants through social networks and the role of movement leaders. Types of movements include reform, revolutionary, Utopian, and resistance movements. Using innovative techniques to promote social goals that can be supported by other groups seems to breed success. However, even revolutionary movements affect the social structure by making the goals of less radical movements seem more "reasonable."

CHANGE AS AN UNINTENDED CONSEQUENCE

Unintended change

Despite the efforts of both voluntary and governmental human communities to engineer patterns of social change, much change occurs as the unintended consequences of human activity. *Unintended change refers to changes that result from social forces that are neither intended nor controlled by people.* The following discussion examines four pre-eminent unintended factors that trigger social change processes: demographic or population forces, technology, the physical environment, and processes of cultural diffusion or borrowing. Let's begin with perhaps the most basic of all social forces, population.

DEMOGRAPHIC FORCES

Demography

It has long been recognized that population size and density, as well as other features of human populations, have powerful effects upon both culture and social structure. Accordingly, *demography,* which *is the study of population size, composition, distribution, and change,* is a well-developed subfield within sociology. It is also a significant area for applied sociological work. Demographers participate in the forecasting of business trends, population-generated needs in the fields of education and health care, and the formulation of governmental social policies at the community, state, and federal levels. The following discussion explores the social change processes stemming from two aspects of population: population growth and changes in the social characteristics of populations.

Doubling time

The first of these two factors, the rate of population growth, is determined by three components, fertility (the incidence of births), mortality (the incidence of deaths), and migration (population movement). Population growth is unique in one very important regard. It is exponential, not simply arithmetical. Thus, each year's growth rate is based upon that year's base population, not the base population in some earlier year. Demographers have incorporated this fact in the concept of *doubling time,* which *is the number of years it takes for a population to double in size.* A population growing at a 1 percent annual rate will double its size in 70 years. A 2 percent growth rate would produce a doubling time of only 35 years, and a 3 percent growth rate doubles a population in a mere 23 years.

When the growth rates for some of the world's less-developed nations are examined in the context of the concept of doubling time, the devastating social consequences of unregulated population growth become readily apparent. As seen in Table 10.1, in each decade between 1970 and the year 2000, the actual and projected growth rates for the less-developed regions are consistently higher than those for the more developed (affluent) regions. In the less developed world as a whole, the projected growth rate of 2.0 between 1990 and the year 2000, means that the very nations unable to feed their populations today, will have twice the number of hungry people to feed in 35 years. In Africa, where hunger and starvation already are widespread, a growth rate of 3.0 means that the population will be twice its present size in 23 years!

Moreover, the longer such nations have their scarce national wealth absorbed by subsistence needs, the less likely they are of being able to muster the capital required for industrialization and development. High population

TABLE 10.1

POPULATION GROWTH RATES FOR WORLD REGIONS, 1970–2000

World Regions	Annual Percent Growth Rate		
	Actual 1970–1980	Actual 1980–1990	Projected 1990–2000
Developed Regions:	.8	.6	.5
Europe	.5	.3	.2
North America	1.1	.9	.7
Oceania	1.4	1.0	1.0
Less Developed Regions:	2.2	2.1	2.0
Asia	2.1	1.9	1.7
Latin America	2.4	2.1	1.8
Africa	2.9	2.9	3.0
Entire World	1.8	1.7	1.7

SOURCE: U.S. Bureau of the Census, 1991

growth rates in poor nations have the consequence of increasing the level of poverty. Each year, more and more persons make demands upon a poor nation's stock of dwindling resources such as food, shelter, and health care.

Ironically, the reverse consequences of population growth patterns are being felt in some European nations. As shown in Table 10.1, Europe, as a population region, had a population growth rate of .5 for the period 1985–90. Some nations within the group, France and the former state of West Germany among them, experienced labor shortages and relied upon substantial immigration to compensate for shortages of skilled workers in the industrial sector. Yet, in some cases, as with the influx of large numbers of Muslim immigrants into the predominantly Catholic France, cultural clashes between immigrant and host communities have occurred. Labor shortages and subsequent conflict between different religio-ethnic communities may be seen as consequences of very low population growth rates.

Demographic transition theory

The long-range consequences of high population growth rates has been a topic of considerable debate and speculation among social scientists. The British economist Thomas Malthus (1766–1834) predicted widespread starvation as the ultimate result of uncontrolled population growth. He reasoned that food supplies, which tend to grow arithmetically, never would keep pace with population growth, which, as we've seen, increases exponentially (Malthus 1798). However, Malthus did not anticipate the widespread use of artificial birth control, nor did he anticipate the extent to which agricultural productivity would increase because of scientific and technological advances. Most importantly, in industrialized nations, where large families are a liability rather than an asset, large families became culturally unfashionable. Thus, the worldwide population catastrophe he foresaw, what modern writers have called the "population bomb" (Ehrlich 1968) has not yet occurred.

Today, *demographic transition theory* has replaced Malthus' view of population dynamics. This theory maintains that population change occurs in three

FIGURE 10.2
Would things be different if they knew the consequences of overpopulation?

stages. In preindustrial societies, high birth rates coupled with high death rates result in population stability. During early industrialism, death rates decline sharply due to better nutrition and improved health technologies while birth rates remain high. The resulting population growth places strains on a society's food supply and other resources. Only in the stage of mature industrialism is population stability again achieved. In industrialized societies, low death rates are balanced by low birth rates. Children no longer are viewed as economic assets, and women no longer are confined to domestic and childbearing roles. From this perspective, Western Europe and North America both have made the transition into phase three, while much of the rest of the world is caught somewhere between phases one and two. Thus, while the United States and other relatively wealthy nations are approaching the point of zero population growth (i.e., population stability and, in some cases, population decline), the poorer nations of Asia, Africa, and South America still suffer the devastating consequences of too much population growth accompanied by too little food production. It is clear that population growth is a powerful basic force in social change processes in both industrialized and less developed nations.

A second aspect of population is the distribution of social characteristics within a population, such as gender and age. When such a distribution is represented in graph form it constitutes a "population pyramid" having a distinctive shape. For instance, many observers have argued that the turbulent period of social change movements that characterized American society during the 1960s was partially a result of the shape of the age pyramid which revealed many more persons under the age of 30 than over the age of 30. American society experienced a "generation gap" in which "youth culture" became a predominant part of the landscape.

In contrast, the 1980s marked the "greying of America," which meant a number of very perceptible changes in American community life. Communities that spent millions of dollars constructing public schools to serve the children of the baby boom during the 1960s, became saddled with empty buildings by the early 1980s. Some of these structures have been converted to senior citizens' centers. Businesses, like the fast food industry which relied upon a large supply of relatively cheap labor (high school students), began experiencing both labor shortages and higher labor costs by the mid-1980s. Thus, it is clear that changes in the proportion of the population (young or old, native or immigrant, male or female, to mention but a few commonly studied population characteristics) can have dramatic effects upon the culture and social structure.

TECHNOLOGY

Technological innovations are so much woven into the fabric of modern society that it is difficult to imagine life without them. Ironically, we also may fail to understand the powerful effects of technologies upon us precisely because we are so totally immersed in them. A useful point of departure is to clarify the concept. What is technology?

Technology

In the generic sense, *technology refers to the ideas and material objects invented by any animal population to increase its control over its environment*. In the context of this definition, it is clear that animal populations vary widely in their technological prowess. Birds, and even insects, are marvelously technological in converting nature's raw materials into protective homes like nests and hives.

However, the human animal is infinitely more technological than any other species. Through the sciences of physics, chemistry, engineering, and even biology, humans do more than rearrange or manipulate the environment. Rather, humans transform their environment.

Most people easily can discern the large scale aspects of what technology does to our ways of life. For instance, the advent of the personal automobile facilitated separation of the workplace (cities) from places of residence (suburbs). Similarly, can you imagine a world without telephones, televisions, airplanes, and computers? Each of these technological inventions has changed daily patterns of living in obvious and subtle ways. Let's consider one small example, the effects of telecommunications upon religious practices.

From the classical-period sociologists, among them Durkheim (1912) and Simmel (1906), to such contemporary sociologists of religion as Andrew Greeley (1972), it has been argued that a key function and meaning of religious behavior is that it provides individuals with a community of belonging. Yet, the advent of what Hadden and Swain (1981) call the "electronic church" has changed this. For individuals whose relationship to God is expressed through "the tube," religious participation is no longer group participation. While such persons may derive some feelings of belonging from watching Pat Robertson, Jerry Falwell, Oral Roberts, or other "televangelists," obviously they do not interact and commune with other persons in their electronic religion. Our point is not to impugn the electronic church. The point is that through technology, the meaning and character of religious behavior is changing. An electronic church may still be a church, but it is not a church in which face-to-face primary group social interaction occurs.

The French social analyst Jacques Ellul has observed that modern humans seem unable to resist using new technologies and do so with little regard for the consequences. Accordingly, he has labeled modern society a "technological society" (Ellul 1954) and warns that technology has gained dominance over people. The issue of whether people control technology or technology controls people continues to be widely debated in the humanities and in the social and physical sciences (Teich 1990).

Clearly, much technological innovation in the modern world, like the proverbial sword of Damocles is "double-edged." For instance, the medical use of nuclear energy makes possible life-saving diagnostic techniques like the cat scan procedure. Yet, in contrast, the devastating and near permanent poisoning of the earth that results from an accident like that at Chernobyl, Russia, represents the "down side" of nuclear technology. In her prophetic book *Silent Spring* (1962), the late Rachel Carson warned that the overuse of chemical substances, especially for agricultural purposes, ultimately would poison us.

Consider one of the small technological conveniences of modern culture, the aerosol spray can. People have sprayed virtually everything—bug killer, hair spray, underarm deodorant, and even paint—onto themselves and into the atmosphere. Unfortunately, at the same time, a large hole has been created in the atmosphere's protective ozone shield. While happily we've begun to address these technological hazards that we've created, their societal consequences will be felt for generations. In the case of Chernobyl, some experts anticipate that in the former Soviet Union alone this accident will result in as many as 250,000 cancer deaths within fifty years of the accident (Barringer 1990).

The use of nuclear materials for both energy production and more specialized applications such as nuclear medicine illustrate the double-edged quality of technological "progress." When these uses of radioactive material were adopted in the 1950s, it was simply assumed that solutions to problems of nuclear waste disposal and decontamination would be found in due course. This has not happened. Thus, the very technologies that have given us "progress," also have created an enormous time bomb of contaminated materials. At the very least, technological advances should not automatically be equated with progress.

Of course, not all the effects of technology are quite this dramatic. For many years, it has been shown that among children in the United States, literacy and language skills have decreased in direct proportion to exposure to one technological invention—television. Americans have become watchers, not readers and writers. Moreover, with the advent of personal computers, handwritten documents are fewer and fewer in our business and personal cultural lives. Many humans, in fact, spend much of their day "interacting" with machines, and little time interacting socially with other humans. Social psychologists are only beginning to study and interpret the qualitative significance of these technologically induced social changes. Yet, clearly, from the invention of the wheel to the electronic digital computer, technologies of all sorts leave their imprint upon social life.

THE PHYSICAL ENVIRONMENT

The members of a highly technological society easily may forget that the physical environment can be a powerful influence on patterns of social life. As was noted earlier (see Chapter 3, pp. 66–68), human culture and social structure reflect the limits, as well as potentials and resources, of the physical environment in a great many ways. Similarly, environmental changes can have dramatic effects on social structures. Let's consider some examples.

Obviously, in modern societies, those places where agriculture remains economically dominant are most susceptible to environmental factors. Invasions of a small insect known as the Medfly in the citrus groves of California during the 1980s and the whitefly in the early 1990s had devastating economic effects on a large number of communities. In order to slow the spread of these insects, large quantities of crops had to be destroyed. The economic dislocations to growers, agricultural workers, and shippers was enormous. Unusual cold spells in recent years in the crop-based economies of Florida and Texas have had similar effects. With luck, these environmental disruptions produce only short-term consequences. However, even on a relatively short-term basis, they require substantial adjustments and changes in the lifestyles of entire communities.

Agricultural communities are not alone in this vulnerability to the physical environment. Communities in which tourism and recreation are tied to the use of the physical environment also are vulnerable. The global warming trend, which has resulted in milder and milder winter seasons in the Northeastern states has had dramatic consequences in upper New York State and in some New England states. The winter ski industries in these states have been devastated by what may be an irreversible environmental change. For some local communities the era of economic growth and social stability has ended. With the loss of an economic mainstay, younger people leave for places where there are more opportunities, thus changing the entire social structure of the community.

The unprecedented forest fires that struck Yellowstone National Park in the mid-1980s had similar effects on the surrounding communities that base their economic well-being on serving tourists. While many now have returned to "normal times," there are always economic casualties resulting from these sorts of environmental events. Communities survive, but are changed.

It may be argued that the less the technological development in a society, the more vulnerable it is to unanticipated and uncontrolled environmentally induced change. Mexico suffered devastating earthquake damage in 1989. Yet, Mexico's recovery does not begin to resemble the recovery of California communities from the earthquakes in that same year. Short-term environmental happenings, be they hurricanes, forest fires, or earthquakes, produce social effects of varying duration, depending on the social and economic capacity to respond.

CULTURAL BORROWING AND DIFFUSION

No study of social change would be complete without considering the role of cultural processes. Moreover, cultural processes may originate from within or outside a society. Studies of these processes tend to be of two types, focusing on cultural borrowing and cultural diffusion. *Cultural borrowing is the initial movement of any cultural unit or complex from one society to another, or from one social unit to another within the same society. Cultural diffusion is the process through which such items or complexes become established as normative throughout a population.* It will be recalled (Chapter 3, p. 80) that a cultural complex consists of a related set of cultural units, ideas, and objects. Let's return for a moment to one such cultural complex discussed earlier, baseball.

Cultural borrowing

Cultural diffusion

Baseball, frequently called the "great American pastime," now has become as much Japanese as American. Baseball leagues and teams have sprung into existence throughout Japan, and have a following in Japan well beyond the sport's current popularity in the United States. The introduction of baseball to Japan occurred during the occupation of that country by Allied nations after World War II. Since that time, baseball as a national sport has become widely diffused throughout Japanese society. There is, in a sense, a cultural congruity here. There has been a nearly wholesale adoption of Western competitive economic values by the Japanese. Baseball is a wonderfully competitive sport. Moreover, it provides a welcome leisure pursuit for a "workaholic" culture. There is nothing about baseball that conflicts with the underlying value system of present-day Japanese society. It is reasonable to anticipate that baseball in Japan will become a valued industry and will be responsible for the creation of new collective rituals like the World Series and the Superbowl in the United States.

Cultural borrowing and diffusion also can refer to the transmission of ideas. A recent example of such processes concerns the popularity of Western political and economic thought in Eastern European communist bloc nations. The dismantling of the Berlin Wall, the reunification of East and West Germany, the fall of the communist regime in Poland, and even the movement toward democratic capitalism in the Soviet republics all reflect in part, cultural transmission processes that ignored national boundaries and physical barriers. To be sure, Eastern European nations could restrict travel and social intercourse between East and West. However, apparently, they could not restrict the tide of cultural ideas. The collapse of the Eastern block governments, while a significant political event, was much more than that. It represented the culmination of cultural transmission processes.

Today, technology intensifies the rate at which cultural transmission occurs. At the time of the American Revolution, cultural transmission was by word of mouth, and as fast as a rider on horseback could carry the most recent edition of the Federalist Papers and other printed words. It has been suggested that the new idea of America, or of Americans as a people, took at least fifty years to become an established cultural fact. Today, the rate of cultural transmission is much greater because of high-speed communications technology.

In summary, this section of the chapter has examined four powerful social change agents. First, demographic changes due to births, deaths, and migration have dramatic effects upon a nation's resources. The low "doubling time" and high growth rates of less-developed countries illustrate these processes. Second, technology has subtle but forceful effects upon people's lifestyles and values. Third, both long-and short-term changes in the physical environment can trigger social change. Finally, cultural change may entail the transmission of specific cultural items or entire cultural complexes which become diffused throughout the entire population.

THEORIES OF SOCIAL CHANGE

As was noted in Chapter 1 (pp. 11–14), all basic sciences focus upon creating theories that explain the hows and whys of their subject matter. The preceding section of this chapter has examined a number of key variables around which theories of social change typically are constructed. Within the sociological literature one encounters demographic, technological, movement-based, and other theories of social change. However, such theories of change tell only part of the sociological story of social change.

Throughout sociology's history, four general theories of social change have provided alternative contexts in which social change processes have been studied. The following section of this chapter examines four historically important theories: evolution, cycles, conflict, and equilibrium. Each of these theories rests upon different assumptions about social change processes. Each provides a unique environment in which different sorts of theorizing may flourish. Let's examine these four theories of social change and some examples of how they've been employed.

EVOLUTION: SOCIETAL PHASES AND MODERNIZATION THEORY

The idea of evolution is one of the most powerful constructs of 19th century scientific thought. It was used first by Herbert Spencer (1820–1903) in his *First*

Principles (1862) and *Principles of Sociology* (1876) to describe social development, and later, of course, became associated with Charles Darwin's theories in biology and zoology. While earlier writers tended to equate evolution and progress, today, sociologists working within an evolutionary framework use the term as an explanatory, not an evaluative, concept.

What are the essential components in an evolutionary theory of social change? First, evolutionists claim a linear relationship exists between time and the phenomena being studied. Thus, over time, the trend being studied gradually moves in a single direction. In the biological theory of evolution, animal species of increasing complexity emerge. In social theories of evolution, societies of greater and greater structural complexity (social differentiation) emerge. Typically, it is argued that these evolutionary trends result in increased functional interdependence within societies and greater human control over the environment through technological development. A second, and perhaps corollary assertion, is that events in an evolutionary chain are not reversible. For instance, societies that embark on the path of social differentiation and industrialism are not likely to reverse direction in favor of a rural-agrarian economy. Third, evolutionary explanations of events typically depict periods or phases in the development of the phenomena studied. For example, societies go through stages of development such as pre-industrial, industrial, and post-industrial. *Evolutionary theory claims that events, once begun, are unidirectional, producing an increase in an all-important phenomenon or variable, and passing through typical phases without significant reversals.*

Evolutionary theory

Many of the institutional processes studied by sociologists have been interpreted in an evolutionary context. It is argued that the division of labor and the processes of specialization in societies generally, as well as in specific institutions, follow a unidirectional course. For instance, as will be explored in depth in Chapter 11 (pp. 320–327), once urbanization begins, neither the rural village nor small-town lifestyle will return. The secularization of religion, accomplished either by the separation of church and state, or the emergence of religious pluralism, means that society will not return to a single set of universally endorsed religious values. The rise of bureaucratic work organizations reflects the rational division of work tasks and is not likely to be overcome. Much of what sociologists have learned about specific institutions as well as about total societies may be interpreted within an evolutionary perspective.

There have been at least two general theories of social evolution proposed by modern sociologists. The first of them is found in the later writings of Talcott Parsons (1966, 1977). In Parsons' view, cultural innovations are critically important triggers in stimulating advances in social structural development. With the advent of written language, societies pass from the "primitive phase" to an "intermediate phase." Written language promotes a sense of tradition and peoplehood. It also facilitates cultural borrowing and widespread cultural diffusion processes. Accordingly, the pace of social change increases. Geographically stable (as opposed to nomadic) societies begin to produce material surpluses and more complex stratification systems. The advent of legal systems marks the transition into the "modern phase" because law is an important way in which social structures become rationalized and predictable. For Parsons, social evolution is the story of how major phases of social differentiation, specialization, and structural complexity result from progressive steps in cultural symbolism (written language, law, etc.).

A slightly different view of social evolution is offered by the theorists Gerhard and Jean Lenski (Lenski, 1966; Lenski and Lenski 1970). In their view, important phases in social development hinge upon changes in the mode of economic production in societies. Thus, advances in technology are seen as the triggering mechanisms that stimulate institutional changes throughout the social structure. They depict four phases of social development: the hunting and gathering, the horticultural, the agrarian, and the industrial. There are enormous similarities between the technology-driven theory of the Lenskis and the symbolic culture-driven theory of Parsons. While they disagree on which aspects of human culture are the triggering mechanism in phases of development, they agree on the significant aspects of social structure that result. In both theories, development and evolution proceed in clearly delineated sequential phases.

Critics of the evolutionary approach observe that there are few empirically testable hypotheses in these sweeping historical schemes. This complaint surely is justified as it pertains to depictions of the early "phases" in societal development. However, much useful debate has focused on the eventual transition into industrialism. Here, the modern world, with so many different societies in various degrees of development and industrialization, may be viewed as a living laboratory for testing social theories. The prevailing evolutionary approach in contemporary sociological work that focuses on these issues is called "modernization" or "convergence theory."

Modernization

Modernization theorists recognize that the movement from a traditional to a modern society requires some form of cultural innovation providing motivation for new patterns of conduct, especially in the realm of economics. Though Weber was not an evolutionist, it is widely accepted that his description of how Protestantism justified a work ethic and an achievement motive in Western nations is a fine case study of just such a cultural innovation (Weber 1904–5). Once a triggering mechanism begins this process, a society will move toward what Rostow (1978) and others call a "take-off stage." Technological change, capital investment, and formal education in turn help to create a new kind of social structure. According to modernization theory, from this point of "take-off," a process of economic development evolves, and in turn, affects other realms of social life, such as family patterns, occupational roles, and, of course, values. In this theory, tradition and modernity are seen as polar ends of a continuum. The emergence of one is associated with the decline of the other. Change may occur at different rates in different societies, but processes of modernization eventually lead all societies to converge toward the same point. Not surprisingly, then, this theory also frequently is called *convergence theory*. It is claimed that these phases or steps constitute a "must" for economic development to occur. The problem of underdevelopment experienced by many Third World nations is perceived as a consequence of failing to adopt modern values and social arrangements.

Convergence theory

Third World politicians and scholars alike complain that this evolutionary model simply is biased toward the Western experience. The question—an empirically open question—is whether emerging nations in Africa, Asia, and South America must arrive at modernity through just such an evolutionary process. All of the data are not yet "in." Developments in postwar Japan and other nations in the region of the "Pacific Rim" appear to support the modernization theory, as does the recent move toward capitalism in the Soviet system and other Eastern block communist nations.

Conversely, in India and elsewhere on the Asian subcontinent attempts to stimulate industrialization have not resulted in a smooth evolution into industrial-capitalism. Nor is it clear, especially in the face of the Iranian revolution and other situations in the Muslim world, that economic development and cultural change move in an unbroken single path. The Iranian Revolution marked a reversal in which the society moved away from the very Western values that are believed to promote capitalism and industrialism. Obviously, it is important for modern sociology to continue undertaking comparative case studies in order to obtain theoretical closure on such questions.

CONFLICT AND WORLD SYSTEMS THEORY

The social conflict paradigm represents a second important avenue of explaining and interpreting social change. *Conflict theory views the unequal distribution of social resources, or disagreements over values (political, religious, or other aspects of lifestyle) as inevitable triggers for social change processes.* Like the evolutionary theory of social change, the conflict perspective was widely used in 19th century sociology. Some of these theories already have been examined here (Chapter 8). While Marx in his classic *Capital* (1867–1894) stressed the conflict over unequal wealth distribution, Weber (1923) emphasized value and status conflicts.

Conflict theory

A diversity of conflict theories have been applied to the study of change both within and between societies. For instance, the classical theorist George Simmel (1858–1918) focused upon the ways in which different objects of conflict (values as opposed to material resources) precipitate certain forms of conflict (Simmel 1890; Coser 1956). Karl Mannheim (1893–1947) studied the connections between the social locations of different political groups and the different styles of ideological claims about social reality they make (Mannheim 1929). Both of these writers foreshadowed the interest of modern sociology in social movements. As we've seen earlier in this chapter, social movements are a common occurrence in modern, pluralistic societies. The questions become how and why some of these groups succeed while others fail and what the impact each has on structural arrangements within a society. Such diverse movements as gay rights, civil rights, The Moral Majority, the prolife and prochoice movements, all are understandable in a conflict perspective. Each of these movements represents the desire of subgroups to promote their cherished values or to obtain a "fair share" of society's resources.

While students of social movements have produced a substantial body of case study literature focused upon specific movements, the German social analyst Ralf Dahrendorf (1959) has offered a general conflict theory for explaining change and conflict processes in modern societies. For Dahrendorf, conflicts over authority (control) are becoming more important than conflicts over class (wealth) or status (prestige) resources. A different application of conflict theory is represented by the writings of Daniel Bell (1976) and Alvin Toffler (1970). Bell focuses upon the force of technology in producing unintendedly high rates of social change. He examines structural consequences, such as the decline of family capitalism and the family's declining control of other spheres of social life. In contrast, Toffler examines what he calls "future shock" or the cultural dislocations that result from rapid change. What Dahrendorf (authority conflicts), Bell (technology-driven change), and Toffler (rapid cultural shifts) all share is the assumption that dislocation and conflicts are inherent in modern structural and cultural systems and that individually and collectively they account for much social change.

World systems theory

World systems theory, also called dependency theory, applies conflict theory to the realm of international development (Wallerstein 1974, 1979, 1980; Chirot 1977). From this perspective the highly developed or industrialized nations achieve their position, in part, by exploiting dependent nations. The so-called "core" nations of the capitalist West derive their high standard of living by extracting the natural resources and cheap labor of the "periphery" nations. Conflict is inherent in these relationships. According to world systems theorists there is no evolutionary process through which all nations will "naturally" become industrially advanced. Rather, development of the Third World nations, through whatever process, must involve altering their relationships with and dependency upon the "core" nations.

Obviously, this theory of social change contrasts strongly with the evolutionary claims of convergence theory. Here, change, or the lack of it, is seen not as a consequence of ties to traditional values and ways of life, but rather as a consequence of the ability of rich and powerful nations to dominate poorer and less powerful nations. While evolutionary theories of development are criticized for ignoring external (i.e., international) factors that impede evolutionary trends, the world systems theorists often ignore factors internal to nations (such as political culture) that retard development. However, this perspective surely provides an enhanced view of why some nations have failed to achieve industrialization.

CYCLES: POLITICAL ELITES AND RACE RELATIONS

Cyclical theory

Cyclical theories focus upon sets of occurrences that follow one another in a precise order and that happen in that order repeatedly. In nature, as with the changing of the seasons, some things do occur in cycles, and, thus, it is not surprising that scholars in various disciplines have attempted to apply cyclical theories to patterns of social life.

The notion that social life and even historical patterns *writ large* follow cyclical patterns was extremely popular in the 19th century, mostly among philosophers of history. Among the so-called classical period founders of sociology, the one writer who argued that important social trends emerge in cycles was the Italian social theorist Vilfredo Pareto (1848–1923). Pareto was especially concerned with patterns of domination and rulership in societies, issues that today fall within the realm of political sociology and stratification theory. He argued that cyclical patterns are formed by the emergence and subsequent decline of different elite strata in society (Pareto 1916). This *circulation of elites* was depicted as a continual process in which specific aristocracies rise and fall. However, in Pareto's view, throughout these cycles, even when apparent revolutions are involved, rulership remains in the hands of elite or aristocratic strata. Today, there is little interest among sociologists in Pareto's "circulation of elites."

Circulation of elites

Within American sociology, the only grand historical scheme to adopt a cyclical approach was that of the immigrant Russian social theorist Pitirim Sorokin (1889–1968). Sorokin (1937–1941) distinguished between types of cultural systems that he called "sensate" (those emphasizing material concerns), "ideational" (those stressing spiritual values), and "idealistic" (a blend of the other two). Sorokin interpreted broad historical changes as cyclical transitions between these three types. His view of cultural cycles did not inspire a program of empirical social research. However, the Chicago sociologist Robert Ezra Park (1864–1944) inspired a substantial body of research with his notion of *race relations cycles.* Park argued that race relations follow a cyclical pattern beginning with conflict, followed by accommodation, and ending in assimilation (Park and Burgess 1924). Much of the debate over Park's race cycle theory has centered upon the question of how inevitable the final stage, assimilation, really is.

Race relations cycles

Why have cyclical theories largely been abandoned in modern sociology? There are several reasons. First, the cyclical theories have been more "postdictive" than "predictive." Cyclical schemes have been imposed more readily upon past events than used to predict future events with any precision. Second, the act of "fitting" historical particulars to the broad outlines of a cycle frequently has meant the blurring of historical events. To make events fit the cycles exactly often requires overlooking many significant facts or events. Third, and most important, cycles ultimately impose a sort of magic hand on historic and social processes. Cyclical theorists typically concentrate on demonstrating that cycles exist, while failing to explain *why* such cycles of events prevail.

EQUILIBRIUM: CULTURE LAG AND MODERN FUNCTIONALISM

Equilibrium theory constitutes yet another category of explanations of social change. *Equilibrium theories depict most, if not all, social processes and institutions in terms of their contribution to maintaining a state of balance in society. Accordingly, most features of social change processes are understood as adaptive and adjustmental.* The guiding concept of equilibrium or *homo statis* is borrowed from the biological sciences. Biological organisms exhibit a tendency to maintain balance or equilibrium in many different ways. For instance, when the human animal begins to overheat as a result of strenuous exercise, perspiration occurs as a mechanism for cooling the body and returning it to a state of equilibrium. A wide range of biological functions in both plant and animal life are geared to the maintenance of a balanced state of affairs. A variety of social theorists have applied this concept to social life.

Equilibrium theory

An early expression of the equilibrium view of social change in American sociology is found in the work of William F. Ogburn (1886–1959). Ogburn formulated the theory of *cultural lag,* in which some parts of a culture change at a more rapid pace than other, related parts. The result is a disruption of the integration or equilibrium of the culture. Ogburn distinguished between material and nonmaterial features of cultural systems (Ogburn 1922). Although Ogburn recognized that cultural lag can result from changes in the nonmaterial features of culture preceding changes in the material aspects of culture, he contended that the more typical case in modern societies is that material features of culture, such as technology, change more rapidly than do nonmaterial factors, such as values and ideas. Thus, there is a continual process through which nonmaterial features of culture are adjusting to material changes. Ogburn maintained that cultural systems, like biological systems, have interrelated parts that work together for the good of the system. Accordingly, he saw

Cultural lag

changes in institutional patterns resulting from the need to compensate for a "lag" as being essentially adaptive and adjustmental. Ultimately, societies are in the continual process of re-establishing equilibrium. While modern sociologists still debate the general claim that societies tend toward equilibrium, Ogburn's specific concept of a cultural lag is widely accepted, although there is some debate over which changes first, the material or nonmaterial aspects of culture.

A more recent and much more elaborate version of equilibrium theory is found in the structural-functional social theory of Talcott Parsons (1902–1980). Parsons (1951) claims that societies are highly integrated systems of institutions in which each particular institution yields a function for the whole system. Social change is viewed as adaptive, with institutional modifications (including changes in functions) contributing to the general state of social equilibrium. Bales and Parsons (1955) specify four kinds of social functions that must be maintained in order for social order and equilibrium to be maintained. Known as the GAIL or AGIL functions, they are: goal setting, adaptation, social integration, and what they call latency, or reinforcement of existing norms and values. It is claimed that every social institution contributes in some way to at least one of these four social processes required for social equilibrium.

Equilibrium theories have been criticized on a number of grounds. The most sweeping criticisms warn that there are great dangers in equating social systems with biological systems. Society is not an organism. Unlike biological systems, the tendency toward stability is not intrinsically built into societies. A second critique of equilibrium theories is that the functional significance of many social institutions is not quite so clear as such theories claim. Indeed, most social institutions do as much to promote change as stability, and not all change can be understood most meaningfully as "adaptive." Some trends really change the system in ways that are much more than so-called adaptive change.

FOUR THEORIES IN RETROSPECT

Each of these four theories, evolution, conflict, cycles, and equilibrium, tells which kinds of phenomena and events are worthy of inspection. Each of these theories take different "facts" about social life for granted. However, the existence of multiple theories, while creating a complex situation, should not be viewed as a negative feature of modern sociology.

Each type of theory contributes to the overall sociological understanding of social reality. Let's return to an analogy discussed in Chapter 1. Persons visiting a construction site readily can see parts of the building scattered around the area. Brick and mortar, steel beams, roof trusts, an assortment of plumbing pipes, electrical wiring, and components of other parts of the building's systems are in evidence. But, how will this building appear when it is done? The riddle of how the parts fit together is solved by a series of blueprints. They show the designs of the various systems in the building and for good reason, it is quite rare to find the structural, electrical, plumbing, and other building systems all on one blueprint. Rather, each blueprint features its system as the paramount feature of the building.

This, in part, is the task accomplished by these different kinds of social change theories. Multiple theories add diversity and variety to the avenues of sociological analysis that may be accomplished. They allow us to see social

TABLE 10.2

THEORIES OF SOCIAL CHANGE COMPARED

Theory:	Change Is:	Change Happens Because:	Examples:
Evolution:	A linear process	Social processes triggered by cultural diffusion, technology, etc., once begun cannot be halted or reversed	Differentiation Modernization Assimilation
Cycles:	A circular repeating pattern	Initiating causes may vary but the options, phases, or outcomes are from a standard set of choices	Race relations cycles Circulation of political elites
Conflict:	Fights over values and material resources	Inequality in society and differences in values make struggles inevitable	Class conflicts Ethnic, racial, and other status disagreements
Equilibrium:	Adaptive processes restoring balance	Unintended social processes create temporary institutional flaws or social misalignments	Cultural lag Generation gap Population pyramid changes

reality, and the processes within it, from a number of perspectives. Yet, it must also be remembered that each type of theory is a selective view, emphasizing different features of the subject matter. In this sense each involves a preselection and a prejudgment about what is worthy of sociological attention. Table 10.2 provides a comparison of these four general social change theories, their basic assumptions, and some examples of their use in sociology.

In summary, of the four general social change theories examined here, the cyclical theory is the least frequently encountered in modern sociology. Evolutionary theory, which focuses upon linear change processes, has been widely employed, with modernization and convergence theory being important examples. Equilibrium theories, which view societies as balanced systems tending toward adjustment and stability also have been widely employed as explanatory models of social change in modern sociology. Functionalism is the leading example. Finally, conflict theories, most notably world systems theory, stemming from the work of Marx, Weber, and others focus upon how struggles in societies over both material resources as well as social values lead to social change. Each theoretical avenue provides different sociological insights.

APPLICATIONS
Cultural Lag and Bio-technology

It has been seen that William Ogburn's theory of "cultural lag" (1922) is one of the earlier expressions of a social equilibrium theory for analyzing social

FIGURE 10.3
What shall we name the baby?

change processes. However, one need not accept the general theory of equilibrium to recognize that cultural lag processes are rather common in modern societies, especially those that are a consequence of the rapid pace of technological change. Ogburn's theory was really quite simple. He maintained that frequently material culture, through advances in technology and science, develops at a faster rate than social values and ideals. Therefore, he argued, people often must "adjust" their norms, values, and beliefs to reflect these material changes. The result is a disparity or lag, which Ogburn maintained could last for considerable lengths of time, sometimes for many years (Ogburn 1922).

The complex technology of medicine epitomizes many of the dilemmas confronting contemporary societies because of cultural lag. Consider, for example, the social issues surrounding the right to die examined earlier (Chapter 1, pp. 25–26). Derek Humphry's book *Final Exit* (1991), it will be recalled, provides precise recipes for committing suicide, and was published as a humanitarian response to the dilemmas of the terminally ill. In an earlier time, people aged, they faltered, occasionally lingered, and died. Generally, dying was not a matter for decision making. Nature made the decision. But today, medical technologies with artificial life-sustaining means have created a decision-making situation. Because people can be kept alive indefinitely, and because life-sustaining technologies frequently are used without considering all their consequences, dying in a technological age creates ethical dilemmas not easily resolved by traditional values, norms, and beliefs. When does death occur? What distinctions should be made between the quality and quantity of life? Who has the right to make these decisions?

Clearly, life-prolonging technology has advanced ahead of the emergence of collective social values and norms for dealing with this changed situation. In fact, ambivalence about assisted suicide exists even within Mr. Humphry's own Hemlock Society (Gabriel 1991). The American way of dying has become an example of cultural lag. The act of dying has become a sociocultural issue rather than simply a medical one.

Ironically, a cultural lag also has developed at the opposite end of the life cycle, birth and parenting processes. In July 1978, a remarkable and seemingly novel event occurred in the world of medicine. Louise Brown, the first "test-tube" baby was born in Lancashire, England. The birth of Louise resulted from the fertilization of her mother's egg by her father's sperm outside the womb. This was the first successful implantation of an artificially conceived embryo in a human mother. Other than the medical technology involved in the process of conception, Louise was like any other baby conceived through more traditional (and enjoyable) means. However, the birth of Baby Brown was the beginning of a new medical technology having enormous potentials for changing the relationships of parents and their offspring. For example, today, pregnancy may result from a donor egg, donor sperm, and even a donor embryo. Such options create what is now called surrogate parenting, a situation in which persons donate eggs, sperm, or womb.

Typically, surrogate parenting involves a woman who volunteers to conceive and/or carry a child for the benefit of a couple who will raise the child as their own. Although surrogacy may be undertaken for humanitarian reasons, more frequently it involves a fee for service arrangement. Thus, surrogacy quickly has become a thriving business. For would-be parents, it represents a miracle solution for having children of "their own." Additionally, for women who cannot afford the medical risks of pregnancy and birth, the surrogate parent is a solution to a dilemma. But, as will be seen, at the present time there are neither social norms nor values to accompany this increasingly widespread practice. Surrogate parenting presently is experiencing a cultural lag. The rapidly expanding reproductive technology has outpaced laws and social mores. Let's examine what's happening.

CASE

Surrogate Parenting

As so often is the case in life, value dilemmas emerge not when matters proceed as anticipated, but when they do not. In the case of surrogate parenting, value questions have emerged when the process leads in directions not anticipated by the participants.

Perhaps the most well-publicized such instance is the case of Baby M (Chesler 1988). In February of 1985, Bill and Betsy Stern contracted through the Infertility Center of New York (ICNY) with Mary Beth Whitehead and her husband Richard for Mary Beth to be artificially inseminated with Bill's sperm, and for her to carry his baby to term. Upon the birth of the child, the Whitehead's would relinquish parental rights to the genetic child of Mary Beth. Betsy would then adopt Bill's genetic child. Although technically Betsy Stern was not infertile, she feared that a pregnancy would exacerbate her condition of multiple sclerosis. The Sterns initially considered adoption but saw potential problems because of their ages and differing religious backgrounds. Thus, a convenient, though not inexpensive, solution was found for the Sterns' problem. The surrogacy contract stipulated a payment of $7,500 to ICNY, and, upon the delivery of the child to Bill Stern, $10,000 to Mary Beth Whitehead.

By now the rest of the story is well-known. Mary Beth had a change of heart and didn't want to part with her baby. Although she reluctantly gave the baby to the Sterns, the child was returned to her when it appeared that she was threatening suicide. Mary Beth then refused to return the child to the Sterns. When the Sterns came to her home accompanied by police to claim the child, she passed the baby out the window to her husband. During the period of time when the Sterns sought a court order, she took the child from her home in New Jersey to her parent's home in Florida, where, four months later, under a court order, the police forcibly removed the nursing infant from its mother, returning her to Bill. By what values and norms would the courts resolve the case? Two biological parents, not husband and wife, who never really wanted to know one another personally, were making parental claims on the same child.

The various court rulings leading to a final determination of this case provide a curious mixture of contract and family law. The initial ruling of the New Jersey lower court emphasized contractual obligations. On March 31, 1987, the court upheld the surrogacy contract and awarded sole custody of Baby M to the Sterns. Mary Beth's parental rights to the infant legally were severed. Immediately following this decision, adoption proceedings were held making Betsy Stern the baby's legal mother in accordance with the surrogacy contract.

In 1988, the New Jersey Supreme Court reversed this decision basing its ruling on precepts in family law. The court voided the surrogacy contract because it involved financial payment, and thus constituted baby-selling, an illegal act in New Jersey. Additionally, the adoption of Baby M violated New Jersey laws, which require that the surrender of child must be voluntary, and that this decision may only occur after its birth and after extensive counseling of the birth parent. Therefore, even though the creation of Baby M was a decision of Bill and Betsy, Betsy had no legal connection to her husband's child under New Jersey laws. She was only the wife of the genetic father, and the baby was Mary Beth's genetic child. Betsy Stern's relationship to the child was social, not biological. In accordance with established family law, the rights of both biological parents are equal. Thus, the New Jersey court awarded custody of Baby M to Bill Stern, with Mary Beth having visitation rights because it is in the "best interests of the child" to know her biological mother.

Complex though the situation of Baby M may seem, it raises only a few of the perplexing social issues that arise from the new technologies of birth. Consider, for example, the case of Mary Sue and Junior Davis. Late in 1988, they decided that their infertility problem was likely a source of the marital difficulties they were experiencing. *In vitro* fertilization of their own sperm and egg and subsequent implantation of a fertilized egg could resolve their dilemma. Seven of Mary Sue's ova were fertilized by Junior's sperm through *in vitro* fertilization, and these fertilized eggs (embryos?) were cryopreserved (frozen) at the Family Center of East Tennessee at Knoxville. Not long afterward, Junior and Mary Sue began divorce proceedings. What's to become of their frozen potential children?

Initially, the Tennessee court ruled that the fertilized eggs are not yet "living," and therefore decided the case on the rights of the "parents." In 1989, it vested joint interest in these fertilized eggs in both Junior and Mary Sue, who by now were no longer married to each other and no longer wished to parent each other's "child." This seemed logical enough, for to allow either individual to control these fertilized eggs could amount to forcing one of them to become a parent against his or her will. However, if the eggs are not yet "living," and have no status as persons, does this mean they are in fact property? This hardly is a public policy position with which most people would be comfortable. Surely, fertilized human eggs are something more than property. Yet, in 1992, the Tennessee Supreme Court empowered the Family Center of East Tennessee at Knoxville to "dispose" of these fertilized eggs as though they were property.

Yet a different set of dilemmas emerged for Crispina and Mark Calvert and Anna Johnson. Crispina and Mark's egg and sperm were fertilized *in vitro*. Their fertilized egg was then implanted in Anna Johnson's womb. As with the Baby M case, the Calverts and Anna Johnson had entered into a fee-for-service contract. However, in the Calvert case, the result was a baby with not two but three parents: the genetic father, the genetic mother, and the birth mother. Ms. Johnson, saying that she had bonded with the infant during pregnancy, refused to surrender her baby and the matter was brought before the courts of the State of California. The lower court ruled in favor of the Calverts, thus upholding the concept of a surrogacy contract. It interpreted the concept of parenthood as genetic, stating that surrogate mothers have no biological link to the children they bear. It compared the birth mother's care and nurturance of the unborn child to that of a foster parent, stating that neither has a legal right to the child in its care. As might be expected, Ms. Johnson is appealing (Tifft 1990).

Although the biological facts of these three cases are different, the three events share an important social feature. Each involves a situation made possible by technological developments for which no clear social norms have been established. All three cases evidence the phenomena of cultural lag. The issues involved are likely to become more complex as reproductive technology advances. In the offing are such things as cloning, male pregnancy, and birth without pregnancy through the use of an artificial womb. These technologies already have been used experimentally with nonhuman populations.

Few states have laws dealing with these reproductive technologies, and those states having such laws are in conflict with one another. For example, in Arkansas couples who contract with an unmarried surrogate are considered the child's legal parents. Yet, in some other states, among them Indiana, Louisiana, Kentucky, and Nebraska, surrogacy contracts are unenforceable. Where there are no laws, decisions are based on the individual whims of judges using laws that were not designed for these particular situations. Inevitably, some of these rulings raise more questions than they answer. For example, the California court's ruling that genetics determine parenthood has the potential for chaos. Does this mean that an anonymous sperm donor has a greater claim to fatherhood than the husband of the woman artificially inseminated with this sperm? One might have assumed that issues regarding such fundamental things as birth and parenthood would follow rather unbending norms in any society. Yet, the ability of technological change to outpace other aspects of culture and to producc unanticipated events shows the fallacy of this assumption. As always is the case with cultural lag, surrogate parenting and related events exhibit enormous value confusion. These moral and ethical issues will not be resolved easily (Fletcher 1988).

Chapter Summary

1. Social change refers to alterations in the norms, hierarchical arrangements, division of labor, and social control mechanisms within a society or its institutions. Unlike change, social progress is an evaluative concept based on the claim of social betterment.
2. While it is instructive to isolate the factors that cause change in order to study them, it must be remembered that most social change processes are multicausal.
3. It is useful to distinguish between social changes that result from human intent and motive, as opposed to those that are unintended. The two major causes of intended or guided change are rational planning techniques and social movements.
4. Planned change, even when done by governments, seems most effective in smaller rather than larger social units. Government planning ultimately results in complex political decision-making processes.
5. Voluntary social movements are of several types, including reform, revolutionary, resistance, and Utopian movements. Resource mobilization theory focuses upon how movements emerge from the interactions of potential recruits and the networks connecting them with each other and their lead-

ers. The most successful movements promote goals consistent with widely held values, obtain the support of third parties, and employ innovative techniques.

6. Four sources of unintended change are population, technology, the physical environment, and cultural transmission and borrowing. Demography is the science of studying population size, distribution, composition, and change. As measured by the concept of doubling time, uncontrolled population growth remains a critical problem in many less-developed nations.

7. Technology represents a powerful source of unintended change in human societies. It is a deceptive social force precisely because people readily adjust to it. Scientists still debate the question of whether we control technology or it controls us.

8. Even technological societies are influenced by changes in the physical environment. Short-term events like hurricanes and earthquakes can severely disrupt and change the way of life in entire communities. Long-term environmental change like global warming can alter communities permanently.

9. Cultural processes can stimulate social change in at least two ways. First, specific cultural complexes may be transported from one culture to another. This is called cultural borrowing. Larger-scale processes of cultural diffusion also may occur. The spread of Western cultural values, including both democracy and capitalism into Eastern Europe, represents a case of these processes.

10. The four major theories of social change are evolution, conflict, cycles, and equilibrium. Each theory offers a useful but partial view of the events being studied.

Key Concepts

circulation of elites
conflict theory
convergence theory
cultural borrowing
cultural diffusion
cultural lag
cyclical theory
demographic transition theory
demography
doubling time
equilibrium theory
evolutionary theory
MBO (management by objectives)
modernization
motivated change
planned change
progress
race relations cycle
reform movements
resistance movements
resource mobilization theory
revolutionary movements
social change
social movement organizations (SMOs)
social movements
technology
Theory Z
unintended change
Utopian movements
world systems theory

Bibliography

Bales, Robert, and Talcott Parsons
1955. *Family, socialization and interaction processes.* New York: Free Press.

Barringer, Felicity
1990. "Chernobyl: Five years later the danger persists." *New York Times Magazine,* (April 14): 28–34, 36–39, 74.

Bell, Daniel
1976. *The coming of the post-industrial society: A venture in social forecasting.* New York: Basic Books.

Berger, Brigitte, Peter L. Berger, and Hansfried Kellner
1973. *The homeless mind.* New York: Doubleday Books.

Carson, Rachel
1962. *Silent Spring.* Boston, Massachusetts: Houghton Mifflin.

Chesler, Phyllis
1988. *Sacred bond: The legacy of Baby M.* New York: Times Books.

Chirot, Daniel
1977. *Social change in the twentieth century.* New York: Harcourt Brace Jovanovich.

Coser, Lewis
1956. *The functions of social conflict.* New York: Free Press.

Dahrendorf, Ralf
1959. *Class and class conflict in industrial society.* Original German edition, 1957. Stanford, California: Stanford Univ. Press.

Drucker, Peter
1954. *The practice of management.* New York: Harper and Brothers.

Duncan, Otis Dudley
1975. *Introduction to structural equation models.* New York: Academic Press.

Durkheim, Emile
1912. *The elementary forms of the religious life.* Translated by J. W. Swain, 1965. New York: Free Press.

Ehrlich, Paul
1968. *The population bomb.* New York: Ballantine Books.

Ellul, Jacques
1954. *The technological society.* Translated by John Wilkinson, 1964., New York: Alfred A. Knopf. (1964).

Etzioni, Amitai

1961. *A comparative analysis of complex organizations.* Rev. ed., 1975. New York: Free Press.

1964. *Complex organizations.* Englewood Cliffs, N.J.: Prentice-Hall.

Fletcher, Joseph
1988. *The ethics of genetic control: Ending reproductive roulette.* Buffalo, New York: Prometheus Books.

Gabriel, Trip
1991. "A fight to the death." *The New York Times Magazine.* December 8, pp. 46–47, 84, 86, 88.

Greeley, Andrew
1972. *Unsecular man: The persistence of religion.* New York: Schocken Books.

Hadden, Jeffrey K., and Charles E. Swain
1981. *Prime time preachers: The rising power of televangelism.* Reading, Massachusetts: Addison-Wesley.

Humphry, Derek
1991. *Final exit.* New York: The Hemlock Society.

Jenkins, J. Craig
1985. *The politics of insurgency: The farm worker movement in the 1960s.* New York: Columbia Univ. Press.

Killian, Lewis
1975. *The impossible revolution phase 2: Black power and the American dream.* New York: Random House.

1984. Organization, rationality and spontaneity in the civil rights movement. *American Sociological Review.* Vol. 49, No. 6: 770–83.

Lenski, Gerhard
1966. *Power and privilege: A theory of social stratification.* New York: McGraw-Hill.

Lenski, Gerhard, and Jean Lenski
1970. *Human societies: An introduction to macrosociology.* 5th ed., 1987. New York: McGraw-Hill.

McAdam, Doug, John D. McCarthy, and Mayer N. Zald
1988. "Social Movements." In *Handbook of sociology,* edited by Neil J. Smelser, 695–737. Newbury Park, California: Sage Publications.

McCarthy, John D., and Mayer N. Zald
1977. Resource mobilization and social movements: A partial theory. *American Journal of Sociology.* Vol. 82, No. 2: 1212–41.

Malthus, Thomas
1798. *An Essay on the principle of population.* Reprinted in 1963 by Homewood, Illinois: Richard D. Irwin.

Mannheim, Karl
1929. *Ideology and utopia.* Translated by Louis Wirth and Edward Shils, 1936. London: Routledge and Kegan Paul.

Marx, Gary
1971. *Racial conflict.* Boston: Little, Brown & Co.

Marx, Karl
1867–1894. *Capital, A Critique of Political Economy.*

Nisbet, Robert
1980. *History of the idea of progress.* New York: Basic Books.

Ogburn, William F.
1922. *Social change with respect to culture and original nature.* New York: B. W. Huebsch.

Ouchi, William
1981. *Theory Z: How American business can meet the Japanese challenge.* Reading, Massachusetts: Addison-Wesley.

Pareto, Vilfredo
1916. *Trattato di sociologia generale.* Firenze, Italy: G. Barbera. *Mind and society.* Translator not indicated, 1963. New York: Dover Press.

Park, Robert Ezra, and Ernest W. Burgess
1924. *Introduction to the science of sociology.* Chicago: Univ. of Chicago Press.

Parsons, Talcott
1951. *The social system.* New York: Free Press.

1966. *Societies: Evolutionary and comparative perspectives.* Englewood Cliffs, N.J.: Prentice-Hall.

1977. *The evolution of societies.* Englewood Cliffs, N.J.: Prentice-Hall.

Rostow, Walt
1978. *The world economy: History and prospect.* Austin, Texas: Univ. of Texas Press.

Simmel, Georg
1890. *The sociology of George Simmel.* Translated by Kurt H. Wolff, 1950. New York: Free Press.

1906. *The Sociology of Religion.* Translated by Curt Rosenthal, 1959. New York: Philosophical Library.

Sorokin, Pitirim
1937–41. *Social and cultural dynamics.* 4 vols. Abr. ed., 1957. Boston: Porter Sargent. New York: American Book Company.

Spencer, Herbert
1862. *First principles.* 6th ed., 1904. New York: Appleton.

1876. *Principles of sociology.* 3 vols. 3d ed., 1910. New York: Appleton.

Teich, Albert H., ed.
1990. *Technology and the future.* 5th ed. New York: St. Martin's Press.

Tifft, Susan
1990. Its all in the (parental) genes. *Time Magazine.* Vol. 136 (November 5th): 77.

Toffler, Alvin
1970. *Future shock.* New York: Bantam Books.

Toqueville, Alexis de
1835–40. *Democracy in America.* 4 volumes.

Trow, Martin
1961. The second transformation of American secondary education. *International Journal of Comparative Sociology.* Vol. 2: 144–66.

U.S. Bureau of the Census
1991. *Statistical Abstract of the United States: The National Data Book.* Washington, D.C.: U.S. Government Printing Office.

Wallerstein, Emanuel
1974. *The modern world-system.* New York: Academic Press.

1979. *The capitalism world economy.* Cambridge, England: Cambridge Univ. Press.

1980. *The modern world system II: Mercantilism and the consolidation of the European world-economy, 1600–1750.* New York: Academic Press.

Weber, Max
1904–05. *The Protestant ethic and the spirit of capitalism.* Translated by Talcott Parsons, 1958. New York: Scribner's.

1923. *Economy and society.* Translated and edited by Guenther Roth and Claus Wittich, 1968, Totowa, N.J.: Bedminster Press.

CHAPTER **11**

MODERNITY: BUREAUCRATIZATION, SECULARIZATION, AND METROPOLITANIZATION

CHAPTER OUTLINE

LEARNING OBJECTIVES

This book has provided a brief journey through the conceptual turf of modern sociology. It has been stressed that sociology provides a rich conceptual apparatus for describing, analyzing, and explaining social structural, cultural, and social psychological processes. This chapter examines three important social processes occurring in modern societies: bureaucratization, secularization, and metropolitanization.

Modernity

Individually and collectively, these three processes are central to the phenomena called *modernity*. The idea of modernity, widely echoed in the writings of 20th century psychologists, sociologists, philosophers, and theologians, is that life in modern times is qualitatively different from earlier eras. The purpose of this chapter is to explore those differences. The experience of modernity is embodied in the broad-scale trends toward bureaucracy, secularization and metropolitanization. While they alone are not the entire story, a recognition of these three trends is a prerequisite to any understanding of the modern era.

After reading and studying this chapter, you should be able to discuss the following issues:

---

1. What is bureaucracy, and what are its distinguishing social structural and cultural features?
2. What factors have caused the rise of bureaucratic organizations in modern societies?
3. What are the consequences both for individuals and societies of the prevalence of bureaucracy?
4. What is secularization, and what is uniquely secular about modern life?
5. What factors in modern society have given rise to secularization, and to what extent has secularization meant a change in the place of religion in modern life?
6. Given the secular character of modern life, what is the future of religion?
7. What does the term metropolitan mean, and how are metropolitan patterns of living different from urban ones?
8. What factors have caused the metropolitan trend?
9. What are the consequences for a society based on metropolitan population settlement patterns?

WHAT IS BUREAUCRACY?

There are few sociological concepts that have become so much a part of our everyday vocabulary as the term "bureaucracy." It is little surprise that this is so, for the phenomenon to which it refers is virtually everywhere in modern societies. Moreover, the term, as it is used in everyday speech, is far from value neutral. Most people believe that bureaucracies are not nice places to work and that encounters with bureaucrats rarely are pleasant. The expression "behaving like a bureaucrat" typically is used to describe inept or uncaring behavior.

The following discussion addresses several related questions about bureaucratization in modern societies. What is bureaucracy, and what causes its emergence? Why is the spread of bureaucratic patterns of social organization viewed by many observers as a cause for concern? How does the prevalence of bureaucracy affect the quality of life in modern societies?

BUREAUCRACY AS SOCIAL STRUCTURE

Iron law of oligarchy

The term "bureaucracy" was introduced into modern sociology by two classical period German writers, Max Weber (1864–1920) and Robert Michels (1876–1936). Michels, in his book *Political Parties* (1911), explains his *iron law of oligarchy*. The basic idea is that *large, bureaucratic, organizations have a way of empowering those at the top*. Once they are in control, the professional bureaucrats value self-perpetuation and self-enpowerment over all other goals—including the original goals of the organization. Thus, according to Michels, wherever there is formal organization there will be oligarchy, or rule by the few.

Michels saw these tendencies emerging in large-scale political organizations (especially political parties) as well as in voluntary associations (such as labor unions). He feared that these bureaucratic tendencies would work against the formation of truly democratic institutions in modern societies. In this sense, Michels foresaw bureaucratic tendencies that would later be studied here in the United States in government agencies (Selznick 1949), labor unions (Lipset, Trow, and Coleman 1956), and even large religious organizations (Harrison 1959). Contemporary sociologists have studied bureaucratic processes in such diverse settings as hospitals, business corporations, and even the F.B.I. (Glassman, Swatos, and Rosen 1987).

While Michels' observations have stimulated much scientific debate about the consequences of bureaucratization, most basic descriptions of the features of bureaucracy rely upon Weber's writings on the subject (1923). On the one hand, Weber saw bureaucracy as a form of social organization or social structure. However, he also understood bureaucracy as a cultural trend in which certain specific cultural values are expressed. It will be useful here to examine both the cultural and structural properties of bureaucracy.

Bureaucracy

Let's begin with a definition. *Bureaucracy is a type of formal organization exhibiting a fixed authority structure with a division of labor based on elaborate rules and regulations and claiming to embody the goal of rational efficiency*. The social structural properties of bureaucracy may be examined conveniently through the four properties of all social structures: a division of labor, norms, social control, and hierarchy (Chapter 4, pp. 89–94). While all social structures exhibit

FIGURE 11.1
Nothing happens without some waiting in modern societies.

these properties, they are given more extreme, complex, and rigid expression in bureaucracies.

First, bureaucracies are formal organizations and therefore, they exhibit a complex division of labor. In bureaucracies, there is an enormous proliferation of offices (or positions within the organization), each with a specific job description, each embedded within a complex of other positions. This complex division of labor reflects the high degree of specialization of organizational tasks in bureaucracies.

Second, in bureaucracies, the pattern of norms is carried to the level of fixed rules. Activities are governed by a consistent set of rules and regulations that define the responsibilities of various offices and the relationships among them. This insures the coordination of tasks and uniformity of performance despite changes in personnel. However, at the same time, the formalization of rules tends to make bureaucracies rule-bound in their dealings with outside clients (customers, patients, citizens, students, and others) as well as in their own internal relations. Numerous observers have characterized this rule-boundedness as "ritualism" (Merton 1940). *Ritualism means a strict adherence to rules, without regard for the attainment of organizational goals.* A related feature of bureaucracy is the requirement for written documentation of all actions. Indeed, in bureaucracies there are written forms for everything. All forms must be completed according to precise instructions, and nothing happens until it happens on paper.

Ritualism

A third feature of bureaucracy is a direct result of this rule-bound characteristic. A rigid system of social control is adopted. Because norms are treated as fixed rules, norm-violation becomes rule-breaking, and as is the case in most social settings, rule-breaking typically is sanctioned by punishment. In bureaucracies, social control of clients is accomplished by the refusal to render service to those not following exactly the rules and procedures. Thus, in bureaucracies, "your application cannot be accepted," or you can "lose your place in line" because "you have not followed the rules precisely." Social control of those within the organization typically is accomplished through the withholding of raises and promotions—and in extreme cases, firing.

Fourth, while all social organization exhibits varying degrees of hierarchy, fixed hierarchical relations are the essence of bureaucracy. Authority structures are complex and layered. Here, Weber's insights converge with those of Michels. Weber recognized that hierarchical structure has the effect of centralizing power and authority at the top of bureaucratic organizations and fragmenting it at the bottom. This is because the pyramid-like structure of these organizations provides only those at the top with a controlling overview of organizational patterns and communications channels. Thus, it may be argued that the rigidly fixed pattern of hierarchy has important consequences that are manifest throughout the organizational structure.

BUREAUCRACY AS CULTURE

Just as bureaucracy represents a distinctive social structural configuration, these structural characteristics are expressions of distinct cultural values. Max Weber (1923) described the cultural component of bureaucracy as "goal rationality." His student Karl Mannheim (1940), later described it as "functional rationality." Regardless of the specific term used, modern writers agree that an emphasis on efficient means is the banner under which bureaucracy operates. Human actions are said to be *rational* if there is an *explicit calculation of the relationships between the means and ends of an activity. Goal rationality is a form of rationality in which efficient means to desired ends are adopted.* This is a uniquely modern cultural emphasis.

Rational

Goal rationality

Value rationality

Goal rationality may be contrasted with *value rationality.* In a society guided by a value rational culture, people's actions are assessed in terms of their consistency with a universal value. The Ten Commandments are an example of a value-rational code that provided enormous cultural stability. In value-rational cultures, persons are expected to act according to a uniform substantive set of social values. To the extent that they do so, patterns of social action are both predictable and reliable. Such a society enjoys rather uniform cultural, and therefore moral, standards that guide human actions.

Goal rationality does not provide adherence to uniform substantive values. Rather, it is a procedural norm—rational efficiency—that permeates the culture. From this vantage point, we now can see why bureaucracies are a distinctive and problematic development. For the bureaucrat, the supreme cultural mandate is to follow rationally efficient procedure, not adherence to substantive values such as "do unto others," "the customer is always right," or "heal the sick." In a goal-rational environment, that which is efficient for the organization is the "correct" path of action. Both Weber (1923), and Mannheim (1940) saw this focus on efficient means as a distinctively modern trend. Weber (1904–5) recognized that its origins were in the more utilitarian contexts, such as work and economic institutions, but that rational efficiency was spreading throughout all sectors of modern societies.

SOME NOTES ON CAUSES

What specific historical circumstances have conditioned the rise of the bureaucratic form of social organization? Traditionally, sociologists have focused upon at least two factors, one demographic and one cultural. As was seen in Chapter 10 (pp. 286–288), population factors are enormously important in triggering social change processes. Surely, the invention of routine bureaucratic processes, including standard rules and procedures, is a response to situations in which large numbers of persons must be serviced in some capacity. As population size and density increase, rationality of means as expressed in bureaucracy also increases.

The Mom-and-Pop grocery store, the small county hospital, the town clerk's office in a rural community, and even the small professional office need not be overly concerned with forms and procedures. However, once the office, firm, agency, or company grows beyond the point where it can keep track of its accounts, clients, or customers on a face-to-face or even first-name basis, the need for rational management techniques enters the picture. Thus, in the first instance, certain thresholds in the size of client populations trigger bureaucratization.

However, ritualized procedures, required forms, and the proliferation of offices in a strict hierarchy are not the only ways in which large numbers of "cases" may be processed efficiently. One might, instead, decentralize the operations of the firm. It is here that the element of rationalism must again be considered. Efficient rationalism dictates a particular solution to the problems of size and scale. It is not so much that bureaucrats invent the idea of rational bureaucracy. Rather, they apply rational principles already available in the culture to solve the problems that emerge from increasing scale and size. Rational management is a control technique. Other solutions to problems of scale do not offer the degree of control that rational management does.

Finally, a third element that greatly amplifies the effects of bureaucracy must be considered—technology, especially in the form of computers. Computers have an enormous capacity to manage information and to do so by rule. This particular technological advance is greatly disposed to increased bureaucratization. This is not to suggest that bureaucracy would not advance without computers. Clearly, present-day bureaucratic structures have their origins in events that predate the widespread use of computers. Nor does it suggest that computers are inherently evil. Much good can be done with them. However, given problems of scale and a cultural preference for rational control, computers provide technological amplification of these tendencies.

SOCIETAL AND INDIVIDUAL CONSEQUENCES

Thus far, the structural and cultural features of bureaucracy as well as the conditions that foster the rise of bureaucracy have been examined. What does it all mean? What are the consequences of the predominance of bureaucracy for individuals and for society? Does it really matter if bureaucracy increases or decreases in society? The consequences of bureaucratization are many (Blau and Meyer 1965). Five of them are considered here.

Alienation

First, the sociological concept of alienation is central to any examination of the consequences of bureaucracy. *Alienation* refers to *the experience of powerlessness* (Seeman 1959). Individuals experience powerlessness when they are confronted with social situations over which they cannot exercise effective control. How does this concept of alienation apply to the phenomenon of bureaucracy?

Consider the situation of the client, customer, or citizen approaching a bureaucratic organization for a service or product. Typically, adherence to the rules, procedures, and regulations takes precedence over the client's needs or problems. Much like the hospital patient being awakened from a sound sleep to be given a sleeping pill, most persons interacting with bureaucracies complain that the organization's procedures have taken precedence over the service allegedly being rendered. Moreover, the patient, client, or customer is left with the feeling that he or she has no ability to alter these events.

A related factor producing such alienation is derived from the excessive division of labor within bureaucracies. No single bureaucrat or office in the bureaucracy (except at the very top) has the authority to "solve" the client's problem, and no single bureaucrat is accountable or responsible for the bureaucracy's failure to respond. Thus, the individual is trapped in a series of regulations that don't "work," and bureaucrats who either can't perform the required service or who seem not to care. Additionally, if the client either can't comply with the rules or won't comply with the rules, the client becomes a victim, bearing the sanctions that result from norm-violation or rule-breaking.

These structural characteristics that produce alienating effects for the customer or client also extract a toll from persons working within the bureaucracy. The responsible employee becomes the object of the client's frustrations. Unfortunately, bureaucrats must work daily with the inability to solve problems and situations that confront them. The bureaucrat, like the client, faces the situation of powerlessness.

A second consequence of bureaucracy concerns the gradual reduction of primary group, face-to-face relationships in societies in which bureaucracy is prevalent. More and more experiences in everyday life involve the partial, rather than the whole, person. Highly bureaucratic societies reflect qualitative

TABLE 11.1

FEATURES OF BUREAUCRACIES

Structural Properties	Characteristics			Analytical Term
Norms	are	Fixed and rigid	not Flexible	Rulebound
Division of Labor	is	Specialized	not Variable	Alienation
Hierarchy and Authority	is	Centralized	not Distributed	Oligarchy
Personnel Relations	**Characteristics**			**Analytical Term**
Bureaucrats	are	Predictable	not Innovative	Ritualism
Clients	are	Powerless	not Respected	Alienation
Activities	are	Task-oriented	not People-oriented	Efficient Rationality
Communications	are	Written	not Face-to-face	Impersonal

changes in the life experience. Shopping in a local family-run grocery store is very different from shopping in a large modern super market. The local "walk-in clinic" and even the group medical practice offer a less personal experience than does the family doctor. With size comes bureaucracy, and with bureaucracy comes impersonality.

Bureaucratic personality

Third, some writers have commented on these developments by referring to what is called the *bureaucratic personality* (Merton 1940). Not only sociologists, but psychologists and psychotherapists have expressed concern about the tendency for bureaucratic organizations to shape the personalities of those working within them (Hummel 1977). The person begins to extend bureaucratic ways of acting into other realms of social life. This means, in part, *a de-emphasis on the open expression of emotion and feelings in human relations. It entails viewing other people as elements of situations or as objects, but not as whole persons.*

Fourth, at the societal level, there is little question that the pervasiveness of bureaucracy has broad implications. Because of the tendency of bureaucracies to promote their own self-preservation, implementing desired social changes becomes difficult. Bureaucracies become structural impediments that thwart change in those areas of social life over which they have domain. It is for this reason that government agencies, once established, are rarely disassembled. While critics and consultants have, for years, called for a redesign of government social welfare programs, little change has been implemented. Bureaucratization retards social change processes.

Finally, as we've already noted, some writers following Michels (1911) have argued that bureaucracy is inherently antidemocratic in its ethos. The formation of bureaucracy in government and in other institutional sectors retards representative or citizen control. The "iron law of oligarchy" prevails. Bureaucracies do not foster participatory democracy.

Substantial research literature indicates that the features of bureaucracy examined here are, in fact, "softened" and mitigated in a number of ways. However, the tendencies discussed here are normative. They happen more often than not. Thus, the trends discussed here are an important part of the modern social experience.

In summary, bureaucracy is a form of social structure exhibiting a complex division of labor, fixed rules, and rigid hierarchical and social control systems. Bureaucracies claim to embody the virtue of efficiency. However, the pervasive goal rationalism within bureaucratic organizations frequently results in alienation for both bureaucrats and clients, a decrease in primary group relations, and the development of bureaucratic personalities. Bureaucracies are resistant to social change, and their tendency to centralize power at the top (oligarchy) may be understood as potentially antidemocratic. Some of the key features of bureaucracies are summarized in Table 11.1

SECULARIZATION

At the middle of the twentieth century in the United States, it was nearly impossible to find a retail store, except perhaps a pharmacy, open for business on a Sunday. Sunday, of course, is the traditional sabbath day, the day of rest and worship in the Christian tradition. Sunday closing laws in America were a reflection not so much of American shopping habits, but of the importance of religion in American culture. Today, a family trip to the regional shopping mall on Sunday afternoon is a popular form of family recreation. It has become part of the American way of life. Similarly, the Sunday trip to "the mall" reflects a change in the place of religion in American life.

There is wide agreement among sociologists that the experience of modernity involves important shifts in the place of religion in society. The specific sociological term used to describe these shifts is secularization. However, exploring the meaning of secularization here, first requires an understanding of the traditional role of religion in societies. Only then can secularization processes, their causes, and consequences for modern living be comprehended.

THE SOCIAL MEANING OF RELIGION

It was noted in Chapter 5 (pp. 117–118) that religion is one of the five basic institutional sectors found in most, if not all, human societies. From this observation, it seems reasonable to conclude that religion provides something quite important or essential for individuals, groups, and entire societies. This is, in fact, the traditional sociological view of religion. Specifically, it is argued that religion has three basic functions or consequences. Religion provides moral beliefs, community rituals, and a sense of identity or belonging. Exactly what is religion, and how does it do these three things?

Religion

While it might be argued that religion is defined a bit differently in every next pew, a basic sociological definition is that *religion consists of beliefs and practices stemming from the idea of a supernatural entity.* (Johnstone 1975; Hargrove 1979; McGuire 1992). Sociologically, it does not matter if the supernatural entity is called Allah, God, Christ, or, Yahweh, or, for that matter, if that entity is a force, being, several beings, or a power. All religions have in common a set of ideas about phenomena that somehow are beyond the strictly empirical, things that are "taken on faith." This is what is meant by the term supernatural. Given this definition, let's examine the traditional role of religion in establishing moral beliefs, community rituals, and identities.

First, from the classical period writings of Durkheim (1915), Simmel (1906), and others to such modern analysts as Andrew Greeley (1982) and Peter L. Berger (1967), there is a sociological consensus that religion consists of a body of beliefs or doctrines that provide moral guidelines for societies. These ideas about what is good, right, moral, and correct provide, in Berger's words, a "sacred canopy" (1967). Thus, for much of human history, religion has provided the beliefs and moral precepts in which social order and social stability are anchored. A religiously unified society is a socially unified society, in which moral guidelines for human actions are easily discerned.

Second, religion provides a set of ritual events through which individuals, groups, communities, or entire societies symbolize meanings and values. Rituals, of course, are patterns of conduct, which, when done in a precise way, convey significant meanings. Obviously, attending church, participating in prayer meetings, and taking sacraments are explicitly religious rituals. But, traditionally religion also has imbued apparently "secular" activities with "sacred" meaning. For this reason, even some persons who do not claim to be very religious will prefer a "church wedding." Similarly, it has been common to have a religious benediction at graduation and inauguration ceremonies. Each year numerous communities on the New England coast celebrate a "blessing of the fleet." Of course, in earlier agricultural and hunting societies, medicine men and shaman were called upon to bless the land and consecrate the hunt. Religion provides ritual events through which sacred meanings are imparted to secular practices.

Third, religion is a powerful force in shaping people's identities and providing a sense of social belonging. To paraphrase Will Herberg (1955), being Protestant, Catholic, Jewish, Muslim, or even a Moonie are essential ways of being an American. Similarly, certain religious practices traditionally have been designed to reinforce the elements of identity and belonging that derive from religious group membership. Consider, for example, proscriptions against religious intermarriage, or the requirement that persons marrying into a religious community be required to undergo religious conversion.

THE RELIGIOUS FACES OF MODERNITY

Having examined the traditional roles of religion in societies, what is the meaning of the term secularization? and what shifts in religious beliefs and practices have justified the claim that modern society is a secularized society?

The term secularization has been defined by sociologists of religion in a variety of ways (Shiner 1967). For the present purposes, *secularization* may be defined as *a shrinking of the influence of religion in society, and thus, a diminishing of the traditional roles of religion in society.* Let's apply this definition of secularization to the three basic functions or consequences of religion.

Secularization

First, traditionally, religion provides moral authority, ideas of what is correct, right, or good in societies. However, in modern societies, religion does less of this than it once did. Many areas of social life in which religious ideas once provided norms of right and wrong now operate in the absence of a religious consensus, or worse in the context of religious conflict.

For instance, clergymen once were viewed as the arbiters for most issues involved in child-rearing, family relations, and domestic life. However, today, few people approach religious professionals for help in these matters. Rather, the family counselor, the psychiatrist, the clinical psychologist, and the school guidance counselor have taken control of such matters. The power or influence of religion has retreated from domestic life.

Sexuality and gender relations provide yet another case of the shrinking of religious authority and control. In most societies, religious precepts and sexual practices have been intimately connected (Newman 1986). Yet, in modern American culture, the religious control of sexuality has all but vanished. While historically, premarital sexual intercourse has been viewed as sinful in the Judeo-Christian tradition, today, over half of all American high school students have experienced out-of-wedlock sexual intercourse before the age of 18. Clearly, their behavior is not controlled by religious doctrines. Moreover, there is an increasing trend by courts and other governmental authorities to grant marital-like legal status to unmarried consenting adults who live together. The point is not that all of this is either good or bad. Rather, the point is that religious control in these matters has diminished greatly.

No issue in contemporary American life has been more divided along competing religious lines than that of abortion. Here, a matter once clearly defined and controlled by religious doctrines is fueled by religious conflict.

Presently, official government policy (both federal and in most states) is counter to traditional religious values.

Second, while religion usually provides rituals through which important social meanings are reinforced and dramatized, in modern American society, the most powerful rituals seem to be more secular than religious. The sanctity of the sabbath in American society has been eclipsed by economic and leisure pursuits. What religious rituals in America compare with celebrations like the Super Bowl, the World Series, the Fourth of July, and Labor Day? Attempts by sociologists of religion to document the religious symbolism inherent in Independence Day celebrations have yielded inconclusive results (Thomas and Flippen 1972; Wimberley 1976, 1979). The inability of sociologists to document the existence of an American *civil religion, a widely subscribed blend of powerful civic and religious values* (Bellah 1967) demonstrates that religious values do not play the role that they once did in American civic culture.

Civil religion

Finally, there is the question of religion's impact on individual and group identity. Substantially high levels of intermarriage between members of different religious communities in the United States suggest that the identity and boundary maintenance functions of religious institutions have become rather weak. Among American Protestants, as well as between Protestants, Catholics and Jews, old denominational labels have decreasing salience. Among Protestants, this is demonstrated by increasing levels of denominational switching (Roof and McKinney 1987).

Substantial literature has emerged showing an erosion of traditional beliefs and a steady decline of membership in American religious institutions (Hoge and Roozen 1979). Some writers depict a general trend toward what they call a secularization of consciousness (Berger 1967; Fenn 1978). The basic claim is that modern humans simply do not impart the plausibility to traditional religious doctrines that characterized earlier times. Fewer people interpret the Bible as literally true. Fewer maintain that official church doctrines are relevant to their own actions or idea of themselves. In all these senses, modernity means religious demystification. Modern *homo sapiens* apparently do not experience the world with the sense of religious awe and mystery that characterized earlier generations.

FIGURE 11.2
What is the religious significance of this?

To be sure, modern society occasionally does supply evidence of religious revitalization, but typically on a small scale. For example, the 1970s produced a spate of religious cult movements ranging from "Jesus freaks" to the Meher Baba movement. However, the numbers of persons in such new religious communities remained quite small. They did not represent a central trend or a normative pattern for the society. While religious cults are both interesting and sociologically instructive (see discussion Chapter 7, pp. 185–187), their appearance does not signal a general return to religious values throughout modern society.

THE CAUSES OF SECULARIZATION

What are the social forces that have altered the traditional place of religion in modern society? Why has the influence of religious ideas diminished in secular institutions? Why do religious values and precepts fail to provide the kind of guidance in our lives they once did? Sociologists of religion have provided at least two different kinds of answers to these questions. One group of theories explains the declining influence of religion as a result of broader societal trends. The other, focuses upon certain changes within the religious life itself. Let's examine each body of theory.

A first general approach depicts secularization as the impact upon religious institutions of the societywide trend toward social differentiation. As we've already seen (Chapter 10, pp. 293–294), Parsons (1971) and other writers have argued that Western societies have been undergoing a gradual process of institutional specialization. As institutions become more specialized they lose some of their social functions. For religious institutions, this has meant a relinquishing of involvement in, and authority over, a wide variety of nonreligious areas of social life. Secularization then is the special term for describing what these structural shifts in modern societies have meant for religious institutions.

If Parson's approach may be viewed as a structural one, a more cultural theory of secularization is provided in the writings of Max Weber. As we already have seen in this chapter (p. 312), Weber described modernity as an expression of the cultural values of rationalism. For Weber, the pragmatic rationalism of modern life is antithetical to religious ways of thought. This is an important aspect of his essay *The Protestant Ethic and the Spirit of Capitalism* (1904–5). Indeed, religious ideas imbue the mundane events of the everyday world with myth, while modern rationalism creates what he saw as a "disenchantment of the world." Simply stated, the culture of modern rationalism makes it difficult to see everyday events as imbued with religious or mythic meanings. This absence of awe and mystery is very much at the core of the culture of modernity.

Weber's themes have been expanded in a number of directions. For instance, the contemporary French analyst Jacques Ellul (1964) focuses upon the role of technology in modern society. The power of technology, human control over the environment, convinces us that the gods never really did control human life. Regardless of whether one stresses the cultural theme of rationalism and the loss of mystery, or the more structural theory of social differentiation and loss of function, social theorists appear to agree upon the diminished role of religious institutions in modern societies.

A second group of writers (Martin 1978; Fenn 1978; Berger 1967; Hammond 1974) focus upon changes within religious institutions themselves. Their common theme is that something has changed in the religious thinking of modern populations. For instance, the British sociologist David Martin (1978) observes that in the Middle Ages, when the Christian Church's ideas dominated the Western worldview, there were no competing belief systems. However, a pluralism of religious ideas is a uniquely modern situation. The presence of a large number of belief systems all claiming the same legitimacy and authority leads to a dilemma of plausibility. Simply stated, as they compete with one another, modern religious idea systems fail to provide societywide authority and legitimation. This situation also has been described as a "secularization of consciousness" (Berger 1967) and a crisis of legitimacy (Fenn 1978). In either case, it is argued that if all religions make similar claims, they can't all be true; or perhaps, none of them are entirely true.

THE FUTURE OF RELIGION

The general theme of this chapter is that the social experience of modernity differs from that of earlier times. One of these important differences pertains to the religious aspect of modern life. Unlike the members of the primitive tribe, or even the population of medieval European society, the inhabitants of modern societies do not dwell within a universe of sacred events. The rising of the sun each day is no longer a mystery greeted with awe, and the social structure no longer is viewed as heavenly ordained. Modern humans live in a humanly invented social environment dominated by technology. No single religion possesses the "truth," in part because there are so many "true" religions. What do these modern social facts suggest for the future of religion? Few sociologists of religion predict the complete disappearance of religious institutions from society? Why not?

First, religious ideas respond to certain categories of questions about reality that are not answered by political, economic, or other realms of life. The theologian Paul Tillich (1956) described these as questions of "ultimate concern." While religious institutions may not have the authority over some areas of society they once did, there still are some questions to which only religion responds appropriately.

Second, while modern humans experience mystery and awe in the secular world less frequently than people apparently did in earlier times, there remains social demand for such occasions. Religious rituals still sanctify birth and death, as well as other "rites of passage" in the life cycle. Moreover, at times of personal or national crisis, religious ideas and religious institutions provide consolation and symbolic unity in ways that other social institutions do not.

It is reasonable to anticipate that the tension between religion and secularity will not disappear. Rather, religious thought and practice will remain a part of modern social life, a part that will ebb and flow in relation to other social experiences, such as wars, economic crises, even crises of political authority and legitimacy. Overall, secularization means not that people in modern societies are no longer religious, but that they experience religion differently than did people in earlier eras. Religion no longer sanctifies the entire social order. Rather, it occupies but one corner of the modern social experience.

In summary, religious institutions traditionally have fulfilled three important social functions: creating social stability through moral values, providing rituals that symbolize important shared meanings systems, and providing identities for individuals and communities. Secularization has meant a decrease in religion's power to do these things, and therefore, a decrease in the force of religion in secular realms of social experience. Regardless of whether this is understood as a result of a general trend toward social differentiation or the specific demystification and rationalism of religion itself, the weakened role of religion in society is a uniquely modern phenomenon.

THE METROPOLITAN TRANSFORMATION

It sometimes is argued that the transition from nomadic communities to settled communities (villages) was a momentous change in the human condition. While this may be so, an important part of the story of modern societies lies in the emergence of different patterns of settlement. At the close of the 19th century, sociologists in both Europe and America marveled at the emerging shape of the city. Yet, while the city once was the entire trend, today it is only part of a larger trend. At the turn of the 21st century, modern life has shifted from the city to the metropolis. Modern social life is at once secular, bureaucratic, and, on a grand scale, metropolitan. Going downtown has been replaced by driving to the mall. Where "taking a trip" once meant leaving the city, it now means crossing several state borders. Where "nearby" once meant in the neighborhood, it now means "less than an hour's drive." In 1820, 72 percent of Americans lived on farms. By 1920, over 51 percent were living in cities. By 1990, over 77 percent would be living in metropolitan areas, with less than a third living in cities (U.S. Bureau of the Census 1991).

The concluding section of this chapter explores the causes and consequences of metropolitan growth. What does it mean to say that the modern experience is a metropolitan experience? What are the key features of metropolitan areas? What has caused the emergence of metropolitan areas, and what are the consequences of the trend toward metropolitanization?

DEFINING THE MSA

What is a metropolitan area? Since the U.S. Census Bureau collects and distributes the statistics by which population areas, such as cities, towns, suburbs, and metropolitan areas are measured, we must turn first to the Bureau's definitions.

As a type of population measure, the term "metropolitan" first entered the Census Bureau's lexicon in the year 1960. At that time, it was recognized that the older distinctions between urban and rural, as well as urban and suburban, while useful, somehow did not describe entirely the events that already were happening. In 1960, a *Standard Metropolitan Statistical Area (SMSA)* was **SMSA** defined as *an urbanized area consisting of a city of at least 50,000 inhabitants and its adjacent counties.* Key to the 1960 definition was the level of daily commuter traffic between the central city and its adjacent population areas. The Census Bureau's term SMSA focused not simply upon populations commuting into the city, but upon patterns of commuting between the cities and their surrounding suburbs. At the beginning and end of each work day, nearly as many people commute into the cities as out of them, and back again. Such patterns constitute complex systems of interrelated events.

Why was a new concept—standard metropolitan statistical era—needed? Previously, the Census Bureau's reporting categories revolved around the distinctions between urban and rural and between urban and suburban. The term urban, nominally defined as a population center of at least 2,500 persons, carried a not so subtle cultural message. Life on the farm is different from most of what's happening elsewhere. Of course, increasingly, most of the American population was living "elsewhere" (cities, suburbs, and towns). Thus, the urban-rural distinction focused upon the apparently ever-growing urban trend.

In this context, the urban-suburban distinction also emphasized the social and cultural centrality of cities. Suburbs were places where people go to sleep, which is why they sometimes are called "bedroom communities." From a sociological perspective, suburbs initially were understood as serving a specialized residential function. However, suburban dwellers still relied upon the city for a host of needs and services, among them employment, health care, entertainment, and social services. In this sense, the Census Bureau's focus on urban populations and what it later would define as "urbanized areas" (meaning population centers of 50,000 or more persons) carried the message that America was an urban society, that the culture of the nation was an urban culture. Understanding American life prior to the mid-20th century meant understanding city life.

The introduction of the new terms SMSA in 1960 signaled an official government recognition of the end of the era of the city in American life. The idea of SMSAs was that cities were now part of a larger pattern and that cities no longer were the central focus of population settlement patterns.

By the early 1980s, the Census Bureau had adopted a new vocabulary for describing population areas. The older term SMSA was abandoned. In its place are three new concepts: Metropolitan Statistical Area (MSA), Consolidated Metropolitan Statistical Area (CMSA), and Primary Metropolitan Statistical Area (PMSA). The metropolitan concept has so eclipsed the concept of city that population experts now speak in terms of types of metropolitan areas.

MSA

Our concern here is with the generic term Metropolitan Statistical Area, MSA. In the Census Bureau's own words, *"The general concept of an MSA is one of a large population nucleus together with adjacent communities which have a high degree of social and economic integration with that nucleus"* (U.S. Bureau of the Census 1991, 3–4). The essence of this definition, of course, is the idea that MSAs represent complexes of social and economic relationships. These relationships constitute a way of life, a pattern of living.

How widespread is this pattern? As shown in Table 11.2, by 1990 nearly 8 out of every 10 Americans (77.5 percent) were residing within an MSA. By 1990, the suburban portions of MSAs contained twice the actual number of people they had in 1960. Moreover, between 1960 and 1990, the proportion of the population dwelling in suburbs increased from 30.6 percent to 46.6 percent. City populations represented about the same proportion of the total population in 1990, as they did in 1960 (32 percent as compared to 33 percent).

TABLE 11.2

UNITED STATES POPULATION IN CITIES, SUBURBS, AND MSAs 1960–1990

	1960		1970		1980		1990	
	N	%	N	%	N	%	N	%
*Total Pop.**	179.3	(100.0)	203.2	(100.0)	226.5	(100.0)	250.0	(100.0)
Inside MSAs	112.9	(62.9)	139.4	(68.6)	169.4	(74.8)	193.7	(77.5)
Central Cities	58.0	(32.3)	63.8	(31.4)	67.9	(30.0)	78.7	(31.5)
Suburbs	54.9	(30.6)	75.6	(37.2)	101.5	(44.8)	115.0	(46.0)
Outside MSAs	66.4	(37.0)	63.8	(31.4)	57.1	(25.2)	56.3	(22.5)

SOURCE: U.S. Bureau of the Census (1991)

*All population statistics are in millions.

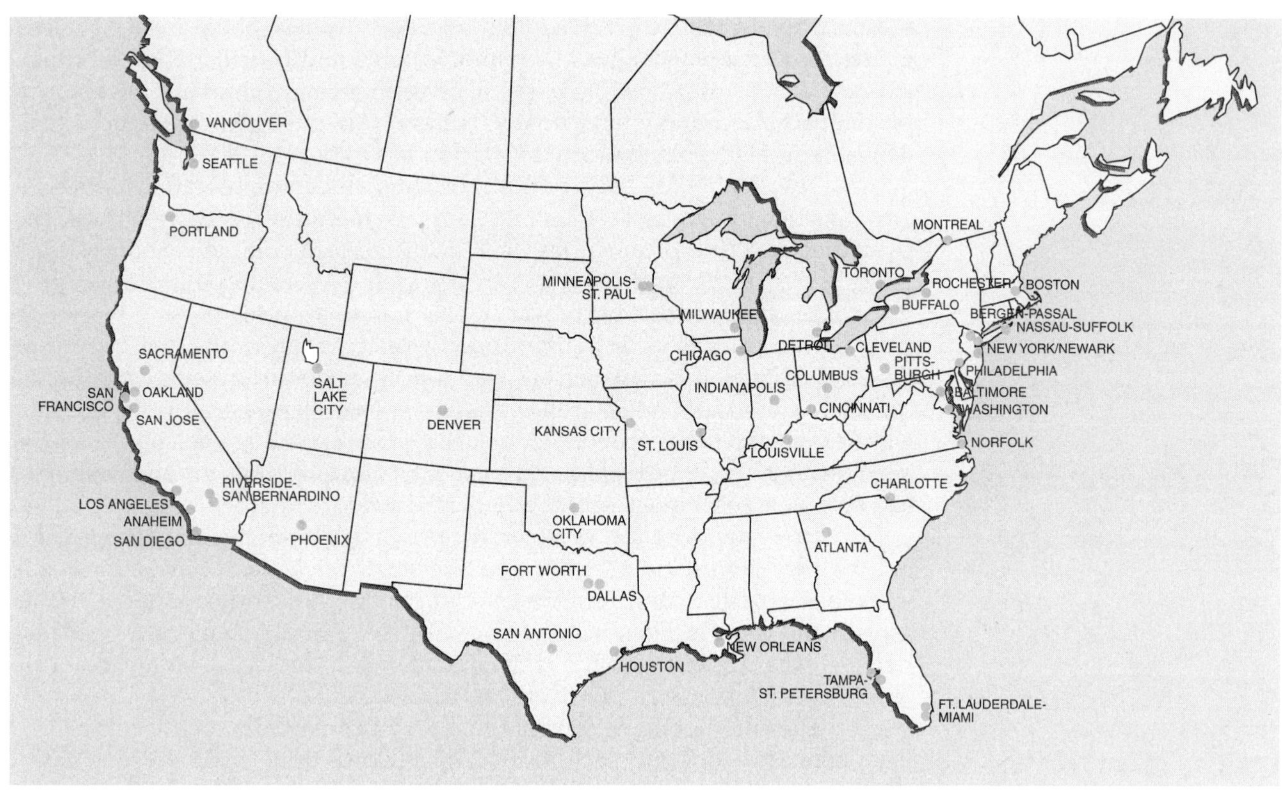

FIGURE 11.3
THE FIFTY LARGEST MSAs IN NORTH AMERICA (UNITED STATES AND CANADA) IN 1990

The Census Bureau lists some 283 MSAs, each of which contains a central city of at least 50,000 inhabitants. *MSAs containing over 1 million inhabitants are called Consolidated Metropolitan Statistical Areas* or *CMSAs.* The New York metropolitan area with approximately 18 million inhabitants, and the Los Angeles, California, metropolitan area with some 14 million inhabitants are the two largest. The Census Bureau also designates *Primary Metropolitan Statistical Areas* or *PMSAs, which in most parts of the nation refers to the county in which the central city and its immediate suburbs are located.* In 1988, the ten largest CMSAs in the nation were New York, Los Angeles, Chicago, Houston, Philadelphia, San Diego, Detroit, Dallas, San Antonio, and Phoenix. Figure 11.3 shows the fifty largest MSAs in North America (the United States and Canada). The remaining sections of this chapter focus upon two questions about these patterns of human settlement. First, what has caused the shift from city to metropolis? Second, what are the consequences of these patterns?

CMSA

PMSA

CAUSES IN HISTORICAL PERSPECTIVE

Every pattern of settlement among human populations can be traced to complex sets of social and cultural forces. Regardless of whether it be the initial transition from nomadic populations to settled communities, the shift from rural life to cities, or the present emergence of metropolitan areas, distinct social forces always are involved. In the present instance, there are at least four interrelated factors: changes in communications and transportation technologies, the actions of powerful government agencies and programs, the rise of a postindustrial economy, and finally, cultural tastes that have produced residential segregation along race, ethnic, and class lines.

The combined effects of transportation and communications technologies constitute one causal element in the rise of metropolitan communities. The paired technologies of the automobile and high-tech communications played critical roles in the shift from an urban society to a metropolitan one. If the place of residence (the suburb) was to be separate from the place of work (the city), a practical means of transportation was required. In the first quarter of the 20th century, this requirement was met by elaborate systems of mass rail transport. Commuter trains, trolley cars, street cars, elevated railways, and subways connected the neighborhoods of the cities as well as the cities with the newly emerging suburbs. The American city, along with its growing suburbs, had become an enormous spider web of rail tracks.

However, with the advent of the personal automobile this changed. All but the very largest cities paved over the street car tracks to make the roads more passable for cars. Rail tracks and cobble stones disappeared under asphalt and cement. Even in New York City, the Third Avenue "El" (elevated railway) was demolished. The subway that was to replace it would never be built. Taxi cabs, busses, and private cars came instead.

The automobile, of course, could do much more than transport people from home to work and back again. The personal auto made possible entire systems of events outside of cities. As we just have seen (Table 11.2), between 1960 and 1990, the actual number of Americans living within MSAs outside the city would more than double (from 54.9 million to 115 million). The advent of the personal auto not only allowed greater distances between places of habitation, work, and play, but also facilitated the relocation of places of work, habitation, recreation, and commerce beyond the borders of the city. Since everyone needs a car anyway, did it really matter where they drove or for what purpose?

Communications technologies also have played an important role in the process of metropolitanization. In an earlier time, the insurance salesperson, stockbroker, and customer service representative all reported to "the office" at the beginning of the work day. Today, hand-held computing equipment that transmits over normal telephone lines is used to report to the office, transmit sales and order information, and receive work assignments. The modern work force is decentralized. While most companies have headquarters, those headquarters are less and less likely to be located in a central city. Proximity to the amenities of the city no longer is a requisite for doing business in the age of high-tech communications.

A second factor in metropolitan development has been the government. It is impossible to overstate the role of government in the life of modern societies. Where money is concerned, government collects and spends more of it than any other single institution in the modern social structure. It is little surprise, then, that both taxation policies and spending policies of government have been involved deeply in the trend toward metropolitan growth. Let's examine both sides of government's taxing and spending ledger as it affects metropolitan growth.

On the spending side of the ledger, two specific policies have had powerful influences in promoting residential and commercial growth outside, but near, American cities. These are the involvement of government in the housing industry and the creation of the national defense highway system.

First, in the depths of the depression of the 1930s, a multipronged government involvement in the housing markets was initiated. Through the Farmer's Home Administration (FmHA), Federal Housing Administration (FHA), Veterans Administration (VA), and later the mega-agencies of the Department of Housing and Department of Health and Human Services, government became the financial champion of the housing industry. The FmHA, FHA, and VA would provide loan guarantees and loan insurance for borrowers. They also provided low down payments and below-market interest rates for first-time home buyers, low-income home buyers, and of course, war veterans. After the Second World War an unending series of housing subsidy programs for developers and builders would be created. These programs were more easily used where land was cheap, and historically land has been cheaper beyond the city's borders than within them. Thus, thanks to a variety of government subsidies, farm lands became suburbs. Population in the cities stabilized and even declined while suburbs grew. If that little home in the country (actually suburb), became an "American dream," the United States government has been the dream-maker.

The second government element in metropolitan growth was the emergence of highway systems. In the early 1950s, an ambitious program known as The National Defense Highway System was launched. The interstate highway system, as it now is called, were intended to serve an important military purpose if the Untied States were ever attacked. But, of course, while Americans were waiting for the Russians to invade, this efficient modern highway system made America a nation of commuters. Thus, government not only subsidized many of the shiny new homes in the suburbs, but also built and paid for the highway system that connects the suburb with the city and other suburbs.

Similarly, on the taxation side of the ledger, government policies have promoted metropolitan, especially noncity, growth. Here the key feature has affected not home builders and home buyers, but commercial enterprises. Through tax credit and depreciation techniques, companies found it more economically efficient to build new factories, manufacturing plants, and office buildings outside the cities rather than expanding their older existing facilities in the cities. As with new home construction, new plant construction was accomplished most efficiently in locations where inexpensive land was available, and where ease of transportation (the interstate) existed. Typically, this was outside the city.

A third force stimulating metropolitan growth has been the shift from a manufacturing to a service economy. While scholars may debate the exact dates of urban-industrialism in America (Miller and Melvin 1973; Yeates 1990), there is no question that the American city that developed between the mid-1860s and the 1920s was an industrial city. Industrialism was the motor force drawing people, immigrants from other lands as well as indigenous farm populations, into America's cities. First along waterways, later through railroads, and finally through road systems, cities grew as central places of manufacturing, employment, and habitation.

However, by the mid-20th century, an enormous economic transformation had begun. The age of industrialism in America was declining. The very jobs (especially in manufacturing) that had drawn workers to the cities were decreasing in number. Instead, a service economy, a postindustrial economy, was emerging. Between 1947 and 1985, the service sector of the American economy (including government) had grown from 53 percent to 72 percent of all hours worked (U.S. Bureau of the Census 1991). Moreover, as Levy (1987) observes, the largest employment gains were in a wide assortment of small-scale service occupations, law firms, hotels, private hospitals, accounting firms, and others in the health care and business service sectors.

The important point is that unlike the factory system of an earlier time, America's growth "industries" in the 1970s, 1980s, and 1990s would not require central locations involving massive labor forces and distribution facilities. America's growing service industries could survive, and even thrive, in small-scale suburban office parks, so-called strip centers, and shopping malls. Cities ceased being an essential ingredient in the American way of doing business. In fact, small-scale locations outside the city became less expensive to purchase, build, rent, and maintain.

Finally, no discussion of causes would be complete without examining the unpleasant realities of housing segregation according to race, ethnicity, and social class differences. The entire history of what some have called "counterurbanization" (Berry 1976), reflects rather conspicuous ethnic, race, and class divisions in American society.

It is, at first, perplexing to understand that while the industrial city in the United States was still in the making, suburbanization already had begun. Clearly, America's new industrial cities were not understood as "Mecca" by everyone. Why not? The answer lies in certain historical developments discussed earlier (Chapter 9, pp. 258–260), and which may be reconsidered here. In the first half of the 19th century, the new rural-agricultural American society was a white Anglo-Saxon Protestant society. While the first great wave of immigration (1830–1860) introduced large numbers of Irish Catholics into the social mix, the remaining immigrants of that period were still Northern European, and predominantly Protestant.

However, the second great wave of immigration, the one that coincided with the urban-industrial shift (1865–1920) was Italian, Hungarian, Russian, Polish, Catholic, and Jewish. It was neither Anglo-Saxon nor even Northern European. As Douglas observed (1925) by 1920, a suburban trend already was in full swing. Those suburbs were propelled by class and ethnic differences. Financially established white Protestants were fleeing the poor ethnic immigrant populations that were entering the cities in unprecedented numbers. Additionally, commuter rail transport made the suburban growth of the early 1900s possible.

In the second half of the 20th century, the players have been different, but the plot is the same. The "new immigrants" of the 1960s, 1970s, and 1980s who flocked to the cities in search of jobs were lower-income blacks, Hispanics, and Asians. The rush to the suburbs correctly has been characterized by numerous writers as "white flight." In the 1960s, the Kerner Commission on Civil Disorders spoke of "two Americas, one white one black" (Kerner 1968). Today, we have a more comprehensive understanding of that trend. There are two Americans in the making, one white and metropolitan, the other nonwhite and distinctly inner city. Class, race, and ethnic preferences have driven this pattern.

CONSEQUENCES OF THE METROPOLITAN TREND

If the modern experience is a metropolitan one, what are the consequences of this trend? There are two sets of consequences that warrant attention here, for they identify problems that are likely to plague American society well into the 21st century.

First, all cities, be they ancient or modern, share an important feature. Many different kinds of human activities occur in relative proximity to each other. In contrast, metropolitan settlement typically creates spatial segregation between important activities of community life. Habitation, education, work, retail commerce, recreation, and health services are located not together, but in residential subdivisions, educational campuses, shopping centers, office parks, industrial parks, and medical centers. Modernity in the metropolitan sense includes a human reliance upon transportation systems.

Presently, the American option has been for the personal auto, and with it a reliance upon an oil-based economic system. This, in turn, mandates at least three important consequences. First, since the United States does not produce enough inexpensive oil to fuel its own automobiles, oil must be purchased from other nations with the political entanglements this entails. The gasoline crisis of the early 1970s showed what could happen, and the Gulf War of the early 1990s was a consequence of the fear of repeating that crisis.

Second, even if American foreign policy can keep gasoline cheap, it will not last forever. Ultimately, other safe fuels, mass transit, or both will be needed. Moreover, mass transit, while a rational and partial solution, will be very expensive to create.

Finally, as many of the world's larger metropolitan areas have demonstrated (on the American continent New York, Los Angeles, Mexico City, and others), a metropolitan area dependent on auto transport is a metropolitan area with dangerously polluted air. Thus, a first consequence of a metropolitan society is its reliance upon personal transportation systems. There are economic, global political, and personal health consequences attached to this aspect of modern life.

A second set of modern problems concerns the fate of the cities. Since these concerns are the focus of the applications section of this chapter, let's first summarize what been said here about the metropolitan trend.

American society has undergone a series of rapid transitions from a rural-agrarian to an urban industrial to a postindustrial metropolitan society. Today, 8 in 10 Americans live within the confines of a metropolitan area, officially defined as a population nucleus together with adjacent communities exhibiting both social and economic interdependence. Among the causes of this trend have been the emergence of new communications and transportation technologies, government spending and taxing policies, a decentralized service economy, and social preferences revolving around racial, ethnic and class segregation in the United States.

A leading consequence of metropolitanization is a life-style involving a dependence on transportation systems. Presently, this means oil dependence with its economic, political, and health consequences. However, the metropolitan trend also has meant a gradual economic and social abandonment of cities. We turn next to the crisis of the cities.

FIGURE 11.4
The problems of cities seem important only once every four years.

APPLICATIONS
Cities in Crisis

In the earliest phases of metropolitanization, the city, in many senses, is the jewel of the metropolitan area. Initially, the city contains the place of work. It is the entertainment center of the region. It contains the "good" restaurants, the "best" stores, and, of course, the most sophisticated professional services, medical, legal, and financial. However, over time, as middle- and upper-income white populations flee the city, shopping centers, medical centers, office parks, and factories follow them.

Who and what is left in the cities? Cities are faced with continuing economic and social decline. The trends of metropolitanization have left cities with an inadequate tax base for dealing with their problems. As Flanagan suggests (1990), the problems of racism, poverty, crime, and powerlessness routinely are associated with cities. Studies of racial segregation from the 1940s to the 1980s consistently show that the suburbs are primarily middle-class and white, while the cities exhibit high concentrations of racial minorities (Taeuber and Taeuber 1965; Van Valley *et al.* 1977; Taeuber 1983).

In an earlier era, cities provided entry-level manufacturing jobs through which workers, especially immigrants, began to climb the American economic ladder. However, today these sorts of employment opportunities no longer characterize the city. Today's urban minorities are trapped in joblessness. At the same time, federal aid to cities and social programs designed to alleviate urban problems have declined. Wilson (1987) has written of a permanent and growing urban underclass in which persons of color are disproportionately represented; and Scott (1984) has described the powerlessness that accompanies the "feminization of poverty" in American cities. While homelessness, poverty, crime, and drug-related violence affect all geographical areas to some degree, they are daily problems in the inner city. In short, metropolitanization has created a frightening legacy, not only for cities in general, but more specifically for inner-city residents.

CASE
The Burning of Los Angeles

The burning of America's cities in the summer of 1967 has become a footnote to history. To young, white suburban-bred Americans of the present generation, the race riots in places like the Watts section of Los Angeles in the 1960s might just as well have been part of the Civil War. The riots happened "back then" when things were different. Then, in the Spring of 1992, it all seemed to be happening again—as if without warning.

A jury of ten whites, one Asian-American, and one Hispanic-American in the suburban community of Simi Valley, California, decided that nothing wrong had occurred when a black motorist named Rodney King was clubbed some 56 times by members of the Los Angeles police force. The home video of the incident that occurred on March 3, 1991, had been shown on virtually every television station in the nation. The media had turned a local incident into a national event. The jury verdict was a shock to the nation, and the "aftershock" of the jury decision was felt not only in Los Angeles, but also in riots as far away as Atlanta, Georgia, and Toronto, Canada. The three days of rioting in Los Angeles left nearly fifty people dead, nearly 4,000 buildings completely destroyed, and ended only with the imposition of a curfew enforced by some 13,000 police and troops.

An apparently bewildered, and understandably upset, Rodney King appeared on national television and asked "can't we all get along?" But the burning of Los Angeles entailed much more than just the problem of different people being able to "get along." The burning of Los Angeles, like the burning of the cities in 1967, was a symptom of the problems confronting those living in America's inner cities.

The largest cities in America today are the most racially segregated, the most economically depressed, the most crime-ridden, and the most dangerous places to live. Gangs control the inner cities because white society no longer cares what happens there. The underground economy of the drug trade is the dominant industry because there is no other industry. People in the inner cities experience an alienating social structure because they truly are powerless in it and are powerless to change it. The burning of Los Angeles was a symptom of these unfortunate realities. The Rodney King verdict was not so much a cause of anything as it was a triggering event for revealing what already was present in the American social structure.

In the very first chapter of this book (pp. 9–11), it was noted that the art of sociological analysis entails looking beyond the surface realities to understand what else is going on. The burning of Los Angeles in the Spring of 1992 was but a reflection of the enduring crisis of America's cities. Rodney King's experience of being beaten down physically again and again was symbolic of the collective experience of inner city minority populations and their experiences of powerlessness, hopelessness, anger, and frustration. For years America's cities, their problems, and their people have been ignored as though they didn't matter. "And then, for a couple of brutal, deadly, frightening, and perhaps, cathartic days, they mattered" (Raspberry 1992). The problems of the city became the problems of the nation.

Chapter Summary

1. The term modernity has been used to describe life in contemporary society. This chapter has depicted the experience of modernity in terms of three prevalent social trends: bureaucracy, secularization, and the rise of metropolitan areas.

2. Bureaucracy is a type of formal organization exhibiting a fixed and rigid division of labor and claiming to embody the goal of rational efficiency. Bureaucratic organizations are a dominant feature of modern social structures.

3. Weber identified four key social structural features of bureaucracy. They are: a highly specialized division of labor, fixed rule systems, a ritualistic system of social control, and a hierarchical system of authority. In addition

to these structural properties, bureaucracy may be understood as an expression of the cultural value of goal rationalism.

4. The rise of bureaucracy may be causally explained by the emergence of problems of scale or size in a society, and rationalism as a solution to those problems.
5. Bureaucratic organizations result in several social consequences. First, bureaucracies result in alienation, defined as an experience of powerlessness. Second, as bureaucratization increases, so do secondary type group experiences. Third, bureaucracies foster the development of what has been called the bureaucratic personality. Finally, bureaucracies are highly resistant to social change.
6. The modern social experience is essentially a secularized experience. Secularization refers to the shrinking influence of religion in modern society.
7. Social theorists often explain secularization as a consequence of society-wide trends toward institutional specialization and goal-rationality. Sociologists of religion have suggested that the competition between religious belief systems has caused a crisis of religious legitimacy or secularization of consciousness.
8. While it is not anticipated that a religionless society will emerge, it is anticipated that the modern social experience will continue to lack the "sanctification" of the social structure of an earlier time. In religious terms, modernity means a lifestyle relatively devoid of religious awe and mystery.
9. The transition from an urban to a metropolitan society has been a key feature of life in the later half of the 20th century. A metropolitan area (MSA) consists of a large population nucleus together with adjacent communities having a high degree of social and economic integration with that nucleus. MSAs represent complexes of social and economic relationships.
10. Four causes of MSAs have been examined here. They are the shift from an industrial to a service economy, the advent of transportation and communications technologies supporting labor-force decentralization, government spending and taxation programs favoring suburban development, and finally, social preferences for class, ethnic, and race separation in the United States.
11. The shift to a metropolitan pattern of life has had the consequence of a reliance on oil-based transportation systems, particularly the personal auto. This reliance has economic, political, and health ramifications. It also has created poverty in the cities. The concentration of racial minorities, homeless, and poor populations in cities represents a serious challenge to the "American dream" requiring solution in the 21st century.

Key Concepts

alienation
bureaucracy
bureaucratic personality
civil religion
CMSA
goal-rationality

iron law of oligarchy
modernity
MSA
PMSA
rational
religion
ritualism
secularization
SMSA
value-rationality

BIBLIOGRAPHY

Bellah, Robert
1967. Civil religion in America. *Daedalus.* Vol. 96: 1–21.

Berger, Peter L.
1967. *The sacred canopy: Elements of a sociological theory of religion.* New York: Doubleday & Co.

Berry, Brian J. L.
1976. "The Counterurbanization Process: Urban America Since 1970." In *urbanization and counterurbanization,* edited by B. J. L. Berry. London: Sage Publications.

Blau, Peter M., and Marshall W. Meyer
1965. *Bureaucracy in modern society.* 2d ed., 1971. New York: Random House.

Douglas, H. Paul
1925. *The suburban trend.* New York: Century.

Durkheim, Emile
1915. *Elementary forms of the religious life.* Translated by J. W. Swain, 1954. New York: Free Press.

Ellul, Jacques
1964. *The technological society.* Translated by John Wilkinson, 1965. New York: Alfred Knopf.

Fenn, Richard
1978. *Toward a theory of secularization.* Monograph Series, Vol. 1. Storrs, Connecticut: Society for the Scientific Study of Religion Monograph Series.

Flanagan, William G.
1990. *Urban sociology.* Boston: Allyn and Bacon.

Glassman, Ronald, William Swatos, and Paul L. Rosen, eds.
1987. *Bureaucracy against democracy and socialism.* Westport, Connecticut: Greenwood Press.

Greeley, Andrew
1982. *Religion: A secular theory.* New York: Free Press.

Hammond, Philip
1974. "Religious Pluralism and Durkheim's Integration Thesis." In *Changing perspectives in the scientific study of religion,* edited by Allan Eister, 115–42. New York: John Wiley.

Hargrove, Barbara
1979. *The sociology of religion: Classical and contemporary approaches.* Arlington Heights, Illinois: AHM Publishing Company.

Harrison, Paul
1959. *Power and authority in the free church tradition.* Princeton, N.J.: Princeton Univ. Press.

Herberg, Will
1955. *Protestant-Catholic-Jew*. New York: Doubleday & Co.

Hoge, Dean, and David Roozen, eds.
1979. *Understanding church growth and decline.* New York: Pilgrim Press.

Hummel, Ralph P.
1977. *The bureaucratic experience.* 2d ed., 1982. New York: St. Martin's Press.

Johnstone, Ronald
1975. *Religion in society: A sociology of religion.* 3d ed., 1988. Englewood Cliffs, N.J.: Prentice-Hall.

Kerner, Otto, *et al.*
1968. *Report of the National Advisory Commission on Civil Disorders.* New York: Bantam Books.

Levy, Frank
1987. *Dollars and dreams: The changing American income distribution.* 1988 ed. New York: W. W. Norton and Company.

Lipset, Seymour Martin, Lester Trow, and James Coleman
1956. *Union democracy.* Glencoe, Illinois: Free Press.

Mannheim, Karl
1940. *Man and society in an age of reconstruction.* London: Routledge and Kegan Paul.

Martin, David
1978. *A general theory of secularization.* New York: Harper & Row.

McGuire, Meredith B.
1992. *Religion: The social context.* 3d ed. Belmont, California: Wadsworth.

Merton, Robert
1940. "Bureaucratic Structure and Personality." In *Social forces.* Vol. 18, No. 4: 249–260. Reprinted in Merton's *Social theory and social structure.* 1968 Enlarged ed. New York: Free Press.

Michels, Robert
1911. *Political parties.* Glencoe, Illinois: Free Press (1949) Wadsworth Publishing Company.

Miller, Zane L., and Patricia Melvin
1973. *The urbanization of modern America: A brief history.* 2d ed. 1987. New York: Harcourt Brace Jovanovich.

Newman, William M.
1986. "Religion." In *Sex roles and social patterns,* edited by Frances A. Boudreau, Roger S. Sennott, and Michele Wilson, 252–79. New York: Praeger Publishers.

Parsons, Talcott
1971. "Belief, Unbelief, and Disbelief." In *The culture of unbelief,* edited by R. Caporalle and A. Grumelli, 207–45. Berkeley, California: Univ. of California Press. pp. 207–245.

Raspberry, William
1992. "L.A. riots were the only way to show they matter." *Norwich Bulletin,* May 12: A-5.

Roof, W. Clark, and William McKinney
1987. *American mainline religion: Its changing shape and future.* New Brunswick, N.J.: Rutgers Univ. Press.

Scott, Hilda
1984. *Working your way to the bottom: The feminization of poverty.* London: Pandora Press.

Seeman, Melvin
1959. On the meaning of alienation. *American Sociological Review.* Vol. 24: 783–91.

Selznick, Philip
1949. *TVA and the grass roots.* Berkeley, California: Univ. of California Press.

Shiner, Larry
1967. The concept of secularization in empirical research. *Journal for the Scientific Study of Religion.* Vol. 6, No. 2: 207–220.

Simmel, Georg
1906. *The sociology of religion.* Translated by Curt Rosenthal, 1959. New York: Philosophical Library.

Taeuber, Karl E.
1983. "Racial residential segregation, 28 cities, 1970–1980." Working paper 83-12. Madison, Wisconsin: University of Wisconsin Center for Demography and Ecology.

Taeuber, Karl E., and Alma F. Taeuber
1965. *Negroes in cities: Residential segregation and neighborhood change.* Chicago: Aldine.

Thomas, Michael, and C. C. Flippen
1972. American civil religion: An empirical study. *Social Forces.* Vol. 51: 218–25.

Tillich, Paul
1956. *Systematic theology, volume I.* Chicago: Univ. of Chicago Press.

U.S. Bureau of the Census
1991. *Statistical Abstract of the United States, 1990.* Washington, D.C.: U.S. Government Printing Office.

Van Valley, Thomas, Wade Clark Roof and Jerome Wilcox
1977. Trends in residential segregation, 1960–1970. *American Journal of Sociology.* Vol. 82, No. 4: 826–844.

Weber, Max
1904–5. *The protestant ethic and the spirit of capitalism.* Translated by Talcott Parsons, 1958. New York: Scribner's.

1923. *Economy and society.* Translated by Guenther Roth and Claus Wittich. Totowa, N.J.: Bedminister Press.

Wilson, William J.
1987. *The truly disadvantaged: The inner city, the underclass, and public policy.* Chicago: Univ. of Chicago Press.

Wimberley, Ronald
1976. Testing the civil religion hypothesis. *Sociological Analysis.* Vol. 37: 341–52.

1979. Continuity in the measurement of civil religion. *Sociological Analysis.* Vol. 40: 59–62.

Yeates, Maurice
1990. *The North American city.* 4th ed. New York: Harper & Row.

Glossary

Absolutist perspective a sociological approach which defines deviance as any objective norm-violation.

Achieved status a social position based on the efforts and accomplishments of the individual.

Adornment term used in dramaturgical analysis to describe all things done to the human body to enhance a performance.

Aggregates some number of persons who share a common location, or situation, but who do not exhibit sustained interaction or a sense of shared identity.

Alienation the experience of powerlessness.

All-weather liberal a person who is not prejudiced and does not discriminate.

Amalgamation a cooperative process by which different status communities through intermarriage mix biologically and culturally, forming a new cultural amalgam.

Anomie a social condition in which the norms governing social behavior are weak, conflicting, or absent, creating normative confusion.

Applied sciences the practical application of basic science findings to real life situations.

Ascribed status a social position assigned on the basis of criteria over which individuals have no control.

Assimilation a cooperative process in which subordinate status populations become more and more like the dominant community and eventually become absorbed into it.

Audiences term used in dramaturgical analysis to describe persons for whose consumption a performance is staged by a team.

Authority the socially legitimated right, by virtue of a social status, to control the action of others.

Back region term used in dramaturgical analysis to describe a location that is frequented by team but not audience members.

Basic science any science that focuses on the goals of understanding and explanation.

Behavioral minorities persons who, because of distinctive behavioral patterns, are assigned a negative status.

Bigot a person who is openly prejudiced and discriminates.

Bilineal a pattern of descent in which kinship is traced through both parents.

Biological determinism the idea that social patterns result from genetically inherited predispositions.

Blaming the victim blaming subordinate communities for the negative circumstances that have been imposed upon them by discriminatory practices.

Blended family a family in which children of one or both spouses from a previous marriage are included in the family unit (also called reconstituted family).

Bourgeoisie according to Marx, owners of capital.

Bureaucracy a type of formal organization exhibiting a fixed authority structure with a division of labor based on elaborate rules and regulations and claiming to embody the goal of rational efficiency.

Bureaucratic personality a type of personality in which the expression of emotions and feelings are de-emphasized.

Business organizations formal organizations primarily designed to benefit owners and stockholders.

Caste a category of persons whose stratification position is determined by unchangeable status norms, and who are powerless to alter either those defining norms or the resulting resource positions they create.

Child abuse violence directed against children.

Circulation of elites a theory of social change that views political processes as circular in which specific aristocracies rise and fall.

Civic ideology the core values of a society as expressed in its political doctrines.

Civil religion a widely subscribed blend of powerful civic and religious values.

Class persons sharing a similar economic position in a society.

Class system of stratification system which ranks groups and individuals according to their possession of material wealth.

Clinical sociology the application of sociological principles and research findings to the solution of human problems.

Closed stratification system system in which upward social mobility either is not possible or when it happens, represents a variation from established norms.

CMSA (Consolidated Metropolitan Statistical Area) U.S. Census Bureau's term for MSAs containing over one million inhabitants.

Coercive organizations organizations people are required to join either for their own benefit or societal good.

Cognitive minorities persons who, because of religious, political, or other beliefs, are assigned a negative status.

Colonialism a type of social conflict in which a population or community is subjugated through economic dependency and, thus, is controlled and exploited by another community or population.

Commonwealth organizations formal organizations primarily designed to benefit the general public.

Comparative reference group any group used by the individual as a basis for making comparative self-evaluation.

Competition a type of social interaction in which individuals, groups, or collectivities engage in mutually opposed efforts to obtain the same resources or reach the same goals.

Complete observer a method used in field studies in which the researcher is not involved with the group or community being studied.

Concepts linguistic symbols representing entire categories of phenomena.

Conflict a type of social interaction in which mutually opposed individuals, groups, or collectivities attempt to neutralize or injure the opposing party.

Conflict theory theory of social change claiming that struggles and conflict are inevitable due to inequality in society and differences in values.

Conflict theory of deviance sociological theory that understands social definitions of deviance as a consequence of political processes.

Conformity a mode of adaptation in which culturally approved goals are pursued through legitimate means.

Content analysis a type of indirect observation that examines written and pictorial documents for the categories of social and cultural experience contained within them.

Contracted labor a migration category in which migrants receive economic compensation.

Convergence theory an evolutionary theory of social change claiming that all societies pass through certain developmental phases which once begun will continue.

Cooperation a type of social interaction consisting of collaboration to achieve a common goal.

Cultural adaptation the process through which culture emerges as a response to environmental pressures.

Cultural assimilation a cooperative process in which subordinate status communities adopt the values and lifestyle of the dominant community.

Cultural borrowing the initial movement of any cultural unit or complex from one society to another, or from one social unit to another within the same society.

Cultural complex a meaningfully related set of cultural practices, ideas, and objects.

Cultural determinism the idea that human life is shaped completely by social forces.

Cultural diffusion the process through which such cultural items or complexes become established as normative throughout a population.

Cultural integration the degree to which different cultural complexes and value systems reinforce and support one another.

Cultural lag tendency of some parts of a culture to change more rapidly than other related parts.

Cultural pluralism a cooperative state of dominant-subordinate relations in which cultural differences are maintained.

Cultural relativism an effort to understand and evaluate other cultures on their own terms.

Cultural unit any singular practice, idea, or material object in a culture.

Culture all of the appropriate and/or required modes of thought, action, and feeling in societies, as well as the material productions that result from people's life together.

Cyclical theory a theory that views social change in terms of a circular, repeating pattern.

Cynical deviants persons who engage in self-serving actions such as theft and burglary.

Deductive method a scientific approach which begins with a theory and uses research to test that theory.

Demographic transition theory a theory focusing upon the relationship between processes of social change and population growth.

Demography the study of population size, composition, distribution, and change.

Deviance actions or attributes that are socially condemned by specific audiences in well-defined social environments.

Deviant career the pattern of an individual's involvement in and identity with a deviant subculture.

Differential association a socialization theory emphasizing the importance of exposure to nonconventional norms in the learning of deviant behavior.

Direct institutional discrimination patterns of differential and unequal treatment that have been incorporated into the formal norms of a society.

Direct observation an array of research techniques for studying readily observable social phenomena.

Direct question methods array of research techniques for studying social phenomena not directly observable.

Discrimination any act of differential treatment of persons that creates a social disadvantage and is based upon the perception of persons as members of a group, community, or stratum.

Displaced persons a migration category in which persons are coerced by situational factors to relocate.

Division of labor an allocation of members into various positions that entail specialized activities.

Doubling time the number of years it takes for a population to double in size.

Dramaturgical analysis analytical perspective in sociology that examines the moment-to-moment social performances of individuals as stage or theater.

Dual-career family a family in which both working partners make professional career commitments.

Dual-earner family a family in which both husband and wife work outside the home.

Economy that institution responsible for the production and distribution of a society's goods and services.

Education that institution responsible for cultural transmission, skill training and occupational allocation.

Egalitarian neither female- nor male-dominated.

Elder abuse violence directed against the elderly.

Empirical availability accessibility of the phenomena to be studied for observation and/or measurement.

Enemy deviants persons defined as deviant because they represent a threat to the legitimacy of the normative order.

Equilibrium theory theory of social change that focuses upon adaptive processes that restore societal balance.

Estate system of stratification system in which groups and individuals are ranked relative to the ownership of land.

Ethnic enclaves a social pattern in which status community members compete by occupying a distinct economic sector.

Ethnocentrism the tendency to view one's own culture as best and to judge other cultures by its own standards.

Evolutionary theory theory that views social change as a linear process triggered by such things as cultural diffusion and technology.

Exchange a type of social interaction consisting of coordinated behavior characterized by the giving and receiving of mutual benefits.

Explanation to tell why or how something happens.

Extended family a family unit consisting of several generations.

Face work term used in dramaturgical analysis to describe work done solely for the purpose of seeming busy.

Face-to-face interview a method of collecting survey data.

Fair-weather liberals a person who is not prejudiced but discriminates.

Family the institution responsible for the emotional and material support of its members, primary socialization, and biological reproduction.

Field experiment a direct observation research technique in which the researcher introduces the experimental condition into an everyday social setting.

Field study a type of direct observation research technique in which the researcher goes directly to the phenomena under study and observes it as closely and completely as possible.

Folkways types of norms with little moral significance.

Forced labor a migration category in which migrants are slaves.

Formal organization a type of social structure, or network of substructures, of comparatively large size created to achieve specialized goals.

Formal social structure the officially designated pattern of social relationships in a social structure.

Front region term used in dramaturgical analysis to describe any location where a team is staging a performance for an audience.

Game stage the stage of self-development in which the child learns that he/she is expected to conform to the rules, roles, and expectations of society.

Gemeinschaft a homogeneous society characterized by primary type relationships.

Generalized other the entire system of "others" or what we call society.

Genocide the systematic killing of the members of a status community with the intent of annihilating the entire community (a type of social conflict).

Gesellschaft a highly differentiated society characterized by contractual and utilitarian relationships.

Goal rationality a form of rationality in which efficient means to desired ends are adopted.

Government that sector of the polity responsible for the allocation of power and authority relations in societies.

High consensus deviance norm-violating behaviors, committed by low status persons who are defined by the majority of people in a society as deviant.

Human nature the collection of traits thought to be intrinsic to the species.

I the impulsive, unique aspect of self.

Ideal type a mental construct used to describe and compare social phenomena in terms of their typical or common characteristics.

Impression management term used in dramaturgical analysis to describe persons attempts to control social interaction.

Indirect institutional discrimination patterns of differential and unequal treatment that rely upon voluntary rather than mandatory compliance.

Indirect observation the use of existing documents, records, and other cultural artifacts to study social patterns both past and present.

Individual facts psychological and biological traits internal to individuals.

Inductive method a scientific approach which begins with the collection of data and forms theories based on analysis of that data.

Informal social structure any pattern of social relationships not officially designated in a social structure.

Innovation a mode of adaptation in which illegitimate means are used to obtain socially prescribed goals (strain theory).

Instincts unlearned, complex patterns of behavior that are common to all members of a species.

Institutional discrimination discriminatory practices that have become routine parts of a cultural tradition and are ingrained in social structural arrangements.

Institutionalized a pattern of activity that happens in a given circumstance with regularity and is accepted widely throughout a population.

Interactionism the idea that human life is shaped by both individual traits and social forces.

Internal colonialism a type of social conflict in which dependency and exploitation is enforced against a community by another community in the same society.

Iron law of oligarchy the tendency of large, bureaucratic organizations to empower those at the top.

Labeling theory a sociological theory that defines deviants as those to whom a label has been applied successfully.

Laboratory experiments a direct observation research technique in which the researcher introduces the experimental condition in a laboratory setting.

Language a system of conventional, symbolic terms.

Looking-glass self the view of one's self that emerges largely as a reflection of how we think others see and evaluate us.

Low-consensus deviance norm violations by persons of high social rank who are not likely to be defined as deviant.

Macrosociology the study of large-scale social phenomena.

Master status a social status having primary significance for shaping a person's life.

Matriarchal female-dominated.

Matrilineal a pattern of descent in which kinship is traced through the mother.

Matrilocal a norm of residence in which a married couple is expected to live with or near the wife's family.

MBO (Management By Objectives) upper-level planning of objectives and translation of those objectives into specific goals and tasks at lower levels of the organizational structure.

Me the self expressed in socially recognized ways.

Mechanical solidarity social cohesion based on similar ways of life.

Microsociology the study of small-scale social phenomena.

Middleman minorities a social pattern in which some low-status communities occupy economic positions that are literally in the middle, between capitalists and workers, between producers and consumers.

Mind the ability to learn and use significant symbols and to think in terms of these same significant symbols.

Minority group people who, because of their physical or cultural characteristics, are singled out from the others in the society in which they live for differential and unequal treatment, and who therefore regard themselves as objects of collective discrimination.

Modernity term used to describe unique features of contemporary culture and society.

Monogamy the practice of allowing persons to have only one husband or wife.

Mores types of norms having strong moral significance, the violation of which elicits strong negative sanctions.

Motivated change social change processes that result from the efforts and intentions of persons to change a society.

MSA (Metropolitan Statistical Area) U.S. Census Bureau's term for a large population nucleus together with adjacent communities having a high degree of social and economic integration.

Mutual benefit organizations formal organizations primarily designed to benefit members.

Myth a collective view providing an interpretation of what a people have been, are, or wish to become.

Natural experiment a type of direct observation research technique in which naturally occurring phenomena provide experimental conditions without researcher intervention.

Neolocal a norm of residence in which a married couple is expected to live apart from both sets of parents.

Nominal definition a definition for purposes of research that identifies a range, type, or category of events or activities that exemplify a specific concept.

Normative organizations voluntary organizations people join of their own volition for nonremunerative purposes.

Normative reference group any group influencing the development of values, attitudes, and standards of behavior for an individual.

Norms shared rules and expectations for behavior.

Nuclear family a family unit consisting of parents and their children.

Objective method a method of measuring social class which focuses upon easily quantifiable (i.e. statistical) measures such as income.

Objectivity in science, an attempt to maintain freedom from bias, prejudgment, and/or extraneous values.

Open stratification system system in which upward social mobility or change in relative stratification position is the norm.

Operational definition the exact specification of how a variable is to be measured in a particular study.

Organic solidarity social cohesion based on the mutual exchanges of a highly differentiated population.

Parallel institutions instances in which status communities create their own self-controlled social structures that address the same community needs as those found in the dominant community.

Participant observation a method used in field studies in which the researcher joins the group or community being studied.

Patriarchal male-dominated.

Patrilineal a pattern of descent in which kinship is traced through the father.

Patrilocal a norm of residence in which a married couple is expected to live with or near the husband's family.

Peer group a group of persons having approximately the same age and status, and frequently the same sex.

Physical minorities persons who, because of physical characteristics such as skin color, age, gender, and body type, are assigned a negative status.

Planned change the rational coordination of human energies and material resources to bring about desired effects in the social and physical environment.

Play stage the stage of self-development in which the young child learns how she/he is by pretending to be someone else.

PMSA (Primary Metropolitan Statistical Area) U.S. Census Bureau's term for or countries the county in which the central city and its immediate suburbs are located.

Polity the institution responsible for such tasks as external defense, internal social control, government, and civic ideology.

Polyandry the practice of allowing females to have more than one husband.

Polygyny the practice of allowing males to have more than one wife.

Population universe all persons or events in the general category one wishes to study.

Power the ability to control the actions of others, regardless of their will.

Prejudice any set of ideas or beliefs that negatively prejudge individuals, groups, communities, or strata on the basis of real or alleged collective traits or characteristics.

Preparatory stage the stage of self-development in which the child engages in purely imitative behavior.

Presented self the self that is presented to others.

Primary deviance deviant behavior committed by a person who maintains a conventional status and role.

Primary group a relatively small and enduring group whose members interact informally in intimate and diffuse relationships.

Primary socialization socialization that is person-centered and entails the acquisition of enduring and holistic features of the self.

Probability the regularity with which events occur.

Progress the idea that things are becoming not just different but better.

Proletariat according to Marx, persons who do not own capital, i.e, workers.

Propositions individual theoretical statements describing relationships among relevant concepts.

Props term used in dramaturgical analysis to describe any physical object used to enhance the management of a role performance.

Purposive sample a selection of persons, cases, or events exhibiting known characteristics of special relevance for the research question being studied.

Race relations cycles theory that views race relations as following a cycle, from conflict to accommodation to assimilation.

Random sample a selection of persons, cases, or events from a universe in such a manner that each one has an equal chance of being chosen.

Rational human behavior exhibiting the calculation of means, ends, and probable consequences.

Rebellion a mode of adaptation in which socially prescribed goals and means are rejected in favor of attempts to change the social system (strain theory).

Reference group any group whose opinions, attitudes, and values are important for individuals.

Reflexes simple, involuntary actions of an organism.

Reform movements social movements that advocate change within existing social structures using legitimate mechanisms such as the established legal and political institutions.

Relativist perspective a sociological approach which defines deviance as behaviors, beliefs, or attributes that elicit some form of social condemnation from others in specific situations.

Reliability the extent to which an empirical measure is consistent.

Religion that institution, based on shared beliefs in the supernatural, responsible for providing meaning and significance to social arrangements, sacred rituals, and a community of belonging.

Religious pluralism a situation in which diverse religions within a society maintain their autonomy and compete with each other for members.

Repentant deviants persons who affirm the social order by admitting publicly the wrongness of their actions.

Replication the ability of different scholars or researchers to arrive at the same research conclusions, independently of one another.

Reputational method a method of measuring social class in which persons are asked to identify the class positions of other persons.

Research hypothesis a statement of the expected pattern of relationships among variables.

Resistance movements social movements that seek either to preserve aspects of the social structure that are waning or to re-established earlier practices.

Resource mobilization theory a theoretical approach to the study of social movements focusing upon how leaders, participants, and social networks become unified.

Retreatism a mode of adaptation entailing withdrawal from culturally shared goals and institutionalized means (strain theory).

Revolutionary movements social movements seeking to completely change a society or social system.

Ritualism a mode of adaptation involving acceptance of socially prescribed means but rejection of socially prescribed goals.

Role distance the extent of awareness an individual has that he or she is either performing a role or presenting a self to others.

Role-taking an imaginative activity in which individuals attempt to see things from the perspective of other persons.

Sample a systematic selection of cases from the total universe or population being studied.

Science a specialized activity having the goal of explaining empirically available phenomena, and employing norms of objectivity and replication.

Scientific humanism the idea that rational science can be used as a tool for social improvement.

Secondary analysis a type of indirect observation that makes use of any existing research data to address a research question not intended by those collecting the data.

Secondary deviance deviant behavior committed by a person who has become labeled as a deviant and who, through individual adaptations, adapts a deviant identity and role.

Secondary group a group of any size and permanence whose members interact in formal, instrumental, and segmented relationships.

Secondary socialization socialization that is role-specific rather than person-centered.

Secularization a shrinking of the influence of religion in society.

Self one's awareness of who and what kind of person one is.

Self-concept a stable set of meanings attached to the self as object.

Self-esteem an individual's overall assessment of his or her personal worth.

Self-esteem theory social psychological theory that emphasizes the roles of culture and social structure in maintaining social psychological well-being.

Self-placement method a method of measuring social class in which people are asked to provide their own subjective view of their class position.

Separation of church and state the independence of religious and secular spheres of authority within a society.

Serial monogamy pattern of marriage-divorce-remarriage.

Service organizations formal organizations primarily designed to benefit clients.

Sick deviants persons whose deviance is politically defined as mental illness.

Sign something that exhibits a natural connection between the object and/or act it represents.

Significant others persons most important to the self.

Significant symbols symbolic meanings, as expressed in language,

Single-parent family a family in which children reside in a household where only one parent, female or male, is present.

Slavery a system of forced labor in which members of a subordinate community are treated as property (a type of social conflict).

SMSA (Standard Metropolitan Statistical Area) U.S. Census Bureau's term for an urbanized area consisting of a city of at least 50,000 inhabitants and its adjacent counties.

Social category a number of individuals who are classified together because they share some trait or characteristic.

Social change the process through which alterations are created in social norms, the division of labor, social controls, and hierarchy.

Social conflict theory theory that focuses upon processes of change and group opposition in societies.

Social control strategies to obtain conformity and minimize deviance from a society's prescribed norms and values.

Social disorganization theory sociological theory that explains deviance as a response to the lack of a consensus over social norms.

Social enclosure the degree of separateness of asubculture from the dominant social structure.

Social facts collective social forces that are external to individuals and exert control over them.

Social group any number of persons sharing a common identity and some common goals, and who interact directly and regularly.

Social institutions the relatively permanent structural configurations centered around the tasks of meeting the important material and nonmaterial requirements of a society.

Social interaction the reciprocally influenced behavior between two or more persons.

Social mobility the process by which social groups and individuals alter their share of status, class, and power resources.

Social movement a voluntary association of persons, formed for the purpose of promoting or resisting some form of structural and/or cultural goal in a society.

Social movement organizations diverse formal organizations representing different versions of a social movement's goals, and often using different tactics and strategies for obtaining social change.

Social organization the process through which social structure is produced.

Social power the ability of a person or group to control the actions of others, even in the face of resistance.

Social problems collective social dilemmas that require collective social solutions.

Social psychology the study of the relationship between the individual and the social structure.

Social ranking the evaluation and ordering of statuses into a hierarchy.

Social role a bundle of expected behaviors for persons occupying a given social status.

Social sanctions rewards for appropriate conduct and punishments for inappropriate conduct.

Social self the term used by symbolic interactionists to mean the personality system.

Social status a socially recognized position in a social structure.

Social strata a category of persons sharing a trait or characteristic which is meaningful both to themselves and others.

Social structure the organized, stable patterns of human social relationships.

Socialization the process through which individuals learn the habits, beliefs, and standards of behavior that make them identifiable members of a group or society.

Socialization theories of deviance theories maintaining that deviance is something taught and learned.

Society a relatively self-perpetuating social structure in which persons may satisfy all the requirements of daily living.

Socioeconomic status a measure of stratification based on a mixture of wealth, status, and power.

Sociological imagination a view of social reality in which causes and consequences of events are understood in a sociohistorical context.

Sociology the scientific study and interpretation of life.

Split labor market a type of social conflict in which low-status and high-status community members are allocated to different economic segments of the labor market.

Spousal abuse violence directed against one's spouse.

Status the honor, prestige, and privilege associated with different positions in a society or with categories of persons in a society.

Status community persons exhibiting a distinctive physical, behavioral, or cultural trait or combination of such traits, that becomes the basis of a relatively stable ascriptive status assignment, either positive or negative, in a society.

Stereotypes negative sets of characteristics attributed to entire categories of persons.

Stigma any attribute that is deeply discrediting, thus making persons different from others, and of a less desirable kind.

Strain theory sociological theory explaining deviance as a consequence of the disjuncture between socially prescribed goals and means for attaining them.

Stratification processes through which class, status, and power resources are distributed in a society.

Stratified sample a selection of subpopulations from a universe in a manner that insures the presence of certain desired proportions of them in a sample.

Structural assimilation the entrance of minority individuals into dominant community-controlled institutions.

Structural-functional theory a theory that emphasizes the functional contribution each social institution makes to social order and stability.

Subculture a social community consisting of persons who routinely act upon beliefs, values, and a lifestyle that differ in socially significant respects from that of the dominant culture.

Survey a direct question data collection technique using a standardized questionnaire, administered either through self-administration or interview.

Symbol an arbitrary invention which bestows meaning, and stands for something outside itself.

Symbolic interactionism a theory that views social life as a shared, symbolic meaning system.

Symbolic meanings a system of shared, humanly invented, conventional constructs which are the basis of self, society, and interaction.

Teams term used in dramaturgical analysis to describe persons who conspire to stage a performance.

Technology ideas and material objects invented by any animal population to increase its control over its environment.

Telephone interview a method of collecting survey data.

Theocracy a form of government in which earthly powers flow from the rulership of gods.

Theory a set of logically related general statements that describe, explain, and predict occurrences in an entire class of events.

Theory Z management planning technique maintaining that rational planning must occur at all levels of an organization.

Timid bigot a person who is prejudiced but does not discriminate.

Underclass a stratum of poor persons who are excluded from meaningful participation in the economy.

Unintended change change that results from social forces that are neither intended nor controlled by people.

Universalism the claim that certain social practices or institutions are common to all societies.

"Unmasking" social reality looking beyond commonly accepted interpretations and explanations of social reality to see what else is there.

Unstructured or in-depth interview a direct question data collection technique in which the interviewer specifies a general plan of inquiry, but has no set question or fixed-answer categories.

Utilitarian organizations organizations joined for the achievement of a tangible, material benefit.

Utopian movements social movements characterized by their highly idealistic social goals.

Validity the extent to which an empirical measure accurately reflects the meaning of a given concept.

Value rationality a form of rationality in which actions are assessed in terms of their consistency with a universal value.

Variable any phenomenon, the characteristics, properties, or attributes of which change (or vary) from case to case in terms of amount, degree, or type.

Voluntary childlessness a situation in which married couples choose not to have children.

Voluntary migration a migration category in which people willingly migrate.

World systems theory type of conflict theory claiming that industrialized nations achieve their affluence by exploiting dependent nations.

Name Index

SUBJECT INDEX